...and a
hard
rain
fell

...and a hard rain fell

A GI's true story of the War in Vietnam

John Ketwig

updated edition with a
new introduction by the author

SOURCEBOOKS, INC.®
NAPERVILLE, ILLINOIS

ISBN 0-7394-2799-1

Published by Sourcebooks, Inc.
P.O. Box 4410, Naperville, Illinois 60567-4410
(630) 961-3900
FAX: (630) 961-2168

Printed and bound in the United States of America

This book is dedicated to John Lennon and Cornelius Hawkridge, each of whom, in his own special way, dared us all to imagine.

This book is based on true incidents. Names (except public figures) have been changed and characters described in the book are composites.

Contents

Illustrations

Introduction

I didn't set out to write a book. It was 1982, fourteen years after I had last set foot in Vietnam, and thirteen years after I returned to The World. I had a family and a career. I'd never written more than an occasional letter to the editor in my life. My twisted insides had spawned ulcers. The nightmares were more frequent. I needed to get Vietnam out into the open, but I couldn't talk about it. Not after all those years.

I think history will, if given half a chance to be objective, regard the Vietnam era as the apogee of the American dream. To most of us who were there, Vietnam was the defining event of our generation, the biggest thing that would ever happen in our lifetimes. Realizing the importance of the experience, the huge changes that the war crafted into one's emotional makeup, it is difficult to let the genie out of the bottle. Suppose one evening after the kids are in bed and the dishes are done, the wife just casually suggests, "Tell me about Vietnam." A reasonable request, I suppose, but where do you begin? It is so huge, so complex and important, you know that to pry up the lid and let just the first few particles escape will trigger an explosion, a mighty dirty geyser of recollections and traumas that have been festering inside far too long. To tell about my Vietnam experiences the first time was not unlike squeezing the pus out from an infected wound. The time was right for me, back in 1982. For others, the time hasn't been right to this day. They shrug, hunch their shoulders, grab a cold beer from the fridge, and change the subject. There will be a better time, they tell themselves.

It just always seems that there will be a better time.

In January of 1982, there were no books about Vietnam on the shelves at our house. I could not imagine divulging the emotions that the subject stirred in me, and I never imagined that others might have written about the war. Our house has always been home to an extensive library, but at that time there were no references to Vietnam. Today, in the early moments of the twenty-first century, thousands of books have been published to expose, investigate, and interpret every aspect of the Vietnam tragedy. This book, my personal story, is being republished, all of seventeen years after it originally appeared. The introduction that I wrote in 1982 hardly feels right today, but I feel compelled to draw from it. What can this book possibly say that hasn't been said a thousand times before?

One Saturday night in April of 1982, I sat down to write out the story of my experiences in the Vietnam War. I wanted my wife to know all I was feeling. I hoped someday my kids, just toddlers at that time, might read it and understand. I expected to fill fifteen or twenty pages; eight months later I had filled more than three hundred fifty. Every character was typed by my right index finger, which grew an enormous, tender callus. My left thumb contributed capitalizations. I was obsessed, banging away on our old manual typewriter until three or four every morning, and carrying on at my job well enough to win awards. I listened to the old sixties music, closed my eyes, and relived some of the most profound experiences of my life. There were no questions or cross-examinations; there were far too many tears and emotional explosions. I can't explain where some of the passages in this story came from. They had to emerge. I am satisfied that this book accurately describes what I saw and felt in Vietnam.

In March of 1986, I attended a symposium on the Vietnam War at Gettysburg College. It was my first opportunity to meet Bill "W.D." Ehrhart, perhaps the most articulate spokesman of all Vietnam veterans. Gettysburg is located near to the Army War College in Carlisle, Pennsylvania, and there were a great many uniformed officers and noncoms from that institution in attendance. Late in the afternoon, after most of us had made our contributions, a graying Sergeant Major came to the podium to have his say. "These whining, complaining veterans will die off," he shouted, his face red with emotion, gesturing angrily. "The history of the Vietnam War your grandchildren will read has been written, and it will not reflect much of what has been said here today!" This book offers only the truth as I saw it, and I hope that a copy will be available to my grandchildren, and also yours.

No, I never intended to write a book. I took no notes while I was overseas; my only goal was survival. I have changed all names (except public figures) and combined some characters. The years have clouded timeframes and dates. All of the incidents are true. I made a conscious decision to structure my story into three chapters. There were no chapter breaks in The Nam, no convenient moments when you could lay the whole experience down, and crawl off to a comfortable bed.

In June of 1965, I emerged from high school graduation brimming with enthusiasm and optimism. I would, I was certain, make the world a better place. Then came Vietnam. Perhaps the most tragic legacy of the war is the damage it did to a generation's, and a nation's, ideals and confidence. The sight of a napalmed child colors one's view of the world ever after. So many young eyes, not yet accustomed to the sight of injustice, were blinded by a flood of suffering the likes of which the world had never known. Almost forty years after, we recall the shock and despair of the Kennedy assassination in Dallas. If JFK's death was overwhelming, the death of a best buddy in the jungle of Southeast Asia was incomprehensible. The staunch anguish of Jackie, Caroline, and John-John would soon be repeated in cemeteries across America as the coffins came home to thousands of broken families.

Our generation has witnessed so much history on the front pages of newspapers. Sadly, too many of the historians have sought to revise the truth, to alter the times as well as the events. Some have attempted to further their individual political or social beliefs, and others simply weren't participants. I am appalled at the way in which the military and political historians ignore the cultural practices of the times, and vice-versa. Very few histories or biographies of the Beatles offer

more than a mention of the Vietnam War. Both simultaneously washed over the history of the times with indelible influ-
ences. The young Americans who were sent to Vietnam were
the first American fighting force to have easy access to automobiles. And oh, what automobiles! The late sixties American
cars were known as "muscle cars," awesome, powerful
machines destined for the nation's drag strips. We acknowledge
that Lee Iacocca and John DeLorean contributed to America's
industrial history, but we have conveniently ignored the impact
that Mustangs and GTOs and Hemi Cudas had on a generation of young men who were taken into the military to fight in
Vietnam. We were the first generation with portable radios.
The transistor allowed us to take our music with us, and oh,
what music it was! No history of the times can be accurate
without examining the role and the impact of popular music.

Much is made of the statistic that the average age of an
American fighting man in World War II was twenty-six, but in
Vietnam it was only nineteen. We cannot afford to miss the sig-
nificance of that fact. The majority of Americans "in country"
were there after the Tet Offensive, or early February 1968. The
Beatles first appeared on Ed Sullivan the evening of February
9, 1964. The average GI in Vietnam post-Tet had likely been a
"Beatlemaniac" at age fifteen. He had been influenced by Bob
Dylan's "Blowin' in the Wind," or "The Times They Are A-
Changin'." By songs like "Eve of Destruction" and "Louie,
Louie," and "People Got to Be Free." We were the first generation of American fighting men to have television! We were
brought up on *Leave It to Beaver* and *Father Knows Best*. We
watched true American heroes like Alan Shepard and John
Glenn ride the first rockets into space, and we were immensely
proud. But, at the same time, we went to school, and the teachers made us talk about current events, and then we went home
and saw poor Americans in the South murdered because they
demanded their right to vote or attend a school. We saw them

shot, assaulted with water cannons, attacked with vicious dogs, and we went back to the current events classes the next day and asked hard questions. And solid, truthful answers were not always forthcoming.

The military of the Vietnam era never adjusted to the history and culture of Southeast Asia, and it cost them dearly. I contend that it's just as important to note that they never adjusted to the history and culture of the young people they inducted to fight for Democracy and American freedoms, and that failure was equally tragic. Looking back, I realized that I feared the enemy, the Viet Cong and the North Vietnamese Regulars, but I never hated them. Today, more than forty years later, I still harbor the deepest resentment and bitterness, and yes, *Hate!* toward the military, political, and business leaders who created, caused, or profited from what I saw in Vietnam. It shouldn't be that way, but my memories and understandings are inescapable. I believe my son died as a result of the war. Wasted, an unnecessary loss, and yet America refuses to acknowledge the damages done by Agent Orange, or the war. I can think of no more important lesson to be learned from Vietnam. I didn't ask to go to Vietnam. I wish I'd never seen the things I did. I think we do our country and the young people who fought in Vietnam a great disservice by covering up the facts.

I love to go to the Vietnam Memorial on the mall in Washington, D.C., and I believe I can "read the writing on the wall." I find it difficult to assimilate the realities of Vietnam with the American "truths we hold to be self-evident." My story is not anti-American. One loves the sick child but curses the disease. I only hope my story will encourage people to read, investigate, and think. Our national priorities require a diagnosis and a cure. I don't want my children, or my grandchildren, to see the world I have known. Sadly, I expect that they might. I could not remain silent in 1982, and I cannot today.

The Draft,
the Decisions,
and The Nam

"I would like to see American students develop as much fanaticism about the U.S. political system as young Nazis did about their political system during the War."

—Lyndon Johnson, 1965

Exactly twenty-three days before I was supposed to leave Vietnam, I stopped worrying about dying. We were called out with a wrecker to haul in some trucks from a convoy that had been ambushed on the road to Dak To. As we neared the firefight, dump trucks loaded with bodies, or overloaded with bodies, swirled out of the dust, sailed past the windows, and retreated the way we had come. Perhaps it was the sight of the bodies in disarray. Obviously, no one had taken the time to stack them like firewood, and limbs hung over the sides at crazy angles. No, that was fitting for the circumstances, understandable. Perhaps it was the very attitude of the limbs; broken, interrupted, torn, and bloodied. Or the mud, like thick brown paste, clinging to rumpled fenders and ravaged jungle uniforms, all-encompassing sticky goo that deformed and defiled all it touched. In an instant they were gone, four or five truckloads of kids going home. A couple of escort vehicles, with flat sheets of armor plate and twin fifty-caliber machine guns, and naked torsos in flak jackets, and the calm, grim, matter-of-fact stares that said these guys had just been to hell and didn't have enough energy left to show emotion. And we were heading into what they had just left!

I was riding shotgun. At twenty-three days you let somebody else fight the fuckin' war. We must have been doing sixty when the shooting started. I simply opened the door and jumped for the ditch. Somehow, I got turned around in midair and landed on a canteen of Kool-Aid that I had riding on my right kidney. I knew, I just knew that I had been shot in the back, and I was going to lie there in that stinking ditch and bleed to death and never see the world again.

• • • •

Sorry! Over two million Americans went to The Nam. Nearly fifty-eight thousand died there. Everyone dreamed about The World, talked about The World, cried about The World. There was nothing more important. The World wasn't a planet. It was your hometown, your tree-lined street in the suburbs, your tenement in the ghetto. It was your wife, or girl-friend, or mom, or just a female with round eyes and swelling bosom. The World was a 427 Chevelle with cheater slicks and tri-power carbs, parked way at the back of the drive-in, with footprints on the headliner and beer cans under the seat. It was fake-proof so you could see the bands, and the gas station where you could buy condoms from a machine on the rest-room wall. The World was where your kid brother lived, and if he ever thought of leaving to come over to this cesspool, you'd chop his toes off with a hatchet, for his own good. The World was flush toilets and doorknobs and fishing streams. A mythi-cal, magical place that had existed once, and would again, and had been interrupted by the Vietnam war as a TV show is inter-rupted by a commercial. Excuse me, I'll capitalize The World. If you were there, you'll know. If you weren't, you never will. And I don't plan to refer to the Vietnam "conflict." LBJ saw it as a "Conflict." To a pfc, nineteen years old, that many dead guys earned it the title of "war."

The World existed. All too often the fantasy became clouded over by the day's events. It seemed far away, intangible, even alien; but you couldn't let go of the fact that it existed, or you might never make it back. You might be lying in the mud lis-tening to some guy beg because his intestines are spilling out of a hole in his belly, and some fool down the line starts singing some old Smothers Brothers thing about falling into a vat of chocolate. The World comes back to life, and everybody strug-gles just a little bit harder, and you make it.

Every single thing I had ever taken for granted in my life was a fantasy. The kitchen. My car. The folks. Clean sheets. Toilet paper. My arms, my legs, my face, even my brain...might not exist ten seconds from now.

Survive. Make it to the next second, it could become a minute. Minutes became hours, and hours, days. A day was an accomplishment, a square on your calendar. One three-hundred-and-sixty-fifth of a year. You remembered every story of survival you'd ever read, ever seen on TV, or at the movies. You became Ben Hur and Moses and anyone else Charlton Heston had ever played.

Someday medical science will discover how many brain cells a man can lose and continue to function. A strong man can learn to live without an arm or leg. A scared kid can learn, if he has to. But brain cells are different; microscopic particles in a group, sorting out life. A lot of brain cells are burned out in a war, overloaded and short-circuited and gone. They don't regenerate. You know they're gone, but the folks back home only see that you've brought all your arms and legs, and the inside hurts stay inside, and there's a void you can feel.

That's if you make it home before you eclipse that magic, terrible number. I came close, twenty-three days before I was supposed to leave Vietnam.

● ● ● ●

I felt the pain. My eyes watered, I couldn't see, and my ears couldn't stand much more of the noise. I ignored the hurt, concentrated on the fear, and on surviving. I pushed every muscle, every tissue, into the brown slime. I wanted to be invisible, to sink up to my nostrils, to buy some time 'til my eyes cleared and I could at least see it coming. God, I didn't want to die without even being able to focus! There was gunfire everywhere. I had to sort it all out, put it into some recognizable form. The M-60 machine guns cracked a snare drum's beat. The M-16s and M-14s rattled the intricate, high-pitched, driving tinkle of thin-ride cymbals. A fifty-caliber thump-thumped a bass beat. I began to get it together. My eyes were clearing. Four or five tiny men in black were moving toward us across the field. They were crouched, firing from the hip. At least a hundred guns were roaring at them, the percussion section of a great symphony orchestra, and they were in plain sight, and they just kept coming closer. Grinning. You could see the white of their teeth. Off to the left, one went down, then reappeared. The top of his head was completely blown away, but the crazy bastard got back on his feet, grinned, and just kept coming!

And then I realized it was over. It was quiet. And I was lying on my belly in the mud, tapping my foot to the abstract rhythm my head had found woven into the chaos of twentieth-century warfare. I had never even shouldered my rifle. I was lying in the dirt tapping my foot to a rhythm only I could hear, and a war happened, and I missed it. I got to my feet. It seemed no one had noticed that I hadn't been shooting. The field had been cleared, and the grass and rubble were only about knee-high. I could see the dead Cong a few yards away. A few of us wandered out to take a closer look. There could have been, should have been, booby traps hidden in the tangle at our knees; fascination made us oblivious. I had seen terrible auto crashes, broken bodies among fenders and chrome. I had never gawked. Twenty-three days before I was supposed to leave The Nam, I walked out into the stubble and looked down on torn men, desecrated flesh, and felt no emotion. It was like walking down the aisle of a supermarket. A couple of guys kicked the gooks. I knelt beside one and removed his belt, canteen, medical kit, and a few empty ammo belts. Another guy picked up his Chicom machine gun. "Go ahead," I said, "I've got one." A few moments before, I had been tapping my foot to the rhythm of death as though I was at a rock concert; now I was handing out the spoils of a war I had ignored! I was aware that I was confused, that somehow this wasn't the way it should be. But I kept that canteen for many years, and I don't have it now, and I don't remember getting rid of it.

The Nam was like that. The strangest things happened, and everybody just sort of shuffled by and accepted it, and you can't explain it to someone who wasn't there. It just happened, and you were a witness to something profound, momentous, but it didn't seem important at the time. You expected to die any minute or any second, and you wondered how you would do it. Tough, grittin' your teeth and pushing the hurt in with your hands; or small and damaged and vulnerable, crying and screaming for your mother, your panic sapping your strength, the very tension rolling out into a stain that darkened the mud. How would you do it? What would the guys say? What would they write to the folks back home? I mean, everybody hopes to die in bed, just go to sleep, but in The Nam, guys were dying and it wasn't like that, and you wondered how you would do at it.

The dead gook was torn up bad. He had been hit twenty, maybe thirty times, and in places there were big holes with bone and tissue sticking out at crazy angles, and most of him was painted with a dark brown stuff that had to be blood, but it was muddy and soaked into the dark pajamas and didn't really resemble the stuff that came out of you. Somebody rolled him over, and I lost the critical brain cell. The dude had the biggest hard-on you ever saw; and it shouldn't have fit the situation but it did. To my mind, his agony was over, and he felt the warm, comforting, electric surge of pleasure a woman brings, and he was happy! I wandered in a numb fog, gazed at gook after gook, torn, smashed, destroyed, but with the telltale bulge to say, "Fuck you, GI, I'm enjoying this!" and I've never looked at death the same since that day.

• • • •

Don't get the wrong impression. I'm not John Wayne. I was nineteen when I arrived in The Nam, and scared to death. Six feet and a hundred and twenty-five pounds of skin and bones, glasses, silver fillings in my teeth. Scared to death; never a hero. I hadn't wanted to come to Vietnam. I was in the Central Highlands. If I'd been on the coast I might have tried to swim east 'til I drowned. The most heroic thing I'd ever done in my life was reassure my family before I left. I wasn't even sure they were real anymore. Nothing existed except right now; and right now was muddy and worn and torn and desolate and hopeless. Barren. The most wretched existence I had ever known; just stumbling through it; and if you survived the day it was an occasion. If you survived the year…well, there wasn't much chance of that, and you wondered how you would die when your turn came. You were so damned, deep-inside-you glad you had made it through a day, you couldn't imagine the relief and joy of going home. It was so far away, so far beyond the imagination. You knew The World existed, but deep inside you knew it was spinning without you, and damned few people had even noticed you weren't there.

• • • •

When I was about six, my family moved to an eighteen-acre farm near one of the Finger Lakes. I was brought up with room to run among fields of corn, alfalfa, and wheat. We had a large fruit orchard and about three acres of garden. My dad was a bus driver and rented the fields to area farmers. He left for work at 4:00 A.M. and returned about 6:00 P.M., so we never spent a lot of time together. Dad had been poor and forced to work at an early age, so he never knew the intricacies of football or basketball. The local school was athletic-oriented, and too far away to allow me to take part in afterschool activities. We played ball in the yard, but I was never an athlete. I have always read a lot, and somewhere I had discovered hot rod magazines. I smuggled them inside my textbooks. I devoured them when I was supposed to be studying my homework. My marks were high until about eighth grade, when I began to know what I wanted to do with my life: cars and drums, drums and cars. I bought a set of drumsticks and beat the paint off the windowsill. I built plastic model cars by the scores. I read the daring tales of the European racing drivers, scarves dancing merrily on the wind. I shoveled snow, mowed lawns, delivered newspapers, and spent my money on car magazines and rock' n' roll records. I think my parents expected my interest in automobiles to wane, and it just never did. I wanted to become an automotive engineer, but there was no money. I washed cars and pumped gas while the other guys practiced football; I tortured my parents with a set of drums while the other guys practiced lay-ups and fast breaks. My marks weren't bad, but I failed chemistry until the final exam. I was in a college-preparatory program, but my mind was on tune-ups and four-on-the-floor gearboxes. I fell in with some older guys who were building a '34 Ford into a dragster and felt more at home studying fuel injectors than algebra. I loved history and social studies, enjoyed literature but disliked grammar, and resented the demands homework made on my time. There were girls and pranks and camaraderie, but I felt school was keeping me from cars.

America had entered the Space Age, and it was taken for granted that a young man would go to college. I had earned a number of scholarships when I graduated with the class of '65, but my heart wasn't in the classroom. I was accepted by Syracuse, Cornell, and the universities of Buffalo and Rochester, but I couldn't justify borrowing money to do something I didn't want to do. Two weeks after graduation my dad fell ill, and I got a job jockeying cars at a Chevy dealership. My scholarships were extended a year. My classmates went off to college, and I found new friends among the mechanics at work. I bought a new set of drums, started playing regularly, and dreamed of being "discovered." The race car was running near national record times. I had money and girlfriends. My employer sent me to a GM school in auto body repair, signed me up as an apprentice, and got me a draft deferment. The news had begun to talk about a place called Vietnam, but I paid little attention. This was the freest, most exuberant period of my life.

The boss suggested a haircut. In 1966, no rock drummer got a haircut. I refused, he insisted, and I quit. I was working at another dealership when I was summoned for a pre-induction physical. I laughed. I didn't want to be a soldier, and I couldn't conceive of being forced to do something against my will. I had little to offer the military, and I knew some way out would emerge.

The physical was in Buffalo. We gathered for the bus trip; fellow classmates, total strangers, a mixed lot. As the bus moved closer to Buffalo, we laughed. I was nervous, rehearsing the proper answers, but the idea of forced servitude was beyond my comprehension. Everyone had prepared himself, carefully wording answers to offer no more help than necessary. Many had medical records to bear witness to medical problems. The inspectors were contemptuous, herding us like animals, poking, probing, laughing about "cannon fodder for Vietnam" and announcing that, "If you are walkin' and breathin', you're going!" They asked for voluntary enlistments, and no one stepped forward. On the way home the bus was quiet, with occasional outbursts of rage and frustration. I still didn't believe they could take me if I didn't want to go. I felt no sense of duty. If anyone did, he didn't mention it. Most of the whispered conversations concerned atrocities and indignities. "Did you see what they did to the kid with polio?" "They told Jackson he's One-A, and he's got a heart murmur." "Can you imagine two years of being treated like that?" "Shit, they couldn't do anything to us. We're civilians. My brother told me about boot camp. That's where they really get rough." Somebody in the back hollered, "Hey driver, do you do charters?"

"Sure."

"We would like to see Niagara Falls...from the Canadian side!"

• • • •

It was a strange time in American history, a time when many seemingly unrelated events were combining to shake the very foundations of our most cherished institutions. It was a time of the Beatles and sub-orbital flights, of civil rights marches in the deep South, and black-and-white TV. After the simple satisfaction of the fifties and the patriotic frenzy of the New Frontier, and after the Bay of Pigs, and the Cuban missile crisis, and that day in Dallas, we all felt some kind of ominous tension. Even our high school teachers had seemed somewhat bewildered. You couldn't watch police dogs attacking blacks on the evening news and believe the United States was the land of the free and the home of the brave. You used to think the Commies were far away, but then they showed up ninety miles from Florida. You used to think boys had short hair, but then the British invaded, and you looked at history books, and there really wasn't anything wrong with long hair. The grown-ups objected, then suggested you go to church, and Christ's hair was on his shoulders, and everything seemed suspect. They spoke of obligations to your country and whispered about tax breaks. They told you to defend freedom and used cattle prods on the Freedom Riders in Alabama. If you were young, it was an exciting world. You worked all week, and on the weekend you watched fuel dragsters or British rock bands or X-rated movies, and you believed you could change the world and make it a better place. Thirteen years of public school had created a generation of believers. "Do your own thing." "The times they are a-changing." "We shall overcome." Born in the late forties, we were the first generation to grow in the shadow of the mushroom cloud. Hate wasn't the answer. Material goods weren't the answer. The church wasn't the answer. Get yourself a surfboard and a girl, ride a wave, do your thing, and don't hurt anybody. There was plenty of world to go around; everyone had his right to a piece of it. They told us so in school. This was a democracy. It didn't always work just right, they said, but your generation will have to get it all together because now there's a bomb that can eliminate the whole population of the planet. So we grew up believing we could do it, and that the answer was peace, or love, or the golden rule, or whatever you wanted to call it.

After all those years of preparation in the schools, you walked out the door and they told you it was your duty to kill the Commies in South Vietnam. If you wouldn't volunteer they could draft you, force you to do things against your will. Put you in jail. Cut your hair, take away your mod clothes, train you to kill. How could they do that? It was directly opposite to everything your parents had been saying, the teachers had been saying, the clergymen had been saying. You questioned it, and your parents said they didn't want you to go, but better that than jail. The teacher said it was your duty. The clergy said you wouldn't want your mother to live in a Communist country, so you'd best go fight them in Asia before they landed in California. You asked about "Thou shalt not kill" and they mumbled. And you felt betrayed. You sat and drank beer and talked to all your classmates, and they agreed, but their folks were paying to keep them in college and they had a student deferment. For thirteen years you had been through it all together, and now they were taking the easy way out, and you didn't have much in common anymore. You only knew it was all a bad dream, that the placid suburban street had become divided into us versus them, and they were copping out on everything they had ever told us. How could it all have gotten so serious so quickly? It was all a bad dream. You tried to wait it out, hoping it would just blow over like the Cuban Missile Crisis. You saw more and more about Vietnam in the papers, a coup against Ngo Dinh Diem, Buddhist monks in flames, a "Dragon Lady." Maybe, if you just waited, it would all go away. Gee, California had all those cool cars, and surfers, and movie stars, and you had never met anyone who had ever been there. Too far away, too expensive. Vietnam? Yeah, you saw the thing in the papers, but right now you were trying to scrape up the bucks to see Sonny and Cher in concert.

• • • •

Jimmy Rollins had been ahead of me in school. He had been on the basketball team, and was always friendly, but we weren't close. I assumed he had gone to college. I was at a Friday night football game. I had a date with one of the cheerleaders, and I watched her strut her stuff. I felt kind of special, a graduate. This year's students, teachers, and parents stopped to say hello. In a small town everybody knows you. Belinda came over to the snow fence to talk about our plans for after the game. Suddenly her eyes darted to the crowd, and she called out: "Jimmy! Jimmy!"

Jimmy Rollins ambled over to the fence. Belinda leaned across the splintered wooden slats and threw her arms around him. He seemed to fall back under the impact. "Jimmy! It's so good to see you!" She said it over and over, and there were tears in her eyes. Rollins was hunched into a heavy mackinaw, his hands buried deep in the pockets. It was cold, and there was a detachment that had become fashionable with the Rolling Stones. He looked at his feet and said nothing. Belinda was rattling on. "I'm so glad to see you! Are you all right?" Rollins mumbled something and wrestled out of her embrace, coming face to face with me.

"Hi, Jim. How ya been?" I held out my hand. He didn't. He looked at his feet. Belinda went back to her pom-poms. I nodded her way. "What was that all about? You been away?"

He looked up now, almost as if he were surprised at the question. His face looked, well, tired, or strained. Different. Older. I couldn't put my finger on it. "Yeah, away." I sensed a tension.

"School?"

"No. How 'bout you?"

"Naw, I'm fixing dents in Chevy fenders." He shrugged himself deeper into the mackinaw, and tilted his head a funny way, as if he was seeing me out of the corner of his eye. Cool. Mature. He kicked at the brown grass with a loafer toe.

"How do you stand with the draft?" He sounded sincere, concerned. It took me a little off guard.

"The army doesn't want me. I had a physical. I'm One-A, but I don't think they'll want me."

His face turned to mine, and it was twisted somehow. "Listen to me, asshole. The fuckin' army wants anybody that's walkin' and breathin'. There's a war on. Get in the fuckin' reserves, man, or the guard, or school, or get married. Do somethin'!" He was getting loud. "This ain't a fuckin' game! One day you'll find your ass in the fuckin' jungle, and you'll wish to God you'd listened!" It was an explosion now, a startling, loud explosion of profanity and emotion that shocked me. His eyes were wild, crazy, and spooky. "Nobody told me! I didn't know! You ever seen your best buddy die? Shit, no! And you better pray to fuckin' God you never do! You think that fuckin' football team is rough? Huh? That's a fuckin' game, and what we're talkin' about is no game! It's serious, deadly fuckin' serious! You gotta do something!" He was screaming now, crazy. People were looking. You didn't use language like that in small towns in 1966. Rollins took a deep breath, looked at me with those eyes, turned, and melted back into the crowd. I was bewildered, and I guess it showed. A teacher from my junior year had been a few spaces away along the snow fence, and he came over to me.

"Jimmy's been through a lot." I liked Mr. Gott, had missed him.

"What's his problem?" I asked.

"You don't know?" Gott's eyebrows arched. "He was an ammo carrier in Vietnam. His arm was blown off at the shoulder."

The earth rocked under my feet. "No shit!" I looked toward the spot where Jimmy had disappeared. "No shit!" I dug for a cigarette. My hand was shaking as it raised the lighter.

Mr. Gott had a reputation for talking too much, but it was informed, insightful talk. The man read the papers, thought about what he had read, and challenged you to do the same. He always seemed to ask, "Why do you think this happened?" as if all the world's news were interrelated.

I was still fumbling when he changed the subject. "You didn't go to college?" Before I could answer, he went on. "I hear you're working on cars. Should've had some auto shop. I didn't really think you wanted to go that way." He paused to light a cigarette.

"I just didn't want to spend any more time behind a desk. I always liked cars. I just couldn't get enthusiastic about going back to school."

"Uncle Sam after you yet?"

"I had a physical. I'm One-A."

Gott dragged at the cigarette, turned, and looked me straight in the eye. "Enlist."

"Mr. Gott?"

"Enlist! You can get some education. Training. How to fix cars, if that's what you want. Guaranteed. They send the draftees to Vietnam. You'll probably go to Germany. Even if you do go to Vietnam, you won't be infantry. Enlist. I did. It'll make you a man, do you a lot of good. Teach you some responsibility, get you out from under momma's apron. You can get out after three years, with benefits. You'll never regret it. Best years of my life were in the army."

I mumbled something, the team burst back onto the field, and Mr. Gott returned to his friends. It all seemed so far away. I looked to Belinda. I would think about it later. Tonight…

• • • •

One night a few weeks later I was driving in a blinding snowstorm when I saw a dark figure with his back turned to the wind and his thumb extended. I stopped. He was half-frozen and very appreciative. As he thawed, we talked. He was heading for Pennsylvania. Coming from Buffalo. He worked at the pre-induction center giving draft physicals. I pulled over to the edge of the road and asked him to get out. He couldn't believe it. I insisted. I left him huddled against the snow and wind, in the night, a long way from home. My friends laughed at the story, but it was no laughing matter. Somewhere, deep inside, it felt deadly serious.

• • • •

I-Feel-Like-I'm-Fixin'-to-Die Rag

C'mon all of you big strong men
Uncle Sam needs your help again
He's got himself in a terrible jam
'Way down yonder in Vietnam
So put down your books and pick up a gun
We're gonna have a whole lotta fun

And it's one-two-three what are we fightin' for
Don't ask me I don't give a damn
Next stop is Vietnam
And it's five-six-seven open up the Pearly Gates
Why, ain't no time to wonder why
Whoopee! We're all gonna die

Well, come on generals, let's move fast
Your big chance has come at last
Gotta go out and get those reds
The only good Commie's the one that's dead
And you know that peace can only be won
When you blow them all to kingdom come

And it's one-two-three what are we fightin' for
Don't ask me I don't give a damn
Next stop is Vietnam
And it's five-six-seven open up the Pearly Gates
Why, ain't no time to wonder why
Whoopee! We're all gonna die

Come on Wall Street, don't move slow
Why, man, it's war a-go-go
There's plenty of good money to be made
By supplying the army with the tools of the trade.
Just hope n' pray that if they drop The Bomb
They drop it on the Viet Cong

And it's one-two-three what are we fightin' for
Don't ask me I don't give a damn
Next stop is Vietnam
And it's five-six-seven open up the Pearly Gates
Why, ain't no time to wonder why
Whoopee! We're all gonna die

Well, come on mothers throughout the land
Pack your boys off to Vietnam
C'mon fathers, don't hesitate
Send them off before it's too late
Be the first one on your block
To have your son come home in a box

And it's one-two-three what are we fightin' for
Don't ask me I don't give a damn
Next stop is Vietnam
And it's five-six-seven open up the Pearly Gates
Why, ain't no time to wonder why
Whoopee! We're all gonna die

—Joe McDonald
(Country Joe & The Fish)

• • • •

The next few weeks were agonizing. Thinking slows the movement of time, and I was going over and over the options in my mind. I spent too many nights in a little bar in the city, sipping wine by candlelight and listening to a rock group called Onja and the Loose Ends. No one called them hippies in those days. They were beatniks or bohemians, they did a lot of Bob Dylan songs, and every night's assembled audience made me feel comfortable. I could hide in the darkness, be soothed by the soft acoustic guitars. I was trying to bide my time, waiting for the miracle that would save me. Time was running out. In a scant sixteen months, the optimism of high school had been replaced by hopelessness and confusion. I would probably be drafted within six months. If I escaped to Canada, my family would be social outcasts. They didn't know what to suggest either. We discussed Canada, and they weren't at all enthusiastic. They insisted they didn't want me to be drafted, but day after day expired, and there were no good alternatives. "Enlist. At least you won't be infantry." But I would have to go for an extra year! "Sure, but you're young." Yeah, and I wanted a chance to get old.

The waiting lists for the reserves and National Guard were too long, but I added my name. I thought about just running away, but to where? Again, it would dishonor my family, and I could never come home. Two years was a long time, but never was forever. I begged a doctor to write something about my damaged right knee. He encouraged me to do my duty. It was too late to register for school and get a student deferment, and I had a car payment to think about. At eighteen, school seemed as much a prison as the army. I only wanted to be free to do what I was doing. Advice came from everywhere. Try to get in the air force or navy, they live better than the army. They weren't accepting any more recruits. I didn't want to join anything or go anywhere. I only wanted to be free.

It was a bright and sunny Saturday in late November. I drove with my parents to Batavia, to a small storefront office. We were greeted by a portly, balding, kindly man who seemed to exude self-confidence and dignity. His clothes were crisply starched, and there were rows of multicolored ribbons on his lapel. He laughed at Vietnam. We've got a few men there, sure, and it makes good news copy, but you'll probably go to Germany. We have bases all over the world. You'll live in modern barracks, like a college dorm. He held out a brochure. How long did I think a bunch of jungle savages would be able to stand up to the full might of the United States? I would be guaranteed months of schooling; chances are it would be over before I finished. Frankly, though, the best advice he could offer was not to let myself be drafted. They'll be the first to go to Vietnam. Second class soldiers. Stand up to your obligation, go along with the army, and it would go along with you. Basic training is a kind of orientation. The hardest part is the physical conditioning, but you're young and healthy and it won't bother you. After basic, it will be just like any other nine-to-five job.

In my eighteen years, I had never been away from home more than a week in my life. I knew I wasn't cut out for the heroics I saw on "Combat," but I could work on trucks and cars. I was scared and confused. Three years. Three years ago I had been a sophomore in high school. It seemed long ago. Three years from now I should be making good money. God, I was scared. I didn't want to shoot anybody, and I didn't want anybody to shoot me. I took a few days to decide. I had to make a decision soon, or not get my guaranteed army training. I met a girl who told me about her brother. He had been totally blind in one eye since birth, but they had drafted him, and he was in basic training. I called the recruiter. Could I at least stay home for the holidays? In order to make the class date, I would have to go in December 30. I signed the papers. The agony was over. I didn't like the outcome, but the terrible question was answered.

It was a strained Christmas. The family tried to make it jolly. Maybe they tried too hard; maybe it was the gifts. A shaving kit. A pocket radio. Traveling things. I was going away. I was dating a girl named Maggy. We went to a concert, the Who, the Blues Magoos, and Herman's Hermits. The teenybopper girls screamed and passed out. I hated that baloney. I had paid a good buck to hear the music. There was something different about that night, and I made some excuse to Maggy and went out into the corridor. Stretchers with unconscious girls were everywhere, while nurses in white uniforms rushed about. I stood and watched a long time. The papers said it was like a battle zone.

Knowing he would have to hire me back, the boss fired me "because my hair was too long." That, I assured him, was what I would be defending: American ingenuity. I sorted catalog orders in a Sears warehouse 'til Christmas, then took a vacation. I tried to cram a lot into those few days, and they ticked

away, one by one. On the morning of December 30, 1966, my
parents drove me to that horrible building in Buffalo. Everyone
was pleasant and respectful while the parents were there. We
raised our hands and repeated some kind of oath. I thought I
would throw up or feel my knees collapse. The parents left,
and we were allowed to get something to eat and meet at the
train station at midnight. I bought a bottle of Scotch. There is
no place on earth as lonely as a train station at midnight.

I drank to the very limit of my endurance, threw up, and
slept on the floor of the train. It was as if my life had ended, or
I wanted it to. I was among total strangers, being carried away,
and the drinking wasn't pleasurable. I wanted to get "dead
drunk." It was self-destructive, the way I poured the booze
down. I never wanted to see the morning, but I did. My eyes
were bloodshot, my headache was immense, and the train
rolled on. In New York City we transferred to buses, and
arrived at Fort Dix, New Jersey, in the early afternoon. I was
digging deep, looking for strength. As the bus stopped, the DIs,
or drill instructors, attacked. In uniforms with knife-edge
creases and their stereotypical Smokey the Bear hats, they burst
through the bus doors, screaming. We jumped, we hustled, we
shuddered, but it really didn't upset me as I had expected. It
was obviously an act. If a person really had that temperament,
he would be committed. Rational adults don't behave like that.
The secret was to act intimidated when confronted personally,
and blend into the background whenever possible.

● ● ● ●

Where does the army get all that ugly pale green paint? It
must be mixed specially and shipped in tank cars, because it
would never sell on the outside. We were hustled through pale
green room after pale green room, accompanied by the ranting
and raving DIs. Uniforms. Bedding. Dog tags. ID cards. Blood

tests. They called us girls, or pussies, or shitheads. Run from station to station, balancing a mountain of gear. Nothing fit. They asked your sizes and handed you clothes that didn't come close, and the DIs screamed that you were to blame and called you "shit-for-brains." Then it was time to eat, and you piled your collection in the parking lot and swung hand over hand from the rungs of a ladder to get into the mess hall. You got ten minutes to go through the line, gobble a few bites, and be back at your pile of army-issue paraphernalia. The DIs circulated through the mess hall, screaming, hollering, ridiculing, and pushing faces into plates of food. I could see they were harassing the overweight guys, and I was pleased to be skinny. I managed to stall the eleven-minute mark, which gave me a great deal of satisfaction. I vowed never to respect their limit on time to eat, and I never did. Even if it was just seconds, I took longer than the allotted time for every meal I ate at Fort Dix. It was my secret, my token individuality, and they were never able to strip it away.

The barracks must have been built for George Washington's troops. Many of the windowpanes were missing, and there were no mirrors, just sheets of metal nailed to the wall. The story was, someone had slashed his wrists with a shard of broken mirror, but it made no sense. There were still a few windowpanes if you were determined. Bright red soup cans hung from the posts, filled with exactly three inches of water. These butt cans, we were to learn, were not allowed to have ashes.

God, it was cold! It was about ten above, and with no windowpanes the famous New Jersey Pine Barrens wind whistled over us, indoors or out. After a session of pushups and screaming, we were taught to make a military bunk. A schedule of fire guards was announced, everyone getting an hour to walk around the building guarding against a fire that was highly unlikely since the furnace wasn't lit. The New Year slipped in unannounced. New Year's Day was a holiday, but we had to swing down the ladder to our meals. The rest of the day we were confined to the barracks. Cigarettes were running low, and the chill made your bones hurt, but we tried to rest. A lot of us had long hair, and we decided to cheat the army barbers of their fun. We hacked each other's hair off with razor blades.

The next morning all hell broke loose. About 5:00 A.M., one of the DIs turned on the lights and hollered. We were supposed to roll out of bed and stand at attention by the bunks, but no one had bothered to tell us the rules. I was a pretty sound sleeper and had spent the night on a top bunk. When I didn't jump, the sarge simply pushed it over. An army bunk is not comfortable, but it is heavy. When you and the bunk hit the floor from about five feet up, it hurts.

They saw our hair and marched us out into the early morning cold in varying degrees of undress to await some officer who would decide whether to court-martial us for "destruction of government property." Fear and intimidation made the cold seep deeper into our bones. Finally, we were allowed ten minutes for the "four S's" (shit, shine, shower, and shave), and swung down that damned ladder to breakfast. We carried our gear to a new brick barracks, on the run. It would be eight men to a room, but at least there was heat. We got our army haircut and tried to stifle a smile.

The cold was incredible, but jackets were not allowed. Our next training was a two-mile run. I'll never forget it. There was a fat guy from the Midwest. He was older than most of us, married. He had flunked out of law school, and the draft got him. We hadn't run very far when he fell. His face was an unhealthy shade of red. We were halted and made to stand at attention in the bitter wind while the DIs slapped him around. He cried, threw up, got to his feet, and tried again. The second time he fell, Sergeant Anderson took off his belt and began to whip him. Anderson was the ranking DI, and mean. He kept repeating, "Get up, Fatso." Fatso had a bloody lip now, and his face was distorted and pathetic, but he got to his feet again.

Anderson flailed away with the belt like a slave driver in a biblical movie. Fatso's giant thighs trembled, and he fell again.

Anderson ordered him to attention. He got to his hands and knees, vomited, and collapsed in tears. Again he was ordered to come to attention. He got to his feet, weaving, but upright. Anderson was inches from his face, screaming. "You puked on your uniform, boy! That uniform should be worn with pride, boy! You can't represent the United States of America looking like that, boy! Take that uniform off! You're a fat pig, and we don't allow pigs to dress like soldiers, boy! Get that uniform off! Now!" He was screaming, red in the face, crazy. Still at attention, we felt the sweat freezing under our arms and across our chests. Fatso's eyes darted from side to side, looking for help that would never come. He unbuttoned his shirt and shrugged out of it. The screaming continued. He dropped to the ground to remove his boots and socks, hesitating, expecting Anderson to say, "Enough." There was more screaming, no respite. The wet T-shirt came off. The poor guy's chest and back were striped with swollen red welts where the belt had landed. More screaming. "Those are official United States Army shorts, boy! You don't deserve to cover your fat ass with shorts some poor taxpayer worked his ass off for. Boy, I told you to get that uniform off. I mean off, now!"

Fatso's eyes begged the other DIs for help. We were on a large grassy field, and traffic streamed up a road at its edge, only a few yards away. The DIs wouldn't meet his eyes. Anderson continued to scream, then walked up to the cowering recruit and smashed his fist into the guy's face. He rolled across the grass, shook his head to clear it, got to his feet, and charged. At that last instant, the sarge sidestepped and drove a fist squarely into Fatso's belly. There was a scream of mixed pain, horror, and defeat. Anderson rushed to the shaking, twisting form and tore his shorts off. The guy was stark naked, out here in the middle of the field where anybody could see.

It was over. Anderson picked up the discarded uniform, tucked it under his arm, an ordered us to run. It was hard to get the cold, stiff muscles going, but the exhibition has served its purpose. You ran. Some guys puked, some tripped. It hurt. The cold air burned your lungs, your legs felt like jelly, but you ran with all the conviction cold terror could muster. If you stumbled, you rushed back into place. If you vomited, you made sure it didn't soil your uniform or delay you. You ran. Around the PX, past the bus station, and back onto the parade field. Fatso was still there, on his knees, covering his nakedness with his hands, shivering. Sarge called a halt. We struggled to stand motionless, gasping, fighting to draw the breath of life into tortured lungs, to control muscle spasms that threatened to throw us to the frozen ground. "At ease!" Anderson had run along beside us, and wasn't even breathing hard. I guessed his age to be near forty, and I was afraid he might look at me. No, he strutted over to the cowering, quivering Fatso. "On your feet, boy!" Fatso rose. "Tay-un-hutt!" There was a crude parody of attention, the position we had learned only yesterday. It seemed so long ago. Fatso trembled so violently he threatened to throw himself off his feet. His eyes pleaded. "I'll teach you to disobey, boy! You'll learn to run. You'll learn when I say, 'Jump,' to get your feet off the ground and say, 'How high, Sergeant?' on your way up. I know your problem. You're fat! Fat! FAT! You're a fat, filthy, fucking pig, aren't you, boy?"

Fatso looked very defeated, smaller. "Yessir!" It was a whisper. Crack! Anderson slapped his cheek so hard we all expected him to go down again. The cold was making our shirts stiff and hard.

"Don't you ever call me 'Sir'! Ever! See those stripes? I work for a livin', pig! I make men out of fucking animals like you. I'm gonna make you a man. You believe that, boy?" There was a pause, but finally Fatso nodded. "Answer me!"

"Yes, Sergeant!"

"Boy, I'm gonna make you a man! You're an animal, boy! A fat fucking pig! A disgrace to the uniform of the United States Army! I'll make you a man, pig! I'll get that weight off you! I'm gonna make you sweat, and cry, and beg, and bleed, and someday you're gonna be a soldier. I'll make you a man, and I'll make you a soldier. No fuckin' college education gonna help you here, boy! You wanna be a soldier, boy?"

"No, Sergeant!" We cringed. God help him. But the Sarge turned his back and strolled toward us. No one dared draw a breath.

"Take a break, troops! Smoke 'em if you got 'em. Anybody got a Camel?" Someone offered a Camel from a rumpled pack. He took it, offered a polite, "Thank you," then turned on his heel and returned to the shaking Fatso. Sarge walked up to him, bent at the waist, and made an exaggerated inspection of the guy's naked privates. Satisfied, he rose and turned back to us. "He's got balls! His fuckin' stomach hangs over so you can't see 'em, but they're there! Long as he's got balls, I can work with him! I'll make him a man. I'll make you all men!" He turned back to Fatso, and his voice became softer, almost friendly.

"Son, you got to lose that weight. You know it, and I know it. In eight weeks you got to leave here lookin' like a solder. You gotta lose that weight, and I'm gonna help you. It's gotta be done, and we're gonna do it. Right, son?"

"Yes, Sergeant." Fatso relaxed a little, but the cold was making him shake uncontrollably.

"I'm gonna help you, son. Will you let me help you?"

"Yes, Sergeant."

"Good." He walked around Fatso and laid the cigarette on the ground, then returned. "We gotta get the weight off you, son. We gotta get the weight off, which means you'll have to exercise, and sweat, and ache, and you're gonna have to eat less and shit more! Do you understand me, son?"

"Yes, Sergeant."

"Good! I'm glad you understand. Then you just squat down there, and you shit on that cigarette. And when I can't see that cigarette anymore you can get up, and get dressed, and we'll go on with our day. And all these young men will watch, and see if they can learn anything from someone with your educational background. Do you understand, son?"

"But…but I don't have to, Sergeant."

Quick as a snake, Anderson's right fist smashed into Fatso's belly, and it sounded as if Fatso sucked in all the air in New Jersey as he doubled up and went down again. He crouched there a minute, then crawled over to that cigarette, raised himself to a crouch, and shit. He cried, and he strained, and he kept his eyes away from us, and when the sarge was satisfied, he got dressed. Then, because "it wouldn't be nice to leave a mess like that on a public parade field," he carried it away in his bare hands. It was intimidating, but not nearly as intimidating as the awful knowledge that this was to be my life for over a thousand more days.

• • • •

We were pushed, pulled, beaten, screamed at, humiliated, and emasculated for eight weeks. Up at five, train 'til six, work details 'til eight, polish and clean and launder and starch until lights out at ten. Always aching, always cold, always scared; never secure. Dig a hole six feet by six feet by six feet, then fill it again. Shovel a foot of snow with dustpans, naked but for boxer shorts and boots. There was freezing rain on the rifle range, knee-deep mud on the way to orientation lectures. Endless lectures in sixth-grade vocabulary. The Code of Conduct. The perils of venereal disease. The evil of communism. Why we were in Vietnam. The Uniform Code of Military Justice. First aid. Tear gas. You had to breathe it so you would recognize it. Fever. Chest congestion. A five-mile run. Aching, tearing cough. I tried sick call one morning. I had eighteen hours of KP and two aspirins to show for it. A few cases of meningitis broke out. They were separated. Exhaustion. Depression. Over a thousand days. Hand-to-hand combat. Charge a dummy with a mock bayonet. "What's the spirit of the bayonet?" "Kill! Kill! Kill!" I rebel and holler, "Peace! Peace! Peace!" and I am punched and kicked into submission. I holler "Kill!" and hate the sergeant's guts.

At the end of basic we had "night fire." We marched to the rifle range to shoot at human-shaped targets in the darkness. "Ready on the right? Ready on the left? Lock and load! Fire when ready! Hold your fire! Clear your weapons! Clear on the right? Clear on the left? First squad, retrieve your targets!" You scramble out of the foxhole and over the frozen ground, take down your target, hang a new one, and return with your peppered prize to seek the sergeant's approval.

Something went wrong at "night fire." It ended abruptly, and we were trucked back to the barracks. Sarge had never let up on Fatso. I guess it just got to be too much. Instead of returning, Fatso just stood behind one of the target forms and waited. "Ready on the right? Ready on the left? Lock and load! Fire when ready!" He had been older. Once, he had been a law student. He had been called to do his duty. He had a wife.

The next day we were "shaken down." They said Fatso had been sniffing glue. No one believed Fatso was on drugs. No one could believe he was dead.

A few days later, Sergeant Anderson was relieved.

My nineteenth birthday came and went.

• • • •

All the ominous signs had been there, and I had ignored them. When I was young, I played soldiers with a wooden rifle and army surplus helmet. I read about the Civil War; John Singleton Mosby, the Confederate guerilla major, was my favorite hero: "The Grey Ghost." I read about Gettysburg and Bull Run, Yorktown and Iwo Jima, and the French and Indian War. It never dawned on me that living human beings were hurt or killed. We visited Gettysburg, saw the wax statues of dying men and the marble monuments, but it wasn't realistic. Now I see the rolling fields of Gettysburg, and I imagine the stink and anguish of fifty thousand dying men.

• • • •

From basic I was shipped to Aberdeen Proving Grounds in Maryland for AIT, or Advanced Individual Training. This was the course I had signed up for, Wheel and Track Vehicle Repair, and I looked forward to the college-like atmosphere the recruiting sergeant had promised. Aberdeen was a humid and desolate place on the shores of the Chesapeake Bay, a relic of World War II vintage slowly settling into the marsh.

The other students were interested in cars, so we had a great deal in common. In general, the training was inadequate and obligatory. Many of our instructors made it clear from the outset that they were "short," and just serving out their remaining time. They did not intend to be burdened with questions. The lesson plan had been prepared by the army and was designed to teach you everything you needed to know. Questions brought ridicule, rarely answers. I scored well, enjoying the hands-on sessions in which your efforts were rewarded when a stubborn bolt turned or an engine purred. So much of army life required great effort with no discernible reward.

We had expected the humiliation and harassment to end after basic, but it had followed us to Aberdeen. We began to appreciate that this was life in a military society, and the number of days remaining in our military careers seemed insurmountable. In addition to this mechanical training, we were subjected to frequent "orientations." These were propaganda sessions, and the subject of Vietnam came up frequently. "This is the enemy," the film said, and he was a fleeting shadow in the trees. We soon learned to coexist with the army. We kept our hair short, our brass polished, and our mouths shut. A question about Vietnam or the Uniform Code of Military Justice was rewarded with "work detail," endless hours of hard physical labor.

Getting sick was a punishable offense. The favorite form of punishment was an "Article 15," usually a fine and assignment to the harshest work details. To lie down from exhaustion was AWOL. Pass out, and when they released you from the hospital you were immediately assigned to work details. We were allowed passes to go downtown, unlike during basic, and we regularly shopped at the drugstore for nonprescription remedies. Of course, a few adventuresome souls contracted venereal diseases, which were labeled "destruction of government property," and were punished.

Your very body belonged to Uncle Sam. You could be punished, even go to jail, for growing a mustache or peeing without permission. A tattoo was "destruction of government property," a court-martial offense. No trial by a jury of your peers here; you were subject to the Uniform Code of Military Justice. "Army Regulations state...Article this...Paragraph that...Boy, do you think a board of majors and colonels, pulled away from their offices to sit in a hot, sweaty courtroom, would view a private's case with kindness and understanding? That what you think, soldier?"

Sooner or later, most of us recognized the hopelessness of it all and quietly submitted. Still they pushed, trying to force a reaction. "Boy, you better forget that hometown pussy. She's fucking your best friend's brains out tonight, and she don't give a damn for your spindly little dick no more." "Trooper, I do believe yo' momma is as dumb as you are. She kept the afterbirth an' threw da baby away. What you got to say 'bout dat, shithead?"

I learned to be nondescript, learned to avoid attention and

serve my time. It hurt. There was nothing to be proud of. So soon after high school, we had expected "army discipline" to be like the practice sessions we had endured in school sports. This was not teamwork. The lifers had stripped us of all dignity and self-respect and seemed to delight in rubbing our noses in our impotence. I didn't respect them. There was no compassion or humanity, just army regulations and ruthless brutality. I learned to roll my socks into balls and press my fatigue shirts until the creases were razor sharp, but the heavy humidity made them limp and sweat-stained before breakfast. I had an unused razor for inspections and another for shaving. I learned that these day-to-day details were not particularly interesting to girls back home, and their letters became rarer. I learned not to think, not to feel, and not to question; and I learned not to write about the frustration of it all because no one cared to hear about it. I wouldn't have called it "shame" or "guilt"; it was merely existence without self-respect, wasting time.

• • • •

It was spring of 1967. I had graduated from high school months before, brimming over with enthusiasm, eager to contribute to mankind. My adolescent optimism had been torn away and replaced with a thousand-day sentence to futility. I wore the uniform of an American soldier. My understanding of American democracy had been crafted in college-preparatory classes with names like Principles of Democracy and Responsibilities of Freedom. Clever teachers had introduced us to the lofty idealism of the Magna Carta, the Bill of Rights, and the Emancipation Proclamation. We had discussed Emily Dickinson and Thoreau. My peers had gone beyond *Walden* and were quoting Thoreau's *Civil Disobedience*. A sergeant with a fifth-grade education was searching among my personal items, his white-gloved pinkie sure to show some trace of dust.

I resented it. Most of us did. In a class of forty-odd, only one or two felt that they were contributing to America's future. We were prisoners, serving time. The acronym FTA was everywhere, in pencil, ink, spray paint, carved into wood or concrete. Fuck the army! Our frustration was often trained upon inanimate olive-drab equipment. Sabotage was widespread. We were incarcerated and angry. Our only crime was to be male, of age, and in good health. The idea that we might face the death penalty was everyday conversation now.

Vietnam was sucking us in like quicksand. You couldn't ignore it. No matter where you looked, there were posters, pamphlets, bulletins. I was reminded of the halls in high schools just before a big football game. "Go Army! Beat Vietnam! Be Tough! Block that Kick!" Every lecture urged us to pay attention so we might perform better in The Nam. Our training was nearing its conclusion. There would be orders. Many of us would be going to war.

I had learned many new skills, but I wasn't ready to bet my life on them. I wasn't at all convinced I could survive hand-to-hand combat with a fanatical Viet Cong, but I wasn't about to admit my fears to the sarge. I could fire a rifle with reasonable accuracy and march in step. I could make a bunk with "hospital corners," shave without water, and tune up a jeep. I hardly felt prepared for combat, but my fears had to remain buried deep inside. The army had sent releases to the hometown papers; everyone knew I had been trained.

Based upon my aptitude test scores, the army suggested I apply for Officer Candidate School. It would be another session of extreme harassment, far worse than basic. I filled out the application. I hated what I was doing, I couldn't hate anything more. Having volunteered, I could endure it. The rewards would be worthwhile: more pay, creature comforts, perhaps a bit of respect. My acceptance was somewhat of a surprise.

I graduated from the mechanical training with high scores. We stood in the street, in front of the barracks, as the diplomas were handed out. It was a pregnant moment because there was another stack of papers to be distributed. The air was electric with tension. As the orders were announced, as the words "Republic of South Vietnam" were bounced off the worn clapboards of the barracks wall, more than one young soldier screamed out in an agony of fear and dismay.

They packed quietly and caught their buses. I was alone, waiting to begin OCS. For over a month I waited, working as an office orderly, fetching coffee, answering phones. Suspended animation. Each dawn brought me closer to the only goal that mattered, the day I would be a civilian again.

The company commander called me into his office. There was a surplus of ordnance officers; my class had been cancelled. I had been assigned to the Republic of South Vietnam. He handed me the papers, the authorization for a thirty-day leave. I felt sick inside, fought back the tears. Now I, too, packed my bags and caught a bus.

● ● ● ●

Thirty days go by fast when they are all that stands between you and doom. I rushed about, eager to see family and friends one more time, but when we came face to face there was nothing to say. I bought a '54 Plymouth for $7.00, added a Chevy clutch disc for $1.50, and entered a demolition derby. I bought a can of fluorescent spray paint and wrote, "Going to Vietnam and ready to raise hell," down the side of the Plymouth. I busied myself chaining the doors and trunk shut. If I was hurt, it would be "destruction of government property." What would they do, send me to Vietnam? My attitude and my vocabulary consisted mostly of "fuck it!"

I was heading home from a friend's, and it was late. An oncoming car didn't dim its lights, and I flashed my high beams. In the rearview mirror I saw brake lights, the red flasher on the roof, and a U-turn. Now the four headlights were overtaking me, and I pulled over to the shoulder, lowered the window, and waited. What was this all about?

"License and registration please."

I handed them to him. "What's the problem, Officer?"

"You failed to dim your headlights, son."

"Officer, I blinked at your high beams."

"Why?"

"Because I couldn't see!"

"Don't be smart, son. I'm on a call, and your bright lights hampered my ability to respond. I'll have to write you up."

I handed a piece of paper out the window. "You better get me to court real soon, Officer. These are my orders. Tuesday I leave for Vietnam."

He read the orders. "All right, son. Get on home." He handed back my license and registration, made a squealing U-turn, and disappeared into the night. Strange.

I tried not to sleep. I sold my drums to a pawnshop to get money for a date. I wanted to get laid, but there just wasn't anyone. My family didn't talk. Everyone laughed nervously and said, "Be careful." Everything looked different, felt different. The TV networks boasted about next week's shows. Next week I would be on the other side of the globe. Tonight's programs stank!

At the airport I kissed Mom good-bye, shook Dad's hand, and punched a brick wall. All the way to New York the stewardess tried to repair the bleeding knuckles.

Fort Dix again! At least it was warm. The barracks had no mirrors or window glass. The light bulbs were in wire mesh cages. You couldn't have sheets, lest you try to hang yourself. Late Saturday afternoon I caught the plane. The last phone call home hadn't brought much relief; no one knew what to say. We took a bus to McGuire Air Force Base and pulled up next to a giant C-5A Starlifter. We sat backward in web seats, without windows. We refueled in Alaska. It was a long walk into the terminal. It was thirty-eight below zero, and we were in tropical uniforms! We refueled again at Yokota, Japan. It was 4:00 A.M., and I couldn't see anything of Japan. No one spoke after that. I sat next to a marine lieutenant who had been trying to strike up a conversation about hand-to-hand combat and artillery coordinates. Even he was quiet now.

● ● ● ●

We dropped quickly, braked hard, and felt the wave of heat when they opened the huge cargo door. "Welcome to Tan Son Nhut air base." We were on the edge of Saigon. From the darkness in the belly of the plane to the harsh tropical sun was a transition my eyes resisted. I made out the yellow-and-red Vietnamese flag and sentries with M-16s. Buses arrived, their windows covered with wire mesh. A captain in dress khakis with wet stains under the arms began a spiel.

"Good afternoon, gentlemen, and welcome to the Republic of South Vietnam. It is presently thirteen-fifty, September five, 1967. We will be taking you to the Long Binh Replacement Center, where you will receive your individual unit assignments. On the way, please do not extend your fingers through the wire covering the windows."

We crept out of the air base, through a main gate with little Vietnamese guards and a sandbagged bunker, into the mainstream of Vietnamese peasant life. We marveled at the ragged hovels and piles of garbage. The stink was almost overpowering, as if trapped to rot by the weight of the humidity. The people were tiny, like caricatures. As they saw us approaching they hurried to the edge of the street. A chorus of "Go home, GI" and "Fuck you, GI" was accompanied by a barrage of assorted garbage and trash bouncing off the wire mesh that covered the windows. Somebody in the back of the bus hollered, "Hey, you fuckin' gooks. We're supposed to be here to save your fuckin' puny asses!"

Someone asked the driver if these were VC. "Sure," he said, laughing. "Everybody in this fucking country is VC. During the day they'll smile and take your money. At night they'll creep in and slit your throat. You'll be staying right near the biggest ammo dump in the world. They blew it last month; killed about thirty. Dropped mortars on it, and sent sappers with satchel charges. They mortar the airstrip every night. You can plan on one thing: Charley'll do any Goddamn thing he wants, then just disappear. Nothin' you can do about it, just hope you aren't in the wrong place at the wrong time."

I admit it. There was a certain fascination with the curious culture. Tiny people in cone-shaped bamboo sun hats, bicycle-powered rickshaws, cluttered hovels built of flotsam and jetsam, and naked children with large almond eyes all seemed to be pages of *National Geographic* come to life. But there was no escaping the omens of danger: olive-drab jeeps with machine guns mounted upon a pivot, the tight-fitting camouflage tiger-stripe fatigues of the ARVN (Army of the Republic of Vietnam) soldiers, sandbag walls, and twisted strands of barbed wire lining the dusty road to separate it from the tranquil-looking paddies. Viewed through a screen of quarter-inch wire mesh, it seemed too alien to be attractive. The humidity was oppressive; and there was a sweet stink that suggested fruits and tires burning together.

We turned left past a well-fortified sandbag bunker and uphill across a steaming beige sand dune. Low barracks of unpainted wood sweltered beneath heavy roofs of corrugated tin, the heavy overhangs shading screened openings desig-nated, obviously, to trap any hint of a breeze. By the orderly disposition in the midst of a land of squalor, I knew this was an American installation. At the top of the rise we reluctantly ducked out of the shade of the bus into the harsh tropical sun. I felt very conspicuous in my dress khakis, silhouetted against the sky, tall and thin in the midst of an environment defensively low and squat. The heat rose off the white sand in prickly waves, and I became aware of wetness gluing my shirt to my back. It was some sort of relief to be here; but fatigue and the harsh sun prevented any joy. This was it, Vietnam; and I dared not miss a word for fear it might be a capital offense.

We were assigned to a barracks, and fled from the sun. I collapsed onto a bunk. I had slept about two hours when a lifer barged in and started calling names. Guard duty. Grab a meal and draw a weapon. The adrenaline had subsided, there was a break in the temperature as the sun slid lower, and I doubted I could move. Jet lag is a civilian condition, reserved for business executives and heads of state. Pfc's rate only duty. I was exhausted and I was scared. Guard duty? I was new here, and there was a war on. If I made a mistake I could get people killed, including myself. Surely the army had some experienced guys for guard duty?

No one ever accused the army of good sense; if they did, the evidence would never convince a jury. I had given three years of my life to my country, and the army wanted its money's worth…twenty-four hours a day, in sickness and in health, for better or worse, 'til death do us part.

I remember being "placed" on my post about nine o'clock that night. I was on a hill, overlooking a distant rectangle ringed with lights. It reminded me of a football field, but the lights faced outward, not inward. Off on the horizon to my left I could see a red glow and hear muffled explosions. Occasionally a trail of tracers would burn a red path across the dark sky, or a far-off burst of small-arms fire would chase away my fatigue.

The sergeant of the guard hadn't had time to talk. The rectangle was the largest ammo dump in the Free World and had recently been blown by sappers. Sappers were VC suicide squads that crawled in and placed satchel charges, or packages of explosives. My duty would be three hours on and three hours off.

As he had bounced away in his jeep, the sickening truth hit me. I had an M-14, six clips, a helmet, and a flak jacket; and I was in The Nam. I heard the war sputtering in the distance, surrounding me. I could see the blazing rectangle and a few shadowy shapes. I didn't know what I was watching for or listening for. I couldn't afford the luxury of thinking about home. I had to learn to concentrate if I was to survive. I wished I had paid more attention to the Kenneth Roberts novels when I was a kid, had gained some insights from the tales of buckskin-clad scouts during the French and Indian War. The slightest noise, the slightest movement might signal a Viet Cong attack. I swallowed grape Kool-Aid from my canteen and wiped my mouth on my sleeve, without taking my straining eyes off the darkness. Surely the army wouldn't put a green recruit on a really "hot" guard post? This was a big camp, with thousands of American lives at stake. On the other hand, the ammo dump had recently been blown. Had the team that did that come through here, slit some replacement's throat, and crawled down to wreak their havoc?

It was hard to pick out one sound over the constant flutter of helicopter blades beating the air. We had been warned that "smoking is hazardous to your health;" that Charley watched for the glow of a cigarette and picked off nicotine addicts at will. I lit them in the shelter of my helmet and kept the glow cupped in my hands, but I needed a cigarette. SSSSS sssssssss...*pop!* I jumped. A guard post on the perimeter of the ammo dump had fired a flare. As it sputtered to life and began to swing gently toward the ground, I realized that I was standing erect on flat ground, casting a shadow that could be seen in

Hanoi. I ducked into the weeds.The flare cast an orange-gold light. Had the guard post seen something? Were a team of VC, frustrated at having been discovered, now crawling toward me? My stomach knotted, and my heart pounded against my ribs with so much force I feared the sound would give my position away. I heard the muffled *whump-whump* of far-off artillery, the clatter of countless helicopters, the rattle of a machine gun. It was chaos, it was enormous, it was everywhere. This was Long Binh, a suburb of Saigon, and supposedly the safest area in all of Vietnam. No matter where they assigned me, it would be worse! How could I keep track of it all, be alert to so many sides, for an entire year?

I could put the barrel of the rifle against my toes and pull the trigger. Instant ticket home. Then I imagined meeting Jimmy Rollins on the street, and steeled for another cigarette. It was my first night. What did I expect? I would learn. The next three hundred and sixty-four days could only end in three ways: better, worse, or the same. I could take better or the same. Hell, I could take worse! I didn't know how much worse, but two out of three chances were, I wouldn't have to find out.

I was at Long Binh a day or two. I remember a beer hall. Someone said a GI had been killed in a racial fight recently. I decided not to have a beer, because nobody was going to send me home in a box due to a damned race riot. I remember seeing my name on an assignment list. I would be going to Pleiku, in the central highlands. Someone said I was lucky; it would be cooler. I remember walking away from that list, looking at my watch. I had a couple hours to get a meal.

I don't remember the trip to Pleiku. There was no gap in days, so it happened in a matter of hours, but what happened? I must have flown, so I must have landed at Camp Holloway. My unit was on the other side of the city, so I must have ridden through downtown Pleiku. A trip through downtown always made an enormous impression on me in later days, but I remember nothing. It's as if something I saw upset me so terribly that I have blocked the experience out of my mind. I don't remember processing in, or drawing bedding or equipment. I only remember being in a tent, struggling to get my gear organized, and the monsoon rains drumming against the canvas. For some reason, the monsoons hit the highlands during dry season in Saigon, and vice versa.

• • • •

The interior of the tent was dark and dismal. There were dim electric lights on the support poles, illuminating six bunks, three on each side. The center area around the poles contained metal lockers and a table of plywood surrounded by wooden shipping crates for stools. The bunks were topped with T-shaped metal bars draped with green mosquito netting. There was a rough wooden floor caked with mud. As the heavy dark green tent flap fell shut behind me, I felt I had entered a damp, dark cave. The rumble of rain beating on the canvas was broken by the fury of a salvo from Artillery Hill on our eastern perimeter. I jumped, but one of the guys came forward, smiling with his hand extended to put me at ease. The glasses on the table rattled, and the suspended light bulbs swung with each burst. I moved deeper into the mildewed cavern, shuddering against the explosions of artillery, shaking hands. They were a rumpled lot, in baggy jungle fatigues and mud-stained T-shirts of familiar army green. Their hair was longer than it should have been, and every man had some highly individual mustache. They made me welcome and pointed out the only unoccupied bunk, but the sadness and fatigue in their eyes worried me. I unpacked my duffel bag and attempted to make some order of the mountain of equipment and bedding, then joined my new friends in a wild dash through the downpour to the mess hall. I was wolfing down fried chicken and powdered potatoes when a familiar face approached the crowd.

Archie and I had been together in basic and at Aberdeen. He was from Boston, pronounced his name Aaaa-chie, and had grown an eccentric handlebar mustache since I had seen him last. Archie hadn't been here long, his eyes still sparkled, and he called to two other friends from our class in Aberdeen. They carried trays of food to my picnic table and squeezed in on the narrow benches, offering big grins and hearty handshakes made slippery by the grease from the chicken. Seeing that these accepted comrades were glad to see me, the guys from the tent opened up and made me feel comfortable. There was hot coffee and a lot of good-natured kidding when they heard I was from New York, and a lot of hurried briefing about the new home we would share. It was good to be with old friends in this hostile and depressing environment, but everyone hurried away to try to get a shower before "rush hour." I needed a shower worse than I could ever remember needing one, and Archie pointed out the rickety shower building and explained the procedure as we tottered back toward the tents on narrow planks laid across the sea of mud. He ducked under a steaming canvas flap with a cheery "Good night. Glad to see you."

I slid out of the rumpled, wet dress khakis and wrapped an o.d. green towel around my waist. Most of the guys wore knee-high rubber boots to the shower. They were available downtown, but I would have to use my canvas jungle boots 'til I got a day off. I gripped the small plastic soap container and ducked under the heavy tent flap into the pouring rain; then balanced on the narrow plank that promised to lead to the shower. The soaking ooze was slippery and often submerged my slender path. Twice I fell headlong into the mud.

The shower was obviously handmade, an unpainted wooden building with a boiler fashioned from fifty-five-gallon oil drums and a network of slender pipes with brass faucet handles. The water poured down from open pipes pointed toward the floor. There were eight openings to drain the fifty-five-gallon drum. During the "rush hour" the water never had a chance to get hot.

Tonight there was hot water, and I felt better as I wrapped the muddy towel about my waist, slid into my boots, and headed back to the tent. I slipped and caught myself with my right arm, coating it with thick mud to the elbow. I met an approaching figure in the midst of a long and narrow two-by-four bridge. He made no effort to move over, and bumped me off into knee-deep goo. As a new replacement, I would learn, I was expected to make way for "short-timers." I returned to the shower, rinsed, and tried again to return to the tent. Again I slipped into the brown swill. It was pouring, a typical tropical rain, and I was disgusted. I stormed back to the tent, where the dim light revealed brown rivers cascading down my arms and legs. From the gloom, I could feel five sets of eyes checking out the green kid. I threw the soggy towel on the floor and ducked back out into the downpour, soap in hand. I sudsed, perched on a two-by-four, and let Mother Nature rinse me. When I felt reasonably clean I ducked back into the dim tent. I was digging out a white towel from home when I was interrupted by a chorus of "Welcome to the Pleiku Hilton!" Five hands reached out for mine, five broad grins signaled acceptance, and a cold beer made us friends for life.

The wind howled, the rain drummed against the canvas, and Artillery Hill roared. The tent was disheveled, crude, and stank of mildew, but it was home. The guys showed me how to tuck in the mosquito net to make it ratproof, how to lay out my combat gear in case Charley paid us a visit in the night, and how to shave in the dim glow of a candle, using a woman's compact and a tiny aluminum pan of cold water. We had a five-gallon jerry can of drinking water. Beer and sodas were available at "the club," a ragged quonset hut that was open for business whenever someone was able to procure a few cases of merchandise. The lifers in Qui Nhon, our supply depot, sold our rations to the black market, so we had to "cumshaw," or swap, needed truck parts for goodies. They taught me to roll socks and underwear inside my rubber poncho to insulate them from the humidity, and to keep matches and cigarettes in sealed glass jars for the same reason. Finally, I crawled into the musty bunk, carefully tucked in the mosquito net, and closed my eyes. My head must have thudded into the pillow.

We were wakened at 4:30, had a formation at 5:00 A.M., then a breakfast of powdered eggs and limp toast. I met Archie for the trip to the shop. We had to be at work at six, and it was a long and trudging walk through the deep mud. At noon, we rode a truck that was in for repairs, and after lunch there was a break of about thirty minutes. I was introduced to the housegirl who would wash my clothes and polish my boots every day for five dollars a month. There was another meal break from five to six, a respite that included both hot food and mail call. Of course, I had no mail, but I was eager to send my address to my parents so things would improve as soon as possible. We worked until ten or eleven and returned to the tents too tired to shower, but too filthy to avoid it. Even if I could stand the grimy feeling, I wouldn't take the chance of annoying the other guys. At Aberdeen, I had seen a guy from California who didn't bathe treated to a "GI shower." A group of classmates waited 'til he was asleep and carried his kicking, squirming form into the latrine, where he was washed with powdered cleanser and coarse scrub brushes. Sleep was to become the rarest and most prized commodity in The Nam, but a shower was a close second, and you were awake to enjoy it. Later, mail from home would downgrade the shower to third place, but I would have to wait a few days for that.

The shop was a giant aluminum barn over a dirt floor. One end was almost completely open. New arrivals worked at the open end, where the mud was deepest and the rain blew in to torment your skin like a thousand tiny insect bites. As your time went on, you moved deeper and deeper into the barn. The floor was dirt, and a four-by-eight sheet of plywood on two saw-horses served as the office. There was a diesel generator to power the trouble lights, but it was temperamental, and we often had to work with flashlights. Of course, there was light outside, but no one wanted to work under the Vietnamese sun. If there were no flashlight batteries, you just waited for a lifer to think of something.

The shop was north of the hootches. (You had to learn the local dialect. It looked like a tent, but it was a hootch.) The compound was laid out around a central crossroads. The main road ran east and west. The entrance gate was at the foot of Artillery Hill. Main Street led from the gate through the cross-roads, westward toward the Cambodian border. At the cross-roads, having entered the gate, the mess hall and our hootches were in the near right rectangle. In the far right, or northwest, corner our parts supply men had a hootch area. Some months before a team of sappers had crept into their area and killed two Americans before being gunned down. The left rectangle near-est to the gate was a field of broken vehicles. Parts were some-times hard to get, so this "boneyard" of scrapped trucks was maintained for salvage. It was just like a junkyard in The World at first glance, but most of these relics had been sidelined by mines or B-40 rockets, not mechanical breakdowns. Back at the crossroads, looking forward to the left would bring battalion headquarters into view. This was a rust-colored tarpaper build-ing. Behind it loomed the shops (there was a separate tin barn for the body shop) and rows of eight-foot metal shipping boxes, which housed the parts. There was another crossroad near the shop. The southernmost third of the compound was unused meadow and swamp, though ringed with guard posts and barbed wire.

It rained every day, starting about nine in the morning and pouring in translucent gray sheets until after midnight. The rain in The Nam was as different from rain in the United States as anything we would encounter in this strange land. The drops were as large as marbles and driven with enough force to sting when they hit you. We were in a wide valley, and there was no runoff. There were areas of shallow mud and areas of deep mud, but there were no areas without mud. Most of our world was under water, and you had to know where to step. The huge trucks we worked with would often sink up to the frame. The driver would try four-wheel-drive, spin the cleated duals at the rear, and dig himself in deeper. The rule was, the driver who "lost" a truck had to swim down and attach the tow chains. *Swim* is an accurate term for the depth of the mud, but hardly describes the frenzied mucking about in zero-visibility goo.

A few days after I arrived, a pfc lost his footing and drowned in a puddle. A five-ton tractor had churned a hole nearly eight feet deep, a hole you tried to remember, but couldn't see. It was in a field of muddy water. I fell into the same hole but was able to tread water until someone threw me a rope and hauled me out. The first sergeant was a kindly man, but I didn't appreciate his humor when he offered to take a picture so I could send it home to the family.

The drowning changed the atmosphere. We were nestled between Artillery Hill and the Ho Chi Minh Trail in Cambodia. The huge howitzers roared at all hours of the day and night. They should have been a constant reminder that a war was raging just beyond the barbed-wire barriers on the perimeter, but, like residents on the flight path of a major airport, we soon grew accustomed to the noise. Our struggle was with the elements. The only way you could cope was to laugh at the adversities—until someone died. No one had known him well, but it was a grim reminder that any of us might go home in a box. The compound grew sullen and quiet, and suddenly we were acutely aware of the artillery again.

A dry spot was at a premium, and we were not the only creatures seeking shelter. Tucking in your mosquito netting was an elaborate nightly ritual. When the lights went out, the hootch was taken over by rats. They scampered, squealed, fought, and chewed. They ate crumbs, boots, plastic, books, even soap. They owned the tent; we staked small territorial claims with the mosquito nets. A solid punch to the filmy gauze would send them squealing into space and convince you these were no field mice. Rats as large as an American house cat were common, perhaps because cat meat was considered a delicacy by the Vietnamese. If a rat managed to bite you, you were doomed to twenty painful injections in the stomach. I swore, if I ever got out of that place, I would never sleep in a tent again. I never have, and I never will.

I was far from comfortable, but I grew accustomed to the new way of life. It was a world of exhaustion, heat, mud, mildew, rot, and few pleasures. You peed into a large tube fashioned from the metal shipping canisters that had brought artillery rounds from The World. You ate powdered eggs and powdered potatoes and drank powdered milk. The water tasted like medicine, and the Kool-Aid tasted like fruit-flavored medicine. Artillery Hill roared, and helicopter blades constantly chopped at the humid air. You couldn't get clean. You couldn't get rested. You grew accustomed to all that; but you never grew accustomed to working on trucks with bloodied seats and giant holes torn in their floorboards. You never grew accustomed to the chatter of a nearby machine gun, or long hours on a guard post, peering into the rain and fog, wondering if a tiny form had crawled through the wire and was behind you preparing to slit your throat. You couldn't grow accustomed to the fear. There was a war all around, and you knew one of these days it was going to ride into town like a gunfighter dressed in black. How would you react? Would you survive? In one piece? Every second brought you nearer to it. How would you die? Loved ones were far, far away; almost a fantasy. In their place you had come to love the guys, your buddies. You knew you were all experiencing the most horrendous, dangerous, profound experience of your lives. As the strongest steel is tempered by fire, you knew the friendships made in this pressure-cooker atmosphere were special. God, you hoped you wouldn't make some stupid move and get them hurt! Or killed. You were aware they might die, any minute, and you fought the normal emotions and didn't let yourself get too close to any of them. And when you didn't see a guy for a few days, or he just got up and walked away, you knew he was thinking the same things and doing what he had to do, and you weren't offended. Long ago, back in The World, you were afraid you might die in The Nam. Now you were afraid you might cause a buddy to die. The change was unsettling, and The World seemed a long, long ways away. You weren't comfortable, but you grew accustomed to living in fear.

• • • •

So I held my breath and hoped the war would continue to stay away from the twisted barbed wire at the perimeters of our compound. Life was far from dull. We were, after all, thousands of miles from home, in an exotic ancient land torn by war. It wasn't pleasant, but it was an adventure and a challenge, and an education.

Our closest contact with the Vietnamese was through the housegirls. Most were middle-aged, but a few were downright attractive. Archie's hootch had a saucy little girl with a Cambodian background. Her eyes were particularly sparkling, and she delighted in sexual teasing. Our girl had buckteeth and wanted no part of the suggestive comments from six horny men. They arrived each morning, in the back of a truck. They gathered the laundry and converged on the shower building, where they beat the clothes on the wooden floor. They laid the wet clothing over the mosquito net T-bars, scraped the mud off your boots with a stick, and spit-shined the toes. They swept, and brought fresh water, sewed on stripes, darned worn socks, and begged us to bring hair spray and Salem cigarettes from the PX. The younger girls were exposed to a lot of sexual harassment, and the older ladies marveled at pictures of America. They had been through a lot, you could see it in their eyes, and most were very kind. If you saw them on the street, downtown, they ignored you; it was not healthy to like Americans.

Of course, there were no flush toilets. We had outhouses. Down below were the top and bottom thirds of fifty-five-gallon drums. We all donated a couple dollars a month to hire a Vietnamese fellow to drag the stinking containers to a pit, empty them, add diesel fuel or gasoline, and burn the waste. I would gladly have paid more to avoid the smell. Our Shitburner was a wrinkled little man with a huge grin. He was probably fifty to sixty years old, strong as a bull, and wonderful. Once, some fool had explained to him what the nickname meant, and his honor was offended. He stayed away from work for a week, a horrible week; and after doing his job, we all agreed to a raise, and to call him Papa-san to his face.

In the center of the compound, a large wire mesh cage was home to two monkeys. In true "monkey see, monkey do" tradition, these two were confirmed alcoholics. Once, my parents sent a package and used saltwater taffy for packing material. The monkeys got more of the taffy than I did, but I enjoyed it more. A monkey with his teeth stuck together, especially if he was drunk and disorderly, was a hilarious sight. Soon everyone was asking the folks back home to use saltwater taffy for packing.

Like all military bases, ours had a barbershop. The barber

was too young for military service, but he was a fine barber. He shaved you with little tin razors that looked like toys, and carefully shaped your eyebrows and shaved the inside of your ears. After each shave or haircut, he urged you to lean forward and "popped" your vertebrae into place one at a time. All good things must come to an end, and one day he announced he was being drafted. He needed three hundred dollars to bribe his way out. A lot of us could relate to that, and a collection was raised. One night we shot him dead, when he was trying to crawl through the wire with satchel charges on his belt.

We eyed the housegirls and their foreign ways with curiosity and amusement. They loved to gather in a circle, squatting flat-footed, picking lice out of the hair of the girl in front, and cracking them in their teeth. Many chewed betel nuts and spat the blood-red juice into the mud. Gold teeth were popular, and many women had their front teeth edged in gold and tiny gold stars or Playboy bunnies or initials inset into the flat surfaces of the tooth.

I was assigned to guard two prisoners while they filled sandbags. They begged cigarettes, and I was kind. I wanted to communicate with them, the Shitburner translated. One of them had killed seven Americans before he was captured. He found a bee's nest in the ground and ignored a thousand angry stings to dig the honey out with his bare hands. I gave him a pack of Marlboros, and he kissed my boots.

Occasionally we would be picked for duties like that. One time you guard gooks, next time you paint the mail hut or help the supply sergeant count canteens. One day I was assigned to the garbage truck; not as a laborer, but as a guard. The truck had been loaded and had to be emptied at a landfill near Camp Holloway. I had my rifle, loaded and ready. As we entered, throngs of peasants crowded around. My job was to keep them back. In the chaos and confusion, an unseen hand could easily plant an explosive charge under our truck. Two boys were allowed up on the truck to throw the garbage into the huge pit. In return for their help, they got first pick of the trash. Below, in the pit, hundreds of ragged people waited in the merciless sun as the torrent of garbage showered down onto them, watching for edible scrapes or unopened cans. It reminded me of a flock of seagulls at a fishing pier.

The next time I was picked for garbage duty, I took my camera. The fighting over scraps had become so vicious, ARVN soldiers were posted to try to keep the crowds away. I saw a young man in a white shirt and snapped a picture. A few seconds later, he found two gallon cans of American food, tucked one under each arm, and scampered out of the pit. He was running headlong toward the barbed wire and the forest when the soldier shouted, "Halt!" "*Dong lai!*" The rifle barked, on full automatic, and the back of the white shirt turned red. The fugitive never missed a step; he dropped to his knees and wriggled through the twisted barbed wire with a finesse that could only have been practiced and disappeared into the jungle still clutching his treasures. I wrote a long letter home that night and searched for words to describe the scene. I needed to tell someone, and knew I couldn't tell the army. The army couldn't interfere with the ARVN, it was "their" country.

Our pleasures were simple. Archie built a barbell from two truck flywheels and an axle shaft. His parents sent jars of wheat germ, and he lifted his weights. Fred embroidered. Simmons whittled tiny water buffaloes and helicopters. Norris bought "pure gold" downtown, melted it down, and molded it into Montagnard bracelets. He spray-painted them with great care and sent them home to his uncle, a jeweler. Poker games flourished. Cockroach races were commonplace. The favorite pastime was sleep, but no one can exist just working and sleeping. A hot shower, a cool beer, or a bottle of hard liquor were popular. Once in a while someone had a marijuana cigarette, and everyone gathered around Ridgely's tape recorder and passed the joint around and listed to his tape of the Doors and the Jefferson Airplane. Ridgely was freaky and wouldn't let anyone listen to his Donovan tape, but we gathered outside the tent. We respected his privacy, but it was music from The World, and if we wanted to stand in the mud and listen through the canvas walls...

The greatest pleasure was escapism, a mental journey home. The booze was an attempt to tune out Artillery Hill and chopper blades, but the ultimate escape was mail. Mail assured you that The World was still turning. Mail was private, and personal, and caring, and concerned, and everything our daily existence was not. A day without a letter from home was only mechanical; your watch ticked and your heart beat and you went through the motions. A letter allowed you to live life again, to turn your attention to loved ones and the familiar things in the neighborhood, to recall insignificant details of an existence that seemed too far away. Once in a while there were photographs of the living room or the flower garden or the neighborhood, and you gazed for hours, wondering what it would be like to be back.

I had dated a girl named Meg. Her older sister dated a guy who was into ham radio. He talked to someone in Cincinnati, and one Sunday my name and address were printed in the Cincinnati newspaper. "Lonely GI in Vietnam" or something. I began to get a lot of letters, sometimes thirty or forty a day. Most were from girls, wondering what was really going on in Vietnam. A few were proposals of marriage, sight unseen. A few had nude or suggestive pictures or offers of carnal delights when I returned. Some were pathetic. An unwed mother had seen her baby die and needed someone to care for. A wife wrote that her husband beat her. Some had lost a loved one in Vietnam and knew how important mail was. All were kind.

Many of the guys around me didn't get mail. Their families were busy or didn't know what to say; and I shared my good fortune. Unopened, like a blind date. Many of the letters were unusual, but most were sincere and honest. I just didn't feel I could look at the letter before passing it on. I wrote to five or six of the girls, and they described rock concerts and snowstorms and Christmas Mass, and helped me more than the writers ever realized.

One evening in October, far away in Rochester, New York, a mother visited her daughter. The daughter was a nursing student, and her classmates gathered in the dorm to hear about a new idea. The mother had a list of addresses of men in Vietnam. The girls agreed to close their eyes, run their fingers down the list, choose three names, and write letters. One of the girls chose a lieutenant, a sergeant, and a pfc. She didn't want to write to a lowly pfc, but rules were rules, so she did.

I had about twenty letters at the mail shed. None from the family, but a pale green envelope from Rochester caught my eye. Inside was a brief note and scented sachet. Her name was Carolynn, and she was a student at a hospital just a few blocks from the Chevy dealership where I had worked. The soft, feminine scent took my mind away like a spring breeze. I had forgotten my sense of smell. My nose had been assaulted by the stink of perspiration and mildew, burning shit and stagnant mud. Her words lifted me, and I scratched a reply. The subsequent letters spoke of life on East Avenue, Christmas decorations, lilacs. Wilmer and The Dukes were playing at the Village Inn. Somehow, in a gloom of mud and silt, I had discovered a nugget of gold! Jacob Sutter could not have been more enthusiastic.

Fifteen years later, she still has my letters. Someday I suppose I'll read them. How did I describe it then? How did we find a common ground? She was studying to become a nurse, to save lives. I was part of an awesome olive-drab killing machine. Many, many nights I slept with my nose tucked inside one of Carolynn's envelopes, inhaling the sachet.

Somehow, the tiny threads woven into her letters moored me to the realities of life back home. She liked Bobby Vee; I liked Chuck Berry. We both liked the song "Cherish" by The Association. She sent cookies at Christmas. I sent a silk robe. Her grandparents lived near Watkins Glen, but she had never seen a car race. I urged her to go, and I remembered. Every pale green envelope brought memories and escape, and a quiet reassurance that life in The World was going on.

• • • •

Life went on at home, and time dragged on in The Nam. I had arrived in early September. It was now mid-November. Over sixty days had passed, and my calendar showed fewer than three hundred Vietnamese sunrises remaining. Things were heating up, especially a hundred miles north near an outpost called Dak To. We had a small shop at Dak To. The surrounding hills were supposedly a staging area for North Vietnamese infiltrators coming off the Ho Chi Minh Trail; and Dak To was a base camp for the Fourth Infantry Division's search-and-destroy operations. In November of 1967, things went wrong for the Fourth Division. All around Dak To, Charley had sprung coordinated ambushes with surprising numbers of well-equipped troops. It became the largest battle of the war up to that point, and the tiny compound of Dak To came under siege. Mortars and rockets crashed in from the surrounding heights, disabling the airstrip. Before it was over, it would become impossible for a helicopter to land in the compound. Supplies had to be trucked in from Kontum and Pleiku.

One morning in late November, our first sergeant asked for volunteers to drive to Dak To. The cardinal rule of a soldier is, don't ever volunteer, but I did. It was an impulse, not a considered decision; but I was relieved to have stepped forward.

For two months I had been holding my breath as the war swirled around me. I knew it would inevitably swallow me. I couldn't be this close to such a mammoth event and expect it to avoid me; it had a kinetic energy that was crushing the life out of kids like myself throughout this Godforsaken land. Once, long ago, I had believed I might escape the draft, the army, and the war. Now, deep in my gut, I knew there would be no escape. In my comfortable youth, I had never been forced to face a situation of such awesome importance. The tension had grown unbearable. I had to know how I would act under fire; and the convoy offered the opportunity to find out. Today. In a few hours. The opportunity to end the agonizing waiting, and to face both Charley and myself, out on the road to Dak To, away from my friends. If I failed, I would not directly threaten the guys.

As I gathered my equipment, I was almost giddy. Archie was incredulous. I felt an exhilaration, a sense of adventure. I had a lot of confidence in my driving ability. In my mind, I was a Grand Prix racing driver at Watkins Glen, or Monza, or the Nurburgring. The Targa Florio. Mille Miglia. No speed limits, no radar traps. High-speed adventure on narrow overseas roads; sneering drivers defying death with scarves dancing merrily on the wind. Nuvolari. Ascari and Stirling Moss. I trembled with excitement. If I had to meet the Viet Cong, let it be at the steering wheel.

The great confrontation would come at the wheel of a dented deuce-and-a-half, or two-and-a-half-ton stake-body truck. It looked tired, sagging beneath too many wooden cases of high explosive. In my mind's eye, the faded olive-drab paint resembled British racing green, a color I had come to love as I had overlooked the pit straight at Watkins Glen. The interior was cramped and uncomfortable, like a Formula One Cooper or Porsche. A layer of sandbags on the floor was protection against shrapnel from mines, but I saw the interior of Surtees'

Ferrari. I had seen Jimmy Clark, Graham Hill, Richie Ginther, Von Tripps, Bandini, and Gendebein before a race. Cool. Calculating. Contemplative. I stayed to myself until my shotgun introduced himself. He had been volunteered and was too short for this crap, under a hundred days, and he didn't relish riding with some green recruit.

"Gentlemen, start your engines!" They probably used other words, but those were the words I heard. The diesel engine responded slowly; the throw of the shifter was far too long. I practiced "split-shifting," simultaneously shifting the four-speed and the high-low range levers, double clutching to keep the rpms up. Like a parade lap, the column crawled out of the compound for the start of the Grand Prix of Vietnam. Soon we were on the open road, churning and grinding, sliding and crawling over a rutted dirt trail that was Highway One, Vietnam's finest highway. Through the torrents of rain and inadequate wipers, I strained my eyes to watch the truck ahead, a tractor-trailer flatbed of ammo. Damned governor; I needed power. Shotgun sucked bourbon and pronounced me "fuckin' crazy."

I was getting the hang of the ponderous truck, making it work, feeling it become one with me and I with it. We passed ragged Vietnamese with crude carts pulled by water buffalo, a column of nearly naked Montagnards with their strange cylindrical baskets, the broken hulk of a bus. We roared through Kontum and beyond, across a pontoon bridge, past a devastated American armored personnel carrier. The army acronym for these boxes on tracks was APC, but we called them PCs. This one had taken a B-40 rocket in the side and was settled dejectedly into the mud, its rear hatch hanging open.

We were on a straight stretch with heavy jungle on both sides threatening to engulf the road. The engine roared. Clumps of mud clattered against the undercarriage, and the canvas top clattered against the wind. Shotgun was telling me about ice fishing in Minnesota, when everything disappeared. There was a giant confusion up ahead, a curtain of mud, a blinding flash, a roar unlike anything I had ever heard. I couldn't see. I couldn't hear. I existed in a slow-motion world turned upside down. The great barrier grew, fire and mud and smoke and noise, and the earth heaved, and I thought I had been shot in the head and what I was experiencing was the final spasm of torn and shattered brain tissue. The wiper cut through the wash of mud, and I glimpsed a dark hole and went for it. We plunged in, and we came out, and I was out of control, and there was a giant dark green truck stopped dead in the road. Nothing to do, nowhere to go, a dead-end tunnel; then limbs and leaves pounding against the windshield, popping, scraping, tearing; and I can't see; and…we were stopped. I sat, deflated and baffled. Frozen. I became aware of a frantic activity and confusion. I became aware that I was alive. Like a surreal movie, a face appeared to my right; a distorted, anguished face, obviously screaming, but I couldn't hear what it was saying. Where was Shotgun? I didn't remember him leaving. I couldn't hear! My hands went to my head, to my ears, and I realized I was hearing the most enormous, crushing, howling, roaring noise of my life. Little noise among the great noise. Crackling. My eyes were okay, I could see the seat, the dash, Shotgun's door hanging open. Where had he gone?

I lay across the seat to look out the door, to see where Shotgun had gone. There was a guy, lying in the mud, with a stick or…and an abstract swarm of golden insects flew away from his head, and I concentrated on the crackling sound because it must be a clue; the stick was his rifle, and he was shooting, and the insects were shell casings, and the roar was a lot of explosive, and we were hit. I was alive, and everybody was down there, and I was up here, where the hell was Shotgun, and what should I do now? Where was my rifle? On the sandbags, muddy. Gotta get down with those guys, gotta shoot.

Can't see anything but muddy splotches on dark green leaves, and vines, and grass. What the fuck is going on? I don't see anybody. The noise. God damn the noise. My head aches. Won't somebody please be quiet? I don't see anybody to shoot at. Big, dark, noisy shadows overhead, the roar again, the mud is shaking and none of this makes sense.

Suddenly, it was quiet. Bodies stirred around me. I rolled over, lay on my back looking up into the gray rain. My head hurt. I felt it, felt wet mud in my hair, and checked my hand. Mud, not blood. Back to my head. There! My ears! There was that roaring sound that wouldn't go away. That's how it had started. What was that? What had happened? A face leaned over, smiled, held out a hand. Pulled me to my feet, and my knees didn't want to hold me up, and the hand held out my rifle. It tugged at my arm, but I'd lost Shotgun, and I didn't know how, so I staggered off to look for him. I had to ask him what that noise was. I'd never heard a noise like that before. I stumbled past the dark form of a truck, and guys were gathered, looking at something, so I should probably look too. There was a crater, a huge bowl-shaped hole, right square in the middle of the road. Wider than the road, stretching the jungle walls back. Twisted, shredded, dark forms, probably metal, a set of wheels, a grotesque steel ladder. Fireworks, or gunpowder. I smelled gunpowder. What was going on? Why hadn't I seen that great big hole? How could I have missed it? What had happened? Must be a clue there somewhere. All those guys, all strangers, all so quiet. Were they keeping a secret from me? No. Most of them looked bewildered too.

Suddenly Shotgun was there, screaming, hugging me, slapping my back, raving at the top of his lungs. "...motherfucker had our name on it, and you fuckin' drove that fuckin' truck and we fuckin' made it, and...and...Fuckin'-A! Fuckin' Christ, man, you fuckin' did it, you fuckin'-A did it, man, and..." I grabbed him, begged him to tell me what had happened. I felt very tired, very confused, and I just wanted to get this all sorted out and get on with it, get home. I didn't like this convoy shit, didn't understand it. What happened? Why were we stopped? What was the noise?

Shotgun stopped jabbering and looked at me. I guess, because he had been in The Nam so long, he realized that I had no idea what had happened. He lit two wrinkled cigarettes, put one in my lips, and explained. The flatbed just ahead of us had hit a mine. The whole load of ammo went off. Somebody said we went through it on two wheels, just from the force of the concussion. Blew that big fuckin' hole in the road. Dented the jungle. The guys in the truck? They were looking for them, for something to send home.

My knees gave out, and I knelt in the road. All the air had rushed out of me, as if some giant had squeezed me. My rifle lay beside me, in the goo. I saw it, but I had no control of my arms to reach over and pick it up. I was numb; everything was numb except my head, and it hurt so bad. I felt the cigarette fall from my lips, saw it land on the stinking mud. I started to tremble, then I started to shake, then I started to cry and to shake, and I almost fell over. Somebody put a bottle to my lips, and the fiery liquid seemed to cut through some of it, but I couldn't control the shaking. There was another cigarette, and they forced me to my feet, but I didn't want to walk. I didn't want to go anywhere, or do anything. Just think. Figure this out. They were screaming at me, and it wasn't my fault. "Go on." I didn't want to go on. "Got to. Got to."

Somehow, I went on. Choppers beat the air overhead. The truck was banged up bad. Shotgun's side of the windshield was gone, mine was starred and cracked. The canvas top hung low. The hood and left fender were buckled back. There were leaves and twigs and mud everywhere. I moved mechanically, stumbling without emotion. My blood had been drained; I was empty inside. The road cleared, the engine fired, and we rolled. Sheets of rain ripped in through Shotgun's broken windshield. He offered the bourbon, and it helped. I was thinking about driving over the torn road. Thought was returning. I went on. I'll never know how, but I went on.

I drove through a dream world. My head hurt, and I kept replaying those few moments. They didn't make sense, wouldn't make sense. My actions were mechanical. I saw my hands but didn't feel them. Just follow the truck ahead. The world situation was crushing in on me! I was shaking real bad, didn't know if I could breathe. Confused. It was happening all around me, and it was more than my mind could accept. Follow the truck ahead. Choppers overhead. Shotgun's booze. Confusion, and the worst fucking headache of my life. I wrestled the wheel.

We arrived at Dak To late in the afternoon. The noise was enormous, and it escalated as we got close. Chaos. Mud. There had been tanks, and PCs, and choppers. I could see a lot of activity, and I was driving into it, picking up momentum, a sense of urgency. Adrenaline flowing. Frantic, chaotic action. Noise, confusion, the smell of powder. artillery roared. Incoming mortars whomped into the mud. There were squat, dark tents sinking into the goo, and men. Stooped, disheveled, frantic men. On the perimeter, firing with unbelievable ferocity. There was an emotion, a need, an intensity that seemed to grip me, as if the world had gone off its axis, and to do anything out of the ordinary might explode it all. It wasn't ordinary, just all-consuming, and you had to be a part of it because it was so enormous, so awesome. The endless rain seemed to beat against the place, driving it, and everyone in it, deeper into the depressing goo. The valley was sliced into horizontal thirds by a layer of blue-gray smoke accumulating fifty feet above the mud, and a huge, dark green hill loomed above the smoke. This was Hill 875, the focus of today's attention. A muddied and rumpled man, his rank or unit unintelligible, leaped onto

Shotgun's running board and screamed orders. In the roar and commotion, most of what he said was lost, but Shotgun leaned over to yell, "No more than ten cases to each gun. I'll be working in graves registration. For Chrissake, don't leave without me." He punched my arm, hollered, "Keep your head down," and clambered out of the truck. After my cargo was unloaded, I would be on my own until the convoy formed up for the return trip in the morning. A nearby mortar round erupted in a huge geyser of mud and thunder, and I kicked the truck into motion.

Frantic men, distorted by wet and mud and fear, waved me toward the perimeter. Figures seemed to loom up out of the sound and fury, then disappear as if consumed by it. The roar never quieted. It banged inside my head in waves, drowning out my thoughts, and I lost all sense of where I was, or where I was going. It didn't matter; it all looked the same. I managed to coax the tired truck through the slime to a gun emplacement. As the gun roared, steam rose, and brown, half-naked men struggled to load another shell. I hesitated, not knowing what to do. Two of the men clambered up onto the truck and hefted the ammo down to their buddies. I pulled the lever out of gear and went back to help. "Only ten cases!" They ignored me, tossing the heavy wooden crates into the soft goo. There was no stopping them. These weren't men; one look at their eyes told me that. These were frightened animals desperate to survive. A slap to my helmet startled me. A face, distorted by clods of wet mud, shouted and pointed at a round erupting about a hundred yards away. "Go! Go! Get out of here!" The clear white of the eyes seemed incongruous against the dull brown mask. "They're walkin' 'em in on ya!" Another round, closer this time, threw swamp into the air. It was closer, and it was on a direct line towards us. Charley was adjusting his aim round by round, closer and closer to me. I had to get out of there. Sweat and debris seemed to cloud my eyes. I couldn't really see where

I was headed, but I made the truck lurch forward. Behind me, I heard bumping and swearing as the gunners dived off. God, the noise was awful! There was so much noise, so much action, but it was a kind of action I had never seen, confusing, and I wished Shotgun had been there to offer advice. I saw another gun crew, figured they could use ammunition, and forced the truck toward them. It bogged, refused to move. I pulled levers, screamed at it, and it ground forward again. I lost sight of the gun when a sea of brown swill washed over the broken windshield. The wipers cut through, and I bounced toward my goal. I ground the tired truck to a halt and burst out the door in such a hurry I went face-first into slime. I pulled myself up and clambered onto the truck, fighting the weight the mud had added to my loose-fitting jungle fatigues. The ammo cases were heavy, bulky, slippery. I managed to get a couple over the side before the guys arrived. Mud-soaked forms rose to help, only their eyes and teeth showing color against the brown. I'm not sure why, but I heard myself shouting, "Only ten! Only ten cases!" again and again. Then the truck was empty and the men were back at the gun. Smack! A blow to the side of my head knocked me off my feet and out into space. I hit the mud on my back, and something heavy landed on top of me, threatened to smother me. I fought.

"Get down, asshole! Get down!" One of the guys had knocked me off the back of the truck, lost his footing, and tumbled on top of me. He put his face inches from mine and screamed. "You okay? You okay?" I said I was. "You were standing straight up in the back of that truck." He needed a shave and a bath.

I was ashamed of my stupidity. "I'm okay. I thought I was shot. Next time, just ask, or give me a shove."

He was grinning. His teeth were stained, and the wet pink of his mouth stood out in striking contrast to the muddy face. His eyes were red, tired. "I'd send ya a letter," he grinned, "but the mail hasn't been dependable lately! You liked to got your-self killed. Where ya from?"

"New York. Rochester, New York."

He motioned toward the frantic bedlam at the wire. "Hell of a show, ain't it? Fuckin' Charley don't give up. Four fuckin' days this been goin' on. Hell of a show!"

A personnel carrier slithered across the slime, track rattling. "Do us a favor," my new friend shouted against the noise. It wasn't so much a question as a statement of fact. "Get that truck outta here. Charley likes to drop mortars on trucks. Stick it over near those hootches, nobody gonna be sleeping in a hootch. Just get it away from here, then come back." I didn't want to move. I didn't want to get back in that truck. Every time I got in that truck, all hell broke loose. "C'mon!" he hollered, slapped the side of my helmet again, but with less force. "C'mon, get outta here. You're gonna bring a whole buncha shit down on us!" There was a crazy, desperate look in his eyes. I struggled to the running board, then turned.

"You didn't say where you're from?"

"Ohio! Near Cleveland! Now get your young ass outta here, New York, and c'mon back so we can show ya how to fuck Charley's head up!" I pushed the lever into low and heard the tires growl.

I wrestled the truck into the little community of tents and struggled toward Ohio. Time after time I tripped or slipped, fighting to lift my sodden legs over ruts and out of puddles. It seemed I was moving in slow motion. The noise, that eternal, indistinguishable roar, seemed to be a wall. I felt that weight of the canteen on my hip, the cartridge clips in canvas pouches pulling the web belt lower. The pant legs seemed glued to my legs, stiff and heavy. I saw my rifle in my right hand, its famil-iar shape distorted by clods of mud. I felt grit in my mouth, sweat stinging my eyes. I tripped again. Goddamn it! An incoming round crashed on my right, a dull *whumpoom* threw up a cone of brown spray. I struggled forward, trying to keep my head down and still lift my legs high. My glasses were covered with filth, and I couldn't make out much of the scenario ahead. It all seemed to be closing in, swallowing me. I felt my right foot slip out from under me, the slow diving toward the muck. I watched the water splash away as I hit. I struggled to get my footing. I was straining, hurting, beginning to panic. Was there no escape? "C'mon, New York! C'mon! You're almost here. C'mon!" I saw the muddy barrel chest rise, the outstretched hand, the white teeth. I fell into the hole, disoriented. He held out that hand, helped me to my feet.

I didn't want to see. I didn't want to know what was going on around me. I wanted to crouch in the mud and slop, sink away, get away from all this. The noise was crushing me, squeezing in on my chest and my head. The weight of my limbs made me wonder if I had been shot, if the life was flowing out of me. Everything hurt, I couldn't pick out a specific pain. There was a glimpse of white, a flash near my head. I ducked so violently I smacked my head. Ohio was tugging me again, laughing. "Clean your glasses." He held out a white rag. It was damp and gritty, but I absent-mindedly rubbed at the lenses. Ohio stuck a cigarette in my lips. They were quivering so badly it fell into the mud. "C'mon, New York! The fuckin' PX is closed. Get your shit together." He laughed, but there was a note of hurt in his voice. He held out another smoke. I held it carefully, pulled hard at it. God, it was good. My hands were shaking. Ohio held out a bottle. I swallowed, and my eyes cleared as my throat burned. I choked a little, then swallowed again. I could feel the heat in my gut now. Ohio had pushed gobs of mud off my rifle, wiping it with the rag. He lifted it over the sandbags, pointed it away, and squeezed off a few rounds without looking to see where they were going. I tipped the bottle again, leaned back against the sandbags. I struggled to control the shaking, lost it, felt heat on my thighs and belly, smelled urine. The bottle again. "Hey, that shit's harder to come by than cigarettes," and Ohio reached for it. "C'mon, meet the guys." The cigarette was soggy, but I sucked at it once more before I threw it away. We met the guys; most had naked torsos stained to the color of the mud. Everyone's hair seemed blond and wet. Stubble sparkled on their chins. I wasn't enthusiastic. They assigned me a post on the sandbags, looking out and downhill across the wire and mud to a dark line of trees. The noise had died somewhat, and the rain slowed to a drizzle. The blue layer of smoke seemed a canopy, pressing down, making it seem we were overlooking the entrance to a huge tunnel. It was nearly dark, but I thought I saw a human form.

"Ohio!"

He was a few feet to my left. "Yeah?"

"Is that a body out there?"

"On the wire? Yeah, patrol got hit last night. Shit got heavy, and that kid tried to make it back. There's about six of 'em right on the edge of that tree line. Probably a few gooks, too."

"You mean that's a GI?" I felt a chill.

"Yeah." Silence.

"How many were there?"

"Gooks? Or the patrol?"

"The patrol? How many American guys are out there?"

"Twelve. Maybe fifteen. I dunno. Poor fuckers got fucked up bad!"

"Hey, Ohio!"

"Yeah?"

"Got another cigarette? Mine got kinda wet."

A voice came out of the darkness behind us. "They're bad for your health!"

The darkness came fast. The incredible noise had died away, grown more distant. Occasionally a flare would pop and swing down on its silken parachute. The golden glow emphasized shadows. As soon as the darkness returned, they seemed to move. I tried to make my eyes avoid that dark form by the wire, but they wouldn't obey. Somewhere, up above the smoky gray ceiling, a distant battle raged. Someone offered a box of C-rations. Ham and lima beans. Shit! I lifted the dog tag chain over my head and set about opening a can of pears with my P-38 folding can opener. It was cold and damp now, the drizzle was getting heavier. Someone brought me a cup of coffee, two packages of C-ration Lucky Strikes, and a poncho. I wrapped the plastic poncho around me and swallowed the hot coffee, wondering how long eight cigarettes might last. I shivered and lit one. My mind struggled to comprehend the enormous events of the day. The explosion on the road seemed long ago. The sounds of distant firing and chopper blades seemed to set a mood, like music for dinner. The chaos of this place was overwhelming. Thousands of guys like myself, torn away from home and family, crouched in the mud, wishing they weren't here. How could all this happen? I pulled at the cigarette and finished the coffee. I moved two steps to the right and peed. What different would it make? I pulled the poncho closer.

"Ohio?"

"Yeah?"

"You drafted?"

He moved toward me, dug into a thigh pocket and offered the bottle again. "Nightcap?" I needed the warmth. "I enlisted. My wife's brother was wasted last year, down in the delta somewhere. I wasn't doing much and wanted to get even. At the time, it seemed like a decent thing to do. She's stayin' with her folks, and I thought I was doing the right thing. Shit!" He swallowed from the bottle. "I was in-country six days and saw half my company get it. Three weeks later they send us here. I got three hundred 'n' seventeen days to go in this motherfucker, and I oughtta write to my wife, but I don't know what to say.

She thinks her brother was a big fuckin' hero, ya know, and I'm gonna tell her about this?"

Did he really want an answer? Before I decided what to say, a voice from the darkness got me off the hook.

"Ho!"

Ohio looked up. Someone was splashing toward us. One of the guys hollered back, and a form dropped into the trench. There was excited whispering, then he moved to Ohio and me. Ohio nodded a greeting. "Lieutenant."

"How ya doin'?"

"All right, sir. Cold, wet, and hungry. What's up?"

"PC's going out after the patrol." He whispered, but belched loudly. "They want to get them in before they swell up and burst. Got some near the gate. It's beehives at point-blank, right?"

"Got it."

The lieutenant splashed on down the trench. I realized how quiet it had become. Ohio shrugged. "Back to work."

"What's going on? What's a beehive?"

Ohio grinned. "Shit, New York, your education's been sadly neglected. C'mon, I'll show ya." We crept through the darkness to the gun. Ohio turned around to face me, holding something my mind interpreted as a watermelon. My eyes tricked me. It was an artillery shell, about four inches in diameter and eighteen inches long, to be fired from a 105-millimeter howitzer. "This is a beehive. Inside there are a couple thousand little steel arrows, about an inch long. Each one as sharp as a tack, and has four little steel quills. We use 'em for human waves. This sucker'll pin gooks to a tree forty deep. None of 'em'll be more than an inch thick. They're goin' out in a PC; to try to bring that patrol in. The shit's apt to get pretty thick. If Charley gets pissed and comes at us, it's gonna be for real. There's a whole North Vietnamese division out there, shootin' up and getting' half crazy. Somebody shouts, 'Go!' and there ain't no stopping them." He patted the dark cylinder. "This'll stop 'em."

I was chilled and shivering. My bones ached. I was bone weary, and wet and dirty. Mostly, I was scared. Human waves? Visions of an army of drug-crazed Orientals in black pajamas, of John Wayne playing Davy Crockett at the Alamo, of hand-to-hand combat all ravaged my imagination. I was getting the shakes again, feeling the cold deep in my gut. In all my nine-teen years, I had never seen anything like this. Hell, I had never imagined this might happen. Maybe it was a nightmare, and I would wake up and go to work. This couldn't be hap-pening. I fought to remember my hand-to-hand combat train-ing at Fort Dix. I had never paid that much attention, never dreamed I might have to rely on that training to stay alive. I wished I had a cup of coffee, a shower, or a few hours' sleep. I wanted to tuck into clean sheets, pull the pillow over my head to make the noise go away, and wake up in the morning to find myself home. As if to answer my thoughts, a flare popped and lit the slope in a golden glow. I saw the muddy hill, devoid of plants, streaming away toward the tangled wire. The tree line was a black wall now, an impenetrable black pit that led to the depths of hell. The sounds of war were distant now, but all around us. Surely, as they approached, we would be caught in the middle 'til Charley squeezed the life out of us. There was no place to go, no place to hide. Thousands of guys were kneeling in the mud, peering into the shadows and awaiting death, and none of them wanted to be here. What power could put so many American kids into a position like this? Why hadn't they told us about this while we were growing up? To my left a voice cut through the damp fog. "Holy Mary, Mother of God..." Were the others as scared as I? They were such a disheveled bunch, brawny and tough, it was hard to think of them as scared.

"Ohio?"

"Yeah?"

"You scared?"

"Fuckin'-A I'm scared. I've been scared since I got off the plane at Cam Ranh Bay. Anybody that ain't scared shitless in a place like this is crazy as hell. You want a belt?"

I moved closer to him, thankful for the bottle. "Where the hell do you get this stuff? We been hittin' this bottle all day, and it never goes dry. You making your own or something?"

"Walker swapped some ammo to some Green Beanies, got us a whole case of it. At the time, we didn't think we'd need the ammo."

"Somebody coulda got killed."

"Yeah, but anything you do in this fuckin' place can get somebody killed. The Beanies must've really needed it, to give up a case of booze. So maybe we saved a life; who knows? Ain't it funny how little you know about what's goin' on around ya here? I mean, there's some heavy shit comin' down. Just listen. And what's it all about? No-fuckin'-body knows! It's fuckin' crazy. If somebody would just tell me what the fuck is going on around here, what they hope to gain, or what they stand to lose, or something…but, no! You see guys all blown to shit, and you don't know why." He tipped the bottle up and drank hard and long. "Hardest thing's gonna be goin' home, and seeing the wife and her family, and her kid brother got blown away over here, and I don't know what to tell them about it. I mean, how the fuck can you describe this to somebody's sister?"

"Yeah, but you're married to her. It'll come." For such a big man, he seemed very vulnerable. I tried to lift him up but didn't know how.

Ohio lit a cigarette. "Supposing we die tonight. What happens then? They put what's left in a body bag and ship you home, and some lifer in a dress uniform tells your wife you died for your country. They have a funeral, and they fold up a flag and present it to her, and they draft the kid next door!"

I hadn't thought about it. If I went home in a box, I didn't want the army involved in my funeral. Fuck 'em. I hadn't asked for any of this. I wasn't a hero. I would have to write to the folks, tell them not to allow a military funeral. Ohio flipped away the cigarette.

"How old are you, New York?"

"Nineteen."

"I was twenty, four days before I left home. The lieutenant's twenty-three, and he's the only guy older than I am. There's nineteen guys, and I'm the oldest. Only three of us are married. Can you imagine? My wife went to the recruiting office with me, and I enlisted to go to The Nam, and she just sat there and listened to the whole thing, and it was almost like she didn't have any emotion. So it's my birthday, right, and we're at her folks', and she brings out this cake with all the candles and says, 'Make a wish.' I wished, just once before I had to leave, that she would say she didn't want me to go. I blew out the candles, but I never got my wish. Look at this fuckin' place, would ya? My wife wanted me here! She thinks I'm doin' some kind of patriotic duty, and it's wonderful. What the fuck am I ever gonna have to say to her? She wanted me to come over here! I've been here a little over a month, and I'm not sure I love her anymore. I can't tell her what it's like, and I can't forgive her for wanting me to be here. Haven't written her a letter in weeks. How the fuck you gonna describe this? Shit! I don't know if I want to see her again. She'd tell her friends I was some kind of fuckin' hero, and I'd have to just tell her to shut the fuck up. I just hope if Charley fucks my shit up he does it right, 'cause I don't want to spend the rest of my life with her pushing me around in a wheelchair, telling people I did what I had to do. If she had asked me not to go, I would have stayed home. I don't need this shit! I don't need to hear what a fuckin' hero I am. I just need a bath, and a drink, and some good pussy. She can keep her mouth shut and her legs open, and we'll get along fine. I mean, I feel bad about her brother, but what fuckin' good am I doin' for him? He's dead, and I'm about to be too, and I ain't seen anything getting a bit better because of it!"

My thoughts drifted away. There wasn't anything I could say to make it better. I thought about Jimmy Rollins, and my family. How would I talk to them? I heard an engine growl behind us, the clatter of tracks. Too much booze on an empty stomach. I had to pull my shit together. Thinking could get in the way. One more cigarette while the PC was going out; then I'd better have my shit together. Goddamn the rain!

The personnel carrier hung close to the trees, moving parallel to us. The sound of its engine, its General Motors three-speed automatic transmission seemed too loud, as if it were inviting the Cong to try something. Suddenly there was small-arms fire, then an explosion of firing. The PC zig-zagged, bouncing and churning a haphazard dance from shadow to shadow. It accelerated, slowed, turned 180 degrees, stopped, accelerated again. The machine gun on top was hurling red tracers into the tree line. Ohio touched my arm, leaned close to whisper. "They find a body, and drive over it. Some poor bastard opens the back door a crack and leans out with a rope; ties it around a wrist or ankle. They play out about ten feet of rope and slam the door, and go looking for the next one. Drag the whole string around; sometimes run over them with the tracks. They'll be all beat to shit, but you can't leave 'em out there. Charley'll crawl in, cut off their heads and stick 'em on poles with their balls in their mouth. In the morning the sun comes up and they're lookin' at ya all day long. Just be glad you aren't in graves registration tonight. They gotta bag 'em up to be shipped home; identify them and everything. Those guys are up to their ass in puke and guts and shit. I'd rather be here." I remembered Shotgun. That's where they had sent him.

A tremendous explosion erupted near the PC. "Mine." Ohio said it without emotion. "They pull a string to trigger it. Charley's timing sucks!" The armored carrier moved to the right, became obscured by rain and fog. The firing died down, and the sound of the grinding tracks was washed out by the clatter of a chopper overhead. A flare popped. Occasional rifle fire made sleep impossible. About three in the morning, a heavy mortar barrage fell behind us. It was amazing. You could actually hear the rounds sizzling overhead. I hadn't expected the explosions to be so loud. In the cold and wet, I was shaking again. I had to pee. I unbuttoned my fly and let go against the sandbags, never taking my eyes off the misty slope. Dawn brought a few more mortar rounds, again over our heads. Ohio suggested breakfast. I was a guest here. There was no question; I got ham and lima beans again. The lieutenant got the beans and franks. A short-timer got the fruit cocktail. We built a small fire and heated coffee in canteen cups, added a shot of booze and a little sugar. Breakfast was the best meal of the day. It meant you had survived the night, you were one day shorter. Two F-4 Phantom jets screamed across the sky, pulled up sharply. We heard a muffled *whuuumppff*. Dak To was open for business.

The sounds of fighting on Hill 875 were intensifying as we got the word to saddle up. I shook Ohio's muddy hand. I was searching for words when he spoke first. "You keep your head down, New York, and thanks for the ammo." I wasn't eager to go back out onto Highway One. "C'mon asshole." Ohio was grinning. "You don't want to stay here, do ya? Shit, in a few hours you'll be taking a hot shower back in Pleiku. In a few days you'll be eating Thanksgiving turkey and all this'll seem unreal. You're over the hard part. Shit, you're a battle-scarred veteran. Now get down that fuckin' road, 'fore ya smoke up all our cigarettes. We'll see ya again." He held out the bottle, and I tipped the neck his way before I drank.

"Hey, Ohio?"

"Yeah?"

"Hell of a party! You take care. Thanks, man."

I ran across the morass to the truck. Shotgun was already in his seat, and he started when I opened the door. His eyes were wild. He looked away. I pushed the starter button. "Ready?"

He spoke out the open window, softly. "Just get us the fuck outta here!"

"You all right?"

"I don't think I'll ever be all right again, but get us the fuck outta here." He was crying. If graves registration did this to an experienced, hardened short-timer, I resolved to avoid it at all costs.

We ground up out of that stinking valley, leaving the sounds of battle behind us. Helicopters clattered overhead, and I kept a big distance between us and the truck ahead. Shotgun stared straight ahead, tears streaking his cheeks. We were rolling hard when he leaned out the window and puked. He was silent all the way back to Pleiku. It was an uneventful trip, if five hours of utter terror can be uneventful. No mines or ambushes, you had to feel fortunate. We ground to a halt at Camp Holloway. Shotgun punched my shoulder and spoke softly. "Good job. Hope ya make it." Then he just walked away, and I looked for a ride back to my compound.

I was in the shower when the shaking started. I thought about Ohio, how he had said I was over the hard part. Suddenly thirty hours of terror exploded in my stomach, and I started bawling like a baby. I rushed outside, stark naked, and threw up on my knees in the mud. It all unwound out of me, like a coil spring. Unraveled. Came apart. I saw the explosion on the road again, the crater, the personnel carrier bouncing around in the dark, the disjointed body hanging on the wire. I hear the sound, that crushing roar that squeezed your ears 'til your brain went blank. I smelled the powder and the diesel fuel and the rot and the death. I went back into the shower, and I scrubbed 'til my skin was red, but it wouldn't come clean. Back at the hootch, I drank too much Scotch and fell on the bunk. When I closed my eyes I saw the road explode. I put the pillow over my head, tucked it tight against my ears, but the roar wouldn't go away. I felt very cold, got the uncontrollable shivers, pulled the heavy wool blanket tight around me. I saw the dump trucks loaded with bodies, the dark shadows trailing behind the PC. Christ, they must have hauled them right in to Shotgun. Never did know his name, or Ohio's. They never asked mine. Imagine experiencing something like that two feet from another guy, and you don't even know his name. You'll never see him again. Either of them. Wouldn't volunteer for another convoy if it was going to San Francisco! My volunteering days are over.

The guys burst into the tent, waving mail and laughing. I made believe I was sleeping. Archie shook me. "Jawn. Jawn." Damned Boston accent, leave me alone. "C'mawn, you gotta eat. Got a meal fit for a king." He whistled for an imaginary dog. "Here, King. Here, boy." How the hell could I ignore that? I sat up.

Archie looked at me kind of funny. "You look like hell. Pretty bad, huh?" I nodded. "Know what you need? Powdered potatoes! Stick to your ribs, give you intestinal fortitude to face the adversities of life in The Nam. Powdered potatoes'll fix anything. Half the bricks in Saigon are glued together with the army's powdered potatoes. C'mon, get dressed." He screwed up his face, made that handlebar mustache twist into a ridiculous caricature of a silent movie star. I had to laugh.

"Anybody ever tell you you're fuckin' crazy?"

He stepped back in mock horror, his eyebrows arched. "Sorry, fella, you got the wrong guy. Just 'cause I enlisted, you don't have to make disparaging remarks."

We ate, and I felt better. We talked about Dak To. I didn't go into detail; no need to get him upset. Every time I thought

I was going to lose it, Archie clowned and got me over it. We smoked and drank too much, and went to bed early. The next day I would be back at the old grind.

• • • •

The return to work did not offer the relief I had expected. For the next few days I raged and cried, laughed and swore. I went through the mechanical processes at work without thinking, as if watching my hands manipulate the machinery from afar. I was a different person trying to ignore Dak To. I was deflated like a balloon, seeking to return to my former dimensions. Like a balloon, I had been stretched, and I could never regain that virgin symmetry. I shook. I shivered as my blood turned cold. I threw things, and hit and kicked at nothing, or no one. Or at everything? I had no appetite, no longing for home. I felt contaminated, as if by plague. The guys tried to help, and I didn't want them to become infected. The wall that separated me from mankind was real as brick and mortar.

Some balloons burst. Some never came home. In a single explosive moment the air rushed out, and the distended rubber membrane was relieved. As a straight pin relieves the balloon, so the bullet or bayonet or shrapnel must have relieved the boys in the body bags. The rest of us were released by the giant fingers to deflate at our own speed. The air rushed from the nozzle with a rasping sound, but the rocketlike propulsion took us on a ride for which we were ill prepared. Then, lying limp on the floor, we saw ourselves. A balloon, once inflated, never quite returns to its original shape. The strain has been too great. Each successive inflation leaves it limp; less elastic, less resilient. And yet, the balloon tries to return to normal. It wants to be normal. It needs to be normal. It is the nature of a balloon to be elastic, to return to normal; but once inflated the balloon can never again be normal. It feels the distension, the stretching to the limits of its thin hide, and it knows it has become more vulnerable than ever before. How many times can it be inflated before that weakened film breaks down, and the explosion leaves the balloon as broken and worthless as if it had been pierced by steel? How many times?

I knew, in the last few days, my protective covering had been stretched to the limit and weakened. How many cells, how many molecules, how many atoms still held me together? Atoms. Particles of matter so tiny even the most gifted scientists refer to them as abstract. Fragile beyond comprehension.

People who endure the extraordinary stresses of life are called thick-skinned. I had survived, but without the resiliency of youth. If this was manhood, I would prefer to have remained a child.

A few days after I returned from Dak To, we celebrated Thanksgiving. There was a turkey dinner at the mess hall and much to be thankful for. The horror on Hill 875 continued, and our frantic efforts to help knew no holiday. After dinner we were granted a few moments for reflection, or a holiday drink. Some had the new *Stars & Stripes*, the army's newspaper. Charley, it reported, had suffered a crushing defeat at Dak To. Over three hundred enemy had been killed, compared to only twenty-three American casualties. We laughed. Some journalist asshole in an air-conditioned apartment in Saigon had bounced his fine French whore out of bed just to get to an army briefing and hear those numbers!

My emotions continued to rise and fall with the force of a roller coaster. Bones had been with the Eighty-Second Airborne until he flipped out and volunteered for an added six months in The Nam if he could be reassigned to a rear unit. He was a big help and managed to get us an afternoon off to go downtown. Bones explained that tension built up in a man until only a woman could relieve it. We resisted the hawkers on the street, with their cries of "Boom-boom, GI? Hand job?

Blow job? You want fuck my sister, GI? Mama-san number one cocksucker. You come three time, only one price. No money, no honey! Solly 'bout that!" Bones took me to the far end of town, up the hill, to a walled and barbed-wired compound with ARVN guards at the gate. Inside we found a dirty pink stucco two-story villa and ordered a beer. You could drink the local beer safely there. This was the South Vietnamese government-operated whorehouse, where our allies expressed their thanks for America's assistance. The girls were among the most beautiful in the area and were checked daily for diseases. It was three in the afternoon. What time was the inspection? Obviously, this was one of the more popular attractions in town. Bones laughed and drank, with a girl on his knee. Best prices in town, he promised. Enjoy yourself. I wasn't really in the mood. The place was filthy, utterly devoid of decoration or atmosphere, and the girls were ridiculous imitations of anything sensually attractive. They wore the usual black Vietnamese silk trousers with garish brassieres trimmed in black lace and stuffed with tissue or rags. They chattered to each other, smoked, spat on the floor. The madam was a heavy woman, wearing a blouse. She waddled up to the table and asked, "You want fuck?" Bones said we did, and she waddled to the bar, returning with a filthy three-by-five file card. Some forgotten GI had obviously hand-lettered it. This was the first time I had ever seen a menu of sexual delights, and I tried to buy the card for a souvenir. Bones was hysterical and Mama-san was indignant. "You want fuck? You want fuck?" Bones insisted, and I chose a harmless-looking girl, paid the madam, and followed up the stairs.

She led me to a tiny cubicle with a wooden crate and an army bunk covered with a poncho. As I undressed, she washed the poncho with alcohol, then pushed her black trousers to the floor. She was naked beneath them, and she lay on the bed and spread her legs. When I was naked I joined her, and as I mechanically pumped at her crotch she struck up a conversation with the girl next door. I was fast losing any excitement I had been able to muster, but the other girl came around the plywood partition, sat on the edge of the bed, and coaxed me with one hand while smoking a cigarette with the other. There was a weak mechanical response, and I thought I knew how a milk cow must feel when the farmer visits in the morning. I was left to dress alone as the girls hurried downstairs to try again. Bones insisted I should feel better, and I grinned and tried not to disappoint him.

Thankfully, I escaped VD. Like everything in The Nam, even lovemaking could be deadly. One member of our company, affectionately referred to as "Champ," contracted gonorrhea seventeen times in twelve months. A legendary superstrain, the "black syph," was supposedly incurable. Fearful of introducing this horror to Hometown, U.S.A., the army supposedly sent "black syph" victims to Okinawa (Camp Crotch-rot) and listed them as missing in action. Rumors of razor blades in a girl's sex organs abounded, though I doubted that would be medically possible. Short-timers warned the new arrivals against falling asleep after sex, for fear of castration. The pleasure palaces in Saigon were legendary; but upcountry sex was a demeaning, mechanical act, a reminder of how desperate and vulnerable the fatigue and loneliness and terror had made us.

I didn't enjoy Pleiku, but I always tried to. It was a filthy and dangerous place, but I always hoped I might find some reason for our presence in Vietnam. Secretly, I hoped to be greeted like a GI liberating France in World War II. The people resented us. Inside our compound, the housegirls were usually pleasant. Downtown, we were treated like an invading army. Try as I might, I was never able to find the exotic, inscrutable Asian culture. Everywhere I looked, I found a society of murderers, thieves, and carnival hucksters.

Nothing about downtown was refreshing. A cold drink might contain ground glass or debilitating drugs. Black market fruits abounded, but an apple might contain a hidden razor blade. Our family home had featured acres of fruit orchards, and I longed to taste an apple. They never made it to the mess hall, but were openly displayed on the streets of downtown, alongside oranges, grapefruit, C rations, and waterproof clothing. Some GIs took the dare and ate the fruit. I reminded myself of the rewards if I returned to The World, and diverted my eyes and my thoughts.

Diversions abounded. Although Pleiku was a large city, the streets were unpaved. Like cities everywhere, traffic hindered movement. The Vietnamese in their antiquated Renaults and Citroens vied for space with dilapidated buses and overloaded Italian motorbike-taxis. Motorcycles and pedal rickshaws swarmed into each nook and cranny. Pedestrians took their chances. Into this swarm of activity America had introduced the machines of war, their heavy armored hulks a stark contrast to the flimsy conveyances re-manufactured by the Vietnamese. Every Viet vehicle appeared to be straining against the concept of mass transportation. I wondered where all those people were going? Why did they always travel with their livestock and firewood, but never a change of clothes?

There was no neon or plate glass. Storefronts spilled onto the narrow sidewalks, beneath brightly painted and elaborate signs. Staples and necessities were nonexistent, but cheap gaudy souvenirs abounded. An open-air market featured a stink so offensive it withered the curiosity and watered the eyes. Only the barest minimum of the stores bore any resemblance to places of business back home. There was a camera store, proudly displaying myriad colorful logos, but no cameras. Its inventory consisted of black-market film and souvenir photo albums. There was a drug store, reminiscent of our Colonial apothecaries, but with a voodoo curse. Small crocks and jars of alien salts vied with the dried corpses of reptiles and rodents. I imagined a sick child, his mother firmly forcing him closer and closer to this chamber of horrors, curing himself through the overpowering energy of raw terror. There were recognizable lunchrooms and taverns, and a plethora of jewelry stores. The rest of this Wall Street of the Weird consisted of souvenir shops, massage parlors, whorehouses, black marketeers. It appeared that the merchants of Pleiku had forsaken their countrymen in a mad effort to lure the alien invaders and their "funny money."

I hoped to glimpse the culture, the way of life, the soul of this strange society. All I found was the snake-pit attitude of a carnival huckster, and a desperation. I marveled at a GI's inherent gullibility. So many young men dreamed of making a profit from the spoils of this ravaged land. They invested in "pure gold" jewelry and watches at prices so low they approached the ridiculous. Once, a beggar offered me a sparkling Seiko watch. It ticked, it was on time, but there had to be a catch. Turning it over, I noticed a slight opening at the edge of the backing plate. Prying it open with a thumbnail, I discovered a crude clockwork fashioned from Lone Star beer cans! I arrogantly tossed it back to the ragged beggar, never thinking of the conversation piece that had eluded me at thirty-five dollars. Some GIs exported opium and marijuana to their friends at home. One quasi-intellectual searched for French "masterpieces" among the silk-screened paintings of tigers and nude women. Some brought rolls of silk.

Most popular were jackets fashioned from black-market poncho liners, a camouflage blanket of silken insulated material similar to a light comforter. Upon the swirls of green and brown, brightly colored embroidery announced proudly, "When I die I'm going to heaven 'cause I've spent my time in Hell. Pleiku, South Vietnam. 1967"; or, "Lo, tho I walk through the valley of death I will fear no evil, 'cause I'm the evilest motherfucker in the valley." I wonder how many thousands of those jackets still hang in the dark corners of the closets of America, the scarred owners unable to say, "I'm a Vietnam vet" in polite society, let alone proclaim it proudly on their brightly colored jackets.

Second in popularity were the gold and silver-tinted aluminum bracelets, supposedly a symbol of kills, like notches on a pistol handle. Silk smoking jackets were "in" for the men, brazen robes for the ladies. As Christmas approached, we sent thousands of sweaters home, to learn later that the metric sizes were incompatible with American bodies. In fact, we accused the Viet Cong of manufacturing all articles of clothing sold in The Nam, because the stitching invariably disintegrated when exposed to American laundering.

So we strolled, and shopped, and shooed away the pests. Pleiku teemed with flies and beggars, and both pissed us off. The flies we could excuse. Sanitation was by the rotting process. There were no piles of garbage, just garbage everywhere. Only beggars outnumbered the flies. "Give me pi!" The Viet money was measured in piasters. "Give me Saah-lem!" Salem cigarettes. (This was decidedly *not* Marlboro country!) All ages, both sexes, everyone begged. You learned never to turn your back. Half of these poor beleaguered souls were Cong, eager for an opportunity to drop a grenade onto a sidewalk crowded with GIs or slip a razor blade out of their belt and slash at an American throat. One of our men was killed when he approached a forlorn dog that had a satchel charge cleverly sewed into its belly. (A stupid mistake. Dogs were eaten in Vietnam. Cats were a delicacy. Pets did not exist, and the unusual in The Nam was usually deadly.) More common, and perhaps the most heartbreaking memory of all, were booby-trapped kids. A tiny child dressed in rags, unaware of the lethal package strapped to his back, approached. Too young to understand his lot in life, his eyes still sparkled. A GI offered candy or a cigarette. The child radiated joy, and innocently came closer to explode in a crowd.

In spite of the obstacles, we could not allow ourselves to become so embittered that we resisted the kids. By age ten the reality of hopelessness haunted their eyes, but the eyes of the very young were a refuge from the inhumanity all around us. Too often there was sorrow born of suffering, but the spark of hope still flickered.

God knows, we ached for those children. We spoiled them as we would have our own. We gave them candy, toys, money, our hearts. We saved the choicest cans of C-rations for them. We wrote to friends and family, asking for clothes, books, rattles, and toys. Once I spent an afternoon on a quiet side street, riding a little boy "horseyback" on my hands and knees across the muddy yard, delighting in his joy. From the shadows of a ramshackle hovel, his mother's eyes seemed to mellow from open disapproval to passive acceptance. I bought a little tricycle, taught him to balance precariously on its seat, taught him to say, "Bike!" He sparkled. Anxious to share his good fortune, he struggled to show his treasure to his mom. I never saw the tricycle again. Chances are, the mother sold it back to a store for a fraction of what I paid for it. It was difficult to bring happiness to these bitter people.

In Saigon, months later, I would see a horde of these kids begging in front of the Vietnamese capitol building, its quarter-inch-thick plates of fourteen-carat gold glowing in the afternoon sun in a heartrending contrast to their dirty, ragged clothes. "Fuck you, GI." "Go home, GI." "Tonight you die, GI." "VC kill you, GI." Never comprehending the meaning, their grins proclaiming a harmony the words decried, they tugged at our pant legs and our heartstrings. Why couldn't their parents teach them the words their eyes suggested? "Help me, GI!"

• • • •

The period following Thanksgiving was lonely and sad, and dangerous. Back in The World, preparations for Christmas were the center of attention. Carolynn had been shopping in the stores I knew so well, and her descriptions of the gay tinsel and multicolored lights were reassuring. Life was going on. It was sad to be away, but it was comforting to hear that all Creation had not been destroyed in the earthquake that had reshaped my life.

Like a miniature society, life went on. The rains began to subside. Jim Gordon was stung by a scorpion and went into convulsions. Chris Noel, a gorgeous blonde disc jockey for Armed Forces Radio, whispered her seductive, "Hi, Love!" and fifty thousand GIs thought back to a time when women were feminine and soft. We ate powdered eggs and drank powdered milk. We prayed that the endless supply of liver and creamed corned beef on toast ("shit on a shingle") would end up on the Vietnamese black market instead of the steaks and chickens and pork chops. The gooks had better taste.

Wounded trucks continued to arrive, in need of first aid. The heat wilted us by day, the rats and vermin took their toll by night. Alexander received a pellet pistol from home, and we developed the rules of a new game. He sat at one end of the hootch with his new toy. A volunteer stood by the light switch, hidden by the metal lockers. Everyone else was banished from the kingdom. Lights out! In moments, we heard the telltale scratching and squealing of the rats. Lights on! *Pop-pop-pop!* One night we killed eleven, but one or two were more common. The injured were stomped to death or clubbed with rifle butts. Then, triumphant, we hauled the corpses outside. Someone lit a cigarette and blew a cloud of smoke to establish wind direction. Upwind from the hootch, the bodies of the rats were stacked and drenched with lighter fluid, then set ablaze. The acrid smoke, blowing over and through the hootch, repelled rats for two or three days. We knew, however, that no system was foolproof, and went through the nightly ritual of tucking in the mosquito netting.

The days came and went. Artillery Hill roared, choppers fluttered overhead. The damaged trucks rolled up in endless lines. The news from home was optimistic, penned in an atmosphere of good cheer. Mutilated boxes of cookies and candy began to arrive. Later, scolded for not sending thanks for boxes that had never arrived, we came to the conclusion that some more attractive packages had been "censored" by the mail clerks in their air-conditioned offices in Saigon.

One of the more trusted housegirls was discovered smuggling an M-79 grenade out, tucked between her legs. The M-79 was a grenade launcher that looked like an oversized sawed-off shotgun. The grenade was about two inches in diameter, and there was considerable joking about Mama-san's physical proportions. (One of the guys claimed to have met a whore who could have stolen a launcher, too, in the same way.) Upon searching the housegirl's shack downtown, detailed maps of our compound were found. The name and sleeping location of each occupant was inscribed on the floor plan of each hootch. Dimensions and distances were exactly to scale. Mama-san was a colonel in the North Vietnamese Army. We never heard her fate. She was probably handed over to the ARVN interrogators. After that incident, two female guards at the gate frisked every housegirl every day, in a very thorough and personal manner.

At the Pentagon, a young soldier with a bayonet fixed and rifle loaded protected the American Dream from a mob of protestors in bell-bottom jeans and tied-dyed shirts. One young hippie girl slipped the stem of a flower down the rifle barrel, a photographer immortalized the scene. I found the photo in a magazine and hung it proudly on my locker door. Peace on earth. Good will to men.

A sergeant in the parts company across the street was found crumpled near the outhouse, trousers at his knees. A poisonous snake, probably a bamboo viper, had bitten his bare backside.

It had most likely been planted. The shitburners were interrogated, but they all returned the next day. The bamboo viper is a small green snake, the size and color of a blade of grass. If you were unlucky enough to be bitten, you had about forty-five seconds to blow your own head off before the agony began. Eyewitnesses described the sarge's face in hushed awe. He had a wife and baby. He would have gone home in February.

As Christmas drew closer, we struggled for a suitable means of celebrating. The elite Green Berets, in order to make them "resourceful," were issued nothing. They had to steal and deal for their needs. The strict army code authorized them nothing. They needed truck parts. We needed a case of steaks for Christmas dinner. A deal was struck.

Two of us loaded the specified parts into a three-quarter-ton truck. We had stripped them off the skeletons in the boneyard, offering to share our booty with the "cannibals" if they looked the other way. This cumshawing was a way of life in The Nam, an elaborate system of collaboration for the common good. The Green Beanies were dug in at a firebase near the Cambodian border. There would be no convoy, no air cover, not even a radio. They assured us it would be safe. I hadn't volunteered; I was drafted. We roared and bounced across roads that were little more than rutted trails for about three nervous hours. Only when we arrived did we find three small holes behind the passenger's door.

The firebase was a hole in the sea of vegetation. Like the eye of a hurricane, a clearing, a grassy meadow had been ringed with barbed wire and sandbags. Near the center, two big guns hunkered down into the soft ooze. M-60 machine guns and automatic rifles stood vigilant at the perimeter, perched on sandbagged bunkers like guard posts on the corners of the stockade in a cowboys-and-Indians movie. I imagined painted Apaches on horseback circling the free-fire zone. There were no hootches, no outhouses, no mess hall. There were only mud and dirt and brackish puddles. A handful of ARVN troops in camouflage fatigues lounged about, their eyes insolent. Numerous vehicles, obviously tired and spent, were scattered in disorganized abandon. To our left we could see the Green Berets, gathered near a conglomeration of boxes, crates, tests, and an olive-drab, dilapidated fire truck. A fire truck? It was, because of its color and the streaked coating of mud, almost logical. Almost, but not quite! In fact, the incongruity of it all made me stop and laugh. Here we were, unprotected, in the middle of nowhere, without a building in sight, let alone a refrigerator. We were after beefsteak and found a fire truck! It was absurd!

Insane thoughts rolled out of me in a release of tensions. We had made it. A giant man approached, grinning broadly. Naked to the waist, he bulged with power. The hair had probably been red once. Now it was bleached and streaked with white. His face was wrinkled and weathered, but the eyes were warm and inviting. He seemed really glad to see us. I had been uncomfortable about meeting these legendary men on their own turf. I had seen them before: wild, uncontrolled men whose sole purpose in life seemed to be violence. Someone once said, "Hell hath no fury like a drunk Green Beret." They marauded, they destroyed, they killed with a fury so intense it was sometimes unleashed upon their countrymen. Proximity could be a capital offense. They were Green Berets because they didn't fit the normal mold, and we could never fit theirs.

"Hey! Good to see you! We've been expecting you! Merry fuckin' Christmas!" His warmth simply melted my reservations. My shotgun found the bullet holes, and we discussed the implications. We were nervous. Our host, who had introduced himself as Lieutenant Frost, scoffed. "Charley can't hit shit. Best you can hope for is a gook tryin' to shoot ya. Can't hit shit!" Nervousness faded away. We were accepted. Frost looked over the truck parts. I was impressed. He was soft-spoken, down-to-earth. He seemed to appreciate the pieces that would get his men mobile again. It had been rough lately. He had lost a lot of men. No longer were the Cong the main problem. There were a lot of NVA around, heavy firepower. "They're bringing in tanks!" he said, his voice tired. "Can you imagine? How's a place like this supposed to stop tanks?" He looked older. We started walking toward the group of Berets.

"How's it going?" As Frost spoke, the circle opened. In its center were three whores, hands bound, eyes defiant. Someone said, "No good." An ARVN, obviously with rank, chattered at one of the girls in Vietnamese. From the tone of his voice it was obvious he was interrogating her. He was growing agitated, angry. It was like something out of the movies. All that was missing was the swinging light bulb. The ARVN officer was frustrated. His hand snaked out to slap the girl's face. Her head snapped. Tears rushed to her eyes. He struck again. They had words; hot, emotional words. She was defiant. The ARVN got to his feet, lit a cigarette. A Green Beret spoke to him in his native tongue. He answered, then turned back to the girl at his feet. There was obviously a question. She spat back an answer. He nodded to two of the Americans. They pulled the girl to her feet, tore her silken blouse open, removed her gaudy brassiere. Their giant hands closed on her upper arms. The ARVN dragged at his cigarette, stepped forward, and pushed the cherry tip to her nipple. I couldn't believe I was watching this. I looked at Jerry, my shotgun. We had never gotten along real well, but we communicated now. His eyes were wide. Frost noticed our discomfort. "You guys don't get to see this stuff where you are." He spoke factually, unemotionally. "One of our guys visited these ladies for a shot of cock. We found his head with his cock in his mouth! Haven't found the rest of him. We tore that place apart. Lots of papers, NVA stuff. These worthless cunts fucked our buddy up bad! Now, we know something big is coming. Real big! These babes are gonna tell us what Uncle Ho is up to, and they're gonna pay for what happened to Timmy. Timmy didn't deserve that shit. You guys want to leave, I'll get the shit out of your truck. You wanna see the war, stick around!" I looked at Jerry. He looked back at the girl. She hadn't uttered a sound. Her eyes were moist, but burning with hatred and defiance. Someone nudged me, handed me a joint. I took a deep hit. My feet were planted. I couldn't have moved if I wanted to. I looked at Jerry. He was staring, mouth open. I took another drag at the joint, passed it back. Somebody handed me a cold can of Coke. It shocked me a little as it touched my hand. I could feel the marijuana. I sat on the sandbags to watch the war. Jerry was swigging bourbon.

The girl was on her back now, and naked. Her bound wrists were over her head, held by a swarthy GI. The ARVN had backed away. There was a flurry of activity. I jumped at the sound of the starter as it brought the fire truck to life. "I couldn't believe a fire truck in a place like this!" I was laughing. Giggling. Frost's voice came to my right. "That's our water supply. We got tired of trying to catch rainwater. Cumshawed the thing in Qui Nhon. There's underground water, so we borrowed a drill and drilled us a well, and that's our pump. Got enough pressure, we shoot it straight up and all get a shower."

The girl's legs were held apart. A burly black man stood over her, screaming. "Where Timmy? Where da resta Timmy? Cunt! Whore! You gonna die, oh, you gonna die bad, Mama-san! You gonna wear you cunt in you mouth, Mama-san! Talk t'me, woman!" He raged. He stormed. He paced back and forth. A geyser of water erupted from the fire truck, falling on us, shaking us out of the spell. Everyone gathered round, moving closer to watch the fun. It was obvious the mood was rising toward a crescendo. The girl lay still, impassive. The ARVN officer barked at the other two, his eyes glued to the scene unfolding. The other two whores had the same detached, far-away look in their eyes. The huge hose was brought into the circle. The giant black, still raging, shook it in front of the girl's face. The ARVN called to her. She closed her eyes, shuddered a little. The tarnished brass nozzle was forced between her legs, forced against the resilient folds of flesh. Her eyes started open. A scream started from her throat, a sound unlike any other! Red and pink and brown and white and green, a torrent of mixed flesh and high pressure steam knocked the intimate circle back. The white flood of water died away, the lifeless hose was discarded.

It didn't matter what the Green Berets thought. I was sick. The sweetness of the Coke seemed to seep up my throat, through my nose. It gripped the back of my tongue, gagging me. I heaved until my insides hurt.

Jerry and I talked about it on the way back. We were afraid of those men, afraid to say anything. We had seen "the real war." We made a pact to keep it a secret between the two of us. If that was the way it was, we weren't able to change it. We were just relieved to have been assigned to the relative civilization of Pleiku. "Aww, shit!" Jerry whispered. "They're gonna take a shower out of that hose tonight." It was the last time either of us mentioned the incident.

• • • •

It took a long time to return from the firebase incident. I'm not sure I have ever made it all the way back. How could something like that happen? How could I stand idly by and allow it to happen? Why didn't I stop it? What had I become? Would I ever be able to return to everyday life in America's mainstream? How often did things like that happen in The Nam? Was that the way of life? Is that the way of life in all wars, or was Vietnam something different? And the most haunting question of all: Having been a monster, what future stress might cause me to return to inhuman behavior?

I knew it was wrong. Why hadn't I tried to stop it? It was easy to point out that I was a visitor, in a barbed-wire circle in the jungle, on the other side of the planet. I was surrounded by Green Berets, professional killers who knew far more about the war than I. A close-knit band of men who had lost a dear friend. Men under stress. Dangerous men. It would not have been wise to step forward and say, "Stop! That's not nice."

But can I deny responsibility that easily? Frankly, there was a fascination to the whole affair. Why do otherwise normal people flock to see horror, murder, rape, blood, gore, and perversions on the movie screen? Why do motorists stop to see the horrible aftermath of an automobile accident? I was nineteen years old. For the past year I had lived in an atmosphere of "Kill! Kill! Kill!" and "I don't know but I've been told, Eskimo pussy is kinda cold. Sound off!" Killing was an art form to be practiced, an established social institution. Morality? What about Fatso? A woman? You respected your mother, your wife, your daughter, and any WAC who outranked you. The rest of the women of the world were sex objects. Your orientation to Vietnam warned about gook whores and Vietnamese women in general. "The only good gook is a dead gook."

What had I become? The army said it would "make you a man." Was this a macho rite? A masculine right? Survival of the fittest? Was this an isolated incident, like My Lai? If all the atrocity stories from Vietnam are to be believed, what does it say about the American kids who were there?

What had we become? Why? Who is to blame? Our parents, who gave us too much? The military leaders, who cultivated an atmosphere of genocide and chauvinism? American society in general, too infatuated with material goods to remember the ideals America was based upon? The Viet Cong, whose methods of warfare reached a new level of barbarism?

Is a human being really in control of his own destiny? Were we victors, or victims? What is a man's duty to his country? To his God? To his fellow man? Which has priority? It is difficult to agree upon the answers to those questions; it was more difficult in Vietnam. The average age of the American fighting man in The Nam was nineteen. The average age of the American fighting man in World War II was twenty-six. A lot of guys spent a year in The Nam, came back to The World, and couldn't legally drink a beer. A lot of values became clouded in Vietnam. Survival became your only goal, the only standard of measure. We debate teenage drinking, teenage voting, and teenage marriage. Vietnam haunts America. When will we debate teenage war?

This was America's first war to be fought with computer support. "Official" estimates of the number of Americans who went to Vietnam vary from 2.2 million to 4.3 million. This was the first war to be televised, and it made Mom and Pop uncomfortable all over America. Supposedly, atrocities have happened in all wars, but never before had they been so graphically reported to the "good" people back home. Nobody's mother wants to think that her son is capable of such a thing. The returning millions sat down at the family dinner table and soon discovered that their problems were unacceptable conversation. All too often, and out of genuine concern, we tried not to upset Mom and bottled up the most violent memories. Over the years a lot of fermented frustration and trauma have exploded like a champagne cork. After all the ages of human combat, medical science has forsaken electric shock treatments and the tag "shell shock" in treating this condition. Today we call it post-traumatic stress, and there are counselors. These advances haven't come without controversy and criticisms. How many mothers have furtively studied the encyclopedia map of Vietnam to find My Lai and their son's base camp and felt relief that "he wasn't near anything like *that*"? Meanwhile, far too many young men walk through life hiding hideous secrets, avoiding *Judgment at Nuremburg* on the late-late show, and scarred inside with the frightening knowledge that we are all just a very tiny step removed from the mindless violence of jungle animals.

• • • •

I drove back to Pleiku with a case of steaks. Jerry and I never talked about what we had seen. We quietly returned to work and the daily routine. We avoided each other, but with respect forged in the hottest smelter.

A few days later, I was putting the finishing touches on a truck. I had replaced the engine, transmission, transfer case, and both rear axles. I had brought it back from the dead. I only had to snug down a few bolts, and it would be ready for another trip to Dak To. It was reassuring to take a tired and broken truck and heal it. I was pulling a wrench when the sarge told me the army had changed its mind. The truck was assigned to salvage. Take all the new parts off and get it hauled out of here. I threw the heavy wrench at him.

I could have gone to jail. Instead, I went to the body shop. The captain had been here a long time and seemed to understand the frustrations. He needed a body man, and I had civilian body-fender experience. The sarge thought I was being punished, but I was glad to be back to something I could relate to home.

A package from home brought a miniature Christmas tree and tinsel. Other care packages contained cookies and candy in holiday gift-wrap. We ventured downtown to do some Christmas shopping. The selection wasn't really reminiscent of an American department store. I had been warned about the metric sizes, and I sent silk smoking jackets to my father and brother, and mohair sweaters to my mother. The stitching of the sweaters disintegrated in American detergent. The smoking jackets were garish, and I doubt that anyone ever wore them. I decided against the "pure gold" jewelry, afraid it might turn

American bodies green. I bought a Vietnamese doll in the beautiful *ao dai* dress and conical sun hat, and an assortment of beautiful Christmas cards with hand-painted scenes of placid villages or a water buffalo pulling a plow through the rice paddies. We laughed and called the water buffalo Vietnamese reindeer.

Half of us would see Bob Hope at the Fourth Infantry Division base camp. The other half would see Connie Francis a few nights earlier. Whenever you ventured outside the barbed wire after dark you wore full combat gear, so we watched Connie Francis with rifles on our shoulders. She was lovely. It was chilly, but we hardly noticed. As she closed the show with "God Bless America," men in wheelchairs and on stretchers from the nearby evac hospital struggled to stand. Their struggles were poignant, and many of us wiped away tears. We stood beneath a full moon, realized that the same moon would be looking down upon our hometowns in a few hours. Thanks to Connie Francis and all the other members of her show, we felt close to home for a few moments. Then the show was over, the huge speakers quieted, and the sound of helicopters overhead brought us back to reality. The personalities who entertained in the war zone will never know how much we appreciated their efforts.

On Christmas, the mess hall cooks prepared the steaks from the Green Beret firebase. I couldn't eat. We had a few hours off; there was a holiday cease-fire. I looked at the miniature Christmas tree and remembered another Christmas long ago. I had found a BB gun under the tree, and I "went hunting" in the orchards, shooting shriveled apples and the o's of "Posted" signs. Scraggly brown weeds jutted out of the snow at lifeless angles, dark pines rose to a turquoise sky, and a distant cardinal wolf-whistled. There was a movement to my left.

A rabbit crouched near a bank of weeds, totally still, hoping I wouldn't notice. I levered a BB into place and fired, and the rabbit erupted in one last celebration of life. My dad seemed pleased. The shot had entered at the base of the skull, killing it instantly. The rabbit's brown eyes were sad. We threw the carcass into the weeds. What had been the point?

Vietnam had many Roman Catholics. Today I wonder if one of them found my little Christmas tree after the war. Might it be some hidden token, like the crosses carried by early Christians attempting to avoid the Roman lions at the Colosseum? The glittering tree couldn't overcome the gloom inside the hootch, and I wandered off to the perimeter. I sat on a sandbag bunker overlooking concertina wire and claymore mines, across the great grassy meadow leading northward to Dak To. Off to the left I could see the deep vee that was the outlet of the Ho Chi Minh Trail. I had cigarettes and a drink, and I remembered every detail of other Christmases, long ago. It was a sad and lonely day.

• • • •

I had been fortunate so far. Except in dreams, I hadn't sighted down my rifle and found a man looking back at me. What would I do? Surely the day was fast approaching. Dak To had changed my dreams. Now there were waves of men, thousands. I picked one, sighted at his gut, then noticed his face. Dark eyes, black hair, a determined grin. If I didn't kill him, he would kill me. Would I fire? I always woke before the situation was resolved. Would I watch him crumple? Or would I feel the fiery impact smash my head? What would that be like? Like switching off the radio and the lights at the same instant? If I squeezed the trigger and watched his grin disappear, would it be right? Would this meadow be a better place? A thousand years from now, which death would best serve humanity? Would the historians say I had died bravely, defending the downtrodden peasants of Vietnam from communism? Is communism a fate worse than death? Why were these poor unfortunates willing to suffer so to bring communism to their loved ones? Were they really unfortunate? The strongest, richest nation on earth was spilling money and blood to help them, and their reaction was a simple "Fuck you, GI." Why should my family's hearts be broken for that? Society had required me to spend thirteen years in school. Now this. I was young. There was a whole world to explore, a million moments to be experienced. If I died, and all those possibilities poured out of me to stain the Vietnamese mud bloody red, would mankind really benefit? I thought back to Fatso. What had he died for? What was his wife feeling, sitting in an empty house watching the Christmas tree twinkling? And the convoy to Dak To; the two guys in that flatbed truck. Did they have wives, or kids? "Merry Christmas, little fella. Don't open this box. Your daddy's inside, but the world is a better place." Hell, they hadn't found a trace of those guys, just a big hole in the road. What does the army do about that? Send an empty box? Fill it with rocks? Is that why they had weighed us so often in basic? I wondered about Ohio and Shotgun. Guys came and went, and you didn't even ask their names. Who would give a damn if they died? Other than my family, who would care if I died?

The recruiter had said, "You probably won't ever see Vietnam. They don't need mechanics in Vietnam. You'll probably be stationed close to home, and be home on weekends." I was a fool. Where was that SOB? He had stripes all over the place. He was a career soldier, with years of training. Why wasn't he here? I had made a big mistake. Would I get the death penalty? Then, if I did go home, I would have a thirty-day leave and have to go back to some army base and shine my boots and polish my belt buckle for fourteen months. How would I ever stand it? What if I was assigned to the Pentagon to use a rifle and bayonet against the war protestors? I knew I couldn't do that.

The girl at the firebase had died so bravely. Just a whore. She must have known she was going to die. The other two must have known it, too. None of them would get out of there alive. She just lay there, didn't cry, didn't beg. If I was a prisoner of war, would I be that brave? Would it do any good? I was a pfc, didn't know a damn thing that would help the Viet Cong, didn't know as much as they did. They knew why they were there. They lived there. They had been invaded by strangers who tortured their women. I understood their rage. Hadn't anybody told them we were here for their own good? Were we?

Since I had been in this place I had been attending church services every Sunday. I made an appointment with the chaplain and explained my problems. I didn't want to kill. I didn't think I could kill. I had never had occasion to find out in civilian life. I wasn't myself. I was losing my values, maybe even my sanity. I was having nightmares. Would it be possible to apply for conscientious objector status at this late date? I would serve out my time, but I had to get out of there!

The chaplain had my records, and there was no mention of being a conscientious objector. He put his arm around my shoulder as he walked me to the door. "It's called battlefield religion, son. You'll get over it. You'll do what you have to, and you'll go home. The worthwhile things in life are never easy, and I want you to feel free to come in and talk with me any time." We parted at the side of his jeep. There were golf clubs.

On New Year's Eve, we had a party. At midnight most of us cheered and turned bottoms up. We were going home this year! I missed formation the next morning. I was found sleeping peacefully. In the monkey cage!

On January 17, I turned twenty years old. I wasn't a teenager anymore.

Nothing relieves depression like a good laugh. Mine started with a note from my dad, with a special enclosure. I unfolded the paper and broke into a fit of laughter. Tears rolled down my cheeks; my side hurt! After days of reflection about the effect Vietnam was having on me, this simple piece of paper symbolized the absurdity of it all. It was official. My draft notice had arrived! I wrote a letter:

Dear Draft Board,

This is to inform you that, due to present circumstances, I will be unable to report for induction as required by your recent correspondence. Believe me, I'd love to. I am in Pleiku, South Vietnam, and the company commander won't give me the time off. I'm sure you will understand.

By the way, I respectfully suggest that, before you send any more young men over here, you come over and see it for yourselves. Perhaps then you can answer the most serious question about the war. Why?

Sincerely,

I signed my name and official U.S. Army serial number and showed it around to all my colleagues. We mailed it and had a beer. A lot of beers. We laughed and joked, and I felt better. In some small way, I had told them.

I never received a reply. I have moved around quite a bit since I was discharged. Maybe they're still looking for me.

● ● ● ●

The replacement company commander arrived shortly before Christmas with a flurry of activity that we wrongly construed as a flair for showmanship. The previous CO had left, and the first sergeant was running the show for a few days until the replacement took over. First Sergeant Parker was a kindly man, with a military brush-cut and forlorn, basset hound eyes. He was fair and honest, interested in getting the job done, but aware of the stresses we were feeling. He formed details, sprucing up for the new commander. Had they met beforehand? Did the new guy have a reputation that preceded him? Rumor was, the new CO needed a combat tour to be promoted to major, and he was hell-bent to succeed.

It was early in the morning. We stood at attention as a jeep approached, flags fluttering from its front fenders. Captain Benedict stretched himself out of the seat, formally accepted command from Parker, and turned to address us. He was short, maybe five-feet-eight. His uniform was immaculate, fresh-pressed to razor-sharp creases, with brass and ribbons shimmering in the golden light of early morning. He was stiff, formal, polished, and as out of place as a neon sign.

"Men," he barked, "the enemy is on the run. You have worked hard, and it is truly a pleasure to take command of a unit with a record as distinguished as the one you have compiled. And yet, apart from those faceless papers, those meaningless statistics, I find myself appalled! At first appearance, in briefings with my superiors, I thought I was inheriting a company that is a credit to the United States Army and the good people back home. Today, standing here, I see that I have inherited a band of ragamuffins! I remind you that you are soldiers, members of the United States Army, the Number One fighting force in the world! I will ask First Sergeant Parker to accompany me on an inspection, and I expect to see soldiers out here! I *will* have a unit I can be proud of. Parker..."

Up and down the rows they came, stiff, turning on their spit-shined heels to stare at each man; asking questions but disregarding answers, or the reasons behind them.

CAPTAIN BENEDICT: "Soldier, are you aware that military regulations allow facial hair only above the junction of the lips?"

UNCOMPREHENDING SOLDIER: "Sir?"

CAPTAIN BENEDICT: "Your mustache, soldier. It extends below the corners of your mouth! Are you aware that military regulations state that mustaches may not extend below the corners of your mouth?"

SOLDIER: "No, sir. Most copies of the regulations mildewed during the rainy season."

A burning look from steel blue eyes, a formal salute, a snapping turn, and he was in front of the next man.

BENEDICT: "Troop, what in God's name has happened to your belt buckle?"

SOLDIER: "It's taped, sir."

BENEDICT: "When was the last time it was polished, soldier?"

SOLDIER: "Sir, with all due respect, I drive a wrecker escorting convoys to Dak To every day. It gets rough on that road, sir, and we cover everything shiny so it won't be a target. I don't wear my watch anymore, I tape my wedding ring every morning." He offered his left wrist as proof.

BENEDICT: "I'm new here, son, but I've been in this man's army a lot of years. This man's army requires a polished belt buckle. As long as you are under my command, I intend to enforce regulations, soldier."

SOLDIER: "Sir, I have a wife and a daughter back in The World, and I intend to see them again…" First Sergeant Parker interrupted, "Sir, some of these boys get shot at every day. We allow some latitude in camouflaging for their protection. The tape is army issue, for camouflage. We use it quite a bit on convoys and patrols."

BENEDICT (his eyes flashing hatred at this insolence): "I'm new here, and I have to learn how things are done. I don't know the requirements of a convoy to Dak To. I *do* know the requirements of serving my command. You will appear in a full and correct military uniform every morning. If your work requires a deviation from that uniform to be performed satisfactorily, so be it. I'm sure you can purchase a second belt buckle at the PX and change to your taped one before going on these convoys. You will appear in military uniform every morning! Do I make myself clear, soldier?"

SOLDIER: "I read you loud and clear, sir!"

Up and down the rows they went, Benedict strutting, Parker taking notes, interjecting comments. Sometimes Benedict asked about a soldier's time in-country, or experience. Finally he had satisfied himself, turned our welfare back to Parker, and stormed into the command tent. Parker asked a few men to stay behind, and sent us off to our day of work.

The next morning at our formation, the plywood wall of the shower building spoke eloquently of our feelings. Large, scrawled letters of red spray paint proclaimed: FRAG YOU BENEDICT. A number of hard-case lifers, both NCOs and officers, died in Vietnam at the hands of their own men. In the bush, a firefight offered a chance to fire a "stray round," and in base camp a fragmentation grenade could be rolled under a cot. Hence the name. No one knows how often it happened. Captain Benedict didn't want to find out. He retired to his sandbagged bunker and never came out. Three men were chosen as round-the-clock bodyguards at the door, armed with an M-60 machine gun, M-16 rifle, and .45 caliber automatic pistol. First Sergeant Parker was, for all intents and purposes, in charge. Benedict started a regimen of spit and polish.

The rains had ended. With their departure, a chill night wind swept through the highlands. Temperatures would reach a hundred degrees by day and plummet to the low forties at night. Tropical-weight uniforms were insufficient against the chill. I asked my family to send long johns. We cumshawed air force parkas and sleeping bags. The greatest challenge was to time your shower, to get clean of the sweat of the day before the chill night wind made the trip back to the hootch uncomfortable. The Vietnamese mud had turned to dust, churned to a pink fog by the endless vehicles.

Still, it was a change of seasons, a sure sign of the passing of time. We were creeping inexorably toward a climax; an unknown, but an end. Any sign of progress was welcome. With the new year I had started a formal short-timer's calendar on my locker door. As the sun rose each morning, I got the greatest pleasure that day would provide by coloring another square. Each day brought me a step closer to the goal. The war had quieted, but the nights were often an ordeal of nightmares and memories. It was fitting to mark progress in the morning as the first light of day sent the demons into hiding.

Letters from home spoke of snow, mornings white and pure. The bands were stretching the limits of rock 'n' roll music; the Super Bowl hoopla was building.

• • • •

In Pleiku, Charley had left us to our internal stresses. From hiding, Benedict issued orders with daily efficiency. The housegirls, on the other hand, buoyed our spirits. The Vietnamese New Year was approaching, and their exuberance and preparations were reminiscent of holiday preparations back home. They pointed off to the northwest, where a valley led the Ho Chi Minh Trail into our valley. "Ho Chi Minh come home for New Year," they predicted. "Ho Chi Minh from Pleiku, always come home for Tet!" Day after day, the smoke and flame of napalm bombs dotted the distant hills. If Ho Chi Minh was up there, he had to be in trouble.

The housegirls gathered in circles, squatting flat-footed, to pick the lice out of each other's hair and crack them in their teeth. We had nothing to fear, they assured us. This was Ho's escort. The holiday would bring a cease-fire, and downtown would be an exciting chaos of drink, parades of ornate costumes, special banquets, good cheer, firecrackers. I imagined a Mardi Gras atmosphere.

From a deep sleep, I awoke, listening. Something was wrong. There! I heard it again! Instead of the familiar *BOOM-SSSSsssshhhh* of rounds leaving Artillery Hill, tonight's went *ssssSSHHHHH-BOOM!* I jumped into action, screaming "Incoming!" and grabbing for my helmet and boots. The warning siren started into its dreaded mournful song. In the darkness of the hootch the sounds of frantic motion, chaos, and swearing assured us everyone was awake. Round after round was coming now, shaking the ground. Shivering with fear and chill, I pulled on my fatigue jacket, buckled the heavy web belt around my waist, grabbed my rifle, and burst out of the tent into a turmoil of milling, shadowy figures and overwhelming noise. Orange-gold flares lit the sky. I crouched and ran toward my bunker.

I crashed into another guy heading to his post. The wind was knocked out of me; I struggled to my knees, then to my feet. Running headlong across the rutted ground, I heard the sizzle of a shell approaching, and hit the dirt. It exploded with a deafening roar but wasn't really close. I ran again. The rounds were falling heavily on Artillery Hill, straight ahead of me. Explosions lit the night, shook the ground. I reached my bunker. There were dark forms inside, probably my assigned colleagues, but I called out to be sure. When they heard me over the din, they urged me to get up with them. There is a safety in numbers. Looking across our area of the perimeter, past the concertina wire to the elephant grass beyond, I imagined figures in black. Artillery Hill roared in answer, then shook as a new wave of shells came in. The ground trembled beneath our knees. To our left, far in the distance, we could see flames leap from the enemy rocket tubes. We heard the faint thumping of their explosions, mixed with the shriek of the rounds overhead. Four flashes brought four trails of sound, followed a few moments later by four thunderous concussions on Artillery Hill. Four more flashes. Anxiously, we counted the four crackling trails overhead, knowing that any less would mean a round was heading our way. I struggled to keep my head down but watched the grass for the ground attack we expected. In our small arena things quieted, bringing sounds of heavy firing from the direction of Pleiku, Fourth Division headquarters on Titty Hill, Holloway, everywhere. I turned to see a red glow rising from downtown, a flock of helicopters, scarlet tracers streaking everywhere, the flash of heavy rounds. Another volley of incoming rockets rattled overhead, landed closer. The noise was tremendous again, the fear overwhelming. "Jim!" I hollered to my companions. "Jim! Al! When you get a chance, look at downtown! They're hittin' everywhere!" The answer came back. "Yeah!" It was an awesome show!

A normal firefight in The Nam was over in a brief flurry of uncontrolled fury. Hour after hour, this one kept reviving itself. Waves of rockets thundered in, bursts of small-arms fire crackled, the clatter of chopper blades mixed with the far-off thunder of artillery. Flashes of golden fire lit the sky behind us. The wind rustled the tall grass, its motion creating images of shadowy illusion that seemed human, deadly. Helicopters circled Pleiku like hornets around the nest; the big guns on the hill seemed louder, harsher than usual. It began to get cold. It began to get light. The fury continued. The VC were night fighters, sneaky, in black pajamas camouflaged by darkness. They had never gone on this long. They should have stopped by now. A voice came from the guard tower above us, to our right. "Hey! It's an emergency! Can anybody take some fresh underwear to Benedict's bunker?" Laughter from the distance. A mocking falsetto answered from our left. "Sorry! My belt buckle is dirty, and I'm just not fit to be seen by an officer of the United States Army!" Another voice growled. "Sure is chilly in The Nam!"

A final flurry of rockets pounded into Artillery Hill, interrupting the hill's endless barrage of return fire. Far off in the bush we saw a flicker of lights. Charley was calling it a night, heading home on his motorbike. Like distant fireflies, they twinkled, heading to our right toward Highway One. In the hours of bombardment, not a single round from Artillery Hill had landed near them. No air support had come to our aid. Charley had pounded Artillery Hill and Titty Hill unmercifully, uninterrupted. The action still raged downtown and toward Camp Holloway. From the distant echoes we knew this was no firefight. It was really getting light; we could see the tiny black outlines of the choppers and fighters, far off but still battling with an incredible uproar. The sounds came on the wind, rumbling and thumping. This was a major battle. When it stretched into the first light of dawn without slacking, we knew it was serious.

Herky-jerky, a jeep bounced along the line, approaching from behind us, to our left. Stopping, starting, stopping again; coming closer; bouncing over the rough dirt. At each bunker muffled, excited voices carried to us in snatches. At our bunker the jeep stopped, Lieutenant Baker ran toward us, crouched in our humble corner. "We stay on the line!" He was obviously upset. "Patrol is surrounded, about a mile and a half out. They had to whisper on the radio, but they haven't been seen yet. At least a battalion of North Vietnamese regulars are heading straight our way. Patrol says they can hear machinery; it sounds big but they can't see it. Might be tanks, or trucks. They're comin' straight down the valley at us, and they're armed to the teeth! Stay on line, stay awake. We're sendin' a truck out with C's and coffee. We don't think the main force'll be here 'til ten or eleven, but they may have advance parties to soften us up. The whole fuckin' country's gettin' this shit! Hue, Saigon, Cam Ranh, everywhere! Pleiku is in enemy hands. We're cut off from Holloway; can't even get to the water point! When it's fully light, one at a time you can go back to the hootches, get your jackets, shovels, all the ammo you got, and bayonets! Fix bayonets! Prepare for a full human wave assault!"

"Lieutenant?"

"Yeah!"

"Sir, are Captain Benedict's boots shined?"

"Captain Benedict won't come out of his bunker. Martinez says he's on his knees with rosary beads! Parker's on the phone, running the show. Benedict just says, 'You know what to do!' Who needs him?! You guys get your shit together, and be ready by nine. Anything moves outside the wire, it's a free-fire zone! Fix bayonets! Got it?"

"Yes, sir!"

Baker ran to his jeep and bounced to the next bunker, stirring a cloud of dust that settled on us.

"Jesus Christ! Did you hear that?" I was shivering. A full human wave assault, in a couple of hours. The ultimate nightmare. Fix bayonets? I'd seen the horror at Dak To. I had been thanking God ever since that I hadn't had to see a human wave attack. I knew I was no match for a wiry little fanatic in hand-to-hand combat. If it was bad in Saigon, this must be the last big one. We would be killed, or taken prisoner! No one was gonna help us. The noise from Pleiku told me that. Everybody was too busy. Everybody was getting the shit kicked out of them, and Charley was saving us for last 'cause he knew we were just a bunch of mechanics and we were cut off. When he got the tough stuff out of the way he planned to just roll over us! I was shaking inside, but trying not to let others see my fear. The sun broke over Artillery Hill, cut through the heavy shroud of smoke and dust. I sat in a daze, watching the sun come up. Maybe for the last time.

When my turn came to go back to the hootch, I got control of my wobbly legs. In the familiar darkness, I gathered my long johns, cigarettes, and bayonet. I pulled it out of its scabbard, examining the heavy steel blade. How the hell could this be?

In a couple of hours I might have a chunk of steel like this in my gut! I dug for fresh socks, found my writing paper. God, I've gotta say something to the folks! Hurriedly, I scribbled the date, and a quick message:

Mom, Dad, Ken,
   It's bad. Supposed to get human waves in a few hours. All hell is breaking loose. Want you to know I love you. Watched the sun come up. It's beautiful! God bless you!

I stuffed it into an envelope, addressed it, and set it on my cot where it would be in plain sight. On the pillow I had so hurriedly abandoned last night, I noticed a familiar, pale green envelope. I lifted it to my nose, breathed in its soft fresh scent. I tucked it under the pillow, took the other letter, the one to my family, and turned it over. On the outside of the envelope I scrawled a feeble P.S.: "Please tell Carolynn how much it meant, and thanks!"

I had written about her, sent an address. Someday, Mom had written, she would stop by and say hello.

One quick look around me and it was time to go. I really wouldn't miss that hootch. Let the rats have it! One more thing. I grabbed my small transistor radio. We could listen to the news on Armed Forces Radio and find out what was going on.

Shit! One more thing! I scratched off another day on the calendar! Two hundred and eighteen to go. If I got through this one.

We filled sandbags and dug holes to pass time. Time was the real enemy in The Nam, and it had shifted to slow motion. Just another day, but a thousand thoughts poured across my mind, and only four minutes had passed when I checked my watch. Time. We waited for 365 days to go by, for the dry season, the rainy season. We waited for the PX to have cigarettes, we waited for R and R, and we waited for a letter from home. We waited for chow, and sleep, and a hot shower, and sex, and cold beer. We waited for progress in this stinking war. We had been waiting for it to be over, and suddenly it seemed it might be, and soon. But we had always thought the United States would win, and the prospect of death or a prisoner-of-war camp offered little relief. We were waiting for a horde of Oriental madmen to storm us, for hell to engulf us. Minutes became hours, and hours became days. The sun beat down, and the dust found its way into our eyes and throats. Drinking water was scarce. Artillery Hill roared, and Charley answered. The choppers clattered, the fighters looped low over Pleiku. The radio told of horror everywhere. We took turns sleeping, but it was hard to sleep while you were terrified, so we smoked and talked and waited.

We spent about ten days in the bunkers, waiting for an attack that never came, listening to news reports of the widespread devastation throughout the country. It was shocking and discouraging.

In December, President Johnson had called General Westmoreland back to Washington and presented him with a shiny new Oak Leaf Cluster. "All the challenges have been met," the president said. Westmoreland talked about "the light at the end of the tunnel." On January 21, North Vietnamese long-range artillery opened fire on the marine outpost at Khe Sanh, about 150 miles to our north. The five thousand marines were surrounded by a North Vietnamese force estimated at eighty thousand. Over a thousand artillery rounds crashed into Khe Sanh every day. President Johnson feared another Dien Bien Phu, where the French had been defeated in 1954. The siege of Khe Sanh lasted seventy-seven terrible days. By the end of January, the plight of the marines was well known to everyone in The Nam. Our confidence was sagging.

On the night of January 30, Charley used the cover of the Tet cease-fire to attack every major city and town in South Vietnam. The Communist losses were heavy; only in the ancient city of Hue did they gain a reasonable foothold. For a few hours they had invaded Saigon, seized the radio station and the American embassy. Had Khe Sanh been a diversionary action in the preparation for the Tet offensive? No, the siege wore on and on. On February 5, the NVA actually broke through Khe Sanh's perimeter, but were repelled in bloody hand-to-hand fighting. Then, on February 7, North Vietnamese troops in Soviet-built tanks overran a Green Beret base at Lang Vei, a few miles from Khe Sanh. Over nine hundred Americans and South Vietnamese were wiped out. Back in The World, Walter Cronkite, America's most respected newsman, exclaimed, "What the hell is going on? I thought we were winning this war."

The Communists had expected a general uprising of the South Vietnamese people, and it never came. Pockets of invaders were systematically cleaned out. Today, one accepted view is that the Tet offensive was a serious military defeat for the Communists. General Westmoreland himself has characterized Tet as "the turning point of the war." Based solely upon the numbers of casualties (and the accuracy of "body counts" in the American effort has never been called realistic), we should have seized control of the war. But in fact, shortly after Tet, America began to slowly disassociate itself from Vietnam. The March 10 *New York Times* shouted across Sunday morning coffee cups:

WESTMORELAND REQUESTS 206,000 MORE MEN

If the enemy had been decisively beaten, why did Westmoreland need so many reinforcements? The answer involves intangibles like "confidence" and "will to win." Momentum, in the lingo of the pro football commentators, had shifted. A West Point textbook printed years later attributed the "complete surprise" to an American "intelligence failure ranking with Pearl Harbor." (Stanley Karnow, *Vietnam: A History* New York: Viking Press, 1983, p. 543.)

On February 13, the Pentagon announced that only 10,500 reinforcements would be going to Vietnam. In the words of the *Pentagon Papers*, "the resources were beginning to be drawn too thin." On February 29, LBJ bid farewell to Robert McNamara, his Secretary of Defense, and replaced him with Clark Clifford, a close personal friend. Clifford had supported the war, but now he advised Johnson that "the one course of action the United States should take was to get out of Vietnam." (Michael Maclear, *The Ten Thousand Day War*, New York: Methuen, 1981, p. 218.)

Although this is not intended to be a history, some of this background is necessary to understand our feelings as we crouched behind the sandbags in Pleiku. We were not privy to the classified, top-secret intelligence. We couldn't get printouts from the computer banks at Long Binh. We were not able to talk to Washington daily, and we did not suspect that our leadership had put a ceiling on the number of enemy troops that could be reported to the powers who would ultimately equip us! Still, despite our lack of specific knowledge, we were as capable as the American people of analyzing what was going on around us.

Walter Cronkite was safe and warm back in The World. We were threatened with imminent death or capture. We were demoralized, tired, hungry, and terrified. But we were not stupid.

Our military training had urged us to have undying faith in America's ultramodern war-fighting technologies. From the enormous computer rooms at Long Binh to the reconnaissance satellites in space, microchips had made every day's actions known and predictable. We had firepower, from the awesome minigun, able to fire fifteen hundred rounds per minute, to the M-16 rifle. A bullet fired from an M-16 tumbles, so that it causes maximum wounding upon only the slightest impact with the human body. A firing-range instructor at Aberdeen had reassured us that an enemy, shot in the palm of the hand by an M-16, would have his chest cavity shredded. There were forty-two different missile systems in use, and a rainbow of chemical defoliants to strip away Charley's cover. We would rely upon tens of thousands of electronic sensors dropped along the Ho Chi Minh Trail. These sensors detected movement, noise, even the ammonia in urine, supposedly allowing bombers to thwart North Vietnamese troop or equipment movements. We had waves of air power, helicopters, fighters, bombers. The awesome B-52. We had napalm and white phosphorous bombs. We had giant bulldozers to destroy forest or farmland. And we had nuclear weapons. Technology had become America's God, and Vietnam attracted the worshippers like a Deep South revival. Hundreds of civilian contractors filled the gaps with state-of-the-art data processing or communication equipment.

President Kennedy helped publicize a new hero to America by reading Ian Fleming's James Bond thrillers. James Bond movies became the great box-office attractions of the era. A great deal of their appeal lay in the futuristic equipment designed for the agents "licensed to kill." The technology worked in movies like *Dr. No* and *Goldfinger*. But in real life, in the jungles of Vietnam, it failed miserably. In 1965, 177 helicopters were lost, at a cost of $250,000 apiece. Only seventy-six fell to "hostile action." (Vance Hartke, *The American Crisis in Vietnam*, Indianapolis and New York: Bobbs-Merrill, 1968, p. 104.) And all the electronic surveillance did little to warn us of the Tet bloodbath. The Pentagon's buying sprees had equipped us, but America's effort in Vietnam was hampered by unreliable equipment, lack of a coherent overall strategy for using the technology (and communicating with other branches of the military), and the failure to successfully convince the average soldier of the need for the war. All the King's horses and all the King's men, and all the dollars the Pentagon fantasy-mongers threw at the situation could not overcome Vietnam's determination. We saw that clearly, seven long years before the war would end.

Yes, we were demoralized as we watched the elephant grass for signs of human activity. From the beginning of our military careers, we had heard that "the only good gook is a dead gook." Surely the planning for this countrywide offensive required inside information coupled with intense security. How could it have happened? We wondered if North and South Vietnam were cooperating secretly. Far from this being the uninformed conjecture of mere foot soldiers, historical literature has given our theory considerable attention. (See Ward S. Just, *To What End*, Boston: Houghton Mifflin, 1968, pp. 57–60; James Hamilton-Paterson, *The Greedy War*, New York: David McKay Publishing, 1971, pp. 108, 1881–191, 214, and 248–253; Frances Fitzgerald, *Fire in the Lake*, New York: Random House, 1972, p. 513.)

To reiterate, this was the common conversation as we waited for the fury of the Tet offensive to abate. It was February of 1968, and a great many of us have grown into middle age with this nagging doubt in the back of our minds. This is what we were thinking then; the references in literature I discovered only after fourteen years of trying to forget the war. We waited, we crossed each day off a short-timer's calendar, and we trusted no one in authority. Tet had made it clear that our leaders couldn't warn us, couldn't protect us, and probably didn't realize that they had failed in their responsibilities to us, our loved ones, and the American people. A feeling of despair fell over us and spread throughout the American military. LBJ continued to draft the kids out of the poorer homes, and green body bags continued to bring them back again. By 1972, despair had become so pervasive that nearly 25 percent of all Americans in military uniform had mutinied, deserted, or were openly defying orders! (Maclear, p. 280.)

We stayed in the bunkers nearly two weeks. The first week was terrifying, then the fighting slowed, and we regained control of the drinking-water station. The mess hall cooks went back to work, and we returned to the workshops in "half strength," half of us repairing damaged vehicles while the other half manned the perimeter. A mail truck made it in, with news from home. A truck went downtown to look for our housegirls. The driver returned with an ashen face. Most of our housegirls had died at the hands of door-to-door death squads. Shitburner was barely alive. His daughter had been raped and shot before his eyes, then his wife, and finally his arms and legs had been riddled with automatic weapons fire. Miraculously, he survived. Months later he was loaded into a jeep and brought to the compound for a visit. His smile was gone, and it was an emotional time for anyone who had known him. We took up many collections to support him. When the Americans left and the war was lost, his chances for survival were not good.

The note had never been mailed to my parents. I tore it up, not wanting them to know how scared I'd been. The words were so inadequate. I wondered what life had been like for them, trying to carry on with their lives while the news of Tet and Khe Sanh assailed them from every newspaper, TV, and radio.

By late February we were allowed to go downtown, in small, armed groups. The destruction was staggering. The rubble reminded me of photographs of Berlin or London after the bombings of World War II. I took no pictures. These were not scenes I would forget, not things I would want to show friends or family. There were elaborate displays of captured weapons in the square, and glossy eight-by-ten-inch photos of hundreds of captive raiders for sale in the shops. Most of the Cong were young, naked, and filthy, their wrists wired behind them with barbed wire. Many were wounded. Throughout the city there was a sickening scent of death and burned wood, but the Vietnamese seemed oblivious to it all and shouted, "Short time, GI?" or "Give me cigarette, GI."

Benedict ordered a spit-and-polish inspection. Things were, as Archie said, "Back to abnormal!" The trucks were hauled in with what seemed to be larger holes and bloodier seats.

• • • •

Early in March, the night was again split by the sound of incoming. This time we weren't so lucky. Running toward the bunker, I heard the whistle of a shell overhead, growing louder and louder. Suddenly, the sound evaporated. Someone had once told me that this would be a sign that a round was going to land on me. In the fury and the fear I recalled that warning and hurled myself to the ground. The explosion, the noise, the concussion are impossible to describe. If I had remained on my feet, I have no doubt that I would have been killed. The explosion wasn't twenty yards away. I was showered by chunks of earth. When I got to my bunker, my colleagues said my body had been tossed into the air like a rag doll. Round after round roared in, all around us. We crouched behind the sandbag wall, peering down the barrels of rifles, watching for the human waves. A round hit, right in front of us. Someone to my right was crying for his mother. "Mom? Mom? Where are you, Mom?" Artillery Hill was roaring. The dust, thrown up by the explosions all around us, created an orange cloud. We strained our eyes, and they filled with the dust. The smell of gunpowder was incredibly strong, taking my mind back to my childhood adventures with firecrackers. In the midst of this confusion, small-arms fire broke loose on our right. All eyes turned that way, to see a figure running headlong toward us, firing out into the tall grass, and screaming incoherently. Rifles swung toward the figure, but cries of "Hold your fire!" held us back. Incoming rounds continued to thunder around us as the shadowy figure flashed past and disappeared into the darkness to our left, still firing and screaming. In a few moments he was gone, like a strange specter, and the shooting stopped. There were anxious cries from the distance, then silence. The firing finally ended, and the familiar, quiet routine of waiting began again. At last dawn broke, and we were called in from the wire.

Spec 4 Andrews had been in Dak To for months, making quick repairs to the convoy vehicles so they could make the return trip to Pleiku. It was a lonely existence, jerry-rigging and making do. Nearing the end of his tour, he asked to be returned to Pleiku. Feeling, however falsely, that he was "behind the lines," this attack had pushed him over the edge. He was apprehended, and sent to Okinawa for psychiatric help. We never heard from him again, and I often wonder if he got it together and got home on time. In a way, he was fortunate. By going off, he got help.

There were thousands, perhaps millions, of bombardments during the long war in The Nam. This one cost Andrews the critical brain cell and earned him a ticket to a psychiatric hospital in Okinawa. In the morning I discovered the sandbag I had been peering over, lying empty and forlorn atop the bunker wall. A two-inch piece of shrapnel had torn it, just inches from my throat. The damage to our compound was considerable. Parts boxes were exploded or torn by shrapnel. Numerous trucks were immobilized. A metal building outside the perimeter took a direct hit.

Not a single round had been fired in return. Artillery Hill had roared, but Charley felt no pain. There were both American and ARVN positions on Artillery Hill, and one of the ARVN positions had dropped nearly two dozen 105-millimeter rounds on us! Andrews lost his mind, and I nearly lost my neck. The rain of deadly shrapnel had been American-made, the gun had been American-made, but the ARVN in charge had been a Viet Cong sympathizer. At formation the following noon, it was announced that he had been interrogated and then executed. We knew little about artillery, the precise calculations necessary to aim the big guns, but we decided that the entire gun crew should have noticed the unusual settings and stopped the bombardment. After all, our compound was less than a mile from the muzzle of that gun, and in plain sight. None of us had been close to Andrews, he kept to himself, but we agreed that his sanity was poorly compensated by the single execution...if, in fact, there had been any execution at all. But there was little time to dwell upon what might have been, and we patched the damage and went on to the next adventure. Unusual occurrences were the norm in Pleiku, and you ignored them or became a victim of them. We had no rank and deserved no explanations. We learned to accept our roles, because to question the authorities brought added grief and nothing more.

• • • •

For power poles, we welded artillery canisters end to end. Carruthers had been climbing one to repair a wiring problem. He fell and broke a leg in three places, and his only comment from the ambulance was, "I'll be home soon, Wife, and it could've hurt a lot worse." He grinned and shook a few hands. They closed the doors and took him away, and we never heard from him again. His replacement was a guy named Justice from Louisiana. Justice was nineteen, but had been a ground-pounder in the delta. One afternoon his squad had been pinned down, cut to ribbons. The lieutenant, fresh from Officer Candidate School, had ordered the survivors to charge across a grassy clearing. They refused, evacuation choppers lifted them out, and the lieutenant court-martialed them for disobeying a direct order. Justice had a jagged scar on his arm and a Purple Heart. He had been found innocent at the court-martial, but the lieutenant received only a verbal reprimand. Justice said, "Only a fuckin' fool'd go back out in the bush with that asshole. He wants captain bars before he goes home, and he don't care how many grunts he gets killed to get 'em. I just said fuck it and extended for an extra year. Used to pull wrenches back home, an' I can damn well pull wrenches for a lot longer'n I could patrol the delta with that bastard." He would not see Louisiana for twenty months, but seemed relieved. Justice bunked in Archie's hootch, and they regularly harassed each other about accents. Soon they were debating the relative nutritional values of grits versus Boston baked beans, or the military accomplishments of Grant versus Lee, or whether it was a "Civil War" or "War Between the States." As onlookers, we rolled on the floor. Archie, feigning total frustration, would throw his hands into the air and cry, "Why our tent? Is there no justice?" and Justice would moan, "Justice is blind!"

Entertainment was scarce, and these two were funnier than Laurel and Hardy. One night Archie introduced a new game. By pulling his pants tight and holding a lighter near his crotch, he could expel gas and create an enormous ball of flame in the dark hootch. Justice waited 'til he was asleep and circled his bunk with lighted candles, "Hopin' he might ignite his foul self like a Buddhist monk." Archie escaped injury, and soon Justice declared, "There ain't nothin' a damn Yankee can do but what a poor southern boy can do it better!" Bets were placed, judges selected, and rules drawn up. There would be two criteria: size of the flame and duration. In order to make his effort "official," the contestant must alert the judges by announcing, "Fire in the hole!" and produce within fifteen seconds after his prediction. I don't remember who won the first contest, but it became a passion. Soon the parts men had a company champion and were challenging our champion, and standings were posted on the bulletin board.

The game was called the "Friday Night Farts," and no one was ever hurt. Of course it was vulgar, but we were living in a vulgar world. Justice wrote to the International Olympic Committee, requesting that our new sport be included in future

Olympic competition, but received no reply. In a land without libraries, movies, TV, or major-league baseball, we improvised.

Captain Benedict, so conspicuous in his absence under fire, demanded a state of "spit and polish" equal to what might be expected in Stateside assignments. A number of us wrote to our congressmen, begging them to investigate his cowardice and dereliction of duty. If First Sergeant Parker was capable of being a company commander, he should have had captain's bars. And the round-the-clock guard outside Benedict's bunker was designed to protect him from his own troops, not Charley. His fear and distrust of us had made our compound tense and inefficient, and Vietnam's climate made his demands for spotlessness impossible. These demands went beyond sanitation; they were harassment. The war effort was not served by starched fatigues; the hardened fabric irritated sweaty skin and the polished brass made a better target for Viet Cong sharpshooters. Our living conditions were crude; we wanted better, but Benedict stubbornly refused to be realistic.

I wrote to my congressman, Barber Conable of New York. I emphasized my fear, that I thought Captain Benedict was shirking his duties and putting all of us at greater risk by refusing to accept the responsibility of his command. A few weeks later, I received a reply from Conable's office. He had made inquiries in Saigon. A general had written that he knew Benedict personally, had eaten dinner with him at an officer's club in Saigon. Benedict was an officer and a gentleman in the finest traditions of the military. Conable considered the matter closed.

I did not. After JFK's Camelot had exploded in Dallas, Bobby Kennedy had become a senator from New York. I had attended a campaign speech, and his concern for the downtrodden had made me a fan. Now, sickened by the bloodshed in Southeast Asia, he was challenging his own party's president for the November nomination. He called the war senseless, a waste. I knew he would understand our fear of Benedict's attitude, our resentment of the harassment. RFK understood that, as Americans, we were all in this together. I knew he would investigate and come to our aid. I believed. And I waited impatiently for his reply.

• • • •

On March 31, 1968, the siege in Khe Sanh ended. The "donut dollies" visited, but there were no games. President Johnson was delivering a major address, to be carried by Armed Forces Radio. As expected, he spoke of Vietnam and the events of the past few months. He would seek a negotiated peace. And he would not run for reelection.

There was a colonel at Fourth Division who was a close friend of our battalion commander. Officers in The Nam had certain status symbols, coded references to their power, prestige, or combat experience. Elaborate swagger sticks were the most obvious, glossy paint on their jeeps was another. This particular colonel had recently been awarded the Silver Star for directing operations at Dak To from a helicopter safely riding thousands of feet overhead. He was detested by the Fourth Infantry troops in his command for many of the same reasons we detested Benedict. As affirmation of his new status among his peers, we were ordered to paint his jeep glossy. It was sanded, wet-sanded, and the special (and unauthorized) paint prepared. To do a glossy jeep, you mixed three parts gloss black to one part olive drab. This gave a very dark shade of green, and of course a jeep in Vietnam had to be green. Two weeks later, the colonel had to go to Dak To to see how the war was going. A glossy black-green jeep would have been an attractive target among the convoy route, so we sanded it and sprayed it olive drab, numbered it, and made it a war machine once again. Five days later, the Colonel returned, and we sanded, painted, and numbered it again. Glossy dark green. This time he wanted the fenders pin-striped in gold. In the ensuing weeks we made seat covers from tiger-stripe ARVN fatigue shirts, a special highly polished shift knob, and an embroidered spare-tire cover. Around Pleiku the colonel's jeep looked like a refugee from a Vietnamese Western Auto, but whenever he decided to visit the troops in Dak To, we had to repaint and strip it, return it to its military appearance. It was disgusting to work on bloody trucks side by side with the colonel's "California custom" jeep. To us, it symbolized the detachment of the officers from the suffering of the grunts.

The army posts guards everywhere. Standard procedure is to assign guard duty by rotation, but now Benedict decided that we could best be protected by a permanent roster of guards. These guards would not be required to work in the garages and would be assigned to the guard towers in three-man teams. Each sentinel would be on duty for two hours and off four, 6:00 P.M. until 6:00 A.M. Guards would be expected to maintain exceptional standards of spit and polish, and would be inspected every afternoon at five. I was tired of the bloody trucks and was willing to accept the responsibilities of guard duty in exchange for a few extra hours of much-needed sleep. I volunteered. The spit and polish was no problem; my gear was already "strac" (ready for inspection), and I could polish a lot of boots in ten hours of free time every day.

The guard posts were a mixed lot. Most were metal "conex" (continental exchange) shipping boxes, similar to the shipping containers of today's sea freight industry. Atop the six-foot cube was a corrugated sheet-metal roof and a sandbagged machine-gun nest with an M-60, telephone, and binoculars. Sandbags covered the walls of the box, which was situated with the closed end against the barbed wire and the doors facing into our compound. Two broken cots inside the box gave the off-duty guards a rainproof bedroom.

Other towers, especially along the eastern perimeter, which faced Artillery Hill across a wide meadow, were considerably taller. These were larger platforms mounted on four telephone-pole legs. The on-duty guard and his machine gun perched in a narrow aisle between two cots, perhaps thirty to forty feet above the ground. Each guard post had a box of flares to illuminate the taller grass beyond the free-fire zone, and I soon learned to sleep through the loud *bang-sssssshh-pop* as a guard fired a flare into the sky, where it would swing gently back to earth from its parachute.

Strange things happened in the middle of the night. Each shift change was overseen by a sergeant of the guard, who made his rounds in a jeep. One night, while driving to a post, a giant black panther hurtled out of the darkness directly into the jeep's path. Thinking it was a VC sapper, the sarge wrenched the wheel and flipped the jeep. We saw the headlights catapult and go dark. There was no sound from the sarge. Expecting to find a group of sappers, a team of off-duty guards went to investigate. The sarge was excited but unhurt. We were scared and concerned. How had the large black cat managed to penetrate the perimeter without being seen? He could have easily been a sapper!

Vietnam harbored a variety of exotic animals, and they were often attracted by our perimeter lights. I once watched an anteater collect dinner for nearly an hour. Bats swooped at us; their sonar seemed to be attracted by the telephones. And there were the reptiles, especially the "fuck-you" lizard. Science calls him the gecko, after his distinctive call. Pale turquoise with orange spots, this ten-inch relative of the dinosaur has sung his mournful song for tens of thousands of years without being understood. Now he crept up to a guard tower in the night, eased up to the silent American guard, and hollered, "FUCK YOU!" The guard jumped out of his skin and, often, out of the tower. The "fuck-you" lizard is as much a symbol of Vietnam as the eagle is a symbol of America. (The National Zoo in Washington, D.C., has a "fuck-you" lizard. He is behind glass. His cage is soundproofed.)

Guard duty was serious business, and the Vietnamese climate didn't help. One night there was a full-fledged typhoon, and I drew a tower facing directly into the biting wind and rain. We wore ponchos but were soaked within fifteen minutes. You couldn't see to the ground, and the fear and responsibility made your stomach upset. In the dry season, the Central Highlands get cold at night. In tropical uniforms, thirty-seven degrees and windy is cold. I wore long johns or tucked inside an Arctic sleeping bag I had cumshawed from the air force. Wind-driven sand tormented our eyes, mosquitoes and rats attacked in waves, and scorpions often made nests in the sandbags.

One night I was gazing across the northern perimeter when one of the shadows seemed to have a human shape. As I watched, I couldn't discern any actual movement, but it was coming closer. I called the command bunker and was ordered to hold fire and "see what he was up to." Frightened, I kept him in the sights of the M-60. He certainly wasn't looking for a pizza and beer! It was the first time I had sighted down a killing machine, loaded and cocked, and watched a human being about to die. It was a chilling feeling, and my chest pounded. He kept coming closer. I kept him in my sights, talking frantically to the command bunker. Again, they ordered me not to fire. The shadowy figure was within forty yards. How far could he throw a grenade? I fired a flare, then another. He stopped. The harsh light from the flares accentuated the shadows; the dark form hardly resembled a man. My two companions were with me now, their rifles trained on our unwelcome guest, watching his every move. They weren't sure if he was human. They hadn't seen him move. A lieutenant arrived. Now there were four of us crowded into the tiny platform, straining our eyes. I fired another flare. When it died, he began to move backward. Still, there was no feature, no silhouette you could describe as human. It was a dark shadow, but it slid silently across yards of real estate. It was uncanny. The form was growing smaller, blending into the taller grass at the far edges of the free-fire zone. And then he was gone.

All three of us sat up all night. We were spooked. No one doubted that we had watched Charley, but the ghostlike lack of form or identity had been uncomfortably hard to see. Had he planned to slit our throats? Blow the wire and lead a dozen of his friends into our area? Just how far might he have thrown a grenade? Would he be back?

I was relieved but shaken. I had not killed, but I had wanted to. Sighting down the machine gun, if the command bunker had said, "Fire," I would have blown him away, and felt good about doing it. It wasn't hatred, simply fear and self-preservation. I had wanted to shoot a man, and I was troubled.

Peace negotiations were big news in Washington, but in Pleiku life just ground on with agonizing slowness. I was waiting for May, the two-thirds mark of my year. I had requested my R and R. Everyone in The Nam got a five-day rest-and-recreation leave in an exotic foreign city. Five days of partying away from the war. Civilization. The land of doorknobs and flush toilets. Wine, women, and song. Safety. No war. No torn or shattered trucks, no bloodstained canvas seats, no pieces of flesh rotting on an exploded floorboard.

The choices were Hong Kong, Tokyo, Manila, Bangkok, Sydney, Taiwan, Singapore, Kuala Lumpur, or an island in Malaysia called Penang. Sydney would have round-eyed women, Bangkok was supposed to be exotic, Manila was hectic, Hong Kong was too crowded. I decided on Penang, the island off the beaten path. A former British colony, it should have civilized touches like TV and toilets. But Malaysia had a large Chinese population. I would never have another chance to glimpse the exotic Oriental culture that hadn't survived the war in Vietnam, and I wanted to get a taste of the Chinese the movies portrayed. Not too big a taste, mind you, so Penang seemed just the ticket. As my departure date grew closer, the days grew longer and longer. The only limit to my fun would be financial, and I saved every available dollar. This was going to be the time of my life! The military flew married men to Honolulu for a reunion with their wives. They flew single men to the other exotic cities and guaranteed return transportation. They explained the local laws and suggested hotels that would offer discounts to R and R visitors from The Nam. Then they turned you loose, and the girls descended. As my friends returned one by one and described their adventures, time crawled. The last week seemed like a month.

• • • •

At long last, I boarded a C-130 to Cam Ranh Bay, where I would catch a jet to Penang. The R and R center was little more than a wooden barracks and a few offices, but it was the essence of civilization compared to our hootch in Pleiku. I stared at the facilities in Cam Ranh Bay for a long while. These guys had window air-conditioners! We would board the plane the next morning, so I took a bus to the beach. Like a Florida resort, the white sand reflected the sun in waves. The bay was blue, palm trees swayed gently in the breeze, and sunbathers stretched on multicolored beach towels. As the bus approached, the driver pointed out a two-story building to our left. This, he said, was a hospital, and during the Tet offensive the Cong had come ashore in rubber rafts, set up automatic weapons at both doors, and rolled a grenade inside. The grenade exploded, and the survivors, despite their wounds, rushed out the doors, to be mowed down. The bodies fell in bloody stacks. I waded up to my ankles, but I could not bring myself to swim in the bay after that story. Even in this bastion of civilization, death lurked too near.

Early the next morning a bus took us to a civilian jetliner. As we settled into our seats, wearing civilian clothes, the stewardesses offered cold washcloths and drinks. Soon we were airborne, headed away from Vietnam.

• • • •

By the time I had devoured a steak, the plane was lowering onto the Malay peninsula. We landed on the mainland, at a former British airfield called Georgetown, then took a ferry to the island of Penang. In the golden sun, the cluster of buildings and the turmoil of Chinese junks reminded me of Hong Kong harbor. Tiny fishing boats hovered around large freighters like honeybees around a fragrant bloom. We docked and were herded into a smoke-filled room for orientation. We would be on our own for five days. The ferry would leave at 8:00 A.M. on the dot; we had best be there. It was a small island; deserters would be rounded up easily. They suggested hotels and reassured us that violence and crime were virtually unknown on Penang. As we converted our savings to Malaysian currency and emerged into a throng of taxicabs, I searched the hotel pamphlets. I chose the Hotel International because it was the most Americanized, and there would be nightly dancing and refreshments on the roof for R and R guests.

The splendor of the lobby made me pause. Wall-to-wall carpet, framed pictures, and soft lighting were luxuries I had not seen in months. I hadn't really missed them until now, but standing in the midst of a room devoted solely to comfort and convenience made me painfully aware how primitive my last few months had been. Safely inside my room I turned the lamps off and on again and again, flushed the toilet, took an hour shower, and searched the television dial for an American show. The two languages of Malaysia, Chinese and Malay, sounded the same to me, and the high-pitched voices superimposed over familiar American TV shows made me laugh. From the window, I watched multicolored cars jolt their way through mid-city traffic, listened to horns honking and tires squealing. A rainbow assortment of neon signs jiggled and blinked in a fascinating display. In the distance, the ships bustled about the harbor. To my left, a large green mountain loomed up over the red tile roofs of the city as if shielding them from ocean storms.

After I had become familiar with the room and all its wonders, I went off in search of a lady. Well, if not a lady, at least a female. I kind of hoped she wouldn't be a lady. I walked across the sedate lobby, through the doors into a maelstrom of activity. Street merchants with overladen carts vied with a bustling sea of humanity, most dressed in neat Western clothes. There were plenty of peasants, but they were clean and courteous. There were a large group of taxi drivers, all trying to be heard over the others. "Hey, man! Pretty girls! You want a girlfriend? Want to buy suit? Many pretty girls! I get you good steak and french fries! Ice cream, Joe? I take you to ice cream! I show you good girls, all kinds. Malay. Chinese. Indian. Make love very good, Joe. You want girlfriend?" The average American confronted by this scene might think it barbaric or primitive, but it was refreshing. In The Nam the language was vulgar: "I take you Mama-san. Number one suck dick, boom-boom, you fuck ass, you fuck cherry girl, number one cocksucker!" Here, the language was civilized, to the point but not vulgar; and the references to food and clothes seemed to reinforce our civilized humanity. I wasn't an animal, and the crudeness in Vietnam, even though GIs had taught the people those words, had always turned me off. I was a human being. I had human needs, but here the hawkers respected me enough to talk about them with some decency. I was aching for sexual relief, but not bestiality. The offers spoke to that need in a way I had not heard for months. In no time I was in a taxi, careening through the narrow streets toward an assignation that would have been considered filthy and degrading in America, but was respectable and benevolent in this scenario.

We squealed to a stop on a tranquil side street. Stucco two-story buildings towered over the narrow sidewalk. There was no garbage, no one carried weapons. We had been told that Penang was 100 percent safe, and this quiet residential neighborhood reminded me of home. I was ushered into a large room, with a Buddhist shrine in one corner and a jukebox to the side. I sank onto an overstuffed couch, sipping a Scotch and water. A group of girls entered, giggling and laughing in some unknown language. Unlike the whores in Vietnam, their actions were demure, virginal. Most were Oriental, Chinese, but there were dark-skinned Malays and Indians, and even a plain and formless Caucasian girl with glasses. Quietly, respectfully, they asked questions. "Where are you from?"

"Pleiku."

They giggled. "Where are you from in America?"

"Rochester, New York."

"Aaah. Upstate. You live near Niagara Falls?"

I must have shown surprise. "About two hours away. I live near the Finger Lakes, in a small farming village."

"Do you have cows? A horse?"

"No. But there are cattle farms nearby. Sometimes the cows get loose and walk in our garden. Mostly it is a fruit area. Apple trees. Cherries. Corn and Wheat."

"How long have you stayed in Vietnam?"

I sighed deeply. I didn't want to think about it. It seemed like a lifetime. "Eight months."

"Oh. Velly good. You short-timer. You like dance?"

I hadn't thought about participating in music, really enjoying music, in a long time. My thoughts raced, and a quick daydream caused a delay. "I don't dance much. I play drums in a band, and I never learned to dance much. I would rather play. It's more fun to make music, especially when you don't know how to dance well." The words, propelled by a torrent of thoughts too long repressed, tumbled out. Hearing myself speaking too loudly, too excitedly, I stopped abruptly.

"We have many bands here. They will let you play. You tell us when you want to play, if you like the band, and we can arrange it for you. You are here to enjoy yourself, to have a good time and forget everything. Just tell us what you like, and we'll find it for you."

I was dumbfounded. No one had given a rat's ass for my feelings, my likes and dislikes, in so long. "Does the army help you do that?" It was a dumb question, blurted out.

"The army?" Everyone giggled. "No. The American army? They don't come here. We have seen many soldiers, talked to so many very sad men. They tell us about America, about the war. It is our job to make five short days as pleasurable as possible, to show you a good time. We try very hard. It is important that we be good to you. You tell us what you like, and we will try hard to make your holiday enjoyable. We are very good. You will see!"

My stupid question had embarrassed me, and the fact that I was relaxing in the company of eight beautiful women, small-talking in a whorehouse, about to negotiate a deal to procure a girl and screw my brains out for five days also made me uneasy. My experience with whores had been in The Nam, and these girls were a totally different breed. Neatly dressed in American-style dresses, but with hints of silken lingerie; hair clean and shiny and, in some cases, carefully styled; restrained, modest, coherent, they were ladies. Again, in this environment, female companionship was necessary and natural. The warm smiles and sparkling eyes were kind, inviting. Life had not been kind for a long, long time. It took me a few minutes to adjust to basic human decency, and I squirmed nervously. My underarms dripped. I was out of my element. These people were so very comfortable with the idea of baring their hearts and bodies for my pleasure, and for months I had thought only of fucking like a barnyard animal! My eyes darted from one to another, focused on a full breast, a shapely calf, a hint of black lace. Another Scotch was eroding the tension, if not the discomfort. Mama-san entered, looking for all the world like a Currier and Ives Chinese grandmother. Her white hair was swept back into a tight bun. A print apron was tied around her waist, bringing an image of homebaked apple pie to my racing mind. Most of all, her smile was soft and warm and motherly.

We exchanged pleasantries. She asked if I was married. No. Was I virgin? It was a matter-of-fact question, important to her. No. I grinned, and the girls twittered. Mama-san was the businesswoman, and she came directly to the point. "Would you like to vacation with one of my girls? Or more! You may have more than one! They are very beautiful, no?"

"Yes. Very beautiful, and very kind. I cannot believe they are familiar with Niagara Falls!"

"These are very good girls, very kind. We have no mean girls here. No VD. My girls are checked every week. Would you like to hire one of my girls? Price is forty dollars American for one night, one hundred and fifty dollars American for five days and nights. The girl you choose will be your companion all day and all night, and can show you Penang, help you find bargains. Would you like one of my girls?"

I was enjoying myself immensely, but it was obvious this lady wanted to get down to business. I had been here an hour, casually drinking her Scotch and eyeing her employees. It was time to get serious. Unsure of myself, wondering how one chose a prostitute in this civilized atmosphere, I muttered, "Yes."

There was a long, nervous pause. Everyone was looking at me. Feeling very nervous, very unpolished, I blurted out my frustration. "I can't choose. They're all too nice!"

Mama-san smiled warmly. "Let me introduce you." She proceeded from left to right, lifting each girl to her feet, having her turn. The girls strutted a bit, smiling suggestively, as their talents and qualifications were described. Again, it was so tasteful there was no hint of vulgarity. "This is Mei-Ling. Mei-Ling is twenty, Malaysian Chinese, has a year of college. She has a beautiful body and uses it well. Mei-Ling is a swimmer and has wonderful muscle control. She is very quiet and thoughtful, but a very popular girl."

"Chao-Da is Indian, twenty-four, and an accomplished seamstress. She makes many clothes for all the girls and sells her wares in the market. Chao-Da loves to dance and is familiar with many positions of lovemaking."

"Ellen is mixed English and Chinese ancestry, although she looks more English. She is educated and very popular. Ellen is a favorite with the GIs because of her round eyes and natural blonde hair, and also because she enjoys making love to a man with her mouth."

"Lin was a secretary but came to us to earn more money. Her father is dead, and she supports her mother and her family. She is eighteen, Cantonese-Malay, and a wonderful cook. The boys tell me she is very adventurous and unpredictable." The dark-eyed girl was beautiful, perhaps a little fuller than the others, but surely this was a body made to provide pleasure for her man. Her eyes seemed alive, mischievous, sensual. More important, this was the girl who had mentioned making arrangements for me to play the drums.

I interrupted Mama-san. "Lin is very beautiful. I would like to spend some time with her." I was not satisfied with the choice of words, but Mama-san did not seem to mind. We made financial arrangements while Lin retreated upstairs. In a few moments she was back, carrying a small bag. Her smile was warm, friendly, reassuring. In Chinese, she ordered another Scotch. "I have to attend to Buddha for a few moments, if you don't mind." I settled on the couch, very aware of the cold wetness under my arms. I watched her body as she knelt before the shrine, holding smoking joss sticks and chanting to the golden image. God, she was so feminine, so soft and rounded! She rose and turned to me, smiling.

"I hope you don't feel afraid of me." I whispered.

"Afraid? No. Why do you say that?"

"Well, you felt you had to pray before going off with me. I don't want to take you to something you find unpleasant."

She moved closer, took my hand. Her eyes reassured me as she spoke. "John, I am Buddhist. I must make an offering to Buddha each evening. I want very much to go with you. I know you will be kind. I enjoy my work, and I want very much to make you feel good." She patted my sex gently, suggestively. "I have known many men from Vietnam. I know the hurt and the frustration you hold inside. I know you want to make love to me. I want to make love to you too, I really do, and to pleasure you. Together, we will work it out. All I ask is that you be honest with me, tell me what you want, and allow me to do my job. We'll have to see if we can do something about that!" Her eyes dropped to my throbbing organ, then darted back up to form a caricature of a wink that pulled her whole face out of shape. "C'mon, let's have a good time!" She took my hand and tugged me toward the door. I grabbed the suitcase and hurried after her, feeling more comfortable all the time. I looked for the taxi. He was gone, but Lin summoned a bicycle-powered rickshaw. "I know you miss cars," she grinned, "but this is Penang, and the rickshaws are much cheaper. We'll take taxis when we need to, but you will see more this way." She spoke to the wrinkled, bearded driver, and we settled into the narrow seat.

Perched behind us, the old man sang softly as we pedaled through the placid streets. I put my arm around her shoulders, mostly because the seat was so small, and Lin cuddled against me. I was in Paradise! The sun had started to fall, and its fiery light brought a feeling of warmth and contentment. We wound through narrow streets, past stuccoed walls with wrought iron gates and carefully manicured lawns. Exotic plants and flowers, always neatly and carefully arranged, burst from every available nook and cranny. Antique gaslights gave a Victorian, nostalgic atmosphere, as if I had been transported back in time and the horrors of the war hadn't yet ravaged my mind. The cars were mostly British, the quaint Austins and Morrises that had been in the background of so many pictures in *Road & Track*. I smelled a meal cooking, heard birds singing. An English-woman in a tweed suit walked up the sidewalk carrying a briefcase, waved, and called out a cheery hello! We rattled over the cobblestone streets, Lin allowing me to retreat into my thoughts and cope with this foreign world. I *must* be in Paradise! The softly sway-ing palms reminded me of visits to my grandparents in the South, and the courteous and genteel people had been as com-forting as the legendary "southern hospitality" of long ago. We were approaching the business center and fell into the flow of traffic, snaking in and out through cars and motorbikes and neat pedestrians. When we got to the hotel I paid the old man, and Lin tugged me into a store.

When we emerged, we had a collection of Japanese beauty products. There were translucent honey-based soaps, bath oil, body oil, and powders. Not particularly comfortable in a cosmet-ics store, I had stared at the bright lights and plate-glass displays while Lin shopped. There were elaborate pastel formations on turntables, bold silver-foil proclamations highlighted by pink and red spotlights. I was fascinated by the glitz and glitter, childish in my delight. Lin tore me away, I paid for the shopping bag full of exotica, and wondered why such a beautiful woman would need such an expensive assortment of beauty products. We bustled through the hotel lobby, into an elevator, and into my room.

Safely inside, I had to try all my toys again, and I flushed and tuned and switched the gadgets while Lin busied herself in the bathroom. It was dark, and I stood at the window, spellbound at the sight of a city at night. Neon signs of red and blue turned and flashed overhead as the peculiar golden glow of a thousand headlights blended into a stream of light. On the banks of the stream the crowd bustled in a multicolored chaos. I watched as they patiently obeyed the "Don't Walk" sign, then dutifully moved as one when the light changed. There was a pattern, a purpose, an order underlying what appeared to be confusion. Chaos controlled. Civilization. All of the sinister sides of the human psyche I had known for months seemed nonexistent. I marveled at these people, so unconcerned while horror and death lurked so near. It was all very real to me, so much a part of everyday life; and yet these people hurried on as if it were insignificant.

• • • •

Lin's touch on my shoulder brought relief from the dilemma my thoughts had created. She drew me away from the window and closed the drapes. "We have to get you ready for dinner," she said softly. "Relax. I'll take care of everything." Again, she patted my groin and it responded. Slowly, sensuously, she unbuttoned and unclasped my clothes, and I felt them fall to a heap on the floor. She caressed me, she poked and probed and stroked me; then she led me to the bath. The air was heavy with steam as she knelt and slid my underwear down. I was excited. I slipped into the water at her urging, recoiling from the heat, but Lin insisted, and I was in her power. Fragrant bubbles parted to receive me, and I tried to settle back in spite of the fear my flesh was being cooked off my bones. Lin guided me into a reclining position, adjusting a large sponge at my neck, bending a knee. Adjusting to the temperature, I allowed myself to be guided. Soft music filtered in from the bedroom. Lin lit a small scented candle and doused the harsh incandescent light. Slowly, carefully, she removed her dress, then her slip. In the golden candle-light, she gathered her long black hair and pinned it into a pile. She wore only lacy maroon underwear. She knelt beside me, leaned close. "Let it heal you, John," she whispered. "The heat will draw the hurt out. Just relax and let me make you feel better." She reached behind her back, and the soft bra slid to the floor as she leaned her breasts against the tub and reached beneath the bubbles. Rubbing the fragrant soap into my skin, she traced tiny circles from my forehead to my toes, then back. I leaned forward to give her access to my back, sweat beading on my forehead. Suddenly, I heard the water receding down the drain. I was puzzled. When it was gone, and I felt a chill, she rinsed me with splashes from a plastic bowl. I blushed, stretched out naked in front of her, as she deftly kept her naked breasts from my view behind the rim of porcelain. I was aching.

"Stand up and turn around, please." I did. I felt her hands on my buttocks, sliding the soft soap in tiny circles, closer and closer to my thighs. She dipped more hot water, and the circles moved lower. More water. One hand slipped between my legs, began stroking. I exploded against the tile, my knees near col-lapse. A splash of hot water accompanied the final spasm. Suddenly I felt weak and cold.

She knelt and toweled me, silently, carefully. She led me to the ready bed, shimmering in the glow of another scented can-dle. Cool oil cascaded over my shoulders and back, and strong but gentle hands caressed it into my skin. She moved to my feet, worked up my legs to my buttocks, slipping one hand under my belly. I rolled over and she knelt between my legs and she pushed the oil into my chest, then lower. She took the pins down from her hair, and swayed her head to let the silken cascade move over me. I was throbbing again, when I felt her kiss. Then, spent, I rolled over and felt the soft talcum being caressed into tired shoulders. Her touch was soft, delicate, and yet insistent.

When I was ready again, she stood, turned her back, and slid the maroon bikini panties to her ankles. She looked over her shoulder and whispered, "Are you ready?" then turned without waiting for an answer and raised her arms to push the mound of hair up on her head. I reached for her and drew her down close to me, feeling her warmth for the first time.

After a shower together, we dressed for dinner, I in my jeans and shirt, Lin in fresh lingerie, a skirt, and blouse. We collapsed into a rickshaw for a chaotic ride to a fine new hotel, where the doorman in a white coat with bronze buttons bowed as we entered. In the restaurant, I was dazzled by the formal place settings, fork and spoons and cone-shaped napkins neatly aligned to enhance the shimmering crystal and china. We had steaks and French wine, and Lin spoke of upstate New York with a little knowledge and a trace of awe. We talked of our family, her background. She was, as Mama-san had said, supporting her family, and she showed me pictures and spoke of her young sister's grades. Why, I asked, was she a prostitute? What's a girl like you...? Matter-of-factly, she gestured at the ornate room. "I enjoy living well," she whispered. "I have money, clothes. I enjoy nicer things. But there is more. I like the GIs. They are so hurt, so vulnerable. I feel I am like a doctor. One guy said I should be a shrink. I do not know this 'shrink,' but I know I am doing something very important. I know how sad it is, to try to live your life in five days. I cannot do so much if I am a nurse in a white dress." She looked down. I reached for her hand, and she looked at me with her eyes pleading, filling with tears. "Last month I met a guy. He showed me pictures of his wife in America. He was very kind, and it was no big thing, you know? He did not go to Hawaii, and I asked why. You know what he said? He said he could not make love to his wife anymore because he felt dirty!" She spit out the last word, and a tear started down her cheek. "He wanted her so much, but he could not face her. He drank too much, but he was so kind, and he cried. He cried all the time. Finally, I told him to write to her and tell her everything. If she loves him, it will be okay, you know? So he writes to me and says everything is okay, and thank you so much, and then I get a letter from one of his friends, and he's dead! That never happened before, but I have to think, how many of my boys are dead? I try very hard to be kind, because everyone tells me about Vietnam, and I know a few days away are very special. I do not feel ashamed. Do you understand? I try to do something very nice for very hurting people."

We left the hotel, and Lin spoke Chinese to the rickshaw boy. We went to the old Victorian British palace, walked hand in hand across the broad parade field to the waterfront. Beneath towering trees a sidewalk lined with gaslights edged the harbor. We sat on the stone wall, watching faint outlines of ships and junks gliding silently into place for the morning's business. Ribbons of multicolored light wrinkled on the swells, weaving a tapestry of color and motion. We walked slowly, discussing movies, music, the meaning of life, war, and peace. In the tranquillity I told her things I never told another human being, and she accepted the burdens willingly. A full, crystalline moon danced upon the water as I sobbed, dredging up the horrors of Dak To and the girl at the firebase. We sat on a park bench and talked about cornfields and the Finger Lakes, lilies of the valley in spring, a Rolling Stones concert in Buffalo, and baseball. By the time we returned to the hotel it was 4:00 A.M., and we were dear friends.

• • • •

Time, the great enemy in The Nam, became more of an enemy on R and R. Time had suddenly accelerated to a dizzying blur. We ate and danced. We toured temples and a park where monkeys begged for bananas. I played the drums, poorly. I shopped for a suit, a guitar, records. I ate ice cream with passion. We rode an inclined railway to a majestic view of the island. Like a kid at Disneyland, I absorbed the multicolored clothes and the orderly chaos of city life. Like Alice, I gloried in a Wonderland of freedom and mystery. For seventeen months I had lived in a perpetual nightmare, and this brief reprieve was so totally different it overwhelmed me. For five days, there was no rank. The maid cleaned my hotel room. The fresh white sheets were not infested with rats or snakes or insects. There was no threat, no artillery, no death. No one barked orders. There was only pleasure, and pleasure proved addictive.

I resisted the urge to sleep. The stimuli that assailed all my senses excited each nerve-ending 'til sleep was unnecessary. When exhaustion intervened, Lin stroked and comforted me. Mostly, as we wandered the island hand in hand, we talked. As I drew her views out, I found them remarkably similar to my own. By the end of the fifth day, we were talking about the future. I promised to return, and to take her home with me. I had found what I wanted, what I needed in life. All of the past would be forgotten. A few days before, I had measured my future in seconds. Now I dreamed of children and the excitement Lin would experience as I showed her America. We wept openly as I boarded the ferry that would take me to the plane. The day before, we had gone to the market, and Lin made a feast of giant shrimp, fresh vegetables, and wine. My laundry was immaculate. My hair was neatly trimmed. My mind was blown, and my heart was no longer my own.

• • • •

Back in the cold dust of Pleiku, I perched on guard towers and relived every beautiful moment in my mind. I dreamed of a peaceful future, of pleasures to be. Almost immediately, as I previewed my return to American suburbia, I realized how alien it had become. The butterfly cannot crawl back into the cocoon and change back to a familiar caterpillar. The image of Jimmy Rollins, his outburst, and Gott's subsequent advice to enlist, although a memory, may have been a harbinger. How could I tell Mr. Gott? How could I tell my own father? How could I put Lin at ease in a new world when I couldn't be at ease myself?

Fuck it! We would help each other. We would, in fact, be two lonely refugees; and we would get each other through. I was too old to live at home with my mommy and daddy. Safe in our own room, our own home, we would help each other. No one I had ever known had been as understanding as Lin. I would teach her about cars and supermarkets and drive-in movies, and she would explain the dilemmas of dealing with people, and we would be happy. It was our lives. If somebody didn't like it, fuck 'em. What did they know? There was more to life than country clubs and church festivals, and if I could cope with The Nam, I could sure as hell cope with The World. I always had. Without a helpmate!

GIs described their adventures with the prostitutes simply and directly. Find 'em, finger 'em, fuck 'em, and forget 'em. The four Fs. Like cigarette butts and C-ration cans, the girls were disposable. You did it to them, not with them. I knew I had to build a defense of lies and half-truths. I had to be "one of the guys." My life literally depended on it, and in retrospect I think this was a major problem for many of us. You had to be a he-man. You drank, you tried drugs, you used woman-flesh. You didn't look back. Sentiment was a cancer, forbidden except within the confines of a letter from home. "Fuck it!" Words to live by, and living was everything. There was no regard for humanity, for respect, for dignity, when you knew at any second you might have to explode a human life to save your own. The most basic tenets of human morality had to be put on a shelf, in safekeeping, until the day when you boarded the airplane headed for home. That day, we told ourselves, we would take the precious package off the shelf and slip into the comfortable dress of respectability, walk the familiar Main Streets of America, and everything would be all right again. Unfortunately, most of us never realized that the contents of that package would be rotted. The "men" the military had fashioned would no longer fit into the raiments of children.

I had changed, and I was scared. I had been living a lie, and I had made it this far. I began to lie to cover lies, spinning a web of intrigue and deceit that I could not escape. I could not control my enthusiasm, the joy of young love. She was a secretary, I said, and had been an exchange student to America. I hadn't really fallen in love in five days. I had known her before. Now, more mature, I had seen something I had missed in Hometown, U.S.A., and I wanted to make it my own. I am not a convincing liar, but if anyone saw through my sham they never let on. In The Nam, you didn't mess with a guy's coping mechanism. If he was one of the guys, he had a right to be strange. We were all strange. If he could cope, he could keep you alive.

As soon as I got back to Pleiku, I went to see a legal adviser to start the paperwork needed to marry a "foreign national." The advisor was a lieutenant colonel, and his description of the obstacles defied my comprehension. The basic papers were a tangle of legal gobbledygook. There would be long and exhaustive investigations of both our backgrounds. It would take months, perhaps more than a year. It would be much more convenient if I extended my tour in Vietnam, so I would be accessible, close to the action. I stepped out of his office in shock. Extend? Ask to stay here? God, anything but that! Anything! I trembled with frustration and rage, and fear. There must be a way. Life cannot be this cruel, this unjust. I had done my part. I was short. I was going home in one hundred twenty days. I had to go home! I had earned the right to go home. I burst back into the Quonset hut, choking back tears. I begged for advice, for help, for some kind of alternative. I was openly bawling now, seeing the dream I had nurtured so long disintegrate.

The lieutenant colonel took pity on me. Perhaps he knew how foreign it was for me to be begging the army for a favor. We talked for more than an hour, and he repeatedly stressed the time required to process a request for marriage. Finally, he softened. There might be an alternative, but it would require some very heavy decisions on my part. The war effort had spilled over into other Southeast Asian countries. There was a large American support effort based in Thailand. West of Vietnam, insulated by Cambodia, Thailand bordered Malaysia. It was the most sought-after duty station outside of Hawaii, but I might apply for a year's tour in Thailand. There would be no leave at home. I would board a plane in Saigon and fly directly to a tour of duty in Thailand. But hell, Bangkok was an R-and-R city. I could get a leave, it was like Stateside duty, and visit Malaysia a couple of times throughout the year. Fumbling through his dilapidated olive-drab filing cabinets, he produced one more piece of paper. "Request for Inter-Theatre Transfer." He wished me luck and invited me to stop by any time. He would do what he could to help.

I agonized. I had to make a decision that would have a profound impact on the rest of my life. I wanted to go home. Everybody wanted to go home. Home was everything, had been everything that mattered for so long. Still, if Bangkok was an R-and-R city like Penang, it must be fantastic in its own right. It was certainly convenient to Malaysia. What would my family say? I had written about Lin, declining to mention her profession. She was the most wonderful thing that had ever happened in my life. This was the only way I could see at the time, but my vision was clouded. There were no libraries, and I didn't know the first thing about Thailand. I sought out every guy who had taken his R and R in Bangkok, and they described a heaven on earth. I would have described Penang in the same terms. I saw pictures of tall buildings adorned with brightly colored advertising, shaded streets lined with tiny automobiles, bars with rock 'n' roll bands. There was television and running water and air conditioning and, of course, pretty women in miniskirts. Elephants carried teak logs, and the king in an ornate ceremonial boat was beloved. There were Buddhist temples, a floating market, and a store that sold original European records by the British rock groups. Heaven!

Somebody's brother had been stationed in Thailand. There was almost no spit and polish. It was as safe as the States, but the army didn't go berserk if your boots weren't shined or your belt buckle wasn't polished. The guys in Thailand were frustrated at being so close to the war without really being able to take part in it. Even the brass felt that way, and they went easy on the "chickenshit" spit and polish to make themselves feel more like war heroes.

• • • •

Like a long, drawn-out "morning after," my days after R and R were filled with suffering. Civilization, so long forgotten, had been a reality; and the return to this world of inhumanity and terror was far worse than my original arrival. Then, I was naïve. Over the months I had seen, and learned, and been scarred. Now, after a breath of fresh air, I recognized the stench and all it stood for, and I hated it more because I had had a whiff of fine perfume. A second lieutenant fresh out of Officer Candidate School inspected our hootch. Our socks were carefully rolled, spare razors and blades and toothbrushes aligned in gleaming formation, and crisp white underwear was precisely folded. We wore olive-drab underwear for camouflage reasons, but had had to buy the whites for these inspections. So this second lieutenant, over-impressed with his authority, wears white gloves and crawls under the tent flaps to wipe his lily-white gloves across the top of the sandbag wall. He came back inside, thrust his soiled finger under my nose, and barked, "What do you think that is, soldier?"

"Rat shit, sir." I had had about all I could take.

"Do you like living in shit, soldier?"

"No, sir! May I have permission to go home, sir?" A nervous giggle was stifled to my left. The lieutenant grimaced at this affront to his authority. I really didn't care.

"No, soldier, but you can try shitburning for a week and see if you can learn anything about housekeeping!" Shitburning, since our little Vietnamese friend had been wasted by the Tet offensive, had become a punishment. A day of the stink and heat and heavy barrels was bearable. A week would be terrible.

"Sir," I said, "may I say something?" I was already in trouble, and I decided to get some satisfaction to make it worthwhile.

"Go ahead."

"Sir, with all due respect to you, the army, America, and Mom and apple pie, we don't like living in rat shit, and we don't like living with rats! I've been here eight months, sir, and I haven't seen the army provide a single goddamned rat-trap, or poison, or any goddamned thing to help us get rid of the rats. We have a pellet gun, and we shoot them, and we burn them so the smoke will scent the hootch and keep them away, and we have beat a few to death with brooms or gun butts. Two men in this tent have had the rabies treatment, sir, and they don't like the rats one bit! But sir, and again, with all due respect, we don't search for rat shit with white gloves, sir. We try to ignore it, and make the best of it, and do our jobs. Sir, we would love to know a way to keep the rats away. Every goddamn man in this camp would like to know that, and I wonder if you have any good suggestions, sir?" I had become loud and had left the position of attention to gesture with my hands. I figured I was in real trouble, but I really didn't care. I returned to attention, shaking with frustration, staring at the cold eyes of the punk kid hiding behind his little brass insignia. Stiff and military, he turned on his heel and moved to the next man. Harata was a hot-blooded Hawaiian, and he spoke first.

"Put my name on the shitburners list, sir, 'cause I feel the same way. We all want to know how to get rid of the rats. Living with the rats is punishment enough!"

The lieutenant's eyes went wide. He hesitated a moment, then moved on again. Forsythe told him the same thing. One after another, every man in the hootch opened up. Nobody wanted to live in fear of being bitten by a rat. Jamieson opened his shirt to show the needle marks on his belly. The lieutenant was nervous now, his eyes squinting, his speech jerky. He had not inspected any of the lockers. He was acutely aware that he was on the defensive, and his defenses were weak. He paused at the canvas door, turned, and said, "I will report your frustration to Captain Benedict. Perhaps there is something that can be done. You will not be assigned to shitburner detail. I understand." Then he was gone, and we cheered and laughed and slapped each other on the back. I felt a tremendous relief. The guys had bailed me out.

It was a difficult time. My thoughts were far away on an island off the coast of Malaysia. Back in The World it was spring. Carolynn sent a photo of herself, standing in front of a lilac bush in full bloom. My Thunderbird got a fresh paint job after a long, hard winter. In the midst of the rebirth of spring, Dr. Martin Luther King Jr. had been shot down, returning everyone's thoughts to the assassination of John Kennedy in Dallas five years earlier. Now Robert Kennedy was rolling toward the Democratic presidential nomination, riding high on a wave of public sentiment against the war that had swelled as an aftermath of Tet. Eugene McCarthy promised to battle Kennedy to the wire, urging young protestors to work within the system to bring the war to an end.

In The Nam, feelings about the news from home ran high. Many felt the protestors were just draft dodgers, rich kids whose parents had bought their way out of the war. Americans were flooding into Canada to avoid the choice of Vietnam or federal penitentiary. Estimates of the number who chose to self-exile in Canada vary. In late 1969, the *New York Times* reported that sixty thousand Americans had crossed the border to beat the draft. Congressman Ed Koch, later to become mayor of New York, used that figure in a New Year's Day 1970 press conference. Canadian officials working with the exiles estimated the number at one hundred thousand in 1970! The February 5, 1970, *New York Times* quoted a State Department official's estimate of two thousand, but with the caution that these figures "vary greatly." (Roger Neville Williams, *The New Exiles*, New York: Liveright, 1971, pp. 85, 399.) Many of my comrades felt betrayed or accused the fugitives of being cowards. It was easy to resent the guys back home, in the midst of such misery.

Still, many of us were buoyed by the protestors. We had tried to avoid the draft. We hadn't volunteered for Vietnam. In retrospect, I think the guys who had volunteered for Vietnam, for whatever reasons, were the most affected by the futility of it all. To many of us, the news that someone back home was trying to end the horror and bring us home was reassuring. President Johnson's speeches weren't comforting. His response to Tet and Khe Sanh had been to order more young men into the meat grinder, replace Robert McNamara as secretary of defense when McNamara had expressed doubts about the war, and then announce his decision to quit, or not seek reelection. Lord, how we wanted to quit! Every moment of every day, we lived with the knowledge that this breath might be our last. Numbed by fear and terror and horror, we wanted it to be over. If the American people marched in the streets and demanded peace, it was a sign that they understood and abhorred our plight. Cowards? Amidst the fear that we lived with every day, it was easy to call someone else a coward. Having investigated the options while the draft was breathing down my back, I knew the anguish they were feeling. It wasn't easy to walk away from your home and family and exile yourself in Canada.

There is nothing glamorous about the life of a fugitive. There can be no return, and there would be the constant knowledge that you had brought dishonor upon your family. It was a very momentous decision for a teenage kid, and it is a tribute to their humanity and idealism that perhaps sixty thousand chose to bear the hardships. Also, these people were watching the agony of Khe Sanh on the television every night. We hadn't been exposed to much of that before we had shipped out in 1967. There were a lot of questions about the war, and no answers. Without a good reason, what young men would want to subject himself to Khe Sanh? Their courage was an inspiration to many of us, and throughout the war I kept that picture of a protestor planting a flower in the barrel of a bayoneted rifle on the steps of the Pentagon.

I had applied for a tour of duty in Thailand. I felt a new fear. I couldn't put my finger on it, but deep inside I realized I could not walk down the street of my hometown and face classmates or old friends. I tried to picture what it would be like, and it scared the hell out of me. What would I say? How could I describe the horror, the fear, the loneliness? The social turmoil at home scared me. Everyone in The World seemed to be heading toward some kind of confrontation, and I was not ready to watch a civil war in my hometown after this.

Lin had become my answer to everything. In her arms, I had felt comfort and security and a sense of worth. I could concentrate on making her life better and politely sidestep the enormous struggles at home. I had had enough struggles. The groundwork had been laid, my momentous decision had been made and announced to the family back home. I struggled to learn to play my guitar.

Early in June, Sarge asked me to go to Dak To for a few days and help patch up some really banged-up machinery. Dak To. The words brought a chill. Things were never really quiet at Dak To. Still, the white-glove inspections in Pleiku were depressing, and the harassment was becoming unbearable. Captain Benedict had decided to move us to the area southeast of the boneyard. There would be formal wooden barracks with concrete floors. We would be closer to the work garages. I knew there would be more inspections, more spit and polish, more harassment. I expected Bobby Kennedy to respond to my letter any day and straighten things out, but perhaps the Spartan existence in Dak To would be a good change until that happened.

We loaded supplies into a three-quarter-ton truck with an electric welder built into the back and drove the horrible road to Dak To. We would sleep in an underground bunker facing Hill 875. As the sun sank low, we sat on a sandbagged wall and watched a B-52 raid to the west. With binoculars, we could see the long wavering ribbon of black tubes dropping from the invisible giants. We watched as the distant hill was engulfed in gray smoke, billowing, changing form, sometimes colored with splashes of orange. Then the rumble came, the ground trembled, and the thundering concussion made it impossible to hold the binoculars steady. Spec 4 Albertson ran toward us, obviously upset, waving his arms. Instinctively, we crouched behind the sandbags. Albertson screamed the news as he ran, news that would destroy so much of America's hope and sanity. So much of mine. "Bobby Kennedy's been assassinated!"

We clustered around a transistor radio to get the details. Bobby Kennedy had been shot to death moments after winning the key California primary. I took it pretty personally. He hadn't answered my letter yet. Benedict continued to issue Stateside harassment orders from his refuge in the bunker, and the only person who could help had been gunned down in California. What the hell was going on back home? Was there a war going on there, too? We were living for the day we could go back, and in two months America had lost two of her greatest humanitarians. There were riots in the streets, buildings burned, people hurt. What the hell was going on? It was a terrible, emotional shock. Would the warlords, the military powers who had sent us here, actually have Bobby Kennedy assassinated when he spoke out for an end to the war? John Kennedy had been killed just three weeks after Diem had been overthrown and assassinated here in The Nam. How large might the conspiracy be? Was there no hope?

I felt hollow inside and tried to fill the void with a dinner of C-rations and Scotch. The guys wanted to go to town, and I was confused. I didn't think there was a town. They were boisterous, overreacting. We could party, get stoned, mess with the whores, put today's tragedy out of our minds. I was not a big partygoer, but the Scotch had scrambled my thoughts. What the hell? I needed to think about something besides the war. Besides, I had the truck. I was drafted again.

Albertson had been here for months, knew all the angles, and explained the procedure. Like furtive conspirators, we piled into the truck and idled quietly toward the perimeter with the lights out. At the wire we stopped while Albertson talked to the guards at their post. He pulled the barbed wire back, and we crawled out into the free-fire zone. I pulled the emergency brake to stop for Albertson, knowing that the brake pedal would illuminate the taillights and draw attention to us. He clambered aboard, and I inched along the dirt road to a tiny collection of mud huts with grass roofs. We parked in a grove of trees and covered the truck with camouflage ponchos. One by one, we ran to the shanty on the far left.

A coarse, fibrous linen hung from the doorway. As I burst inside I saw a small room illuminated in the golden glow of a single candle. Altogether, five of us had made the trip, and the fifth rushed in behind me. As my eyes adjusted to the dim light, I saw the others already sitting in the corners, swigging beer or Vietnamese whiskey, or rolling marijuana into sausage-shaped cigarettes. Mama-san and two filthy girls bustled about, bringing beer and matches, grabbing crotches, offering all manner of forbidden delights. Surely, these were the three ugliest women in the entire world. Dirty, with stringy hair and burned-out eyes, all three wore the usual black silk pants. Two wore filthy cotton blouses, the third only a muddy black bra. The lacy cups overflowed with dirt-stained toilet paper, crudely wadded into some semblance of the shape of a female breast. She had the dark teeth of a betel nut chewer, and an M-16 bullet on a gold chain around her neck.

I took a beer and settled into a corner, sitting on a stack of C-ration cases. The sweet smell of pot filled the room, and when the joint was passed my way I took a deep hit. I hadn't come for sex, and I wouldn't have touched any of those women with a broom handle. I had come to forget, to escape the reality of my situation that was beyond comprehension. I had come to mess up my mind, and I drank Bam-Be-Bam beer and sucked at the powerful homemade cigarette with a conviction born of frustration. I could feel the waves of numbness beginning to wash over me. Mellow, I wriggled into a more comfortable position and sat back to watch the others get bombed and paw at the piggish women. I was relaxing. My mind wandered away to another guy, so long ago, when I had found myself at Dak To. "Hey, you guys know a dude from Ohio?" Funny how pot makes you talk slow.

"I'm from Ohio," came a reply from my right.

"No, man. When I was here on convoy, when the battle of eight seventy-five was on, I met this guy from Ohio. And you know, I don't know his name, but he's definitely a fuckin'-A cat, man, and him and me smoked a packa his Camels and watched the fuckin' war one night, an' I wonder if he's still around, ya know?"

"Shit, man, there's about a fuckin' thousand guys around here from Ohio. Maybe you'll run into him."

"Yeah. Maybe..." I watched the candle flicker. For what must have been an hour, I watched as the flame swelled and shrank, leaned left, grew tall, and died away. About eight feet away, Albertson was negotiating a blow job. To the right, the guy from Ohio was peeing on the dirt floor, right in the middle of this lady's living room. "Hey, man," I drawled, "this ain't no fuckin' urinal. We're in this lady's living room, and you're pissing upon her fucking brown carpet!" I spoke carefully, mimicking a professor speaking to a class of esteemed scholars. Giggles bubbled out of the darkness.

"Awwww, sheeit, ma'am. I'm sorry!" With more seriousness, he turned toward Mama-san and proceeded to splash her bare feet. She jumped away, mumbling, *"Domommie!"* which was the Vietnamese equivalent of motherfucker. Suddenly, in an explosion of action, she was back. "MP! MP!" Everyone erupted into motion. One of the girls grabbed my arm and tugged me back into the darker recesses of the shanty. I imagined Jonah being swallowed by the whale. Deep in the shadows there was an army cot with an old man snoring contentedly. She fell to her knees, pulled at a filthy rag, lifted a wooden panel, and pushed me toward a gaping hole under the cot. Desperate, I stretched my feet, then my legs, down into the blackness. The girl was cramming my head and my shoulders down. There was no light. Absolute, total darkness swallowed me. The wooden platform scraped into place above me. My left leg felt room, and I reached out investigating. There was a horizontal tunnel. I tried to scrunch back into it, expecting an MP to lift the wooden panel and look down on me at any moment. Farther and farther back I went, on my hands and knees now, crawling backward. Suddenly, there was no support for my feet. I had reached another vertical section. I lowered my legs down, felt a ladder rung beneath my foot.

Totally blind, panicky, I struggled backward and down. Rung by rung, I retreated into the opening. Dirt fell down on my neck and shoulders. It was a tiny, tight opening; difficult to pull my shoulders through. As I felt myself fall free, I moved my foot to explore the tomb. God, how it stank! I moved again, silently testing the floor under my feet. At the precise moment I came in contact with human flesh, the lights exploded on.

I sucked in all of the air in that tunnel. My hand flew to my throat. My heart nearly jumped out of my chest. I stared down into the giant room hewn out of the earth. Staring back at me were four North Vietnamese Army regulars in full uniform, with AK-47 automatic rifles, grenades, and hand-held rocket launchers! I froze. I did not dare breathe. I looked again, hoping to God the marijuana was playing tricks on my head. Sure as shit, they were there; and they looked as surprised and panicky as I felt. One of them, with a whole assortment of glittery brass oak leaf clusters on his collar, grinned broadly and put his index finger to his lips in the universal sign for quiet. Another, also breaking into a broad grin, held out a bottle of Bam-Be-Bam. I dared to exhale. I bent silently at the knees. I took the bottle, tipped it back, and felt the icy wave wash down my parched throat. I handed it back, but the smiley one pointed to his buddy to my right. I offered it, and he took it and silently expressed his thanks with a toasting motion before he drank. I sat back on my ass, dumbfounded, and leaned back against the dirt wall. All four were grinning now. They were just kids. The oldest one, the one with all the oak leaf clusters, couldn't have been over twenty-two or three. I saw the olive drab, official U.S. Army-issue flashlight in his hand. I pointed up toward the black opening through which I had entered, and silently mouthed "MP." They grinned and nodded. They understood.

We sat there a long time. Occasionally, muffled voices filtered down from above. There was a long silence. The beer was empty, discarded. Suddenly we heard the wooden trap slide open. Oak Leaf Clusters tightened his grip on his weapon, but a female voice whispered down in Vietnamese. He answered, then looked at me, motioned toward the hole, and said, "Okay." All four of them started to their feet. I froze again. Smiling, one of them offered a hand to help me to my feet. Another was already climbing the ladder. They motioned for me to go next, and I did. I probably shouldn't have offered them my back, but the flashlight illuminated my path courteously, and I climbed back up, over, and up again until I was crawling out from under the old man's cot. Mama-san hovered next to me, repeating, "Okay. Okay. No VC. No VC." I gulped at the fresh air. Someone put another beer into my hand, cold and wet, and I jerked my head back. Now there were about six of us crowded into the tiny dark alcove near the cot, and all of us broke into spontaneous laughter. I grabbed the frozen beer and followed into the candle-lit room. Albertson's eyes bulged when he saw our guests, but Mama-san continued to chant, "Okay, okay," and we all grinned. Hands extended, and we shook hands all around and exchanged names, giggling at the poor attempts at repeating alien pronunciations. One of the girls arrived with more beer and a package of joints. In no time we all sat cross-legged on the floor, around the candle, swigging beer and passing a joint around and laughing and slapping each other on the back. Mama-san interpreted, and each of us in turn took out our wallet and showed dilapidated pictures of girlfriends, wives, children, a '57 Chevy, my T-Bird, a stucco house in Hanoi. They explained, through Mama-san, that they had also been drafted and taken away from their families and loved ones. Three were teenagers. They did not like the war. They were lonely, afraid, dirty, and tired. I drank, I smoked, and I listened. I could feel something happening to me, something foreign, and it grew and grew until it possessed me. I knew I was going to be sick, and I tried to rise to run for the door. I didn't make it, and the horrible flood boiled out of my guts onto the dirt floor. Choking, coughing, with the burning slop threatening to melt my nose from the inside out, I crawled out into the moonlight. A flare overhead cast an eerie, flickering glow. Fighting to regain control, I heaved again and again until I thought my guts were going to pour out into the dust. On hands and knees, I started to get scared that I would never stop puking, and never regain my breath. I started to cry. I crawled back to the door, pushed the filthy rag away. The others still sat around the candle, laughing, drinking, smoking. "Albertson!" I choked, heaved again. "Albertson! Let's go. I want to go back!" Albertson came out, handed me a beer.

"Wash the taste out of your mouth, man, and come on back in. We're partyin', and partyin' in Dak To don't quit 'til the sun comes up!"

"Please," I begged. "Please, let's go back."

"Shit, man. Don't fuck up our party. You been sick before." He led me to the truck, helped me crawl in back. "Lay down here, get your shit together. We'll head back pretty quick." He was gone. I fell asleep or passed out. I entered a swirling, multicolored world of lizards and snakes, rivers of blood, screams of agony. Floating on the waters, I felt myself lifted and dropped, lifted and dropped. Great dragons with rows of knife-like teeth snapped at my legs. Winged dinosaurs attacked from an amber sky, breathing fire, crying out their savage intentions as their great wings beat the air. In a whirlpool of fluorescent slime, I tumbled helplessly, watched worms creep out of my belly, felt snakes slither over my feet.

Albertson shook me awake. "Hey, man! Hey! You okay? You were havin' a nightmare. It's okay. It's okay." I heard the others clambering aboard the truck. "C'mon, man. You've had some sleep, and we're fucked up. I can drive, but you ride shotgun." He led me to the passenger's door, put a .45 caliber automatic pistol in my hand. It was cold and very, very heavy. We began to bump back toward the compound. With the swaying motion of the truck the nausea returned, but I held it back. I could feel myself riding the waves of goo again. We stopped to go through the wire, then started with a jolt. The monsters tried to attack, but Albertson's voice beat them back. Suddenly, to my right, a mammoth creature loomed out of the fiery haze. *Tyrannosaurus Rex!* I opened fire with the .45. The lights went out.

I awoke in the glare of an electric light, stared at the sandbags and heavy timbers. I tried to rise, but felt powerless. The familiar face of Rossini looked down at me. "You okay?"

"Yeah. I think so. What the fuck happened?" I still couldn't move. Rossini bent over me.

"You freaked out, man! You really freaked out! We had to tie you down, stuff socks in your mouth. You were fucked up! Must have been opium in the joints!" My mouth felt cracked, parched. Rossini removed the bonds that had tied me to the cot. I needed water. I got to a sitting position. He offered me a beer, and I drank heavily.

"What time is it?" Had I made it in time for the morning's work?

"Shit! It's three-thirty. You been out for hours, twistin' and turnin' and fightin' and cryin'. I was afraid you was gonna die on me. I got elected to stay with ya. Couldn't take ya to sick call 'cause you were out of your head, and we'd all be in deep shit! Sure am glad to see you come to, I swear I am!" I sucked at the beer and lay back to focus my eyes on the dark timbers overhead.

The next morning I was up early, ready for work. Throughout the long, hot, dusty day I dwelt upon the fantastic events of two nights before. What had happened? If I had been zonked by a joint treated with opium, why had it not affected the others? If that wasn't the reason, what was? Was I losing my sanity? Could it be the news of Kennedy's death? Or a letdown from the tension of deciding not to go home? Maybe R and R had so relaxed me, I was overreacting to being back in the stress of The Nam? Maybe I was crazy for asking to go to Thailand, and my subconscious was revolting? I had mixed Scotch and beer and marijuana. There had been a lot of shock. It wasn't every day you discovered yourself in a hole with NVA regulars. Whatever it was, I no longer trusted my sanity. I would have to be very careful to keep it under control. I was shocked, frightened, and ashamed.

That evening, Albertson took me to see my *Tyrannosaurus Rex*. A dirty olive-drab forklift with its steel jaws raised six feet off the ground sat forlornly on a flat tire. I could remember the terror of seeing the monster, then nothing more. Albertson explained that I had emptied the .45 into the forklift, screaming about dinosaurs in the midst of our stealthy escapade. He had knocked me unconscious with one blow, but the damage was done. The compound had gone on full alert, with sirens and flares and small-arms fire. We were goddamned lucky no one had opened up on the truck! They left me on the floor as they ran to their places on the perimeter. Later, when the alert was called off, they found me still unconscious. When they had splashed water on my face to bring me back to reality, I had started screaming and fighting. They had to tie me to the cot, and finally I settled down. In the morning they had been unable to rouse me, so Rossini had stayed with me.

I had been out of control, and I almost got my buddies killed. I found it hard to live with myself. For the next few days I worked and thought, thought and worked. When I returned to Pleiku, I was an official short-timer. In less than ninety days I would be leaving The Nam.

The nightmare in Dak To had sewn strong seeds of doubt in my mind about my mental state. As the days ticked away, I became more and more careful, more and more afraid. I wouldn't touch marijuana, and was careful not to drink too much. I cleaned my rifle with extra care and piled more sandbags around my bunk and my bunker on the perimeter. I didn't go downtown. I had gone back to the body shop after Dak To, preferring not to be at a guard post when the oncoming monsoon would make it easier for Charley to crawl in and cut you down from behind.

Beneath it all, I was concerned. Why had I been so lucky so long? I could not allow myself to get overconfident. It had been luck, pure and simple, and I had been a damn fool a few times. It would be a shame to get wasted now, but the possibility seemed to be growing. Even my lifeline, my indestructible lifeline to The World, seemed forebodingly changed. The letters from Carolynn and the girls in Cincinnati were still upbeat, still supportive; but times had changed in The World. The assassinations and protests were bringing the innocence of teenagers to ruin, and I found it difficult to judge how deep the decay had gone. They knew I loved the pop records, and they wrote about the Top Forty as if I had my radio tuned to a local Cincinnati station. References to the Iron Butterfly and Gary Puckett and The Union Gap were discomforting to me. I had been on top of the music scene, and it was leaving me behind to rot in a stinking jungle on the other side of the planet. What else had changed? How alien would it be? New replacements brought horror stories of returning Vietnam vets being called baby-killers and spat on or stoned by the protestors. If my request for Thailand was disapproved, I would have to deal with all of that soon. It could get bad, because I would have to wear the uniform of the army I so despised on the streets of America for another fifteen months. If ordered to a peace protest, what would I do? I prayed for the reassignment to Thailand, to be away from Vietnam, and insulated from the civil strife in America. At the same time, I grieved for my family. God, how I wanted to flop on the couch with a bowl of popcorn and watch a baseball game on the tube! How I longed to tell people what was really happening in The Nam, to help get it over before my kid brother came of age for the draft. I ached to take out my frustrations on a set of drums, to wear colorful, flowered clothes and long hair and beads, and watch a race car scream down the straightaway at the Glen. I wanted a cup of coffee from the familiar stainless steel pot on the familiar stove in the familiar kitchen. I imagined someone asking, "What would you like to eat?" instead of standing in line at a mess hall and getting powdered eggs and powdered milk.

I wanted to go back, but there was no return to innocence. If I walked down the street, people would know I had come from The Nam. It showed, like a brand on my forehead. I could see it every morning while I shaved. My eyes were tired, changed. Once, I thought I could change the world. Armed with a high school diploma and college scholarships, I had been ready to attack the dilemmas of all mankind. Now, having been attacked with real-life bullets, I knew I was vulnerable and insignificant. I wanted only to crawl into bed with Lin and be left alone, and it was gonna be damn difficult to do that. The world's problems would have to wait for someone else. I had problems of my own, and Number One was to survive the next couple of months. It started to rain. Dark clouds rolled in, obscuring the light of the sun. The puddles began to fill. The new guys couldn't believe someone had drowned in a puddle. Fuck 'em. They'd see a lot of things they wouldn't believe before they got out of The Nam. Sure was chilly!

● ● ● ●

Captain Benedict ordered a search-and-destroy patrol through the marshland outside what would be our new perimeter. I tried to talk my way out of it, to no avail. We lined up about six feet apart and headed into the tall grass in a pouring rain. Even at six feet, it was hard to keep track of the guy next to you. It was imperative that we maintain eye contact on both sides, because if you got ahead you could be blown away by your own guys. I soon discovered that the elephant grass hid a tangle of twisted vines, thorns, and razor-sharp leaves. You couldn't see your feet. You couldn't tell what you were stepping on, if it was solid or not. The wall of vegetation hid everything. We inched forward.

Whump! To my left, an explosion. I crouched, listening to sickening, heartrending screams. "Oh my God! Oh, God, it hurts! Momma! Oh, please! Momma, please! Oh, it hurts so bad! Pleeeeease help me!" I could feel my heart thumping against my ribs, the familiar shaking starting again. From the left came the cry, "Stay in place! Don't anybody move! We got a booby trap. Look for thin, clear wire, trip wire! Don't anybody move 'til we find out what they want us to do!" I could feel the cold rain dripping down the back of my neck, adding to the shivers already wracking my body. A thin clear wire. I strained my eyes at the tall grass inches from my face. Crystal-clear beads of water clung to the edges of the vertical blades, gathered, and trickled downward. The movement resembled a wire. A million straight edges of a zillion six-foot fronds, and I had to trust my water-spotted army-issue glasses to pick out a thread of clear wire or be blown away. If there was one booby trap, there were bound to be more. Jesus Christ!

"Move out! Stay awake!" Who the fuck could fall asleep? We edged forward, trying to inspect each waving blade of grass but not wanting to take too much time and fall behind. You sure wouldn't want to be out here alone. We came to a stream. "Count off by twos. Ones cross, twos cover 'em. Then ones cover while the twos come across!" I slipped the safety off, and aimed blindly at the wall of shimmering green and brown while the two guys on my flanks plunged into the muck. I took off my ammo belt and held it and my rifle, safetied again, above my head. The stream was reddish-brown, swirling in and out among the base of the grasses. I waded forward, gritting my teeth, waiting for a pongie stick's point to drive itself into my leg or groin. Waiting for the big bang that would cut me in half. Praying for it to be over. My head went under. I clambered forward, more than a little panicky. There was a sharp bank of slimy mud on the other side, and I slipped twice before I hauled myself and my heavy wet clothes up out of the goo. I wiped the grit off the lenses of my glasses, buckled the belt around my waist. I could only half see. In the distance I heard the approach of an ambulance siren, coming to pick up the wounded. I thought they used helicopters. Next time I would tuck a clean rag inside my helmet so I could clean my glasses. We reached another stream. I was soaked. It was surprising how much heavier the wet gear had become, and how the belt seemed to have stretched 'til it was dragging my pants down off my waist. The pant legs were glued to my skin, a ponderous extra layer pulling my tired legs into the goo. My feet seemed to have shrunk, and the slipping from side to side was wearing blisters. Christ, how did some guys do this every day for a year?

"Hold your position! Nobody move! We got a wire here!" I sucked in a breath, felt a droplet of sweat trickle down off an eyebrow, spread out, and burn my eye. I hesitated to wipe at it, as if any motion might upset the delicate balance and set off a catastrophe. Time stopped. I heard myself breathing, felt the pounding in my chest. Voices came from the left. "We're gonna blow it with grenades. Take cover, but be careful. Anderson to Raleigh, back off and find cover. The rest of you go forward, try to get low." I was in the group to move back. For some strange reason, the wall of grass that I had just come through now seemed more threatening than the tangle ahead. I inched back to the stream, dropped into the water where my head would be below the bank. I hollered that I was in position, everyone did. Again, the voice came from the left. "Okay, here it goes! Keep your heads down. One! Two! Three!" *Wooomp!* "Gotta try again! One! Two! Three!" *Whoomp.* I watched a fragile butterfly in the weeds. "Again! One! Two! Three!" It seemed unreal. The heat baked the back of my shirt to stiffness. The butterfly left one blossom for the next, her yellow wings flickering against the breeze. She was so naïve, so oblivious to the chaos about to erupt in her garden. Floating on the wind, she seemed to represent all of Nature, about to be torn by human foolishness. I wanted to reach out, push her down out of harm's way. It would have been suicide to rise. Knowing there was about to be an explosion was worse in some ways than a surprise. It took so long, and my mind raced as I waited. You hope it won't happen, and you know it's inevitable, and, like thunder after lightening, it makes you jump. You feel foolish, but you're glad you've never gotten used to such a thing.

The third grenade exploded the mine, so the first explosion was followed by a second. We clambered back on line and inched forward again. The sun was out now. I swore I saw steam, wrinkled my nose at the smell of rot. Goddamn it, I wished I could see. One minute we were in the grass, straining to see a thin clear trip wire. Then we were on solid ground, a roadbed, able to see far into the distance. It was over. We followed the roadbed around to the right, back to the compound. It had taken over three hours to walk about a mile. In the hootches everyone shed the heavy wet clothes like memories of terror in physical form. Many of the guys had leeches, and I felt sick in my stomach. They were shiny black worms about three inches long and half an inch thick, and the only way to get them off was to touch them with a lighted cigarette. They fell to the floor and coiled in pain, and when you stomped on them with a boot blood sprayed. By the time I got to the shower the hot water was gone, but it felt good to soap up and wash the scum off.

I had escaped again. A new guy, eleven days in-country, had taken a load of steel balls in his legs and gut. He probably wouldn't make it. The trip wire had triggered an American-made claymore mine, a curved tray of explosive with hundreds of half-inch steel balls glued on the face. Our perimeter was ringed with them. Obviously, Charley had crawled in, stolen one, and used it against us.

Archie came into the hootch as I was dressing. Someone had sneezed, and he had dived into a stream and gotten a leech on his cheek. We were in no hurry to go to work, so I dug out two warm cans of Pearl beer. Archie had been near the new kid when the booby trap exploded. Tiny pieces of shredded grass had flown by him, and he was obviously shaken.

"I realized something today," he began. "I used to think the VC were savages, primitive savages. They're absolutely amazing! I mean, one of them stole those claymores right out from under some GI's nose. They set up the booby trap in that field and got one of us. Charley one, Uncle Sam nothing. But think about it! They want to take over this compound. Shit, they want to take over the whole country. They've got booby traps planted all over, and they must have a map of where they are. Have you ever heard of a sapper crawling in, in the middle of the night, hitting a booby trip and tipping off the guards? You're goddamn right you haven't! These aren't scattered little bands of primitive guerillas. There's an army out there, and they're good! They got one of us today, and they're home sleeping. The house-girls will tell them, and they'll cross those traps off their map. Now they know that field is clear, and they can hit us from that corner. But they have to know where every booby trap is and tell their men. Somewhere, some high command office probably has a big book, a collection of all those little maps. When they finally take over, they'll just go out and disarm them. What good would it be to conquer a country and not be able to walk in it? Shit, John, they want to grow rice. They've got this whole thing figured! How the hell are we gonna beat people like that?"

I laughed. "How long ago did you suddenly realize we weren't going to win this war?"

"Yeah, I know." Archie was serious, and it was unusual for him. "I couldn't imagine how, but I guess I still thought we would win. Do you realize what we're saying? Can you imagine Vietnam defeating the United States in a war? Our kids will read about this shit in history books!"

"Archie, did you forget Tet? Uncle Ho can do anything he wants, and he will."

"I still thought we could win. Isn't that incredible? All this time, I thought somebody would come up with something! Then I laid in the grass out there today and heard that kid cryin', and I had a long time to think about it. We're going to lose this war! Isn't it great to be short?"

"Easy for you to say. I'll be here damn near a month after you're home!"

"Thirty days is all right. It will take a while, but I would not want to be arriving today. Some of those guys are apt to find themselves POWs in Hanoi! We'll get out of here before it gets that bad, but it's a spooky thing to think about. My replacement might not make it! My mom read a book, and do you know the army says we've killed more VC than the total population of North and South Vietnam combined? She doesn't understand and is really worried about me. How do you explain something like that to your mother? How can I go home and matter-of-factly tell everybody the Viet Cong are going to beat us?"

"Arch?"

"Yeah?"

"I think we better go to work. Ours is not to wonder why, ours is but to do or die."

He finished the warm beer. "Yes, for fifty-seven more days. Then the army better watch out!" We wandered up the road to the garage.

A few days later I was summoned to the command bunker. I couldn't remember doing anything wrong, but I was concerned. In the strict army class system, we were rarely summoned to meet with the brass unless it was for some sort of discipline. I crushed out a smoke and stepped into the dark interior of the tent. A first lieutenant who looked like a college kid welcomed me into an inner office, shaking my hand.

"Ketwig, I have something for you." He handed me a stack of papers. "Your request for Thailand has been approved." My heart skipped a beat. "On behalf of Captain Benedict and the entire company, I want to congratulate you. I know it's difficult being away from home, and your decision to extend for an extra year in Southeast Asia is a patriotic and admirable one." He shook my hand again and winked. "I hear Bangkok is quite a place. I'll probably take my R and R there, but you're going to spend a year in Paradise!" I thought of Lin, and of the demonstrators at the Pentagon. "Captain Benedict has been talking with Sergeant Phillips, and I'm pleased to tell you that you will be going to Thailand with Spec Four stripes on your sleeve. Your promotion to Spec Four has been approved and will become effective the first of the month." I was grinning. He shook my hand again. "Congratulations! Of course, you will be properly promoted in front of the men on the first, but we wanted you to know we're proud of you. Just promise me one thing, Specialist."

"Yessir?"

"Don't wear out all that Thai pussy before I get there. Okay?"

"Yessir. I mean, no sir. Thank you, sir."

"Thank you, soldier." He saluted, I returned it, and walked out into the bright sunlight. I looked at the papers in my hand. I wouldn't be going home! I went to the hootch, sat on my bunk, and read each paper carefully. Work could wait. The army wouldn't have given me this stack of orders unless they wanted me to read them.

As I digested the brief conversation, I began to laugh. Not only had they agreed to send me to Thailand, they were so impressed with my "patriotism" they were promoting me! I looked at the picture on my locker door, the white daisy protruding from a gun barrel. Did they really believe I was patriotic, especially in the army's sense of the word? It was hilarious. I want to go to Thailand to escape the chickenshit army inspections, and they promote me for being such an outstanding soldier.

I couldn't wait to tell Archie. He rolled out from under a truck, heard the news, and turned his head away. When he looked back, there were tears in his eyes. "If it's what you want, I guess I'm glad for ya. But, Christ, John, everybody wants to go home! How can you go to another country full of gooks? It just doesn't seem right, that's all."

"You know why I want to go to Thailand, Arch."

"I've heard all your reasons, but you're a ninety-day loss. Shit, I can almost smell my mom's cooking. How can you get so close, then kiss it all good-bye?"

"I can't face a Stateside base. You know that. Some lifer would climb my case because my socks weren't rolled right, and I'd tell him to go fuck himself, and go to jail. I can't put myself in that predicament. Shit, I'm gonna go get married and go home a civilian with a little girl to rub my aching back...and my front! I really want to do it, Archie. I'm high as a fuckin' kite. You want to go home, and I'll be glad for you the day you leave. I'll miss you, but I'll be awful goddamn happy for you. This is what I want. Malaysia is my home now, too, and I'll be there in a few weeks. Don't be sad about that!"

He grinned. "Okay! Some guys'll do anything for a promotion!"

• • • •

I needed a passport to get into Thailand. The company clerk made arrangements for me to fly to Saigon, where I could get a passport from the embassy. I caught a C-130 to Qui Nhon early one morning. There was a long wait in a sheet-metal air terminal, and it was late afternoon when I boarded a flight to Saigon. Most of the other passengers were Vietnamese, but I had passed the day chatting with a bearded magazine photographer. He was fascinating, outrageously independent, with long hair, love beads, and a collection of Nikons around his neck. We settled into the nylon webbing seats, trying to arrange the center strap so it would fit into the cracks of our butts and allow our tailbones to support us. A C-130 is a cargo plane with little in the way of creature comforts. Cables and hydraulics groaned all around us. A pretty Vietnamese lady tried to soothe her baby. An ARVN officer stared at a *Playboy* foldout. A young man in a dark blue business suit settled his briefcase onto his lap and sneered at me with obvious disdain, smoking American cigarettes from a gold case. The lights were red, surreal. Somewhere in the back I heard a chicken. The air was foul, thick with cigarette smoke and the stink of rotten-fish sauce. It was incredibly hot, and I was famished. The heat and stink made me nauseous, but my photographer friend offered a stick of chewing gum. An attendant hollered that we were nearing Tan Son Nhut. Charley was dropping rockets on the airstrip, so we would have to sneak in. The red lights disappeared. The baby screamed in terror. I twisted to look out the tiny window. Incredible red explosions erupted below us. The photographer tried to reassure me. "It's always like that."

The cables and pistons creaked and groaned. You could feel the strain through your feet, a twisting or stretching. The sounds became louder, and we were thrown against our belts. The engines were roaring, then they dropped to an idle, and we plummeted. I heard vomiting, crying, whispers of fear. We bounced hard on terra firma, the engines strained to stop us, and the sounds grew painful. In total darkness, swaying on canvas webs, torn by inertia, with vomit hanging heavy and chickens screaming, we arrived in Saigon. We heard the rockets exploding outside the paper-thin aluminum fuselage. A nearby explosion hurled a flash of light through the windows, momentarily exposing the squalor surrounding us. The baby howled. The strain was electric, our plane a prison. Cables ground, fluid squealed through pipes. We stopped with a jerk, and everyone crowded toward the door as if eager to confront the incoming rockets. The air was cooler, and the stink in the plane was displaced by the acrid scent of explosives. I burst out of the fuselage, crouching low, and rushed to the sandbag-and-pressed-steel barrier at the edge of the parking slot our plane commanded. The rocket bursts seemed to come in salvos of three, shaking the earth but lighting the night. A bus arrived, and I elbowed my way on. There were too many passengers for one bus, and this was no place to be waiting. Fuck the gooks, I wanted to get out of here. This was their capital city, not mine; let them enjoy it in all its glory.

Inside the stucco terminal, MPs with flashlights guided us to another sandbagged wall. The photographer and I leaned back against the revetment and smoked until the attack ended. He helped me negotiate for a taxi, then disappeared without a word. At the gate an MP advised me to stay low. I scrunched on the smooth vinyl, felt the seat springs prodding my thighs. The driver sang along with a Vietnamese rock tune from the radio. I had never been to Pleiku at night, but only the pavement of Saigon's streets surprised me. At the entrance to my hotel I saw two MPs in a sandbag bunker listening to the Four Tops on Armed Forces Radio: "Seven Rooms of Gloom." The hotel was Vietnamese, leased by the American army. This was an enlisted man's hotel, nothing fancy, but I found a hamburger and a beer. My room was small and unclean, but the sheets were fresh and the shower was warm. The toilet had a tank of water high on the wall and a pull chain; I watched the whirlpool of a flush with fascination and more than a little nostalgia. I analyzed the sound, trying to compare it to memories of the commode back home. Finally I collapsed onto the sheets, clad only in my underwear. It was hot and muggy in the room, but I was uncomfortable and soon rose to pull on my fatigues and socks.

I thought about the photographer. We had spent hours, two Americans in a sea of gooks. We had been under fire. We had talked, and laughed, and wondered out loud. He had talked of cameras and politics. I had been privy to photographs that might someday explain the war to my grandchildren from the pages of history textbooks. He had seen Dak To and Hue and Khe Sanh and the siege of the American embassy. He was crazy-wise, tired but cheerful, burned out but compelled. He had shared the day with me and then walked away. I couldn't recall his name. If Charley had been on his toes at Tan Son Nhut, our names might have graced the same obituary column, and moments later we had just walked away from each other. "That's just the way it is," I decided, but it shouldn't be that way. The experiences we were living were beyond most people's comprehension. We would do anything to keep an American alive, based solely upon the fact that he was an American. Having endured the onslaught, were we not members of some secret fraternity? Why couldn't we show that? Why didn't we?

Suppose I was back in The World some day, flopped on the couch watching a ball game, and the door rang and the guy said he was the photographer from Qui Nhon? For a few brief moments we would recall the harrowing hours. After that, what? We had been thrown together by the strangest winds of fate. Other than citizenship and a few nightmarish memories, we had little in common, and we knew it. Right now he was probably in a luxurious air-conditioned hotel room with a beautiful woman and a bottle of expensive French wine, and I was a pfc in an enlisted men's hotel room. As my lids sagged, I resigned myself to the fact that I would meet many people in my lifetime. A few would be friends, a few would be miserable, and a lot would wander by without really being noticed. Why should The Nam be different?

The next morning, I went upstairs for breakfast and was surprised to find powdered eggs. This place had closer ties to the military then I had imagined. I brushed my teeth, got my papers together, and took a taxi to the American embassy. It was familiar, strangely familiar. The pockmarks in the high white wall were grim testimony to the ferocity of the Tet invaders. In the courtyard, many of the palm trees had gaping wounds. I was surprised at the plainness, the lack of ornamentation. I gazed up at the building in awe. This was where the secret lay hidden, where the answers to a million questions were catalogued and filed away. Somebody here had to know what it was all about. I had seen plenty of pictures of Ambassador Ellsworth Bunker, and if I recognized him idly standing around I resolved to walk over, introduce myself, and ask him point-blank what the hell was going on.

I had never been to an embassy before. Mercifully, Ambassador Bunker did not greet me at the door. I was assisted by a businesslike young man in a sweat-soaked white shirt. All my papers were in order. I could pick up the completed passport at 4:00 P.M. It was 10:30 in the morning. How should I spend five hours in Saigon? I took a taxi to the famous USO, where I could make a telephone call to home.

The Saigon USO was in an old building on famous Tu Do Street. It was obvious the French had been here. Bright umbrellas mushroomed over wrought iron tables at the sidewalk cafes. There were flowers in ornate urns, and slinky women in miniskirts or *ao dais*. The *ao dai* is a Vietnamese dress, slit to the waist and worn over black silk trousers.

Probably the sexiest garment ever devised by man. The sidewalk was crowded. This was the land of opportunity for Saigon's beggars, and I burst into the USO to escape their outstretched hands. Now that I was here, I was in no real hurry to call home. I had five hours, and what should I say? There were donuts, and real milk, like used to come from cows before the army had gotten involved. A Vietnamese band was mimicking the Beatles. "Stlawberry Fields Foal-ever." For Crissakes! Why weren't these guys in ARVN uniforms, wading through a rice paddy? Most of the GIs were "Saigon warriors," in spitshined low quarters and starched khakis, clean-shaven and far too polished to know a sapper was not a guy in Vermont making maple syrup.

The telephones were upstairs, and the military had managed to fuck them up, too. They were connected through ham-radio operators. You could only talk a few minutes and had to say "stop" at the end of each exchange. There would be a pause, then (by the grace of God and the wonders of modern science and technology) your mother's voice would travel halfway 'round the globe. When she finished a thought, she would have to say "stop" too.

It took quite a while to make the connection after you put in a request. I watched the guys talking to loved ones. Some were casual, but most were very tense and emotional. A few had wet eyes. Funny, there were damn few Saigon warriors here. What should I say? What would I say? I would have about ten minutes to describe all that had happened since September, and it might be the last time I ever talked to them, ever. They knew I was going to Thailand. Would they give me a hard time? Would I change my mind after I talked to them? Could I if I wanted to?

The loudspeaker crackled. "Ketwig, John. Booth Forty-three."

I hurried to light a cigarette, drew some comfort from it, and lifted the receiver to my ear.

"Mom?" There was nothing, then a series of clicks, and the familiar "Hello?"

"Mom? It's me. John. I'm at the Saigon USO, and I had to say hello. Listen, when I say, 'stop,' it's your turn. When you finish what you want to say, you've got to say 'stop.' Got that?" No response...Oh, shit! "I haven't got that! Let's try it again. Stop!"

There was a short delay, then a very tentative, "How are you?" A big pause. "Are you okay? Stop."

Pause. Click. "Yeah, I'm okay. Sweaty and tired, but that's just a way of life around here. I'm really getting' short, you know? Seventy-two days. I even had donuts this morning. Saigon is almost civilization. Stop."

Pause. Click. "Yes, we've seen pictures on TV. We have a calendar on the refrigerator. Are you sure you're all right? Your letters have been a little, well...strange lately. Stop."

Pause. Click. "You're getting good at that stop business. I'm fine, really I am. How's Dad, and Ken? Stop." A lump was growing in my throat, and my eyes were getting wet. Strange? What the fuck did she think they would be, coming from a place like Dak To?

"Everyone is fine. It's Saturday, and they're at the store." There was a long delay. "John, why don't you come home? Are you sure you're doing the right thing? You mentioned smoking pot in one of your letters, and we're really concerned about you. We think you should come home, and if it's right, things will work out so you can go back and get married." Pause. "Stop."

Pause. Click. "Listen, I'm fine. Everybody smokes pot here. If you don't, you go crazy. We never smoke after dark, or when there's any chance of gettin' into the shit. Charley only works nights, and I don't even drink too much. But Mom, please don't ask me to come home. I can't, you know that. This wasn't an easy decision, but I made up my mind. Please don't ask me to change it now. Just wait 'til I bring Lin home.

You'll understand five minutes after you meet her." The lump had grown so big I couldn't go on. I croaked a weak "Stop."

"Well, we are worried. I know you'll be all right, but your father worries himself sick. He really wants you to come home and talk with him before you get married. Stop."

"Well, I wish he was home so I could talk to him now. You've got to understand. When you met him and decided to get married, would you have gone to Vietnam? Hell, no! I can't just jump on a plane and go thirteen thousand miles from Lin. Hey, my time's about up. I hope you know I love you all and miss you. Oh, how's my car? And have you seen Harry? Stop."

"Your car runs fine. The new paint looks great. We haven't seen Harry in a long time. We love you, too. You take care. Dad will be real sorry he missed you. Please be careful. We really are worried about you. Stop."

"I'm telling you, I'm fine. Just give everybody a hug, and I'll send you pictures from Thailand soon. Believe me, I'll be careful. Things are pretty quiet around Pleiku now. Listen, my time's up, I gotta to. I love you all. 'Bye! Stop."

I waited for her final "Good-bye," but the line was dead. I walked out to the stairs, my eyes blurred with tears. I had tried not to think about home that much, but I could picture the telephone on the table by the maroon armchair. I could picture the woodwork by the stairs, and the philodendron, and the phone book with an ashtray on top.

I couldn't let myself think about home. It could get me off on some kind of self-pity trip, and I couldn't go home, so I better get my mind on something else. Did I word things right? Christ, I don't know if I'm all right. What's normal here ain't exactly your common everyday kid next door back in The World! I'm still in one piece, and that's about as good as it gets around here. Better not go into it any deeper than that. I was in Saigon, an exotic oriental capital, full of intrigue and mystery and French influence. Oughta take some pictures to show the people back home. I shaded my eyes as I burst back into the southern sun. I sure had been lucky to get assigned to the highlands. The sun hit you like a fist here. Sure was crowded on the sidewalk. I shot a few pictures of peddlers crouched on the sidewalk, of slinky women in *ao dais* and gooks in white shirt and tie. There must be a million motorbikes. Garbage everywhere. I walked down the street about two blocks. To my left was a line of black marketeers, sitting cross-legged against the wall, their piles of American-made plunder laid out on low tables. The variety was incredible, everything from Beatles albums to hair spray, Kodak cameras to C-rations. Laundry detergent and Salem cigarettes were the most popular. I couldn't believe my eyes. There was an M-16 rifle! I had carried an obsolete M-14 for these many months, which was a blessing because it resisted jamming from sand better than an M-16, but this was supposed to be the latest, greatest weapon in the world, and this wrinkled-up gook lady was selling one on the street in Saigon. If a Charley had the piasters, he could buy it and use it on a GI tonight. "How much, Mama-san?"

"Three hundred American dowrar, four hundred funny money." I declined and backed away into the swirling sea of humanity. I bumped into a couple of passersby, turned, and rushed back to the USO. I burst into a conversation between two MPs, erupting with indignation. "There's an old lady about two blocks from here, with an M-16 for sale! She's got the thing laid out on a little table, and she wants three hundred bucks for it, and anybody can just walk up and buy it and shoot some GI with it."

They didn't seem to care. In fact, they seemed more upset that I had interrupted them. "Listen, man, there're probably ten thousand M-16s for sale in this city, and claymore mines, and anything else you can name. If we walk down there dressed in our uniforms she'll be gone. We're off duty, and even if we were on, we wouldn't stand a fart's chance in a whirlwind, so why don't you just forget it? This ain't the bush, and a lot of strange shit comes down in Saigon, and there ain't nothing we can do about it. I appreciate you tryin' to help, but it's a lot bigger problem than you or I can handle."

It wasn't the first thing I had seen in The Nam that bothered me, but I wrestled with it quite a while. I had heard of the black market, but I never realized it was this bad. I was familiar enough with the Vietnamese that I knew the old lady would sell that rifle to a Cong if he had cash in his hand. Soldiers already had a rifle. Who would her customer be? A rich Vietnamese businessman who wanted to protect his family with style? Possibly, but if he was rich he had already taken care of that. She was looking for a VC, and she would find one. Chances are, she sold it to him for fifty or a hundred dollars and threw in a box of ammo to boot. Every item I had seen had been stolen from the American army, and it would be pretty difficult for an MP to decide where to begin. I should be thankful the old Mama-san hadn't jumped up and wasted me with her prize.

The loudspeaker crackled through the darkness of the USO. In five minutes there would be an ice-cream-eating contest in another room. Ice cream. I could get into that. I put the black market out of my mind and headed for the action.

I got lucky. There were four of us and four two-gallon cardboard drums of vanilla ice cream. When the lady said, "Go!" you shoveled it in for ten minutes. At the end of ten minutes, the drums would be weighed, and the lightest drum would win. It was a heavy responsibility. I was representing Pleiku, New York, and skinny people. Well, skinny people, I only came in second, but at the end of ten minutes my drum had less than an inch of ice cream left. My stomach didn't bother me, and before I left Saigon I would return for a banana split.

Four o'clock was drawing near, and I trudged out into the brilliant heat to hire a taxi for the trip to the embassy. My passport was ready, and I hired another taxi for the ride back to my hotel. On the way, we passed the South Vietnamese capitol building, and the taxi driver took advantage of a red light to point out the huge decorative panels. I peered past the crowd of peasants and ragged children to catch a glimpse of a building paneled with plates of gold! I gave the taxi driver a couple extra dollars to go around the block and allow me to snap a picture. At the time, I thought I was photographing a landmark, a tourist attraction. I hadn't been reading the American newspapers. I learned later that they had never mentioned a gold-plated capitol building with starving beggars in front and an American-built Huey helicopter parked on the lawn.

At the hotel, I took the elevator to the roof to get a few pictures of Saigon. The roof was divided into two ornate sections. The largest featured a swimming pool lined with multicolored tiles and ringed with carefully manicured flowerbeds and stylish Oriental lanterns. A walkway at the edge of the roof offered a panoramic view through plate-glass windows. A wrought iron fence led to the second room, a formal garden in white stone, with a pretentious tiled dragon, ornate flower beds, and topiary, bushes trimmed into animal shapes growing out of huge antique vases. The elaborate decorations clashed with the squalor and poverty on the streets and seemed lonely and desolate. I was the only person there to see it.

I got my pictures and went to dinner. This was to be a special treat, a celebration. I settled at a table near the window, overlooking the bustling city streets from ten floors above. There were tablecloths and linen napkins and two forks. A waiter took my order for a Scotch and water, and I lit a cigarette and tried to appear blasé as I marveled at the variety of the menu. I ordered a big steak with mashed potatoes and salad. I was sipping my drink and dreaming of Lin, stroking the passport in my shirt pocket and trying to imagine married life, when an air force enlisted man asked if he could join me. The restaurant had gotten crowded, and I motioned him to a chair.

He was from Tan Son Nhut and ate here often. When my steak arrived, he broke out laughing. As I started to cut it, I learned why. The knife had no effect on the steaming piece of meat. It was a water buffalo steak! I ordered another drink and sawed with a passion. This steak was as expensive as any I had ever eaten, and I was determined to get my money's worth. The potatoes were powdered, no doubt from the black market, and the salad contained vegetables I had never seen. I worked at the steak silently, relentlessly, determined to enjoy myself. The airman was cracking up now, laughing loud enough to bring a flush of embarrassment to my cheeks. I strained at the dull dinner knife. When it bent, I knew my steak would have to wait 'til I got out of The Nam. The airman summoned a waiter, conferred in Vietnamese, and the waiter disappeared with my steak. In a few minutes he returned with my precious piece of meat warmed up and ground into hamburger.

It was dark when I finished dinner, and I went back to the roof to see Saigon by night. In the distance, somebody was involved in a ragged firefight, and a large group of guys were gulping beer and watching the tracers and flashes. In their own peculiar way, the red tracers and their diverse gradual arcs were graceful, beautiful. artillery rounds burst in a yellow-gold display. From afar there was a beauty to the battle, but the distant THUD, THUD, THUD of the exploding shells reminded me of the death and suffering I was watching. I could, for that few moments, understand the attraction a career military officer might feel in battle. From this distance the explosions were fascinating. Isolated from the horror by miles, it was impersonal, detached. Disgusted with myself for having been mesmerized by the death of other men, I retreated to the bar for a drink.

It was pitch-dark, impenetrable. A Vietnamese waitress showed me to a table. Another sat down next to me, asked me what I would like to drink. Scotch. She asked if I would buy her a Saigon Tea. I was startled. I had heard about this scam, it was a legend from the bars of Saigon, but I hadn't expected it in an army-contracted hotel. I declined. Saigon Tea was served in tiny liqueur glasses. It was nothing but weak tea; the five-dollar charge allowed you to talk to the lady about more important matters. I wasn't in the mood for a whore. I paid for my Scotch and wandered to the jukebox. It had been a long time since I had been able to choose my music. I was reading the list of records when a sexy female voice at my left ear whispered, "Boom-boom, GI?" and I felt a hand on my crotch. In the split second I took to turn my head left and say, "No," I let my guard down. From the right, I felt my wallet being lifted out of my pocket. I whirled to see half a dozen girls darting away in every direction. I saw the one I thought most likely to be the thief disappear through a hanging cloth door, and I burst through it on her heels. My wallet flew back at me, over her shoulder. I stopped to pick it up, and, of course, it was empty. Unable to find her, I attacked the bar. The bartender was wide-eyed, incredulous. Surely I was mistaken. Things like that didn't happen there.

I took the elevator to the lobby and complained to the girl at the check-in counter. She telephoned the bar and, after a long conversation in Vietnamese, explained that the bartender said I had had too much to drink and probably didn't realize how much I had spent. Really pissed off now, I exploded out the door to the MPs standing at the sandbagged bunker. They were sympathetic. It happened every night, but this was a Vietnamese hotel, and they had no jurisdiction to tell the Vietnamese how to run their business. In the morning I should see some major in an office on the other side of town and fill out a complaint. It was hopeless. Fuck it! I went to bed.

It was impossible to sleep. I had hit upon the point. It was, indeed, hopeless. From my first moments in Vietnam, on a bus with windows screened so that the Vietnamese couldn't toss grenades or garbage, it had been hopeless. The beggars on the street, the guards at the landfill, the whore at the firebase, the barber, even President Thieu and the girls tonight: the Vietnamese people didn't care about our noble mission, and until they cared it was hopeless. Our leaders didn't care about saving the peasants from communism, they cared about promotions and medals and the feelings of power and authority. In broken English, grade school dropouts issued orders to college graduates. Harsh, inhumane, degrading orders. Orders with no purpose but to stroke the ego of the powerful. Until they gave us a reason why, until they felt some responsibility toward us and our families, it was hopeless. One could only hope to survive, but to what end? America, in ordering up this holocaust, in conferring the prestige of rank upon these incompetents, must be deeply infected by the cancer. Where did it start? I hadn't seen it on the tree-shaded streets of suburbia, but perhaps it was there. People cheated on their income tax. The local papers were full of stories of child abuse, violence, suicide, social struggle. In the South, people had died for the right to drink from a water fountain in spite of the color of their skin. Martin Luther King Jr. and the Kennedy brothers had been silenced. Appalled, a few were marching in the streets, chanting, "Peace!" and dodging the blows of their neighbors. It was a criminal offense to refuse to take part in the killing of Orientals, but Captain Benedict would be decorated with colored ribbon for service to his country. Was his country my country? Could I ever fit in again? What had changed? Me? America? God? I was not alone in my confusion, my skepticism, my despair. I was in the land of despair. I had come to the army in the full bloom of youth, with faith in the future and the goodness of man. Perhaps some day I could be president of the United States.

In a few short months I had become disillusioned with myself, America, all of mankind. The president of the United States was ordering thousands of young men into this meat grinder, and it was all so hopeless. Vietnam was the land despair called home. Like a tourist, I had welcomed this journey to Saigon, hoped to see something new and exotic. Instead, I saw scars disfiguring the embassy walls and a rifle for sale to the highest bidder. If only money was enough to keep us alive, that M-16 might be a symbol of something. The money America sent to Vietnam gilded the walls, but the children begged. The money bought a presidential helicopter for the palace grounds, but rockets rained on Tan Son Nhut. A piece of meat bent my knife, and a woman stole my money. Back in Pleiku a kid from Kentucky had walked into a trip wire and bled into the dirt. The rains were returning to wash away the red stain, a few shovelfuls of Kentucky mud would cover the silver coffin, and the rockets would fall at Tan Son Nhut again tonight. The local draft board would send a replacement, and the children would be hungry until they learned to steal.

Oh, Mom, if only you could understand why the letters seem strange! I'm not the boy you raised; I'm not the teenage kid you kissed good-bye. You sit in front of the TV waiting for the flag-draped coffin, bearing a burden I will never fully appreciate. I don't call your letters strange, but I see a tension in the script, feel it in the carefully chosen phrases. I'm not the same, Mama; and I don't like the person I've had to become. I don't want to explain it to you. It's best if you and Dad never know what I've discovered about life. I know you love me, and I guess you would have told me if you'd only known. I was happier then, and if you've lived all those years without learning what I've learned...well, I don't want to be the one to tell you how fortunate you've been. On the nightstand are a picture of Lin and a passport. In a very special way, she understands. Until I find the words, I'll turn my back on you and escape toward the setting sun. My eyes can't bear the light of a new day dawning just yet; so I'll go west into the twilight and the shadows. I'll take refuge in bed with a woman, and I guess you think that's obscene. Maybe I can help a little while I'm in Thailand. There are a lot of kids here who need help. If I fly east, it will be a flight to another army base, and the army doesn't seem to be helping anything right now. Yes, I guess it is strange, but I can't go back to being the kid who left. I want to, but I've learned to get by without the things I want. I want Lin, too, and I've got a chance at that. I need the tranquillity, Mom. I'm so tired!

• • • •

Early the next morning I boarded a plane for Pleiku. When I got back they assigned me to a detail, stringing a new concertina perimeter outside the new barracks area. There were three of us in the back of a deuce-and-a-half: Riverson, a new guy, and me. We were in the field where the other new guy had screamed. The belly his mother had diapered and powdered and cooked for was only blood and torn flesh among the weeds now, and I hoped we wouldn't drive over the spot where he had died. We completed a section of wire and bounced toward the next area to be fenced. Riverson was a Texas farmer, older than most of us. He never had much to say. Maybe it was the new kid with us, or the memory of another new kid a few days ago. Riverson was silent. The truck lurched to a stop. We tossed off the fence posts every few feet, then returned to the first post and rolled a coil of the heavy, bladed wire off into the grass. The new guy jumped down, pulled a coil off the loop of wire, inserted a post through it, and Riverson and I took turns lifting a heavy metal cylinder and lowering the open end over the post, then lifting and dropping it until we had banged the support solidly into the earth. Now the new guy lifted the coil and pulled it to the next post, stringing a lethal cylinder of wire across the grassy meadow. We had it down to a system. We had been doing it out here in the weeds and the rain. We finished another section, and the new guy climbed aboard. We distributed more poles and rattled back.

The new kid pulled on his leather gloves and pushed another coil of wire over the tailgate. He placed both hands on the metal truck body, tensed his body for the vault over the side. That's when I saw it, and I dove into him and sent all three of us sprawling onto the jagged wire.

"What the fuck?..." The other two were angry as they struggled to their feet.

"Snake! Right below you! A little green snake!" We rushed to the edge for a look. Had my eyes played a trick? We were in tall grass, thousands of narrow, green, vertical spears dancing in the rain and the breeze. Somehow, with a casual glance, my eyes had picked out a bamboo viper. The color and size of a stalk of grass, he was coiled around a single leaf, searching with his tongue. From the safety of the truck bed, we knocked him down with one of the metal poles. Our driver was on the running board with his rifle, but we were afraid of a ricochet. We speared with the heavy poles until Riverson got lucky and chopped the snake in two. There was a head and about two inches of body. We hooked the rest of the body and flung it far into the weeds. Carefully, we jumped down for a closer look.

Even without his body, the viper tried to strike. He jumped forward an inch at a time, his eyes searching frantically, his tongue dancing. The new guy used a pole to lift the head onto a wheel rim, we flattened the head into a sticky paste. The new guy pushed the heavy weight back onto the truck, then turned to me with a huge smile and his hand outstretched. "Thank you, man!" Riverson was grinning too, and slapping me on the back. How had I seen that snake? The driver threw his arm around the new guy's shoulders and told about the agony of dying from a bamboo viper bite. The rain was heavy now. We called it a day and drank many a cold beer that night. Even Riverson was rowdy. It was my finest hour.

• • • •

As preparations for the move progressed, the war seemed to slow. The brass warned of another offensive, but in the meantime we worked on moving. These were agonizingly slow days, like the last few days before Christmas when you were a kid. The closer my day became, the more I worried about living to see it dawn. It was raining hard now, as it had been when I arrived. The engineers had built a tank farm about a mile off our southeast corner, and we expected Charley to use the cover of the foggy mist to try to blow it. You could feel the tension building. Charley was coming into season, and I knew he cared little about the number of squares on a short-timer's calendar.

As we prepared to move into the new barracks, all of the outbuildings had to be moved. Someone built a new mailroom, but the officer's club, our club, the motor pool tent, and the bone-yard warehouse all had to be dismantled and reassembled at our new home. I was helping with the motor pool equipment when a cable snapped and a heavy metal table crashed into my back, pinning me to the ground. I was scared because it didn't hurt, but when they lifted the table I was able to crawl out and walk. There was soreness, but I thought I had lucked out again.

The next morning I could barely lift myself out of the bunk. My lower back had turned an ugly dark blue. Sarge sent me to sick call, and they sent me to the hospital for X-rays. I was able to find a ride with a supply sergeant from Camp Holloway. With typical army logic, they expected me to walk to the hospital, a distance of at least a mile. Once there, I could be checked to see if I had a broken back.

At the hospital, things were bustling. Because I was not seriously wounded, I would have to wait for the medical people to get a few spare minutes. I was ushered around a row of linen curtains to a line of chairs. Numerous Vietnamese and a few GIs waited. I settled down for a long wait. Outside, the monsoon rains drummed against the steel building. The evacuation hospital's job was to patch up the wounded so they could be evacuated, to Can Ranh Bay or Okinawa or Tokyo. It was basically a giant steel barn on a sea of pressed metal to facilitate the landing medevac helicopters. The rains thudded against the building and the steel plating with a ringing roar, muffling the urgent hustling sounds inside. It was refreshing to see such cleanliness, and yet the overwhelming contrasts of Vietnam appeared once more to boggle the mind. The inside walls of corrugated steel had been painted a grayish dark blue. The curtains and much of the linen were a lighter, robin's-egg blue. Gleaming chrome-plated instruments and white enameled sterilizers glistened like Christmas ornaments on a clear, snow-covered night. The doctors and nurses wore olive-drab fatigues and jungle boots, a stark reminder of their military status among these hospital-white surroundings. In a country where everything seemed to be colored a muted shade of brown, red, or olive-drab, this seemed an oasis. In spite of the turmoil, I could hear behind the screen, the pale blue curtain soothed my eyes.

In the midst of this sterile and businesslike cleanliness, to my left a knot of Vietnamese civilians waited in various degrees of filth and misery. A pathetically skinny boy of about seven or eight, shirtless, tore my eyes away from the tranquil sea of pale blue. He sat motionless, lost in thought, in shorts and Ho Chi Minh sandals. Ho Chi Minh sandals were made from discarded army tires, the tread serving as soles. The little fellow had an unruly patch of jet black hair, and dark eyes that seemed to recede above his cheekbones to burrow into deep, dark sockets and hide from the horrors of his world. There was no reflection, no childish sparkle to those eyes. The reason was obvious. His legs were a horror of blackened, crispy shards of burnt flesh. Above the meager shorts, his torso, also black, seemed bubbled like an over-baked pizza. His right shoulder disappeared into the horrible mass of his chest, a diagonal lump of melted black putty that fell to his navel, then rose on another diagonal to exit near the left shoulder by way of four stubby pink protrusions. His right arm had been melted to his chest in a searing ball of flaming napalm. The boy's right fingers jutted out of his chest like pink worms, clawing uncontrollably. The dry black bubbles rose up his neck and chin, angling off to obscure only half his mouth. I watched him nod to shoo a pesky fly. I thought of kids in America, in Little League uniforms, carrying leather gloves and collections of baseball picture cards. In an agricultural, war-torn society, this kid's chances of survival were nil. There was a cluster of peasant women near him, squatting and chatting. I didn't know which might be his guardian, but it didn't matter. None could offer him a chance at a normal life. Like a curious motorist at a traffic accident, I stared, lost in thought.

The activity picked up beyond the screen. There were raised voices and the sound of equipment being moved. There seemed to be an urgency. I heard a chopper coming in and wandered around the screen toward the door to watch. This would be an experience: watching a medevac chopper bring in the casualties and the frantic attempts of the hospital to patch them together. Morbid curiosity. A few months later a movie about one of these hospitals in Korea would make millions aware of the fascination.

The chopper settled onto the steel plating, its rotor blades driving the gray water in hammering sheets that made the steel walls resound. A door slid open horizontally, and the medics ran forward into the wash. A dark, broken hulk of a man lowered himself to the metal floor, hunched below the whirling blades, and dragged a wounded leg toward me. A second form loomed out of the mist, his arm bandaged and misshapen. A third, naked to the waist, with an olive-drab field dressing held to his ear, blood washing over heavily-muscled shoulders to a hairy chest. The medics, some women, frantically worked at a stretcher, lifting it to a gurney and rushing toward sanctuary from the stinging rain. Another broke out of the mist at the front of the chopper. A final dark figure came out of the wash, holding a wadded fatigue shirt to his side, his torso a dark brown. I stepped back out of the way as the distorted troupe moved nearer, as the stretchers bumped and wobbled toward the overhead door. It was chaotic, messy. The door slid down, muffling some of the clatter of the rain and the ascending chopper. A new sound rose in the metal room, banging off the walls, pitiful in its painful, morphine-clouded misery. "My leg! My God, my leg! What am I gonna tell my wife? Oh, it hurts. I can't feel my foot, my knee hurts so bad! My God! My God! Help me!" He was young, but big and muscular. A red trail ran off the stretcher to the floor, to mix with the water there. Two soaking medics, one male, one female, attacked the leg, cutting shredded wet fabric, tying off the stump of leg. It was gone below the knee, a gory stump of red-and-pink meat. The soldier screamed with more terror than pain. The boy with the melted chest appeared at the side of the stretcher, grasped the struggling GI's giant hand. "Okay, GI! You go home. You okay. Can do, GI! Go home!" The morphine was slurring the screams as they wheeled the stretcher deeper into the building. The misshapen boy stood alone; very much alone, watching it disappear.

In some inexplicable way, the armless boy and the legless grunt symbolize the Vietnam I saw. The emotion of loss, the despair of hopelessness, the horror of disfigurement, and the deep common bond of two people destroyed by forces they could neither understand nor escape. The children saw their world through innocent eyes and admitted the hurt that the adults fought to ignore. The shot and shrapnel-tore flesh and bone created ugly, gory scenes that television showed in American living rooms. The adults pledged allegiance to this flag or that, rationalized the suffering, called it duty or insignificant compared to national interests. The children hadn't learned about flags or complex ideologies. They accepted human beings as equal and anguished over the senseless brutality.

Children are unaware of race or class. Adults have analyzed and developed hatred and bigotry until they evolved into war, and warfare has developed into an art form. We have a War College, but no peace college. We point with pride to megatons as the measure of our civilization's achievements. It is an all-pervasive influence; and when an explosion sets your body aflame or tears away a leg, the emotional trauma is universal. Dying, or being disfigured, is not a patriotic act. It is a waste, an unnatural and abhorrent affront to human decency. It is painful, and you can't change a channel selector and make it go away. The grunt would never tie his shoe again, nor walk through a field of wild flowers. The boy would never button a shirt with his right hand, nor scratch his ear, nor write his name. His shirts would never fit correctly, because those uncontrollable pink fingers jerking out of his left shoulder would create a bulge no shirt manufacturer has allowed for. In a few brief seconds, two total strangers with nothing but pain and suffering in common had spoken eloquently.

The stretcher disappeared into the labyrinth of pale blue curtains. The boy with the boiled body stood silently and watched it vanish. He stood silently for a long time. I wanted to reach out to him, to say something comforting. There were no words to make it better. After all the ages, the progress of civilization had amounted to this, and the sacrificial lambs communicated in a language I hoped I would never know.

The X-rays showed only severe bruises. It was almost awkward to wait for the medics. Compared to the wounds I had seen, I didn't want to bother them, but my back hurt. They gave me a bottle of Darvon, and I hitched a ride back to the compound. The bubbled, black flesh of the boy had painted an image upon my eyelids. There would be no sleep; I had to tell The World about what I had seen. Vietnam was an insane asylum, and I had to get word back to The World. I wrote a letter to an underground newspaper in Boston, then considered the enormity of the situation and added a postscript: Please don't print my name or address. Some lifer might blow me away for criticizing the war.

The boy haunted me. I tried to concentrate on Lin, to turn my thoughts to decency and kindness. My letter asked many questions. How would I react to a wife and children of my own? A nine-to-five job? I couldn't bear to see my child disfigured like that boy. Did I really want to be a parent? How could I prepare a child for the realities of adult life? Suppose I molded and shaped a child, only to see him snatched away and disfigured? How does a parent prepare for that? Could I allow myself the luxury of loving? Life, even outside The Nam, was short and uncertain. Could I watch Lin sick or dying? Could I find the comforting words I had been unable to put together today? Or had I become callused, unable to comfort because suffering is universal? I never remembered feeling this way before Vietnam, but there sure is a lot of suffering here. The responsibilities of parenting are just too awesome right now. I want you, I need you desperately; but let's wait to have children.

• • • •

The war had been quiet. I was uneasy, sensing an approaching climax. We had to face the fact that the final outcome might be very final indeed. I joined a group of guys to take supplies to a friendly Montagnard camp. The day was clear, sunny, and hot. We were in sight of the guards on the towers, but as we walked between the banana trees and into the village the twentieth century disappeared like a memory.

The population of Vietnam consisted of three groups: the haves, the have-nots, and the Montagnards. The Montagnards lived in Stone Age seclusion in the highlands. They had been nomadic until the war. Now they had become our only true allies. Trained by the Green Berets, a Montagnard warrior never ran under fire. He might forsake an M-16 for his crossbow, but he never forsook a friend. He didn't steal, and he didn't beg. He asked nothing, but offered a sense of family and community found nowhere else in The Nam. The Montagnards suffered horribly. Despised by the Vietnamese, they had been banished to the mountains, where they had developed a culture not unlike that of the American Indians before Columbus. As European weapons had spelled doom for the North American Indian, helicopter gunships and jet fighter air-support missions signaled the end of the Montagnard civilization. Regardless, they embraced the Americans.

They didn't care much for clothing. As we carried canned hams and soap powder into their village, topless women and men in loincloths gathered. A throng of naked children pressed in around us, knowing we would have candy. No one begged, and no one said, "Fuck you," or, "Go home." There were only toothless grins and warm embraces. In the center of the thatched huts the chief accepted our gifts and distributed them to his delighted but orderly followers. He offered us coarse hand-woven shirts and rice wine. He would be offended if we did not drink with him.

Drinking Montagnard rice wine requires a ceremony. It sits, uncovered, in the tropical sun, fermenting in heavy crocks. A slender bamboo is notched and laid across the opening of the jug with a tiny bamboo sliver dangling down into the liquid. The chief adjusts this sliver, to half or three-quarters of an inch. You kneel at the jug, and it is filled to overflowing. You drink through a huge bamboo straw, and it is an insult to your hosts if you rise before the liquid falls below the dangling sliver. A quart of this rich brew, the hundred-degree sun, and the motion of rising caused more than one GI to pass out.

The chief lined up the women and girls of the village and offered them to us. They were near naked, unwashed, and primitive. Still, some were pretty, or attractive. In the tranquil and friendly surroundings it was difficult to refuse, but we blamed time. Venereal disease was rampant among the "'yards." I gazed at chunks of meat drying in the trees, at primitive baskets and pottery, at an old man in a loincloth plowing his garden with a pointed log. We pointed to our wristwatches, the position of the sun. We must get back. As we walked out of the village, I remarked that I had not heard a single helicopter all the while we had been there. Strange; no one else had either.

•   •   •   •

Fifty days. I complained about my back and went on sick call three or four days a week. Archie would be leaving in about three weeks. He forged my sick slip, and we headed for the air force enlisted men's club. Due to the varied flight schedules, the air force club was open around the clock. Archie and I would drink a half-dozen screwdrivers and hitch a ride back to our compound. As soon as you were a "ninety-day loss," the lifers expected you to relax a little. It was your responsibility to develop a reasonable excuse, but a certain amount of goofing off was allowed.

I was an oddity. The others would fly to Cam Ranh Bay, board a "freedom bird," and might arrive in the family living room within twenty hours. The army had no debriefing or adjustment procedure. A grunt might fly to Oakland or Portland in fatigues he had worn in the bush, still caked with Vietnamese mud. In the Stateside processing center he would grab a shower, a dress uniform, and a pay envelope. The army paid for a taxi to the airport. By crossing the international date line, it was almost possible to watch a buddy get wasted at 2:00 in the afternoon of a particular day and be in your living room at home at 2:15 of the same afternoon. There was no orientation; the army did not want to admit your head might be screwed up by Vietnam. Most airports had peace protestors waiting to greet you, and there was a legend of a marine who had survived thirteen months in The Nam only to be gunned down at his home airport. Frankly, I think the sergeants realized the strain and shock we would face and, especially in the non-combat units, tried to allow some adjustment time. Official army policy tried to rush a returning Vietnam warrior home as soon as possible. The army had torn him away from home, promised to "make him a man," used and abused him. Now, when his time was up, he could no longer be used, and as he struggled to get it all straight in his head, now, suddenly, what he really needed was home. It might have worked, but both home and the boys had changed. After a year of confusion in The Nam, the vets found themselves home, and confused again.

• • • •

About a mile off our western perimeter, a giant guard tower loomed over the rolling fields and marshes, offering a view to the very border of Cambodia. Unused, it had deteriorated, but now it had to be rejuvenated. The metal roof supports were broken and had to be welded. I was chosen to do the job. My oxyacetylene welding had become flawless, my contribution to the war effort. I saw it as an art form, peering through dark goggles into the bubbling pool of liquid metal, watching two melt into one, filling the void with the rod, dipping, coercing, pushing the tiny bead forward. If, out on the road to Dak To, some kid needed my repair to hold in the agony of a flight from death's door, I was determined not to let him down. I wasn't gonna walk around with that on my conscience for the rest of my life. Insulated from my surroundings by the colored goggles, I lost myself in the golden pool of flame, marveled at the reds and greens. And, as each tear or crack filled and was healed, so, I thought, was my long and jagged line of days being filled. I watched the tiny flares jump away, I felt the heat and smelled the acrid fumes, and it was a miniaturized Vietnam visible only to me, through my special glasses. If it ended successfully and was stronger than before, it boded well for my future.

I fastened a tank of oxygen and a tank of acetylene into the rear of Sarge's jeep, attached regulators and long lines. I wasn't worried about the job. I was upset that I would have no shotgun, no eyes to protect me. My goggles would offer no vision to the outside world, only to my delicate flame. I would be a mile from the nearest GI, perilously close to the Cambodian border, high atop a structure, silhouetted against the sky. A sniper couldn't miss. Besides, I was deathly afraid of heights and needed some help hauling the heavy equipment up and down the long ladder. Why, I thought to myself, couldn't a few VC pop out of the tall grass to surround the base of the tower, and simply point their rifles and take me prisoner? "Shit," the sarge drawled, "you don't know nothin' that would help 'em." Sure, you know that, and I know that, but they don't know that. And I bet they could use the equipment. If I can't have a shotgun, how 'bout a guy to walk around carrying a big sign in Vietnamese saying, "This guy doesn't know anything, and the equipment is worn out!" The guy could bring his rifle, what the hell? Sarge looked back with weary eyes, missing my humor. "I can't spare anybody. Now get your young ass out there and get it done."

Unused, the path out to the tower had grown up into an obstacle course. I kicked the jeep forward, bouncing and splashing through a tunnel lined with elephant grass. He said get it over with, I'll get it over with. The drive first. C'mon, little jeep, we're gonna have some fun.

At the base of the tower, I turned on the tanks, adjusted the regulator, unraveled the hoses. It was raining, and darker clouds formed over Cambodia. I bent the rods into miniature shepherd's crooks, hooked them into my belt. Goggles. Striker. Hammer. Wire brush. Rifle. One last nervous look around. It seemed quiet enough. I grasped the brass body of the torch and started up the ladder, rung by agonizing rung, silhouetted against the gray sky, expecting to feel hot metal tear into my back at any moment. Made it! I scoured the bush spread out below me, looked off to the familiar compound so far away, the garage, the guard towers, unmanned in the daylight. Better get it done.

I lit the torch, took one last look down, and pulled the goggles over my eyes. It was raining harder now, and the hot metal sizzled. Inch by inch, the tiny puddle of fire moved along the cracks. I was cold and wet, and hungry. The dark clouds were advancing hard now, a wall of heavy rain visible beneath the dark overhang. I hurried. The wind pushed me toward the edge. Damn high places. I bent the last bar back into place, pushed the tiny puddle upward. The rain hit the tin roof with a roar. Lost in my darkened world, I thought I had been shot. Raindrops stung my face like a thousand angry honeybees. It was finished, but I couldn't drive back in this. I huddled behind the faint protection of a crumbling sandbagged wall, avoided most of the stinging rain, and lit a cigarette to wait it out. Damn, it was cold. The old tower creaked and groaned in the wind, each sound telling my mind a VC sapper was coming up the ladder with a grenade. I listened to my heart pound. The fury subsided.

I tossed the equipment off the tower, hearing it land in the sea of mud. One last look around, and I climbed down. Gritted teeth, slippery wet metal, the silhouette again. I jumped past the last two rungs to the safety of terra firma. Terra wasn't too firm. It was a swamp. I threw the equipment into the jeep, gunned the motor to life, and hauled ass toward the east. *WHUMP! SPLASH!* The road was a sea, and its contours invisible. I had swamped the jeep. With four-wheel-drive, four geysers of brown mud rose whenever I gunned it. No motion. The frame was on a high spot, all four wheels suspended in midair and muddy water. It would not move. Only one answer. I grabbed my rifle and helmet and jumped clear. I would have to walk in and get a wrecker. I started trudging eastward, eyes peeled for any movement. Charley. Snakes. That damn black panther. Anything.

"Sarge, I got good news and bad news. The good news is, your fuckin' guard tower is fixed. The bad news is, your jeep is hung up out there, restin' on the frame. All four wheels hangin' in puddles. We'll need a wrecker to get it."

"Awwww, shit!"

"Yeah. You know, you got a real way with words!"

We had a new wrecker operator, a Tennessee country bumpkin who had never had shoes 'til the army, and Sarge summoned him. In his gangling way, "Hill William" resembled a marionette. He had volunteered for The Nam and had been adding his peculiar brand of color to our muddy existence less than three weeks. Already, we knew his family history and had learned to love his naïveté but loathe his devotion to the army. "Mah great-gran day-uddy done served with Gener-al Lee, mah greay-un day-uddy done rode up Say-un Joo-ann Hill, an' mah day-uddy got shot at D-Day, an' you can steel see the place on he-is leg! Now, the army done gave me all them nahce clothes an' all them boots an' shoes, an' pay me a real fine salary, an' if they want me to haul trucks out the mud in Veee-Yet Naaam, I be most proud to help 'em."

William wanted to "go fetch the li'l feller rot quick-like," but I slowed him down to talk about the situation. A lot of elements combined to make this a risky operation. A Cong could easily creep up to the stranded jeep and booby-trap it while I was gone. Seeing it loaded with the welding gear, Charley knew we would be back for it. The rain would make it easy to plant a mine on the path and would wash away the evidence in a few minutes. "If you see any freshly dug dirt, stop immediately. When we get to the jeep, I'll cover you while you hook up to it, 'cause it's heavy grass and there's apt to be a sniper. Once the chain's on, and you're back in the truck, I'll get in the jeep. Pull me off the mud, I'll throw the chain in the jeep, and we run for the compound as fast as that thing will go, understand? Don't stop for anything! There's a chance Charley has stuck a satchel charge up under a fender somewhere. If I go bang-o, you don't stop. Just get back in the wire. Understand? You won't be able to help me, and you'll be a sitting duck.

"Now, when we get there, and you're getting the chain, I'm going to look around the jeep. If you see a string, or any footprint that doesn't match mine, you holler, okay? They take an American grenade, pull the pin, and hold the spoon down with a rubber band. Then they drop it down the gas filler (on army vehicles there is about a four-inch gas filler so they can be filled from a jerry can), and when the gas dissolves the rubber band, your lights go out. If you see anything, or hear anything, or *anything*, you holler. I'm too fuckin' short to start with, and I don't want to go home with my pant legs rolled up to my knees. Understand?"

Charley must have had an off day. I was a bundle of nerves, but our expedition was uneventful. Sarge had his jeep back and the guard tower was fixed. I tilted up a bottle of Scotch, and Hill William thought I was exaggerating. It was a great relief to fall into bed. Forty-six more days. I started low and built up volume until my voice could be heard throughout the mildewed hootches. "Shoooooooooort!" From the distance, other voices responded. "Seventeen!" "Thirty-three!" "Six and a wake-up!

Can you fuckin' lifers stop by in the morning and lift me outta the rack? My legs don't reach the floor anymore!" "You think six is short, lifer? Try two an' a wake-up!" "My wife don't believe me when I say I'm short! She's too used to seein' nine inches of a real man!" "Yeah, I bet she'll sure miss him when you get home!"

• • • •

Archie's day arrived in early August. We went to the air force club for "one for the road" and spent the morning drinking and reminiscing. We had been together for nearly two years, from basic at Fort Dix through Aberdeen Proving Grounds and now this. In a few hours we would shake hands and Archie would board a plane, and we might never see one another again. You learn a lot about a person sharing an experience like Vietnam with him. We had become confidants, confessors, morale boosters. We were friends. Once again, something precious was being taken away. We drank far too much, then returned to the compound. Archie had to make noon formation before riding to Camp Holloway. We stood at attention under the Vietnamese sun. I was drunk. Suddenly I went foggy and fell over onto my back, rolled onto my side, and vomited into the mud. The sergeant, of course, did not consider this proper military behavior. I remember the sickness, the heat, the sarge screaming over me, and Archie pleading on my behalf. I was allowed to shower and change and to shake my buddy's hand one last time, then I had to go to work the rest of the day.

Less than thirty days to go. I was holding my breath, waiting for the minutes to become hours and the hours to form days. Every round from Artillery Hill made my skin erupt in cold goosebumps. I jumped when someone closed a book or opened a beer. You don't get used to the terror. I doubted I would live for the four weeks. We had moved to the new barracks, unfamiliar surroundings. I was sleeping when the overhead *hissss* cut through the drumming of rain upon our tin roof. Before I could react, the explosion ignited a panicked race for our trenches. This was it! Ol' Archie had escaped just in time. I had my gear carefully laid out and was one of the first out the door. The alert siren moaned, gained intensity until it squeezed my head. *HISSsss. BAWOOM!* It was raining rockets at the new tank farm, but there were explosions and small-arms fire behind us as well. Golden flares lit the fog and drizzle, reflected off the drops on my glasses. There was a lot of commotion behind us. Too much. Word came that sappers were inside our compound, on the west perimeter near parts supply. Inside the wire. My chest pounded; I could hear the pulses of blood coursing through my temples. Yes, this was it. Eleven months of waiting, of fear so all-encompassing you cried out in your sleep; and tonight Charley was inside and something was going to happen. I would never see home, or Penang, or Thailand. Gawd, a Viet Cong might be crouching between my trench, here in the rain, and the hootch. It might be that I would never see even a photograph of home again. The explosions were thunder now, close enough that I smelled the explosive on the wind. My mind raced back to an eighteen-acre hillside in upstate New York. I had run to every corner of that field; now I stored my life in a small green footlocker and to venture toward it tonight might cost me my life. I was trapped. The incessant rain trickled off my helmet, and my body turned cold and gritty. It was too enormous. Whatever would happen would happen. God, I was tired.

The golden mist of flickering flare-light faded into gray. The explosions died away first, then the rattle of automatic weapons. Choppers beat the air, Artillery Hill roared. The gray became translucent, then dawn. The trench was a pit of slime. I wondered if my shaking was caused by the chill or the terror.

I wondered how I could bear thirty more nights. At 6:00 A.M. the all clear sounded. There was a full inspection at ten. No excuse for wet gear or mud. No excuse for a scratchy cheek or a dirty fingernail. A few yards away bodies were being loaded into trucks. Four GIs had been wounded and seven VC killed. The satchel charges had done heavy damage to our parts supply, but the rockets had missed the tank farm. No harm done; life went on.

Twenty-eight days. How can you describe terror? Adrenaline makes your body electric, but you are terribly aware of its limitations and shortcomings. Your blood thunders in its travels, your eyes ache from strain, your hair becomes acutely sensitive. Time stands still. A moment is forever, but forever may never be. Terror includes desperation, and you claw for escape.

Twenty-seven days. Escape? After three hundred and thirty-eight days of terror, you don't really believe the end is approaching. Fear has been convulsing you from the inside out for so long it has become normal. There is no other way to be. Letters from home or a can of beer may take your attention for a few moments. Your buddies sense that it's getting to you and force a laugh. R and R should be a vacation, but the awful knowledge you're going back is terrorizing in itself.

Twenty-six days. The rains have formed puddles again. You think back to a boy who drowned. The rats are especially noisy tonight. Is that chopper lingering, has he spotted impending doom? Your mouth is dry, you feel the tension in the taut cords on the sides of your neck. You're going to the bathroom, bare thighs resting upon splintered plywood. Someone tosses a rock onto the tin roof, and you scream. They laugh. You shake and cry.

Twenty-five days. A letter from home. Please come home. You try to find words. You are clawing for escape, bloodying your knees and pushing mud up under your nails. It really doesn't matter where you go, as long as you get out of here!

Will they understand? How could they? How dare they think this letter is strange? How else do people react to this pressure? How dare they blame marijuana? Once in a while you have to escape, even if your body remains and only your brain escapes. You don't smoke when there's a real danger. You don't even drink beer or take a pain pill for your back for fear it might take an edge off you that you will need to stay alive.

Twenty-four days. Dak To was clobbered last night. Charley appears to be building another offensive. Oh, God, I can't take that again. You've smoked three packs of Marlboros today, and it is only 9:00 P.M. There is a scream forming inside, building.

Then there are twenty-three days, and a convoy to Dak To has been hit, and they need a wrecker to haul in a corpse of a truck. Please not me! Fuck it! There is a second ambush, the noise crashes into your ears until it forms surreal patterns. You wander among the dead like a tourist, notice the grotesque, obscene positions. The bodies thrust forward at their pelvises in one final, improper gesture of defiance. You lose that one last, critical brain cell. Fuck it! We're all going to die. Dying is escape, and escape has become total obsession.

Three weeks. Eternity. Two weeks. Each breath uses time, brings escape closer. Maybe, just maybe, I might make it? Can't afford to be careless. Details. So few of the guys around me understand. The ones who understood made it; but there's no guarantee.

A week. "On the three hundred and sixty-fifth day," the legend goes, "God created the Freedom Bird." I have a piece of paper, orders to Thailand. I read it again and again. I'm going to start the rest of my life. I've got to get my act together.

Four days. A clipboard of papers, to be signed by this officer, that sergeant. A last trip to the air force club. A silent toast to Archie. I happen upon a *Playboy* magazine at the PX. Is that a hint of pubic hair? I suppose the weirdos will protest, want it banned. Pornography! I wish I could tell them my definition of obscenity. Soon I'll be lifting Lin's skirt, sliding my palms into her panties, pushing them down over her thighs. Some of those righteous old farts would think I should be proud of my time in The Nam and repentant about kissing a woman's breast. How would I deal with that?

Three days. I'm so short I've packed my shadow for fear I might lose it. There are no thoughts of the future; I can't comprehend a world without Artillery Hill.

Two days. In the morning I'll fly to Saigon. Tomorrow night I'll eat dinner in Thailand. I should walk around, take a last look at this place, but I don't want to get that far away from my helmet and flak jacket. What's to see? My luck, I'd drown in a puddle. Fuck this place. I don't even want to eat, for fear of being caught unaware. I almost begrudge the time spent packing; I should be concentrating upon the sounds, the first warnings. I sit in the darkened hootch. Christ, these new guys think this is a hootch. They should've lived in the tents. Those were hootches! I swear, I'll never sleep in a tent again, as long as I live. I shouldn't have had so many beers. I should try to rest.

● ● ● ●

On the morning of the three hundred and sixty-fifth day I made formation, ate powdered eggs at the mess hall, and signed a book in the office, then shook hands all around. I hefted my duffel bag and guitar into the back of a deuce-and-a-half and climbed aboard. I had a picture of Lin in my breast pocket. The truck rumbled to life, bounced across the mud. There was a pause at the guard shack. We lurched into motion, rolled straight toward Artillery Hill, turned right. Off the right side of the truck a huge steel barn was silhouetted against the gray Cambodian hills. I watched the road ahead. We rolled toward Camp Holloway, and I never looked back. My eyes were searching for a grenade from the brush, or a dog with explosive sewn into its belly.

The flight to Saigon was uneventful, save the pounding of the blood in my temples. I was nervous, excited. I felt like a kid on Christmas morning at the top of the stairs, about to investigate a world of fantasies come true. I was leaving The Nam today! Short? I didn't even have a wake-up! Just step on the Bird and be whisked away. So many had bled here, or died here, or suffered here. I was going to make it. I was about to survive Vietnam without a scratch! A few burned-out brain cells, but none of my blood in the Vietnamese earth. Short was waiting to board the plane.

At Tan Son Nhut, I went to the army desk and told an overweight sergeant I needed a flight to Bangkok. I presented my orders and expected to be whisked up a red carpet to the waiting plane. I was so short I was counting time in minutes. In the truest army tradition, there was no plane. Flights to Bangkok left from the civilian terminal. I wandered over there, lugging my heavy gear through the stifling heat and humidity. A sea of Vietnamese swirled around the terminal as I made my way to another overweight sergeant behind another paper-strewn desk. The stucco building with its glass front facing the airstrip was stifling. The sarge looked at my orders, shuffled through his papers, and announced that there were no flights to Bangkok scheduled that day. I would have to wait.

For three hundred and sixty-five long days I had waited for this moment, and the world had been tumbled down around my ears. Instead of mere moments, I would have to sit and swelter and wait for the army to get its act together. The most solemn of agreements, the time required in The Nam, had been violated, and there was nothing I could do about it. So long as I was wearing this uniform the army reserved the right to do with me as they pleased. Like a robot, I was required to do their bidding regardless of right or wrong, common sense, human decency, or written agreement. The army held the power of life and death. Through this overweight, slovenly sergeant, the army exercised its power. Short? It wasn't a military term.

The shadows grew long inside that Tan Son Nhut terminal. The swarms of bustling Vietnamese with their rotten-fish odors and woven bamboo baskets of produce began to ebb. I was hunched in a corner to the left of the entrance, within easy shouting distance of the perspiring sergeant's chaotic desk. The heat was so intense it had mass, banging against every pore with bone-wearying force. My jungle fatigues were wet and sticky, and I could smell myself. I had commandeered a bench, a simple two-inch-by-twelve-inch slab of dark wood on two verticals, and leaned my duffle bag into the corner as a backrest. I leaned the guitar carefully against it, then settled back with my feet up to wait and watch. Passing time. Perspiration hesitated at my eyebrows, then drained into my eyes in a blinding, stinging torrent. My chest dripped onto my belly each time I leaned forward. My hair lay like a heavy wet cap. I had watched the comings and goings all day, the tearful Vietnamese maidens in their graceful *ao dai* dresses slit to the waist, watching ARVN troops go off to war, and fashionable businessmen in three-piece suits, clutching leather briefcases, hurrying to conclude some financial transaction. I enjoyed the children, out of their element, hot and uncomfortable, clinging to their mothers' thighs. The majority of players on my small stage were peasants, poorly dressed, spitting scarlet betel nuts on the floor, shuffling by with hopeless shoulders hunched against the horrors of life in the midst of a great war. I was hot and hungry and uncomfortable; I felt betrayed, but I saw a flicker of purpose in these people.

Perhaps, in spite of all I had known for the past twelve months, perhaps there was good here. Perhaps these people needed the blood of American boys to fertilize their ground, that a brighter tomorrow might grow. I wanted to believe it, but I thought back to Ohio in a bunker in Dak To, and to the sounds of rockets crashing upon us during Tet. I remembered the barber, who had seen so many kindnesses at American hands and had died in the barbed wire trying to kill us. I thought of Shitburner, of the pain in his eyes. I watched an ARVN guard in camouflage jungle fatigues trying to make time with a pretty young Vietnamese girl, strutting and thrusting his rifle to make his points. Where the hell had he been the night the gooks hit us with our own shells? Why wasn't he out in the bush, instead of some kid from Tennessee with a wife and kid waiting at home? I knew the answer. If somebody stepped on a stick and it cracked, this strutting warrior would throw his rifle in the mud and run home. And if he didn't care about his country, why should we? War had been Vietnam's history, as war would be Vietnam's destiny. There was no hope for peace, only a resolve to make the best of it. To a peasant, the most to be hoped for was food for a starving child. To a worker, there were the tons of incoming supplies to plunder and sell on the black market. If that cost the peasant child a meal, both parties accepted the fact without remorse. The Vietnamese had long ago abandoned compassion. Above the workers, the wheeler-dealers plundered at a larger scale, the Army of the Republic of Vietnam at an even greater scale, and the government most of all. Perhaps, I thought, if war came to America it would be the same. But war had not come to America. America had come to war. Back in The World, our families were hearing about military successes and a poor, downtrodden people striving to be free. Surely, accomplishment of freedom for the downtrodden was a goal as lofty as the quest for the Holy Grail. That these people didn't care was immaterial. We were in Vietnam for our own good. To be made men. To protect our mothers from the creeping Communist menace. To pump up the economy. A fly flew into my eye, flapping and fighting to get free. I slapped at it, knocking it to the filthy floor. I squashed it with my boot, heard the tiny crunch. For our own good! To be crushed like flies. There would always be war in Vietnam, there would always be flies in Vietnam. And, for our own good, there were going to be a lot of Americans here for a long, long time.

The flow of Vietnamese stopped. The sergeant gathered his papers and cleared his desk. "Sarge!" I called impatiently after him as he started to amble away. "What's happening? I need to eat, and I need a plane to Bangkok. You aren't gonna leave, are you?"

"Listen, boy, it's 6:30, and there ain't gonna be no plane to Bangkok today. You've processed out of here, so there ain't no way the army can feed ya. You're gonna have to wait and find a meal where ya can. I'll be back tomorrow at 7:00. Make yourself comfortable." He turned and walked away. The last of the Vietnamese ticket agents were straightening up their papers and hustling out the door. The strutting guard was gone. The shadows were longer, the interior of the dark building growing faint. To the rear, I heard a voice speaking English. I hurried down the hall to an area painted in the familiar army pale green. A sergeant and a spec 4 were tidying up a tiny office. I explained my problem. The sarge could care less, but the spec 4 told me to hang on a few minutes and he would get me something to eat. The lifer issued a few terse orders, ignored me completely, and hurried off.

The spec 4 grinned and held out his hand. "Franklin. Chicago. Where's your shit? Leave it here, and you'll never see it again." I hauled it from the deserted terminal, and he placed it gingerly in the crowded office and snapped a padlock on the door. "C'mon." he nodded toward the dark hallway. "Dinner is now being served in the main dining room." He led me through a maze of wooden buildings, down alleys, across a wide parking lot. "Don't worry 'bout the sarge. He's got a shack-up and don't like to be late. He's a lifer, but he'll take care of ya. Fucker knows everybody on this damn post. In the morning he'll be in first, and see your stuff, and keep an eye on it for you." We burst into a crowded mess hall, with both army and air force personnel. I was surprised to find real milk and took three glasses. We settled down to eat. Franklin had been infantry, in the Ashau Valley, and couldn't take it. He had extended six months to get his duty here, processing in replacements. He had over a year to go but figured his chances of surviving were good. Better than in the bush. Charley dropped rockets on the airstrip every night, but nobody ever seemed to get hurt. After our meal, he showed me to a shower, then led me back to the deserted terminal. "Sarge'll be in about 6:30," he said. "Be here. There aren't many flights to Bangkok. Be ready, and don't let anybody forget you. See you in the morning."

"Hey, uh, Franklin?"

"Yeah?"

"Somebody's missing something here. Where the hell am I supposed to sleep?"

"You mean nobody told ya? Here! Shit, man, you just did a year in The Nam. You've slept in worse places than this!"

"Awww, shit! I'm supposed to be in Bangkok, R-n-R city, with booze and broads and here I am, in a fuckin' gook airport, smelling raw fish and trying to make myself comfortable on a wooden bench. Fucking army! My fucking year is up!" I was hollering at the top of my lungs, to no one in particular. "Three hundred and sixty-five days they said, and I been there three hundred and sixty-five fuckin' days, and I'll sue the motherfuckers for breach of fuckin' contract!" I felt better just getting it out of my system. I turned to Franklin, hoping for a little understanding. "You know, this just ain't right. My time is up. There aren't any more squares on my calendar, man. Most important fuckin' day of my life, and the army screwed it up. It just ain't right!"

Franklin knew as well as I how things went in the army. "You been here a year, right? You seen anything in that whole fuckin' year you'd say was right? I'd let ya bunk with us, but the chickenshit outfit I'm in would court-martial both of us. I'll get your stuff outta the office, maybe you can make yourself comfortable. In the morning I'll watch it for ya while ya get some breakfast. Think of it this way. Your last night in The Nam, and you hate the fuckin' army more 'n ever! Would ya really want it any other way?" He grinned.

"Franklin, you gotta admit one thing. Minus one is SHORT!"

"Yeah."

Franklin left, and I sat in the dim light watching the airport bustling with activity. I smoked a few cigarettes, thinking about home, and Lin, and what a pleasure it would be to fly out of this screwed-up place. I pushed a bunch of wooden benches together to make a sleeping platform, folded my field jacket into a pillow, and tossed a last cigarette onto the filthy floor. I offered up a single finger salute to the army and stretched out on my hard and uneven bed. Fuck it!

I was fatigued. It had been an eventful day, an emotional day, and the heat and boredom had drained me. I fell asleep easily. Suddenly, I was awake and scrambling, disorganized. *Boom. Boom-boom! Ba-Voom! BA-VOOM!* Explosions lit the room, shook the floor. An alert siren rose to a ghostly wail. I was awake now, aware of where I was. There was no place to go. If I crept outside to a bunker somebody might see me and mistake me for a sapper. I crawled in under the benches, under my heavy duffle bag, close to the wall. I lay in the stinking rubble, the sound of explosions shaking the walls of my chest. My heart pounded. My eyes teared. "God damn, you guys, I'm too fucking short for this shit!" No small-arms fire, must be just a rocket attack, no sappers. I lit a Marlboro, dragged at it with a passion. VA-ROOM! A patch of ceiling plaster crashed to the floor near me, causing me to jump and bang my head on the roof of my feeble shelter. Damn! Then there was silence. Total, unbelievable silence. Was it over? I heard aircraft screaming down the runway. I flipped the cigarette away, reached for my jacket.

Might as well make myself comfortable. In a few minutes I was asleep, huddled under a half-dozen wooden benches, on the floor of the Tan Son Nhut air terminal.

Something hard struck my arm, and I was awake and in motion all at once, without direction. My eyes opened to the sight of a little old wrinkled gook, prodding me with a long stick. To my bleary eyes it was a bayonet, and I was about to become a prisoner. Not without a fucking fight! I jumped to my knees, benches and clothing tumbling in every direction, blinking against the light to find some escape, some way out. The door! The weight on my back kept me crouched, scrambling, fighting for that door. I heard a noise, a long anguished cry, and suddenly realized it came from my own lips. At that same instant, I also realized where I was, and that the old gook was far too feeble to hurt me, and that the bayonet was a push broom. The janitor had bumped me with his broom. He had jumped back, startled to the edge of a coronary at the animal that had exploded out of this lair. We stopped mid-motion, staring at each other. I grinned, realized what had happened. He showed no reaction, turned, and went on with his sweeping.

At the ticket windows, three young Vietnamese in white shirts stared in disbelief, then looked away to shuffling papers when my eyes turned their way. I was embarrassed, and just a little sore from numerous collisions with the heavy wooden benches that had blocked my escape. I busied myself setting the benches back on their feet, stuffing clothes back into my duffle bag. I turned back toward the counter to find everyone staring again. I bumped the heel of my hand against my temple, and grinned. *"Dinky-dow! Dinky-dow!* Crazy!" They grinned and went back to their papers. The old man turned and grinned a toothless acceptance. *"Dinky-dow!"* He echoed me and shook his head. I was still collecting myself when Franklin arrived. I put my bag in his office and headed for breakfast.

I was standing in line, smelling coffee, when someone tapped my shoulder. "Hey, Troop! You're out of uniform!"

I turned to face a stocky little sergeant in a drill inspector's Smokey the Bear hat. His fatigues were razor-sharp, his belt buckle glistened, and the strap from the hat settled into a crease in his double chin.

"I said you're out of uniform!" His eyes were cold, nasty.

"Well, Sarge, I'm held over at the terminal, waiting for a plane to Bangkok, and my sleep was kinda disrupted last night, and I just need something to eat."

"What unit you with?"

"Well, Sarge, I don't really have a unit. See, I processed out, my year is up, but they don't have a plane to take me to Thailand, so I'm just kinda betwixt and between."

"Lemme see your orders!"

"All my stuff's over in the terminal. I just ran over here to get a bite to eat."

"Son, I'm gonna give you some good advice. Number one, you are a soldier in the United States Army and are expected to wear the uniform of the United States Army at all times. Do I make myself clear?"

"Very!" I was losing my temper.

"Yes, Sergeant!" He was enjoying this. His chest swelled.

It was very quiet. We were providing entertainment for breakfast. I wanted to tell him to stick his stripes where they'd do the most good, but I couldn't blow it now. I decided to humor him. "Yes, Sergeant."

"Can you read, boy?" Oh, he was a rare one. What the hell had I done to deserve this?

"I can read, Sergeant."

"The sign out front says this mess serves Company C, First Battalion. Are you in Company C, First Battalion, boy?"

"Sergeant, with all due respect, I don't know where the Christ I am. I was supposed to get out of this stinkin' country yesterday, and the highly efficient United States Army can't find me a plane. I slept on the floor, I listened to a bunch of rockets land outside the door, and I came over here for a cup of coffee. Now, I am painfully aware that I am in the United States Army. I'm very, very aware of that! And I seem to recall a recruiter promising three square meals a day, among other things that seemed to get real negotiable about the time I raised my right hand and repeated after him. Now, if you don't want me to drink your coffee, just say so. I'll try to be quiet and not lead any of these guys astray, but I would be very, very grateful if you would allow me to eat my last meal in Vietnam in your mess hall!"

The entire mess hall was frozen, listening. "Eat your meal, wise guy, and get on your plane and get outta here. If I see you back here I'll see your ass in a sling! Do I make myself clear?"

"Yes, Sergeant!" And with more than a touch of sarcasm, I added, "Thank you, Sergeant!" He turned on his heel and strutted away, confident he had done his day's duty for God and country. As I ate, a thousand eyes watched me. I knew all too well the life these guys must be leading. There was only a swallow of coffee left. I got to my feet, raised the plastic mug in a parody of a toast. It was quiet again. "Here's to Company C, First Battalion!" I bellowed. "And here's to three hundred and sixty-six days in The Nam, and here's to the plane that's gonna take me outta here today!" A cheer went up as I walked out.

I spent three hundred and seventy days in Vietnam. For five days I sat at Tan Son Nhut, sweltering and waiting. Franklin brought me meals. No sense taking chances with the crazy lifer. I didn't take showers. I smoked endless cigarettes and watched the new replacements come in. They were just kids, scared, tense. Had I been like that? It seemed so long ago.

I was dozing when the big moment finally arrived. Charley had dropped rockets every single night since I had been there. I stacked the wooden benches every night and crawled under them, up close to the wall. It was uncomfortable, but I was determined to get out of this place. During the day I wrote letters, prevailing upon Franklin to mail them. I watched the Vietnamese civilians, and I napped. I was napping when a hand on my shoulder shook me awake. "How bad you wanna go to Bangkok?"

It was a warrant officer. "Bad! Real bad, sir."

"We've got a load of mail. You'd have to lay on your belly on the mail sacks. You wanna go?"

I got my guitar from Franklin, shook his hand, and wished him well. How could I thank him? The warrant officer and his copilot were in a jeep at the door. I hoisted my gear into the back and hung on for dear life. The Vietnamese driver raced across the tarmac to a tiny, olive-drab, single-engine plane. Hardly the Freedom Bird I had imagined, but if it would get me out of The Nam it would be just fine. We squeezed my gear into the back, on top of a sea of gray mail sacks, and I crawled back into the fuselage. There was almost no room, and my head was scant inches behind the two pilots, and slightly above them. At the end of the takeoff strip they gunned the engine and shouted "Hold on!" The thrust threatened to push my horizontal frame out the tail. There was a bump, and we were airborne. I strained to catch a last glimpse of Vietnam. I had survived.

• • • •

American Tune

Many's the time I've been mistaken
And many times confused.
Yes, and I've often felt forsaken
And certainly misused.
But I'm all right, I'm all right.
I'm just weary to my bones.
Still, you don't expect to be
Bright and bon vivant

So far away from home,
So far away from home.
And I don't know a soul who's not been battered.
I don't have a friend who feels at ease.
I don't know a dream that's not been shattered
Or driven to its knees.
But it's all right, it's all right
For we've lived so well so long.
Still, when I think of the road
We're traveling on
I wonder what's gone wrong.

And I dreamed I was dying...

—Paul Simon
Copyright 1973 Paul Simon

Thailand and The World

"Our brave young men are dying in the swamps of Southeast Asia. Which of them might have written a poem? Which of them might have cured cancer? Which of them might have played in a World Series or given us the gift of laughter from the stage or helped build a bridge or a university? Which of them would have taught a child to read? It is our responsibility to let these men live….It is indecent if they die because of the empty vanity of their country.

Do you suppose that ten years from now we will all look back and wonder how the American people ever went so far with something so terrible?

—Robert F. Kennedy, 1968

As we landed in Bangkok, I was struck by the patterned terrain: square green rice paddies divided the land geometrically; tiny hovels of weathered wood lined the white sand streets, their corrugated metal roofs reflecting the hot Southeast Asian sun. The terminal building I watched as we taxied was typical, gray concrete walls with square windows. The reality of my flight out of The Nam had been disappointingly uneventful compared to my anticipations. I was unshaven, unwashed, and uncomfortable. I had dreamed of overwhelming joy and relief. Instead, I felt tired and dirty and apprehensive. I was, after all, going to another army post. I dragged myself out of the plane, retrieved my luggage, and stretched in the familiar heat.

The warrant officer pilot grinned widely and shook my hand. "Congratulations! Welcome to Thailand! You're gonna like it here." During the flight, he had talked about the differences between The Nam and Thailand and had urged me to talk about my experiences. I liked him immensely, but I didn't want to think about them, let alone talk about them. He was probably in his early thirties; tall, strong, and confident. There was a very unmilitary shock of sandy hair and a flamboyant handlebar mustache that reminded me of an Old West gun-fighter. Despite his formidable physical size, he had been kind and soft-spoken, and incredibly enthusiastic about Thailand. I was welcoming of his reassurance.

Inside, the terminal was unlike anything I had experienced in Vietnam. It fairly swelled with people: Orientals, and a surprising number of round-eyes. There was no fear in their faces. Overhead, brightly lighted signs advertised the logos of the world's great airlines, once familiar, now exotic. In a corner, I found an army counter and another overweight sergeant. I handed him my orders.

"Saigon, eh?" His eyebrows arched. "How long were you there?"

"A year and five days."

"Got a lot of time to go?"

"Fifteen months."

"Well, son, you'll be awful glad you decided to do it here. This is the nicest place in the world to be in Uncle Sam's o.d. green army. Nobody'll fuck with you here, and you'll get three months early out and be back in The World in no time."

"You get an early out here? Really?" I was incredulous. In The Nam, if your tour ended within ninety days of the end of your term of service, the army processed you out and sent you home to stay. I hadn't dreamed that they would do the same thing in Thailand. If that was true, my remaining time would be shortened by 20 percent, and I would never have to serve on a base in the States! When I went home from here, it would be as a civilian.

"Sure! Look, I won't have a plane to Korat 'til about eight o'clock tonight. Nothin' personal, but you look like hell. Why don't you try to get cleaned up a little and crawl over here somewhere and get some shuteye? I got your seat reserved, and I'll see to it you get on the plane…"

He was interrupted by the warrant officer who had just

flown me out of Saigon. "Sarge, I got some time, and I thought I'd take my man here on a quick sightseein' tour, get him a shave and a bath and a decent meal. That okay with the army?"

"Sure! Just get him back by quarter to eight, and don't get him a dose of nothin'. Leave your guitar with me, son, and you won't have to lug it around. You got some fresh clothes in your bag?" His smile was warm, kind.

"Well, Sarge, they were washed in The Nam, but they're a hell of a lot cleaner than what I've got on."

"Take your bag and get yourself cleaned up so's you'll make a good first impression when you check in to your unit tonight. And, son, I meant what I said. You're gonna like Thailand. I came here from The Nam, too. You relax. You've done the hard part. The next year's gonna be fun!"

My warrant officer hefted my duffle bag to his shoulder and nodded toward the door. We waded into the sea of swirling humanity. My mind raced. How 'bout that? Not only was I going to get out of the army early, I had an officer carrying my luggage through the airport. I had *arrived!*

He tossed my duffle bag into a topless jeep and motioned me to the passenger's seat. The tires squeaked as we catapulted into motion. The sun beat down without mercy, but the rushing wind was slightly cooler. We roared down a wide concrete boulevard, past the familiar stucco houses. The roofs were notable, steeper, with long, shady overhangs at each end. The people were familiar, and yet imperceptibly different. The styles of clothing were different, more colorful, with frequent Western touches like jeans and T-shirts. Tiny Japanese cars and trucks were, for me, an exotic change from the dilapidated and ancient French relics of The Nam. The houses were arranged in neighborhood colonies around open courtyards, and flowers and tropical plants were landscaped; a small difference, but a sign of tranquillity. Still, many brown teakwood shops with corrugated roofs crowded the very edges of the road, and naked children with black hair and dark eyes played with the simplest of toys. Graceful palms swayed above broadleaf plants, motorbikes blatted, and it was obvious I was still in Southeast Asia. As we turned off the main road and wound through clusters of poorer shanties, I began to grow nervous.

"Uhh, aren't we getting a little off the beaten path?" I was on edge, expecting a grenade or a quick burst of small-arms fire, and feeling very naked without a weapon, flak jacket, or helmet. The warrant officer grinned.

"You aren't in Vietnam anymore. It's safer here than your hometown. Relax and enjoy. We're almost there."

I sat quietly. I was hot, windblown, uncomfortable. I hadn't had a shower in four days, and my lower lip felt sparkling to my tongue where it hadn't been shaved. I struggled to convince myself I was out of The Nam, in Thailand, and this was the first day of the rest of my life. I was in the company of an officer, an unheard-of treat, and he obviously knew where he was going. If he was this casual, it must be all right.

But it wasn't. I was sweating. My eyes bored into every shadow, every dark corner. I analyzed each person, watching for weapons, waiting for the explosion. Relax? It was out of the question. Typical officer! Didn't even have sense enough to be scared.

We turned up a narrow alley. Jesus, this guy is really nuts! A quick left, and we scrunched to a stop in the midst of a small compound, surrounded by the weathered teak single-story houses with broad porches facing the courtyard. There were banana trees and flowers, and a tiny church on a pedestal, decorated with patches of gold and red and white and blue, and the twisted remains of joss sticks long ago burned. My officer hefted my heavy bag and nodded toward an open door. "C'mon."

We mounted the porch, and I looked around one last, nervous time before I followed him into the dark interior. There was a formica-and-chrome dinette set with a vase of flowers to our left, and a bed to our right. On the bed, a woman slept. The officer roused her, in her own language. Vietnamese was a short, punctuated, chattering language; Thai was more singsong and flowing. I heard "Vietnam" in the unintelligible torrent and the girl's eyes turned to me. She questioned, he answered, and I stood in the middle of the room feeling very conspicuous.

The girl smiled. She was probably in her early twenties, and pretty, with large dark eyes. She wore a T-shirt and a bright cotton print wraparound skirt. She handed us cold beers from the tiny refrigerator, then quietly worked at twisting her long black hair into a bun. I held the cold beer bottle, afraid of ground glass. The warrant officer noticed my delay.

"The beer, too?"

I jumped. "Yeah. They put ground glass in it, or inject poison through the cap with a hypodermic syringe."

He opened the bottle, took a long swallow, then paused a minute with his eyes rolled up and his arms outstretched. Slowly and purposefully, he opened his lips and burped. He broke the pose and handed me the bottle with a merry grin. "It's okay."

I swallowed, and it was good. The girl came back from the room, said something to my friend, and he grinned. "Get some fresh clothes. Su-Nee is gonna clean you up and make you presentable when you check in to your new unit tonight."

My eyes must have been wide. "Yeah, that's right," the warrant officer said, grinning. The handlebar mustache made him look more like a Mexican bandido than ever. "She's gonna give you a bath, and a shampoo, and a shave. She's my *tee-loc*, my girlfriend, and there's no sex involved, but you need a bath, and Su-Nee knows how to make a man feel like a king. You've been out of The Nam a couple hours, you had a bunch of bad days, and, well, I guess this is just my way of saying I appreciate what you guys are going through over there." He tipped the top of his beer bottle my way in a small salute and grinned again. "Listen. This ain't Vietnam. This girl is excited. It is a great honor for her. Her brother is with the Queen's Cobras in the delta. You need to learn to relax and enjoy this country, and this is the way it is here. Nobody's gonna hurt you, the war is over. C'mon, man, enjoy!"

I was stumbling, uneasy, confused. The warrant officer rose out of his chair, set my duffel bag squarely in front of me, and sat back down. "Get your clothes and your razor," he instructed, reading my mind. "Go back in the back, and she'll tell you every move. Just sit back and enjoy. I'll be right here. When your beer goes dry, holler, and I'll bring you a fresh one."

Why not? I needed a shave and a shower. I dove into the bag. The girl smiled and went to the rear door. I gathered a change of clothes, razor, shave cream, and comb, swallowed more beer, and tipped the top of the bottle toward this unbelievable character. He smiled, winked, and gestured toward the waiting door.

Still a little unsure of myself, I went to the door. There was a concrete patio, about twelve feet wide and eight deep. This end had a tin roof reaching to the six-foot wooden fence that surrounded us. About half the area was open, and there were large, broadleaf plants and smaller decorative shrubs in an orderly garden arrangement at the far end. A drain spout led down the cabin wall to empty into a huge dark brown earthen jar. A plastic hose dangled from a faucet, and there was a tiny three-legged stool and a heavy wooden bench. Over the open wall at the far end, I could see distant palms.

The girl was kneeling near the large jar, arranging her utensils. She smiled when she saw me and rose. "Come." She motioned me toward her. She took the clothes and laid them carefully on the bench. She took the razor, shave cream, and soap, then put them near the jar. I didn't know how I was supposed to act, so I just stood, feeling dumb. She stood again, grinning. "Take off clothes," she ordered, and I blushed and started unbuttoning my shirt. To my surprise, she knelt at my feet and started unlacing my boots. I had to break the suspense, to make myself comfortable.

"You speak English?" I couldn't think of anything more profound given the situation. She looked up, smiling, and held her thumb and forefinger close to each other. "*Nit-noi.*"

"*Nit-noi.*" I echoed. "Little bit?" I mimicked her hand sign.

"Little bit." She answered, returning to the boots. I had my shirt and T-shirt off now and was wondering where I should go next. In answer, she pushed me back onto the bench. As she worked the boots and sweaty socks off my feet, she tried to make conversation. "You go Vietnam, eh?" The damp cement felt cool to my feet. My boots and heavy wool socks hadn't been off in four days. I was relaxing a little. If this pretty lady wanted to pamper me a little, who was I to argue? "Yes," I answered. "But no more! No more go Vietnam." She smiled. There was understanding in her eyes.

"No more. One year? You one year Vietnam?" She was unbuckling my belt. "Yes, one year."

"Stand up." She was kneeling in front of me, unbuttoning my fly. Damn! She slid the trousers down, worked the elastic blousing bands over my feet, removed the pants. I was in my o.d. green jockey shorts, with a beautiful girl slowly stripping me. I was becoming excited, and when she slid the shorts down she noticed. "Ahh, *tsk-tsk-tsk.*" She looked away, shyly, and wrapped a towel around my waist. I could feel the blush heating my cheeks again. She pointed to the tiny three-legged stool. "Sit here."

I perched on the stool, trying to figure out how to arrange my long legs and the towel to allow some modesty. The warrant officer had specifically said, "No sex!" and I wasn't about to get him mad. The girl knelt beside me, with a small aluminum bowl and my shaving gear. She took a washcloth out of the bowl and wrapped it around my chin. It was hot. She lathered me and began with the razor. Against four day's growth, it pulled and I winced. As she worked, she told me her brother was a Queen's Cobra. (Later I would learn that the Queen's Cobras were a Thai military group fighting alongside the GIs in the Mekong Delta. Unlike the ARVN, the Queen's Cobras were brave and efficient.) This girl was a craftsman, shaving my chin, the back of my neck, my ears, even shaping my eyebrows. She tried to speak to me, and I tried to understand and make conversation. She was charming, and gentle, and very pretty. She laid the hot washcloth over my chin, wiping away the shave cream. Next, she shampooed my tangled hair. The water was cool this time, dipped from the big jar. I jumped, and shivered, and she giggled. When she rinsed my hair, I jumped again. It was probably a hundred degrees, and the cold water was startling. She shampooed me again and then rinsed my hair. With a washcloth, she tenderly washed my face twice, caressing and stroking the skin under my eyes. She dipped the aluminum bowl into the jar, her eyes mischievous. She motioned toward my body. "Okay?" I grinned. What the hell! I nodded. Okay!

The water hit me like a frozen wave. She splashed me four or five times, then began sudsing my back. She went on to my chest and arms, lifting each arm to scrub the underarm. I wondered how she would handle the area under the towel, but she bent to my feet and legs. The moment of truth was fast approaching. "Stand up," she said, and took the towel away. She was behind me, working on my bottom and thighs. I was embarrassed, excited. She moved to the front, and my hands tried to cover me. She giggled and pushed them away, and began working the soap over me. I was straining. She cooled things down with the bowl of cold water, then turned on the plastic hose to rinse me all over. She toweled me dry, paying particular attention between each toe, then helped me into my fresh clothes. I sat on the stool while she combed my hair and even cleaned my fingernails. Back inside the tiny house, the warrant officer pushed a cold beer into my hand. I tried to thank him, but he would have none of it.

"Look," he said, "I've seen a lot of guys come back to the States from The Nam. Most of them are all screwed up, and in the States nobody gives a shit. You don't know how lucky you are to be here. You've got a year to relax and get your head in shape. You'll love Thailand. Get the fear out, relax, enjoy yourself. Get a girl. They call a shackup a *tee-loc*. Get one. The sex is good, but, well, you can see. The fringe benefits are outta this world!" I agreed. "Thirty bucks a month. You believe that? Thirty bucks a month gets me this house, and Su-Nee. Get yourself a bungalow and a sweet young thing; eat their food, drink their beer. It's heaven on earth, and you earned it. Enjoy!" Su-Nee brought food, a rice, egg, and meat mixture on a banana leaf I would later learn to call *cow-pot*. It was delicious, and I ate it with a real enthusiasm. I could feel the tight knots unraveling. I thanked the girl profusely, and we threw my bag into the jeep for the return trip. I had to catch a plane. Korat, according to the warrant officer, was a large city in an agricultural area. People would be simple, hardworking peasants. The pace would be slow and natural, just what I needed. Get downtown, he urged. Dig it! Tourists flocked to Thailand, and I would have a year, free of charge, to explore to my heart's content. Forget Vietnam, it was past. Enjoy today.

I was refreshed. I had nothing to offer in thanks but feeble words. At the airport, the sarge approved of my appearance. I gathered up my guitar and boarded a familiar C-130 to Korat. It was a strange flight, with too many recollections of my trip to Saigon. A jeep met me at the air base. As we rode to the new unit, I noticed carefully manicured lawns and elaborate floral displays. I signed in, and the night staff was immensely hospitable.

• • • •

I was escorted to the barracks, my new home. I was aghast! Tile floors. Flush toilets. Magazines. A TV set. Everyone was casual and relaxed. More laughter than I had heard in months. The sarge suggested I sleep late, then come over to the office to process in. Sleep late? Overhead fans stirred a soft breeze. I stripped and sat in the middle of the shower room, letting eight streams of water embrace me from every direction. I leaped to my feet, laughing hysterically, and rushed down the line of toilets flushing one after another. Back to the showers, then another flush raid. I laughed and gurgled like an infant. The occupants peeked around corners, fascinated. I toweled and dressed. They were watching. Hell, I'll give them a show! I shouted at full strength, "Anybody know where I can get ice cream? Show me ice cream and I'll buy for everybody!" They came out of the woodwork. Somebody said I could get ice cream at the club. Where the hell is the club? I offered to buy the second time, and several of them scattered, looking for shoes. In a few moments my exuberant little band of merry men bustled out the front door. No puddles to drown in here; we followed a carefully edged and landscaped sidewalk between flowers and shrubs. The club was only a few hundred yards away, a giant building. We entered at the bar, a horseshoe-shaped expanse of polished wood, red button-tufted vinyl, and brass lamps, about fifty feet long, crowded with laughing men. We swept right into a cavernous room, mostly turquoise, but dark and noisy. At the far end, a band played on stage, highlighted by pink spotlights. Between us, at least a hundred wooden tables sat in order, crowded, their turquoise-and-white checkered tablecloths covered in the center with candles, salt and pepper shakers, sugar and napkin dispensers. Chrome lids reflected the lights. Damn! We found two tables, pushed them together, settled in. Another round of introductions and hand-shaking. We were loud. Fuck it! I was delirious. I couldn't believe this place. A pretty Oriental girl in turquoise uniform with a white apron brought menus. I flipped out. Pizza. Hamburgers. Steak. Ice cream. Milk shakes. Wow! I'll have a hamburger, a chocolate shake, and a banana split!

Everybody ordered. The questions started. Where were you at in Vietnam? Is it really as bad as they say it is? Did you ever see a Viet Cong? Did you kill any?

"Wait a minute! Look, you guys, last night and four nights before that, I was sleeping on the floor under wooden benches, listening to rockets land outside and scared shitless. I was five days late gettin' out of The Nam, and they were hard days. All of a sudden I look around and find myself here, and I just ordered a hamburger and a banana split! I don't want to be weird or anything, but I don't want to talk about Vietnam, or think about Vietnam. It's kinda hard to explain. I was in Pleiku and Dak To, I never killed anybody; thank God I never had to do that. I saw Viet Cong, I saw a lot of real bad shit. I don't know what you've heard, I've been out of touch for a while. I was there, and I survived, and now I just want to enjoy a little."

There was a pregnant pause, and nobody wanted to look at me. I had to break the spell, be one of the guys. "All right! C'mon you guys. This is a fuckin'-A *party*! If I'm buying, you can at least cheer up."

The girl arrived with a tray loaded with the wonders of modern science and technology. I stood up to get a better look. Damn! She put my hamburger down, with a bottle of catsup. The mood was improving, as everybody tried to sort out hot fudge sundaes and banana splits. I poured catsup onto the burger 'til it rolled off onto the little white paper plate with the side of pickle. I crammed it into my mouth, and I chewed, and

I enjoyed. A huge wave of emotion swept me away, and I started to cry like a baby. The quiet returned. Fuck it. I ate, and I drank, and I cried. They ate and watched. I decided to play it straight, let them in on all the emotion I was feeling. I cleared my mouth, dried my eye. "You gotta understand," I blurted out, "I really didn't think I'd ever order a hamburger again." Silence. "It just feels awful good, you know?" They looked at me, but nobody said anything. How could they know? My party wasn't working out. I dug into the banana split, scooping huge spoonfuls of the delicious mess into my mouth. Pretty soon it was gone, and they were done, and we quietly headed back toward the barracks. I had a million questions. Were you ever hit? Did they issue rifles? If we got hit tonight, where did we go? How could they not know? Up by that fence? The Thai army would protect us if anything happened? Did that work? No shit?

In the light of the barracks, everyone began to prepare for bed. I tried the flush toilets again and drank from the water cooler. Damn! Cold water! They slept in jockey shorts. I hadn't slept without my pants and boots in months. Tonight I would sleep in just my undershorts. Somebody turned off the lights. I lay in the darkness, listening. No artillery. No choppers. No flares popping. It was silent, except for a distant rock 'n' roll record and the soft whirring of the fans. Too quiet. Much too quiet. What a hell of a day! I tossed. Much too quiet.

Sometime during the night I fell into a deep sleep. It had been an eventful and emotional few days. Tired bone and tissue melted into clean white linen and transported me to a land far away. I floated on an indefinite cloud.

Boom! Lights flashed. The roar of a masculine voice. I sprang to my feet, crashed into a dark object head high, recoiled without bearings or direction, felt my unaccustomed nakedness, spun and crashed again. I was frantic. Bumping, banging, screaming, fighting for survival, with no place to go.

Confused, disoriented, I saw but one escape. I tore the familiar dark green bedding and mattress toward my pounding chest, flattened on the floor, covering myself with the mattress's protective weight. Where am I? A hand stretches toward me, helps me to my feet. I've got it. Thailand. This is Thailand, my new unit, Korat.

"You okay?"

I connect the sound to the speaker. "Yeah! Yeah, I guess so." I'm still a little amazed to find myself here. "What was that?"

"Wake-up. Every morning they slam the door, turn on the lights, and holler. It's six o'clock. Formation's at seven."

Damn! There's a twisted tangle of bedding clutching at my ankles. The faces are concerned, laughing. Depends on where you look.

"You sure you're all right?"

I sat on the mattress on the floor, rubbing my eyes, shaking. Yeah. Yeah, I'm all right. I think I'm fine! Let me get my bearings, and I'll be fine. Thailand. Somebody waking us up. The army. It slowly fits together. Just a wake-up. Damn! I started to laugh. The concerned faces broke into grins. Yeah. Yeah, I'm fine.

"You were supposed to sleep in this morning."

Now I'm laughing hysterically. "Yeah, I was trying, when I was so rudely interrupted."

Breakfast was an adventure. The food wasn't powdered. We ate at tables, not plywood benches. There were napkins, and chrome-topped dispensers. There was soft music, not sounds of artillery or helicopters. A meal here was a pleasure, not just a necessary refueling stop.

Seven o'clock. Formation. I followed everyone outside like a puppy dog, fit myself into line. There was no sergeant for our platoon, just a spec 5. I was surprised at the number of guys and what appeared to be their youth. The formation was breaking up, and the specialist suggested I take the day to get processed in. The others marched off to work, leaving me alone on the crushed gravel field behind the barracks. A flock of housegirls arrived. I went back to my bunk, sorted my orders.

One of the tiny housegirls came forward, asked if I would be staying. "Give me laundry and boots. Three dollars every payday." I dug out the rottenest batch of filthy clothes the poor little girl would ever see. She smiled and gathered it all up, tucked my boots under her arm, and trotted off. In a few minutes she was back. "You go to Vietnam, GI?" Yes. "How long?" One year. "Oh. Vietnam number ten." (The Thais rated things from "Number One," excellent, to "Number Ten," undesirable). Yes. She returned to work.

The office was housed in a low building. The grass wasn't doing well, but I was amazed by a gravel parking lot in front. White two-by-two posts supported a black chain along each side of the sidewalk. Inside, an air conditioner hummed, and papers threatened to squeeze out the people. What a reception! The first sergeant offered a mug of coffee, and the company commander, a young captain, came out of his office to shake my hand. My papers were added to the various stacks. Like a reunion of old friends, the questions were casual and laid-back. A few of my papers had to go to offices on the other side of the post. A pfc was ordered to drive me over there. When we returned, I went to supply and drew new jungle fatigues and boots. I was issued a rifle, another M-14, and helmet, but they would be kept in the armory. By noon, my chores completed, I was told to take the rest of the day to get settled. They pointed out the PX, the movie theater, the swimming pool, and the club, and suggested I just relax and enjoy myself there. I was beginning to think I could manage that. I piled my new wardrobe into my locker and headed for the PX.

The PX on Artillery Hill had been a small shanty with unpredictable supplies of rationed necessities. This was a department store with no limits, no ration cards, and a fantasy selection of chromed or brightly packaged luxuries. I investigated the wonders like a bee scurrying from bloom to bloom. Through the day, I flitted gloriously between the PX, the barracks, the swimming pool, the mess hall, and the club.

Finally, I fell into bed, bloated from overindulgence. My mind journeyed back to Pleiku. It was 9:30. Artillery Hill would be bombarding Cambodia, shaking the table with every round. Guys would be sloshing across the sea of mud, balancing on the precarious two-by-fours, hoping for hot water at the showers. The guards would be trying to tuck their ponchos around them to keep the wind-driven rain from trickling down their backs. Would Charley try to blow the new tank farm again tonight? Was Ohio in a sandbagged trench? How could I justify a belly swollen with ice cream while that was going on? How could I sleep, feeling the swelling of my gut and knowing any one of those guys would pay fifty bucks for a slice of hot pepperoni pizza? I was ashamed, saddened at my disregard for others. Some guys would die in the mud and never see ice cream again; I had eaten two banana splits today. What right did I have to be acting like this while somewhere in The World a heartbroken mother was explaining to the kids that Daddy wasn't coming home anymore? How very goddamn wonderful! Fascinated by a flush toilet! In the morning I would crawl into canvas jungle boots and o.d. green army fatigues with my name stitched across the breast and wait for permission to eat. I could have been home on the couch, watching Johnny Carson and raiding the refrigerator. All I had really accomplished was to return to day 364. A "fuck-you" lizard shouted in the distance, and a Phantom jet roared overhead on its way to Hanoi.

I dreamed I was a Ping-Pong ball. Generals and colonels and majors were standing in the surf, throwing balls into the surging ocean with fanatical determination. Army Intelligence and Air Force Weather had told them the time was right. Orders had come down: float a thousand Ping-Pong balls across the Pacific. According to their calculations, about 3 percent might make it. I was one of a half-million hollow white spheres at the mercy of the tides. If one thousand reached California, the order would have been obeyed. Thousands would leak. Sink, or blown off course. Devoured by sharks, or crushed by military ships in the dark. The lifers didn't care; they tossed the balls with careless abandon.

I dreamed of a photograph in a local paper. I saw a Ping-Pong ball in an army uniform, photographed from the waist up because the trousers didn't fit. I saw an elaborate description of the training the hollow ball received. His parents were proud and fulfilled, and patriotic as hell. Now, cast adrift in threatening seas, the brass turned their back on him and strutted for the cameras. One thousand Ping-Pong balls had washed ashore in California; victory was its own justification.

I was at the mercy of tides and currents, wind, and predatory monsters. Now I had floated up onto the beach and gasped for breath. I heard the voice echoing from afar, another order; another thousand balls. I knew I was helpless, and I knew I was expendable. Every five-and-ten-cent store in America had hundreds of balls like me. A giant hand lifted me out of the sand and tossed me into the surf again.

• • • •

As the days went by, I adjusted. Every day I felt more at home, more comfortable in my new surroundings. Two weeks had passed, then three. The guys badgered me to go downtown after work, but I couldn't bring myself to go to town at night. I shied away from shadows on post and did not trust myself downtown. The guys didn't understand, and I didn't care. I just didn't want to go, and I felt that was my right.

Work was fun. When I had arrived, the warrant officer in charge had watched me a few days, then called me into the office to talk. There was no platoon sergeant, although no one wanted to talk about that. Spec 5 Hennesy was the ranking member, but not leadership material. I had been welding, and if I put in the proper paperwork my army job category could be officially changed to welder. As soon as that was accomplished, I could be suggested for promotion. A welder could be promoted to sergeant E-5, not specialist, which would make me the platoon sergeant. It was never put into words, but the impression was definitely that my combat experience made me more qualified to lead men. I signed the papers to change the job classification. I liked welding. I was not interested in a military career, but if the army wanted to give me a raise I would take it.

The change of job classification came back approved almost immediately. It seemed the army really wanted to woo me, and I was leery. In the back of my mind I knew I couldn't expect any favors. Now I was the only official welder. The promotion paperwork was submitted. I thought it was just another step in the promotion process when the warrant officer and I were summoned to a meeting at headquarters.

We were ushered into the captain's office, and the door was closed. Now I was scared. Had I done something wrong? Everyone was cordial, cheerful. I was on guard. They wanted something. It started with compliments. Next came a round of questions about my experience in Vietnam. I didn't want to talk about that. Well, was I familiar with 105-millimeter self-propelled howitzers? Yes. They had a problem. When fired, the cast aluminum body and fuel tank cracked from the impact of the barrel's recoil. The well where the barrel recoiled would fill with fuel, and firing the gun again often set it on fire. This, of course, gave Charley a fine target. The fix was to extinguish the blaze, bail out the fuel, sop it up with rags, and weld the crack. The problem was, the welding glow was a better target than the fuel fire.

According to this meeting, firebases in "the north" were having that exact problem. Since I was officially the welder, the army needed me to fix a couple guns from time to time. I asked if I would be under fire. Well, they couldn't rule out the possibility. This was a guerilla action, and anything was possible. Of course, with my experience, it wouldn't be anything I hadn't seen before. I pointed out that I had absolutely no desire to see it again. I really didn't have a choice, and I was to treat this as a "classified" conversation. It was not to be mentioned in letters home. Oh, by the way, my date to go before the promotion board would be in late November. As the meeting broke up, I felt the sickening fear rising inside me, but there was no further mention for a few days and my comfortable surroundings took my mind off the whole affair.

One afternoon the warrant officer invited me to go for a ride. He unlocked a corrugated metal garage and showed me a three-quarter-ton army truck with full-arc welding equipment. In the side toolboxes there was a shiny new aluminum-welding outfit. The truck had no markings. I was told to draw a new set of jungle fatigues and sew no insignia on them. If I should be ordered to go out to one of these guns, I should wear the unmarked fatigues and take nothing with me that might contain my name, address, unit, etc. I was beginning to sense that this was more sinister than I had been told. No wallet, no dog tags, no letters from home, nothing. They even asked me if I had any tattoos.

Meanwhile, my everyday existence was anything but threatening. I worked with two young Thais, laughing and joking and learning their language. At break times we converged at a small soda stand where two Thai girls sold soda pop and candy. It was a comfortable, relaxed place, and the girls tutored us all in our feeble attempts to learn the Thai language. They were such happy people, perfectly contented with life. I began to be intrigued, to want to learn more. I agreed to go downtown with a few of the guys.

At the end of work we showered and ate dinner, then caught a bus for downtown. Thai buses were incredible machines, festooned with myriad colored lights and chrome doodads inside. Decals and stickers vied with religious trinkets and colorful vinyl leis, Christmas lights, and pastel paints to create a surreal surrounding. The seats were narrow, and the leg room was nonexistent. These gaudy cattlecars were manned by teams of two, a driver and a ticket taker. Ticket takers could have moonlighted as tightrope walkers, and the drivers as stuntmen. The buses were equipped with only two positions, stop and go. Nothing in between. There was no limit to the number of human beings that could be crammed inside, regardless of whether their basic proportions in any way fit the contours of the packaging. There is but one traffic law in Thailand. At an intersection, the driver who blows his horn first has the right of way. A Thai bus driver leans on the horn button a full half-mile before an intersection, then, at full speed, depends upon the steering wheel to deal with emergencies. Brakes are to be used only for stopping. To the driver's credit, accidents are rare. But when they happen, they take on the appearance of a massacre.

At the end of the day, the Thais went home, and we returned to the barracks. Most of the guys went downtown every night. I went occasionally, but it was discomforting. The dark bars, thundering music, explosions of colored light, and bar girls were too reminiscent of The Nam. I wrote letters, ate burgers and ice cream at the club, watched movies. I hadn't written to Carolynn or the girls in Cincinnati; they were too closely tied to the person I had become in Vietnam, a person I no longer wanted to be. I was, of course, waiting to visit Lin, and the long days apart from her were a torment in their own way. I was closer in miles, but still separated by my army "duty." I had applied for a leave to Malaysia but could not go until November. Meanwhile, the other GIs wanted to hear about Vietnam, and I didn't want to talk about it. They didn't understand my questions about life in The World. They were unable to see that I needed reassurance that the assassinations and protests had not plunged America into a second civil war. Most of them had left home only a few months ago. I had been away a lifetime, had seen things they could never imagine, and they couldn't appreciate my apprehension and confusion.

My emotions cycled without warning. Day by day I relaxed and melted into friendships with my colleagues, both American and Thai. The sun was warm and the skies were blue, and we were doing fine quality work. Our work area became known for the close cooperation between ourselves and our Thai employees, and an atmosphere of friendliness and good cheer. We laughed, struggled with each other's language, and sampled foreign food and drink. They explained customs and holidays; we described cowboys and freeways.

I struggled to put The Nam out of my mind. I was usually successful during the day, unless a flight of fighters roared overhead on their way to Hanoi or the radio brought news of more battles. I chose magazines carefully, trying to avoid the bloody pictures that were everywhere now. I shunned TV and read only the comic pages of newspapers. Awake, I could tune it out and deal with it, but the war ravaged my nights.

I dreamed I was bringing my family up the porch steps. It was sunny, a crisp autumn day with the aroma of burned leaves in the air. Lin was hesitant about meeting my family, but I was swelling with pride. In spite of mountains of paperwork and red tape we were together, home, and about to start the rest of our lives. We paused on the porch. She checked the baby, our son, and I kissed her cheek and pushed the doorbell. Mom and Dad exploded out the door. There were embraces, tears, kisses. I was eager to show them my greatest achievement in life. "I want you to meet your grandson!" I said; then I gently lifted the blanket back, and the most beautiful thing I'd ever seen had been transformed by napalm into a bubbled and black monster with an arm melted across its chest.

And yet, sometimes I was almost homesick for The Nam. Life had been pure there. Simpler. You had to do things correctly or you wouldn't survive. You ignored the most horrendous flaws of character in your buddies. All that mattered was survival, everyone's survival, and that pressure created a close-knit society without room for petty bigotry or prejudices. Now, here, the blacks assaulted the whites with loud soul music, daring some "honkey muthafucka" to say something. There were black-power closed-fist salutes and complaints that too many "brothers" were getting wasted in The Nam. What did they know about "brothers"? Over there, we were all "brothers." When you're so scared you piss yourself, skin color doesn't matter much. You need the guy next to you, and survival becomes the only real value in all of life. Why couldn't everyone see the simple truth in that?

The entire post was excited; a new movie was coming to the theater. John Wayne starring in *The Green Berets*! I didn't want to go, but my friends insisted that it might do me good. They wore their jungle fatigues and jungle boots and I wore civies, and we joined the lines in front of the theater. In their fatigues, under the same tropical sun with the F-104s screaming overhead, they were almost a part of the war. After all the training classes and orientation meetings, the rhetoric and the "Go Army!" signs, they wanted to know what The Nam was really like. *The Green Berets* was absurd. Lots of helicopters and sandbags, a few Oriental kids and a booby trap. But where was the filth, the stink, the open garbage piles swarming with flies, the beggars? Where was the fear? No one in that movie was afraid. The Vietnamese were so polite and grateful, and the GIs were a bunch of good ol' boys on a turkey shoot. The gooks didn't look Vietnamese; they were fat and nourished, and there was no hurt or anger in their eyes. Then the camp was attacked by a faceless human wave, and it brought back all my deepest fears. Late that night I was able to calm myself and fall asleep on my bunk, but someone slammed the door, and I screamed and hurled myself and my mattress to the cold tile floor.

I lay on the floor, peering out from under the mattress and bedding, whimpering like a scared puppy, heart pounding, trying to chase away hordes of ghosts in black pajamas. A voice mocked me from the darkness. "Big fucking war hero! Scared shitless when somebody slams a door!" I recognized the voice, a kid who wanted to be a tough guy. Still, it hurt. I wanted to cry out, "Leave me alone," but the barracks was silent now. They were all waiting to see what the freak would do next. I put the bunk back together and pulled on my jeans, grabbed my cigarettes and Scotch, and went out to sit on the back steps. I was terribly alone. A lot of horrible demons lived in my head, and sometimes they crept out when I wasn't prepared. Why couldn't people understand, or care? If I let a little of the pain out I was a jerk, and if I tried to hold it all inside I'd explode. Was I going crazy? Had I already gone? Just when things seemed to be getting better, I would have a bad night. I had been out of The Nam forty-five days. How long would this last?

• • • •

I was sitting out back one night when a guy named Jake wandered up and said, "Ever smoke any grass in The Nam?" and offered a joint. We got a little high, and talked, and went to his barracks to listen to his stereo and drink a Coke. There were six of us, and we became friends. Jake said I should meet Digger, and everyone agreed. Digger was a local legend, but would be going home soon. The stereo played "Inna-Gadda-Da-Vida," and we journeyed to the club for banana splits. There was no further mention of Vietnam. We talked about music, the army, Korat, and the fine grass in Thailand. I was still scared of Korat at night. I explained my fears without going into detail. Jake asked if I had seen any of Korat beyond the honky-tonk strip? No, I admitted I hadn't. I agreed to visit Digger with him, the following evening.

We took a bus. It was easier this time. We went far beyond the honky-tonks, deeper into the city, and by the light of the moon I saw graceful temples beneath gently swaying palms, and stately houses beyond ornate walls and gates, with cars in the driveways and the familiar steel-blue glow of the television from the windows.

We were in another world when we got off the bus. There were no Americans, no beggars, no hawkers. It was a city street, bustling with activity, but exotic and not menacing. I was surprised at my lack of fear. Jake spoke to a *samlaw*, a bicycle-rickshaw driver, and we got in and headed even deeper into the city. Around a corner, and there were no streetlights, just dark shadows of houses and alleys. Now the fear was coming, my mouth was dry, and I was on the alert. I took some comfort from Jake, crammed into the seat beside me, casually carrying on a conversation with our driver in Thai. We stopped, got out, and Jake paid. Down a dark and narrow alley that made my skin crawl, left into an invisible doorway, and up a flight of wooden steps. At the top there was a door, and Jake's knock was answered by a pretty Thai girl in the familiar T-shirt and cotton wraparound. They exchanged a few pleasantries in Thai, and it was obvious she was glad to see him. As I followed Jake into the light, she joined her palms as if in prayer, bowed, and wished me a warm hello in Thai. I had learned this much, and responded, and she smiled and waved me deeper into the house.

Digger rose from his book and chair to greet us in a southern drawl. He was tall, and thin, with curly hair the color of the weathered teakwood walls, and round glasses. He wore a T-shirt and army fatigue pants, with rubber flip-flops. Hardly the stuff of which legends are made, I thought, but a warm and animated character who seemed easy to like. I was introduced to the girl, who seemed distressed at the lack of groceries. It wasn't groceries she was searching for, however, and in a few moments we bustled back out the door, down the stairs and through the alley en route to a place Jake and Digger spoke of reverently as "Granny's." A *samlaw* appeared from nowhere, then a second. I rode with Jake, following Digger through the dark streets. I told myself it was all right, but the wetness at my underarms felt cold against my ribs. We bumped our way across an ornate white stucco bridge, dashed across to the opposite shoulder of a four-lane highway, then dropped off down a dark hole into the undergrowth. I was totally panicked now, but Jake reminded me, "This ain't The Nam, man. It's cool. Dig it!" and as he said it, we burst out of the bush into a silver fantasyland.

It was a warm, clear summer evening, the kind of evening when kids back in The World stretch out on the grass and look at the stars and tell ghost stories or talk about sex. The moon was full, giving everything a soft, silvery glow. It was probably seventy degrees, not hot, not humid, just comfortable. As we scrunched up a gravel path I drew a deep breath and whispered to Jake, "It's unreal, like something Walt Disney would do. Is this what I think it is?"

He answered in a whisper, possibly as a safety measure, but I took it as reverence. "It sure is! A Buddhist cemetary. You ever seen anything like this?"

On both sides, concrete obelisks reached toward the moon, creating a miniature city beneath a splintered canopy of palm boughs. There were stone columns, with tiny flickering candles or smoking joss sticks. In the moonlight, I could see blood-red silk buntings on some stones, embroidered with strange characters or flowers or Thai lettering, the embroidery thread glittering like faded gold. It was totally still. The scent of the joss sticks filled the tunnel with sweetness. The only sounds were the insects, and the constant rush of our tires over the fine gravel. We lurched around a huge pine, up a steeper, bumpier path, down and across a wooden bridge to a tiny house on stilts. There were no electric lights, but candles on the porch cast a warm and inviting glow.

Up the stairs, a heavy old mama-san spoke to Digger, raised her voice to the inside, then eagerly bid us welcome. I joined the others, still a little uneasy. Up the stairs, across the porch, through the door into a dark room that appeared to be a warehouse. Couldn't miss that scent anywhere. There must have been two tons of grass in that room! Digger negotiated in Thai, while a wrinkled papa-san sitting crosslegged on the floor offered us a huge joint. Wow! Very nice stuff, smooth, no seeds popping. Digger called for financial aid. I kicked in a few bucks, no more than three. Everyone took a big hit off the huge joint and hurried outside. Digger paused to speak Thai to Mama-san, then she threw her arms around his neck and kissed him. Our *samlaws* waited patiently, and I noticed that the one Jake and I had ridden now had a series of multicolored lights, like tiny Christmas tree lights, across the rear of the passenger bucket. Had they been there before? Funny, I hadn't noticed them.

We moved forward, slowly, bumping over rocks. I gazed across a silent pond, its surface mirroring the dark swaying palm trees and the huge golden moon. Beautiful! Graceful, stately, tranquil; I searched for a word to describe the scene and there was none. I felt mellow, loose. No fear, no anxiety, just awesome peace and quiet and beauty. And a friend. Jake whispered, "You okay?"

"Okay?" I answered. "I haven't been this okay in a long time!"

Our strange little caravan bumped through the city, now quiet; the stores had closed. We handed a few coins to the *samlaws*, hurried down the alley, up the stairs, into "Digger's hole." The girl had Cokes and cookies. I hadn't noticed how dry my mouth was. Digger had a shopping bag, and he emptied the contents onto newspaper spread on the floor. As he cleaned the shriveled weed, it was obvious this was a craftsman at work. With a giant butcher knife he cut and recut the leaves. I watched the bright blade dance across the cutting board until the crackling leaves had been reduced to a pile of olive-drab powder. No seeds, no husks, no stems, just clean marijuana.

As he cut, Digger and Jake spun a wondrous tale. Digger was an Arkansas farm boy, drafted, and a clerk-typist. He had worked in battalion headquarters and had chanced upon a plot in which some of the highest-ups were selling jeeps and trucks to the black market in Bangkok and declaring them unserviceable and salvaged. They found out he knew. One day they sent him to the post office and asked him to stop by the mess hall on his way back to get coffee. He mailed the letters, got the coffee, and returned to the office unaware of the ordeal waiting for him there. A classified envelope was missing, and he had been seen carrying it out with the mail. He had mailed all the envelopes. A phone call to the post office, and a long wait for a reply. The phone rang. It wasn't there. Where was it? He didn't know what they meant. MPs arrived. Was he selling classified information? The mess hall sergeant swore he had had it at the time he got the coffee.

He was court-martialed and sentenced to fifteen years' hard labor at Leavenworth. He appealed. His mother and her lawyer sent him legal books, he acted as his own lawyer, and won! He motioned to the vast library behind him. Incredible. How had he done it? His answer was clear. "Stoned! I just got stoned and freaked on the books. I knew I was set up, and there had to be a way out." It had taken over a year and a half, and his two years had become three, but that was a lot better than fifteen.

We were smoking now, eating cookies and drinking Cokes,

and I was spellbound. He was awaiting orders to go home and process out. And he was accepted to law school!

Wow! But there was more. Digger looked at me, his eyes sparkling. "You don't have a platoon sergeant. Do you know why?" Nobody had wanted to talk about it. "Right. Your old sarge's name was Ramirez, and he was in it up to his ears, but the real bigwigs decided this was too good for a low-level sergeant, so they just kind of dealt him out, double-crossed him. He threatened to spill his guts, and a couple weeks ago he was heading on post on his motorcycle, and somebody stretched a piano wire across the road, and Sergeant Ramirez lost his head over the whole thing! They were stupid, though. They had hired a couple Thais, and they did it on post. They got held up at the gate, got scared, and admitted what they had done. That was at 6:00 A.M., and by two that afternoon the colonel and the major were on the plane back to the States!"

It was incredible. "You mean," I asked, "they paid the Thais to waste the sarge?"

"That's the common opinion," Jake answered. "They weren't around long enough for anybody to ask too many questions. You gotta wonder what kind of connections they had, to get out of there so quick. Think about it. Somebody's going to notice when thirty or forty trucks just vanish. If some MP brass is in on it, he can cover it up. And when Ramirez shows up dead, he'd be the first to know. So his buddies go home right now, 'for their own protection.'"

Digger turned on a reel-to-reel tape recorder, and we got lost in the cookies and the cold drinks and the guitar. We smoked some more, and it was time for Jake and me to go back on post. It was the only time I would ever meet Digger, who went home and probably became a lawyer.

The day he left, Jake brought me a gift from Digger. It was wrapped in newspaper. In black ink neatly lettered, I read a short message. "Think good thoughts. Digger."

• • • •

There was something symbolic, almost religious, about smoking Digger's stuff. He had beaten the army system. Lifers, intent upon gaining power and wealth, had considered him expendable. But Digger had burrowed into his books, put his mind to it, and survived. He was a hero in Korat, a fine and comfortable place. In my mind, haunted by ghosts of dump trucks heaped with the bodies of American expendables, he was a shining star of hope in the ominous night sky. I hoarded that collection of crumpled leaves, savoring the R and R effect it had on my scarred brain cells. Digger survived, and I felt transfused by his mental capacities. More than the pain of memories, the smoke clouded the realities of everyday life in the crankcase of the great olive-drab machine.

• • • •

The World waited to see if Hubert Humphrey or Richard Nixon would be president. I waited to see Lin. In the meantime, I was growing accustomed to my new workplace.

We had a machine stop inside a metal box mounted on the rear of a deuce-and-a-half. The machinist was a quiet Swede. When repair parts weren't available through supply channels, he fabricated them. He could carve a block of metal into a gear for the elevating mechanism of a howitzer or a freeze plug for a truck engine, or a decorative swagger stick for an officer. The new colonel appreciated the swagger sticks more than the mechanical parts. He ordered one after another as gifts for visiting officers and dignitaries. Johannsen couldn't keep up with the demand. He was working sixteen-hour days and being ordered to let mechanical parts wait while he fabricated swagger sticks. Ego massage for the lifers had higher priority than critical parts that might save a man's life.

Along with the welding and machine shops, we also had wrecker service for all of Thailand north of Bangkok, and we repaired glass, shoes and boots, canvas, and radiators. We were supposed to have fifty men, but operated with fewer than forty. We had a half-dozen Thai employees and occasionally a trainee from the Thai army. It was constant chaos in two languages, but we laughed at the chaos, worked together in spite of the languages, and produced an unprecedented quantity and quality of work.

My boss was a warrant officer named Smithfield. Warrant officers were the class of the Vietnam-era army, granted officer privileges because their particular technical skills "warranted" something special. Their insignia were bars, similar to a lieutenant's, but with brown stripes.

The hard-line officers, the lieutenants, captains, and majors, had graduated form West Point or ROTC or Officer Candidate School. They had been mind-raped by courses in military history, theory, and obedience. These were the corporate climbers of the New Frontier and the Great Society, and they didn't want anyone to forget it. Theirs was an awesome responsibility. Since time began, man had documented the atrocities he has perpetrated against his brother. Today we have war colleges to teach military science. With Armageddon a button's touch away, the authority of a career military officer is overwhelming. In order to keep Armageddon at bay, everything must be "by the book."

The warrant officers, having learned their crafts in the "real world," got the job done. All too often they found it necessary to relax the irrelevant portions of "the book," and the career officers found it blasphemous. Smithfield fought for us. He was a warm, soft-spoken man. He assumed I would soon be the platoon sergeant and groomed me. As we pored over the inevitable avalanche of paperwork, he often pushed the thin strands of hair across his balding scalp as if bewildered. He was a kind man, concerned about his people. He agonized over Johannsen and the swagger sticks. To provoke the colonel could jeopardize his own retirement. He was concerned for his wife's future. Finally, he requested an audience with the colonel, explained the situation, and was disappointed at the pompous lack of what he called "realistic priorities." He shut the office door and helped Johannsen draft a letter to his senator.

• • • •

I was beginning to go downtown more often, each visit inspiring a bit more confidence. Thailand is exotic and sensuous. The women are petite, with dark eyes and friendly smiles. I dreamed of Lin, but I ached for a woman. I discovered massage parlors. My favorite reminded me of a turn-of-the-century bordello, the kind you see in Western movies. The walls were covered in red-and-gold brocade wallpaper, and the windows in heavy silk drapes. There was a restaurant and lounge with black wrought iron tables and scented candles. The girls sat behind a huge one-way glass, sewing, watching TV, or conversing. An attendant in a tuxedo kept a book of each girl's special "talents" and the girl put down her embroidery and stepped through a curtain. You met in a hallway where she bowed, smiled, and led you upstairs to a room. The lights were dimmed, and scented candles gave a sense of soft sensuality. While you undressed, she filled the bathtub. Again, scented oils tantalized the senses. The water was hot, but you soon relaxed. She shampooed your hair, drew firm fingers from the forehead to the shoulder, stretching the scalp and soothing the mind. You grew drowsy. She rubbed fragrant soap into your body, spending time on each finger and toe. She cleaned your nails, clipped or filed them if need be. All too soon she pulled the stopper, rinsed you, and toweled you dry.

Then you lay on the table, on your belly, and she demurely

laid a towel across your backside. These girls were trained like chiropractors, and she pushed, poked, prodded, twisted, and stroked each bone and muscle into place. Her fingers could be tender, stroking just the tips of the hairs on your thighs, or harsh, her palms pushing wayward vertebrae against each other until you cried out. Soft music and the scents of exotic candles and oils took your mind away, and I often imagined I was a Roman emperor. With you on your back now, she found sensations at your breasts only a woman could know, then stretched and prodded your navel 'til it tingled deep into your belly. She pulled each toe 'til it cracked, rearranged the bones in the sole of your foot, forced calcium deposits out of the ankle joints. She did the same to your arms, then returned to your forehead, eyelids, and cheeks. (One girl actually cracked my ears.) She returned to your feet—you were lazy and limp now—and moved slowly upward. Suddenly you realized that her hands were under the towel. She was an artist, painting mountains and valleys 'til you plummeted back to earth. She washed your belly with hot towels, patted it dry, and powdered you 'til your time was up. She helped you into your clothes, knelt to tie your shoes, combed your hair, and cleaned your glasses. It was a physical caress, but it seemed mental somehow. In the hallway she bowed and thanked you, and by the time you returned to the lounge she was already engrossed in her embroidery. Five dollars, no threat of disease, and I told myself I was single and far from home and Lin would understand.

• • • •

As the trip to Malaysia approached, I bought a diamond ring at the PX and sent it to Penang, accompanied by a many-page letter of promises and dreams. So much had happened in six months. I hadn't really believed that I would ever return. In spite of Pleiku, Dak To, Saigon, Tan Son Nhut, the United

States Army, and Thailand, not to mention my family's misgivings, in spite of everything I was coming back to Lin. Surely she would appreciate all of that and know my promises for the future would also come true.

The day came at last, and I stumbled through, bus to taxi, taxi to the railway. I was nervous, but I wanted to see the country and meet the people. Obviously, not many Americans had felt the same. I was an instant celebrity, and armed with my English-Thai dictionary, I chatted and was rewarded for my efforts at international understanding with a feast of shared food and drink. The locomotive was a steamer, belching a great cloud of black soot that entered the windows and darkened faces and clothes. We rolled through hundreds of tiny hamlets, rising from the rice paddies like oases of humanity. Someone must have wired ahead that this train contained a special celebrity, for children lined the tracks and cried, *"Felong! Felong!"* A *felong* is a white guy, and the people on the train said many of these kids had probably never seen a *felong*. The conductor made a point of coming by to tell me each time we approached a village of any size, and I waved to the kids as they jumped up and down and clapped their hands in glee. A lot of parents had come too, wrapped in their colorful cotton clothing to protect them from the unrelenting sun. They waved and pointed me out to the kids, their faces smiling and friendly. Within the confines of the railroad car, the people gathered in the aisle to watch the fun, and they fortified me with sugar cookies and rice balls, even a little Thai Leaping Deer whiskey.

The countryside was spectacular, an endless flat plain of rice divided by two-foot dikes, occasionally broken by a cluster of stately palm trees or huge black stalagmites of volcanic rock jutting out of the flatness like lofty perches from which the gods could keep an eye on the laboring peasants. As we rolled south, the paddies were transformed into mountains, giant dark green cones shrouded in humid mists.

By nightfall we were deep into the mountains. The rice paddies had given way to pineapple plantations, which in turn gave way to tin mines. I was growing impatient. At the border crossing, the customs officials spoke little English, and we were soon bumping over Malaysian rails. The homesites were lovely, the architecture decidedly different from the Thai or Vietnamese. The rust-colored teak cottages perched on stilts were surrounded by broad porches and picket fences, which reminded me of Victorian gingerbread. I leaned out of the train's window to buy lunch, a barbecued fowl on bamboo skewers and a plastic bag of coconut juice. The excitement consumed me now. We reached Georgetown in the early afternoon, my heart pounding in my chest. Across the bay I could see Penang, my island paradise.

Aboard the ferry, the view was the same as I had experienced so long ago (in reality, only six months), and I moved to the foremost vantage point to absorb it all. The ferry headed directly west across the channel, directly into the low-slung afternoon sun, which cast a golden glow on the lush green swell. I could make out the freighters, then the busy junks, and finally, the city clustered at the water's edge. We were in the shadows of the freighters now, and I recognized flags from many lands. The wharf hurried closer, and I made my way to the gangplank, eager to find my ultimate goal before dark.

The familiarity was reassuring. I recognized the hotel, the guitar shop, the flashy restaurant where I once realized I had fallen in love. The taxi raced through the languid streets I had seen from a rickshaw, and I nearly stopped the driver and walked, not wanting to miss a single part of it. There was a left turn, and that street I had dreamed of stretched before me. As I paid the driver, my eyes blurred and watered, and I felt a pressure in my chest that became an obstruction in my throat. I knocked at the door, as so many GIs had done, and it opened with painful slowness.

"Aaahhh!" Mama-san's giant form burst through the door, a great smile wrinkling her features. Her arms went around me, and she danced, nearly catapulting us both to the sidewalk. Then, just as quickly, she shooed me inside, hollering excitedly for Lin, rushing to put a glass of Scotch in my hand. I was crying now, and she hugged me again, held me back at both arms' length to examine me, then threw her arms around me and turned me again. It was a dizzying, unexpected, wonderful emotion, and I was riding it blindly when it stopped and there was a moment of hush. I had lost my bearings a bit and turned away from Mama-san, to be crushed again. My eyes were teary, the room was dark, and I hadn't seen her coming. There was no mistaking it; the perfume, the soft, rounded curves, the touch of her lips devouring my throat, my cheek, my lips. I choked out, "You're so beautiful!" through my tears. I couldn't talk, I didn't want to do anything but hold her and smell her and feel her and never let the moment end. Forever is a long time, but it wouldn't be enough.

Mama-san brought my suitcase, carelessly discarded in the wave of emotion. "Sit," she said, pushing us toward the couch. "Sit. Talk. I get food." She kissed my cheek tenderly and bustled off to the kitchen. I searched for words, fought to regain some composure. God, Lin was beautiful! She turned serious. "Mama-san can cook, we don't have to spend so much money."

"Money! Don't worry about money. I want to be alone with you, to love you and hold you and talk to you 'til the sun comes up. I don't want to have to be quiet, or be on time, or be anything but with you." I had lived with the fantasy so long, pictured the room in my mind, the view of that bustling street, the hotel lobby, all of it; I wanted to relive what had taken place before.

"What happened before happened." She must have read my thoughts. "You want to marry me, you must be smart with your money. This is not R and R from Vietnam, we must be together, but you do not need the hotel." She had a way of lowering her head and arching those beautiful almond eyes up at me, twinkling, teasing, and yet somehow letting me know that this was her truest wish. In her Oriental way she would bend if need be, but the practicality in her had to be expressed. She leaned close, whispered into my ear. "Many men have taken the whore to the hotel. Tonight, the lover wishes to take the man to her bed. This is a lucky man, to be granted such a favor, don't you think?"

I was a lucky, lucky man for a week. I insisted upon buying my meals, which usually meant a trip to the open-air market to purchase shrimp or fish, fresh vegetables, and pastries. We rented a motorbike and toured the island, the sun and salt breeze washing over us in a way that seemed so clean, so natural, so spiritual it must have been a gift from the gods. We sat on a white sand beach with our ankles in the foaming surf, watching the crimson sun set over the placid sea. I brought a new record, "Hey Jude," Lin had the soundtrack album from the movie *The Graduate*, and together we discovered Peter, Paul, and Mary's "500 Miles." We giggled at Shirley MacLaine as *Irma la Douce* in Chinese with English subtitles in a theater where they served giant Singapore Slings. I took out the garbage and replaced the plug on Mama-san's radio.

The other girls came and went, giggling and chattering. Most were entertaining GIs, a few hadn't been chosen this week and spent their days sewing or shopping. I hadn't met any of the guys from The Nam, but Lin suggested we attend a beach party that would be their last big blowout before going back to the war. We rented the bike again, motored to the northern end of the island. In Hawaii they would have called this a luau, huge platters of food, open bar, a band, and exotic dark-haired women laughing merrily under the palms. A snake charmer swayed with his flute as a king cobra towered out of the basket. I saw the GIs splashing in the surf, paddling the native outrigger canoes, trying to climb a palm tree to fetch a coconut. Unfortunately, I saw others, the ones with the Vietnam eyes sunk deep into their aged cheekbones, sitting in the sand surrounded with bottles, staring at nothing, seeing more than was good for them. It was sobering. Most had lovely women sitting nearby, filing nails or chatting with each other as if unable to break into the shell of their boyfriends. Had they spent five days like this? I hadn't noticed when I was here last.

Time after time, a couple would sink into the sand near us, and the guy would ask what unit I was from. I answered something about having spent a year in Pleiku (I had to mention that), but now I was stationed in Thailand. Couldn't handle the chickenshit in the States, and this got me an early out. "You mean you live in Bangkok and you came here?" They would be filled with wonder.

"Bangkok's a couple hours away, I'm up-country. Tell me, wouldn't you want to come back here someday?"

"I wanna go back to The fuckin' World, man. I've seen all the slant-eyed fuckin' women and palm trees I ever want to see."

"You know, the closer I got to goin' home, the more it scared me." I figured I could lay it on the line with these guys. They knew where it was at. "I just figured if I got back to some army shit-hole back there, and they told me to get a bayonet and go play GI Joe to some guy that was saying 'Stop the war,' I couldn't handle it. So I'll just try to sit out a few months, try to get my head straight, then go back and be a civilian and see if I can get my shit together."

Time after time, the guy would look at me almost apologetically, and say something like, "You know, I talk about goin' home all the time, but I hadn't thought about it. I ever get outta this motherfucker an' get back to The World, ain't nobody gonna give me no shit, or he's a dead man. See, you can do that shit, go to Bangkok an' stay fucked up fer a year, but I got a wife…" And the words kind of trailed off, and he got up and got a drink or a swim or a hamburger. My thoughts went back to Pleiku, to the guy who had taken his R and R in Taiwan instead of going to Hawaii to spend five days with his wife. We'd asked him why time and again, and he just drank too much and said, "'Cause I'm too dirty now to touch her, so I'll go get laid by some whore." Somebody, with all the best intentions in the world, would say, "Yeah, but sooner or later you gotta go home," and he'd just take another long drag out of his bottle, spit in the dirt, and say, "Yeah! Sure is chilly in The Nam!"

I tried swimming and eating and playing drums, and when even sitting on the drums didn't make it fun, I grabbed Lin and kicked the motorbike to life and roared away. I wouldn't see guys from The Nam again until I arrived in Oakland the very last day of my army career. I didn't want to see them. They were worn, bruised, tired, crude, hopeless ruins, all fucked up inside, and I didn't want to be reminded that I was one of them. I didn't like what I saw, and I saw a reflection of myself.

I rode a while, enjoying the wind in my hair and the crush of Lin's breasts against my back. There were tears in my eyes, but I thought it must be the wind. We were in the city now, and I had never been so confused, and we passed a park and I stopped near a bench. A few yards away there was a penitent. A penitent was a member of some crazed religious sect, Indian or Pakistani, showing his devotion to his God by enduring great suffering. This guy was short, wiry, with twisted salt-and-pepper hair that reminded me of Medusa's snakes. He wore only a scrap of rag at his loins, and his rods, rising three feet above him in two parallel half-moons, the end of every rod imbedded into his flesh. His arms, like the dying Christ's, were spread wide, impaled upon steel rods. A half-dozen rods swept downward from the hideous framework, forming a knee-length skirt that prevented kneeling or sitting. A vertical rod swung from the loincloth to a point between his knees, where sharpened spikes extended outward toward his bleeding calves, and a heavy steel ball swung it into deadly motion with each movement. From his ankles, long lengths of heavy chain trailed behind for three yards. At the puncture of each rod I saw the familiar maroon stain of dried blood. His lower legs were raw and torn. Fascinated, moving closer, I saw long, thin needles through his eyelids, earlobes, and even the scrap of cloth at his loins. His tongue was extended, pierced with a chain leading to a weight. What got me were his eyes, eyes I had seen before. Lin pulled me away, but I gripped her arms and thrust her toward this pitiful creature. "Look at his eyes!" I told her, and beneath the distended lids and the silvery needles, back deep and dark as night, those eyes told a story of a man who has been there and was just trying to cope with it, and it had nothing to do with religion or steel rods or Vietnam or anything, but yet it had everything to do with all that and much more.

"I don't want to look." She walked off across the carefully manicured lawn without me. I hurried after her, apologized, tried to explain. She turned to face me, upset and angered. "I do not want to look at that." She hissed, a side of her I had never known, "I am Buddhist, Chinese. What do I care about that? He chose to do that. I don't feel sorry for him. If he is so unhappy, let him stop. He is not my concern!"

"Don't you wonder why he chose to do that?"

"No. He is crazy."

"But why? What happened to him to make him decide to do this? He must actually feel his life is better this way than it was before. What could it have been before?" I was getting nowhere. "Many men volunteer to go back to the war when they don't have to. Many men who are suffering live their life in silence, with eyes like his, feeling hurt inside that is just as painful as his. Don't you see? His religion doesn't matter, he is human, and we are human, and that could be you or me. I could be hobbling around without a leg, feeling the same pain. There's no reason why I have both of my legs, and there's no reason why he should be living like that, but there must be a reason, a plan or something, and it's important."

She looked at me with concern and pity, and spoke softly. "I think you are crazy too. I think all Americans are crazy. Why are you so sad? Everyone says America is a wonderful place, but Americans are so sad. I'm puzzled. Why do you care about that man? Why do you feel sad? You are so fortunate to be born in America, to be alive. I have tried to be kind to you, and you are sad. Have I made you sad? Tell me."

I felt tired, deflated. I couldn't describe what I was feeling, but it surely wasn't her fault. She was my refuge, the sane oasis. I thought she understood, and I was worried and hurt that she would ask.

We made a deal. We wouldn't talk about it. We would enjoy our short time together. I was relieved, I hadn't been sure what the problem was, and it was far too complex to be solved here. I resolved to tuck it away, ignore it, and have a good time. For the next two glorious days I wrapped myself into a cocoon of food and relaxation and Lin's lovemaking.

• • • •

I planned to leave a day or two early, to allow some time to explore Bangkok. Lin saw me to the ferry early one morning, and I promised to be back soon. On the ferry, watching my exotic home-away-from-home shrink into the distance, I felt an old sense of loneliness returning when I was approached by a tall, thin Englishman with an overloaded backpack. We seemed to hit it off right away. He was Australian, not English, and soon we were joined by his two friends, a guy and a girl. When they heard I was going to Bangkok, they pleaded with me to join them. They were also heading toward Bangkok, but by hitchhiking instead of the train. All three were Australian high school teachers who had taken a two-year leave of absence, hopped a steamer to Singapore, and were planning to hitchhike around the world to England. I declined, but they insisted and overcame every objection I could think of. On the mainland, I cashed in my train ticket and, filled with a sense of adventure, joined my new friends at the side of the road, thumb extended.

I think the Malays stopped for us more out of curiosity than assistance, for we were an odd-looking bunch. I was a little concerned, but their carefree and casual humor put me at ease. The Australian accent was reminiscent of my years before the army, inundated with British rock music. They were, from all appearances, hippies, with beards and round glasses, faded denims, and love beads. Flower Children, filled with kindness and curiosity and liberal "do your thing" attitude that I had missed since Fort Dix. Their hair was long and flowing, tied down with colorful headbands, and I felt self-conscious in my almost-military short hair and clean-shaven chin, but my mustache seemed to make everything okay.

We perched in the back of one produce truck or another, stretched out among tobacco or tree trunks, my suitcase and their backpacks supporting our heads so we could watch the unbelievable scenery unfold around us. The sun was hot, but the rides stirred a cooling breeze, and we sipped wine from a goatskin pouch and talked of life and its mysteries. Early on, I had admitted to being a Vietnam veteran. Australia had a force in The Nam, and my friends had known a colleague who had come home "a bit daft" from the war. Our laughter ranged over many subjects, most notably to aborigines and their strange tribal propensity for "walkabout." You could educate an abo, my friends explained, make him a doctor or lawyer; he would buy a Mercedes or Jaguar, marry, live in a beautiful home, play golf, and be a pillar of the community. One fine day he would inevitably drive the Mercedes far out into the bush, strip off his clothes, and walk out into the undergrowth to live a prehistoric and barren existence. They would all do it sooner or later, and the Australian government simply made "walkabout" a legal excuse for ignoring financial obligations, family responsibilities, or any other ties.

The dark green mountains leveled off abruptly to become a pattern of tranquil rice paddies, with giant outcroppings of rock, and mysterious little villages nestled among the palms. Our ride ended south of Bangkok amidst the flaming oranges and golds of the setting sun. We found ourselves in the midst of a small city open-air market, quite the center of attention from the grinning Thais, famished and surrounded by unusual and colorful things to eat. Giggling at our pathetic efforts to communicate through my dictionary, the Thais guided us to a restaurant and managed to order up an unbelievable feast that cost us a total of about four dollars.

We found an inexpensive room, and drank Thai beer and talked and laughed, smoked some grass, showered, and collapsed after a long day. The girl, Mary, emerged from the bathroom with her long hair and her hips wrapped in towels, and her bra filled to overflowing. She worked at her hair with the towel, stopping occasionally to swallow the beer. She carefully turned down one of the beds, then finished her beer and announced very matter-of-factly that she had never slept with a "Yank," and knew I hadn't had a blonde with round blue eyes in a while, what with Vietnam and all. High as a kite, I watched everyone finish their drinks and cigarettes, and the two guys flopped on the other bed. I said something about being engaged, and Mary led me to the other bed and proceeded to remove my jeans. She shrugged out of the bra, turned off the light, and slid in beside me. The cold wet towel had to go.

In the morning we caught a ride to Bangkok, where we parted. I was feeling an odd mixture of guilt, disappointment, and shame. How could I have made love with Mary just hours after pledging my undying love to Lin? I should have loved Lin so deeply that I wouldn't want any other woman, and I was routinely unfaithful. There was nothing deceitful about it; Lin had urged me to "stay in practice," but I still felt guilty and uneasy with myself. It shouldn't be so meaningless.

There was beginning to be doubts, despite my attempts to deny them. Lin insisted she had never received the expensive diamond ring. The scene with the penitent bothered me. I could not accept her indifference or her argument that the penitent was neither Buddhist nor Chinese. I was neither Buddhist nor Chinese. Would she really be able to fit into my family and my life back in The World?

• • • •

I settled back into the work routine and tried not to think after hours. In spite of the attractions surrounding me on post, I grew bored and restless. My fear of downtown had been replaced by fascination, and I rented a room in a house with three guys from my platoon. That grew old. I met a guy, Will, who had been a guitarist with a famous San Francisco acid rock band until the draft took him away. He had parlayed a few tickets to rock concerts into orders for Thailand instead of The Nam, and was sitting back, stoned, waiting for his time to go by. We sat at his bungalow marveling at the incredible new record, *Sgt. Pepper's Lonely Hearts Club Band*, smoking and talking about the Haight-Ashbury hippies. Will would get letters from Grace Slick or Janis Joplin, and his great purpose in life was to smuggle home as much Thai pot as possible. He was weird, an LSD veteran, and I stopped sleeping on his floor the night we killed a scorpion there. I spent a night with a neighbor of a friend, a Thai nymphomaniac who was between shackups. I went back the next night to find she had pawned my clock radio. We had a hell of a fight, she stabbed my foot with a carving knife, and I knocked her senseless and escaped before the Thai police arrived. I had never dreamed I was capable of sinking into such a sordid situation, and I stayed on post a few days, ever mindful that a man could be killed for a couple cartons of cigarettes in this strange land.

The mood was broken when my promotion came through. I was suddenly a sergeant E-5, the ranking NCO over forty young Americans far away from home. A plywood partition transformed the center area of the barracks into a private bedroom, and I was issued a double-width wall locker. That night we partied hard, and I was nervous about the reaction of my men. The next morning they let everyone know how they felt when, as we marched to work, they broke into song with an impromptu version of "Sergeant Ketwig's Lonely Hearts Club Band."

As a sergeant, I was ineligible to enjoy the enlisted men's club any longer. With three shiny yellow stripes on my sleeve, I ventured into the NCO club for a bite to eat and found that the atmosphere was decidedly more alcohol—and less ice cream—oriented. Talk centered around "the old army" when "men were men, and boys quaked at the sight of 'em." I munched my burger and fries and sipped a chocolate shake, feeling very small and out of place. At a nearby table a group of overweight bigots argued loudly about which race was the most backward, drawing upon many years of experience to nominate the "fuckin' Germans" or "fuckin' Koreans" or "fuckin' Panamanians." Somebody nominated the "fuckin hippies," and the issue seemed settled. A few years later, as the wisdom of an all-volunteer army was being debated, I couldn't help but think back on the few times I visited the NCO club. Why would an intelligent and educated young man volunteer to be bullied and harassed by those fat and lazy, ignorant bigots? If he tried it once, who could blame him for rejecting it as a lifestyle?

The holidays were fast approaching, and I missed downtown. On a bright and beautiful Saturday morning, I caught the Thai bus and rode it far past the honky-tonks to the area I had glimpsed the night I had visited Digger. I wasn't in a big rush to buy Christmas gifts, and I wanted to wander the exotic streets and explore. I was amazed at the selection, especially of Japanese household appliances and the latest rock 'n' roll records. I found a bookstore with hundreds of hardcover volumes, all in indecipherable Thai, but with elaborate and beautiful artwork and photography. In the rear, I found a real treasure, a genuine Siamese cat, a huge male that would have made a fine dinner for a whole family of Vietnamese. Moving on, I discovered shops swelling with the most unbelievable flotsam and jetsam, incredible everyday household paraphernalia crafted from wood, aluminum, or fluorescent plastic. Colors melted into flaming colors in a brilliant montage of creativity and joy. I hadn't smoked any grass in days, and yet the surroundings took my head on a surrealistic joyride.

I wound in and out of the clustered shops, moving deeper into an area in which I felt strangely comfortable and at home. The train, the week in a Malaysian home, and the adventures with the Aussies had combined to give me a new outlook. I had jumped in over my head and learned I could swim. No longer content to hide in the shadows, I embraced the exotic and fascinating Oriental culture. The Thais welcomed me, struggling to understand my feeble attempts at their language, explaining customs or holidays, and inviting me into family meals and discussions.

This Saturday, I wandered deep into the shopping district, until, late in the afternoon, I turned a corner onto a narrow street that would have a profound impact on my life. It was a nondescript street of two-story stucco-and-wood houses, lined with broad porches covering the sidewalk; a middle-class street of small businesses catering to the needs of the common people. Tonight, however, this simple avenue had become a glittering spectacle, an elaborate canyon of surreal Oriental mystery, beauty, and curiosity. I turned the corner and walked into a festival, and as I fell in with the flow of the crowd, I was swept into an assault on my senses.

I recognized the golden figures upon red backgrounds. This was a Chinese neighborhood, a culture not unlike Lin's. I watched a wrinkled old man with a drooping mustache and wispy beard as he lighted his pipe. A child, her almond eyes filled with joy, leaning nearer to a cluster of candles, clutching her bewildered little brother's hand. The street was lined with joss sticks six feet tall, their soft sandalwood fragrance so reminiscent of Lin's rituals. Red silken tapestries hung like bunting, dazzling the eye with embroidered dragons and demons. Thousands of tiny white candles warmed the night, while enormous red paper lanterns floated like ponderous dirigibles. There were tables of pastry and fruit, dark earthenware jars that could only have contained powerful liqueurs. I paused to admire a decorative jug, and a twinkling mama-san pressed a cup into my hand and poured it full. The husband offered strange hors d'oeuvres that tasted of fish. I pushed on. A group of weathered musicians tickled ancient wooden instruments, sending the sounds of strings into the night like a pocketful of coins tumbling down a stone stairway.

There was a cross street, and a glittering Buddhist temple in the midst of the intersection. Only six feet square, its brilliant reds and golds flickered in the light of a thousand candles. In front, people thronged around a giant concrete urn to place joss sticks into a smoking forest of offerings. Others attached slips of gold leaf to the walls or tied scraps of prayer paper to the branches of potted trees. Deep inside the shrine, more flickering candles highlighted a myriad of golden shapes surrounding a dark stone image of Buddha gazing off into the frenzy with timeless detachment. Balded monks in brilliant orange robes sat cross-legged in meditation, chanting and clutching smoldering joss.

Suddenly I was standing at the open gates of a courtyard, and a sign in English said, "Room for rent." I nervously approached a group of celebrants at a concrete table, viewed the room, and rented it. It was upstairs, overlooking the courtyard. There was a double bed, an American-style toilet, a table and chairs, and garish vinyl flooring. Three windows caught a cross breeze, and in the light of day I could see a graceful temple across the canal.

I purchased bright curtains, blankets, dishes, wall hangings, and a stereo. I bought American records from the PX and even a few pirated record copies with exotic labels from downtown. It was so wonderful to have my own room again; I relaxed in the peaceful neighborhood. I began to carry Thai food wrapped in banana leaves onto the army post for lunch, and visited the dark Chinese and Thai restaurants for dinner. I wore silken Thai clothing at home and walked deep into the darker sections to find the unusual and exotic life of the peasants. The more I looked, the more open the people became. They were fascinated by my height and hair, but even more intrigued that I cared about the lives they led. I, too, was fascinated. These were penniless peasants, but their joy in life was inspiring. Since The Nam, I had become bitter and confused. I sensed that their happiness in the midst of poverty was a treasure, and that there was a lesson I should learn. I spent hours sipping tea, listening to three ancient Chinese men playing antique instruments.

I played with the children and talked with the parents about the terrible responsibilities the children presented. We spoke of gardening, automobiles, government, and God. They wondered about cowboys, the America we had exported, and the Mafia. I tried to gain some understanding of their complex religion, with myriad grotesque demons and ancient wars in the heavens. I experimented with their food, language, and housing, and began to appreciate their innate happiness as derived from an incredible sense of community. They dreamed of the finer things, of riches and televisions and motorcars; but cooperation with nature and fellow man was more important. In a crowded, rural, agricultural society under a relentless tropical sun and surrounded by cobras, leopards, and poisonous scorpions, it would be shortsighted to antagonize your fellow man.

• • • •

As I settled into my room and learned to relax, I looked down upon the courtyard, where an air force enlisted man from Indiana was preparing to take his Thai wife and baby home to The World. He was the only other American in the area, and I delighted in the joy their first baby was bringing, a joy I hoped to share with Lin. Mai-Lee was a devoted mother, and I often turned off the stereo to hear her softly singing Thai lullabies to her precious bundle. Once in a while I would eat with them, and we began a tradition of coffee and sweet rolls on their porch every Sunday morning. I had no cooking facilities in my room, so a hot breakfast with a loving family was a particular treat.

One morning, over scrambled eggs and fresh melon, Jack told me an unusual story. He was a very down-to-earth person, never smoke or drank, so I believed him. He asked if I had heard anything the night before. No, I had slept soundly.

About three in the morning, Jack had been wakened by a noise outside. He grabbed a machete and crept to the door. His porch was about two feet above ground level, and he was shocked to see a huge man, all dressed in white, standing on the ground but towering over the porch. The dog cowered in the corner, and Jack said the strange figure just gazed at him. "He was dressed in all white, about seven feet tall, and his face was kind of distorted, like a zombie." Jack had been frightened and crept off to the bedroom to get his pistol. When he returned, the figure was gone. He sat up for hours waiting for it to come back, not wanting to scare Mai-Lee or the baby. "John, you'll think I'm crazy, but I think I saw a ghost!"

We shrugged it off, but Jack was obviously upset. Strange things began to happen in our compound. One of the Thai girls saw the figure and burst into the courtyard screaming in the middle of the night. Lights turned themselves off and on. People heard moans and cries. The ghost appeared to a third girl. Everyone was scared. Mama-san asked me to move into a ground-level bungalow at the same rent. I didn't see how I could be much help, but I moved. Ever larger offerings of fruit began to pile up around the Buddhist shrine in the courtyard. One of the housewives went to the library and discovered our compound had been the sight of a Japanese mortuary during World War II, where coffins were stacked to be shipped by train.

I mentioned the strange occurrences at work, and a friend begged to spend a few nights in my apartment. We slept in shifts, the sentry watching the courtyard. We put up signs in English and Thai, boasting that we did not believe in ghosts and asking the mysterious visitor to knock on our door. As luck would have it, I fell asleep. Noi, our *samlaw* driver, burst in to wake us for work and was wearing a white shirt, and I'm sure we surprised him with our reaction.

Mama-san decided we were not adequate protection. When the ghostly visitor appeared again, she asked everyone to contribute to bring Buddhist exorcists from Bangkok. They were a splendid group in their brilliant orange robes. After an hour of meditation, they announced that our visitor was a young Japanese soldier who had died without ever seeing his newborn child. They began an elaborate procedure of chants, lighting joss sticks and candles, offering sacrifices of food and flowers, and splashing holy water. They stayed for dinner, and our strange visitor was seen no more. Had it been a ghost? The Thais believed; I will never know. Jack and his family left for the States. He insisted what he had seen could not have been human.

• • • •

I scoured the PX for the latest records from home, and the downtown stores for overseas or pirated music. My bungalow was a rock 'n' roll oasis, and a steady flow of guys came by to fill their musical canteens with the latest sounds from home.

We had been the Beatlemaniacs of 1964. There are many books about Vietnam, most with only passing references to the pop music of the era. Likewise, the biographies of the Beatles or Rolling Stones barely mention the war. Neither is entirely accurate; young America was saturated with both, simultaneously. American society changed drastically after John Kennedy was gunned down in Dallas. A scant two months later Ed Sullivan introduced the Beatles. Throughout the next decade, America endured unprecedented turmoil and a popular music explosion that was ubiquitous to a confused generation. Buoyed to respectability by artists like the Beatles, Bob Dylan, and Simon and Garfunkel, rock 'n' roll became the definition of social progress and conscience. Dustin Hoffman's poignant portrayal of unsure youth in the movie *The Graduate* was defined by the background harmonies of Simon and Garfunkel. *The Graduate* was the masterpiece portrait of sixties youth. Television newscasts brought home the agonies of Khe Sanh and Tet, then entertained the baby-boom generation with rock music. Paul Revere and The Raiders were regulars on Dick Clark's *Where the Action Is*. Ed Sullivan had a different group every Sunday. There were all-rock variety shows like *Shindig*. The Flower Children dared to try new lifestyles in the Haight-Ashbury, and Scott McKenzie's "If You're Going to San Francisco" was a monster hit record. The Monkees became stars of a TV show and rock superstars, although at first they only mouthed another band's music. It was a time of defiance, the sneering of Mick Jagger, The Who smashing their instruments on stage. Staid businessmen grew their hair longer and wore flowered shirts, and Bob Dylan's "'The Times They Are A-Changin'" was discussed over cocktails at the country club. It was an era of sexual revolution, of love-ins and the nudity of Broadway plays like *Hair* and *Oh! Calcutta!*, and the Young Rascals scored big with a song called "Good Lovin'." Blacks were feeling the first inklings of self-respect, and Motown made soul music popular. But there were racial frustrations too, and Black Panthers, and James Brown's "I'm Black and I'm Proud!" The drug culture spawned Jimi Hendrix and Janis Joplin and Iron Butterfly. Good Lord, Joplin didn't sing, she cried out in anguish; we loved her because we were all in this together, and the Robert McNamaras and Spiro Agnews of this world couldn't offer us anything we could relate to.

We marched in the streets to the beat of Dylan; the Byrds; Peter, Paul and Mary; Buffalo Springfield; and Country Joe & The Fish, not John Philip Sousa. Donovan wore white robes like his mentor, the Maharishi. It was time to "do your own thing," and the musicians dared, and the result was an explosion of serious, high-quality pop art that defies description. Crosby, Stills & Nash. The Mamas and the Papas. The Association. Richie Havens. Sonny and Cher. The Four Tops. Gary Puckett and The Union Gap. Vanilla Fudge. The Temptations. Eric Burdon and The Animals. Sly & The Family Stone. Blood, Sweat and Tears. Smokey Robinson and The Miracles. Lovin' Spoonful. Otis Redding. Cream. Tommy James and The Shondells. The Buckinghams. 1910 Fruit Gum Company. Spanky and Our Gang. Kenny Rogers and The First Edition. Linda Ronstadt and The Stone Poneys. The Fifth Dimension. Electric Flag. The Bee Gees. Manfred Mann. Steppenwolf. The Chambers Brothers. The Steve Miller Band. Canned Heat. Wilson Pickett. Unprecedented in quantity, and exhibiting a quality that demanded serious recognition, this tidal wave of sound permeated every aspect of American life, including its war in Vietnam. One day we were dancing or listening to the car radio; the next we were in Southeast Asia. Somebody always had a transistor radio, able to pick up Armed Forces Radio and Chris Noel's sultry reminders of home: "Hi, Love!"

Julius Caesar came, and saw, and conquered. Alexander the Great subjugated the known world. We know little of the peasantry of the times, their hopes, their fears, their emotions. The music, the social commentary of America's Vietnam era are recorded that future generations might understand. No portrait of the period would be complete without them.

The music took us away, and it provided insights. As my friends visited, we analyzed the Beatles' latest offering, the "White Album." There was a cacophony of sound titled "Revolution 9." Why was it there? It must contain a message. "Hey, Jude" had been a clue, telling us something important was on the way. Jude is the book in the Bible immediately preceding Revelation, the description of the end of the world as predicted by Saint John. Jude proclaimed "peace and love be multiplied"; then came Revelation. Or, perhaps, revolution? Revelation 9 speaks of the "sound of their wings was as the sound of chariots of many horses running to battle," and "they had tails like unto scorpions." A reference to helicopters, the war machines that symbolized Vietnam? In the next cut, ominously titled "Good Night," Ringo sings of the sun turning out its light. In Southeast Asia in 1969, with rumors of nuclear weapons "in-country," it all seemed plausible. Even while listening to rock 'n' roll, the war consumed me. I was struggling to forget it, often with too little success.

• • • •

The best diversion seemed to be my expeditions into the local culture. I was totally fascinated with the color, the apparent happiness of these people, the strange and unique architecture, music, and ideas. Tired of running a marijuana-inspired

USO for my friends, I took a weekend away. About twenty-five miles north of Korat was the tiny town of Phi Mai, site of an ancient Khmer ruin said to have been built by the same people who created the awesome and fabled Angkor Wat in Cambodia. The Thai government had begun restoring Phi Mai, and I wanted to see it. I had my camera, my dictionary, and a few dollars, and a lot of faith in my ability to get by. I managed to convince the Thai bus ticket salesman where I wanted to go, and I boarded the bus with what seemed to be half the population of Thailand, and all their livestock! I got a seat next to a huge open basket of geese, and the Thais seemed to enjoy my effort to avoid the half-dozen hissing, squawking heads threatening to devour my left ear. It was hot, and the windows were open. By the time we got to Phi Mai I was coated with dust from the dirt roads. I got lunch and headed into the ruins.

With my upstate New York upbringing, I had no preparation for this. I thought relics from the 1700s were "old," and this building had been built six centuries earlier. It was basically just a broken-down pile of rocks, although decorated with many elaborate stone carvings. After the wholesale destruction of The Nam, it impressed me that something had stood for eight hundred years in Southeast Asia and was untouched except by the ravages of time and climate. I sat for a long time, just imagining what it must have been like centuries ago.

I had no responsibilities, no time limits or boundaries. When I had drunk my fill of the intoxicating ruins I strolled back into town hoping to find a new fascination. Thailand never failed to offer new experiences. I found a group of boys, probably eight to ten years old and totally captivated by my red hair and blue eyes. I motioned to them to group together for a picture, and they scrambled into place, eyes wide and faces beaming. I got an idea. Down the street we went, the Pied Piper with his flock trailing, to a shop that had one of everything if you looked hard enough. I bought a rubber ball and a meter of bamboo. When the sun set on Phi Mai that evening my dictionary was dog-eared, my body was dusty, and my forehead was sunburned, but those kids and some of their dads knew how to play baseball. We drew a crowd on the dusty street, and regardless of language or culture, we all learned something. A group of the fathers helped me find dinner and a room, we drank beer and laughed, and there was something so special and intense you could feel it deep in your chest. I did more to benefit the United States and peace on earth, good will toward men that day than I did in a year in The Nam.

• • • •

I felt refreshed. The holidays were upon us. Bob Hope brought Ann-Margaret, Miss Universe, and Rosey Grier. There was a turkey dinner at the mess hall. I went to a New Year's Eve party (should I say New Year's Eve orgy?) at one of the big hotels, but the fireworks made me nervous, and I retreated to my house and my stereo.

At work, my guys were busting their humps, and it was obvious everyone was proud of us. I was under a truck when the warrant officer came to get me. "You're going north," he said. I hadn't thought about this possibility, and I shivered as all the old fears settled in my chest. "Don't say anything to anybody, just go get your civies and go over to battalion. They'll drive you to the truck. A chopper'll pick you up. Sleep in in the morning." He started to walk away, then came back and put his arm around my shoulder, leading me out onto the parking lot, away from everybody. "I just want you to know, you've done a hell of a job around here, and I need you. You be careful and get your ass back here in one piece." He shook my hand.

The chopper stirred up a lot of dust. It was a Chinook, or "shithook," a giant olive-drab banana with oversize rotors at each end. The crew wore no insignia, the chopper had no lettering. While the crew fastened down my truck, I was given a helmet, flack jacket, web belt with plenty of ammo, and an M-16. "Where the hell are we going?" I asked. "Don't ask," came the reply. My pounding heart drowned out the *whump-whump-whump* of the rotors. We stopped once for fuel.

The next time we came down, it was obvious everyone was excited. I knew the tone, the atmosphere, the stink of the place. Oh my God! I was back in The Nam!

It was dark and frantic. The truck rolled down the ramp. Shadowy figures whispered and pointed the way. I crept over the rutted mud to the shadow of a big gun, a 105. I crawled on top to take a look. Most of the fuel had been bailed out, and a shirtless body hung down into the hole sopping up the rest with rags. I didn't like the diesel fuel smell. It didn't fit the surroundings.

I worked as fast as I could, the brilliant green glow of the Mig welder shielded by ponchos that held the heat. I couldn't see for the sweat dripping into my eyes, and stopped for a cigarette. I gazed off across an unbelievable landscape, silvery in the moonlight. There was nothing. Nothing standing, nothing growing, nothing natural. Craters. Hundreds, no, thousands of craters, large craters, small craters, craters overlapping craters, an endless sea of devastation. The shirtless guy offered a bottle. I had to ask. "Where the fuck *are* we?"

He whispered, as though it was a big secret. "We ain't anywhere. Nowhere at all. You can't get here from anyplace, and you can't get anyplace from here. You're in nowhere. Can't be L...A...O...S 'cause that's neutral, and we ain't got anybody there, so I guess we're just nowhere."

Jesus Christ! I took another belt and dove back into the bowels of the gun. I knew I'd better get this over with as quickly as I could.

Then it was done, I was back in the chopper, and we went up, and down, and up again, and then it was daylight and we were in Korat, and everything looked familiar, and it was as though nothing had ever happened. Problem was, I couldn't stop shaking. I took a shower, tossed my filthy clothes to a house-girl, and tried to sleep. It didn't work. I walked down to the parade field where Bob Hope had been just a few days before, took out some grass, and got totally and completely zonked.

I stayed stoned every waking hour for four days. On my twenty-first birthday I did twenty-one pipefuls of potent Thai marijuana and then visited friends. When it wasn't dulled, my mind raced. I had survived a year, and five extra days, and had survived The Nam. Not content with that, they sent me to Laos. Laos! We weren't supposed to be there, and they had ordered me not to write about it in letters home. The North Vietnamese on the receiving end of those shells knew we were in Laos. The only possible reason to "classify" these operations was to keep people in the States uninformed. This was clearly illegal and immoral. Was there no end to this outrage? They could just pluck us away at will, take away our identities, and ship us to the horror. The enormity of it boggled my mind. I preferred to just drift away on a cloud of smoke, quietly waiting until my days ran out and I could slip out of the army's grasp.

I dotted every *i* and crossed every *t*. I made every deadline. Every paper was neatly typed and correct. Every job from our shop was the highest quality, and delivered on time. We had an understanding, almost a conspiracy. We would do such an out-standing job that the lifers wouldn't risk fucking with us. If I had a problem with one of my guys, he and I resolved it. I wouldn't have dreamed of referring one of my men to the mil-itary system of pseudo-justice. They were thousands of miles from home and family, and I was responsible for them. I knew the names of their wives and children and felt a great respon-sibility to each.

Every morning I religiously crossed off a block on my short-timer calendar, then waited. Two hundred and fifty days of green clothes, green trucks, and jungle boots seemed like an eternity. There was no escaping the fact that I might have to "go north" again. Totally powerless, I could be sent back to The Nam at any moment. This fear, this terrible knowledge that I was just another number, another body to fill a slot, drove me to drugged oblivion. It was hopeless, and I was the only one aware of it, and if I said anything to these naïve kids I might go to jail, or worse. The truth was classified and I had been ordered to guard the secret. When I came off the pot the nightmares reinforced the reality of my fears, but to tell anyone would put me in even graver peril.

Artillery never roared here. There were no firefights or rocket attacks. The quiet was hard to get used to, but my room and stereo helped with that. I could sit quietly, but inside I was churning. I was powerless, we were all expendable, and the terror was difficult to escape. If the most powerful country in the world wanted me to die, I knew I was helpless. I kept their secret, but I couldn't look at my friends in their olive-drab jungle fatigues without blurring the realism of our plight.

I knew how long ten seconds could be. I realized how quickly men die. Two hundred and fifty days was too far in the future to make plans. A lifetime. I had to get through today. If, by some miracle, I survived, I would work out relationships with my family and friends, and, yes, Lin.

If I never got out of here alive, it wouldn't do to have her back in The World alone. I never quite got around to submitting paperwork seeking permission to marry her. There would be less paper as a civilian, less hassle.

• • • •

At the end of the day I showered, caught a bus, and retreated into my room. Friends came and went, GIs or Thais. The Thais laughed with us and explained, and we pointed out things they had never noticed, and there was never a cross word or ugly incident. We were inconsequential specks on the surface of a huge globe, staring in wonder, amazed but at peace with each other.

Sunday mornings I shopped for groceries at the neighborhood open-air market. I learned to curb my middle-class American revulsion as flies crawled over raw meat and people ate huge beetles called *mangdie*. Far more of the planet's population sustained themselves from markets like those than from our gleaming chrome-and-neon supermarkets. I realized my stomach was not acclimated to such things, so I chose carefully. My room had no refrigerator, so I concentrated on fruits and vegetables and canned foods. I had to have a watermelon, pineapple, bread, peanut butter, ornate tins of delicate European sugar cookies, oranges or bananas, Dutch chocolate, and a few cases of Coca-Cola. There was a small Chinese restaurant near my compound, and I had learned to order a breakfast of scrambled eggs, toast, and orange juice in their language. They trusted me 'til payday if I was short of funds, and I brought them American pickles or catsup when times were good. Noi was our *samlaw*. We paid him once a month also. He became our tour guide, interpreter, and dear friend. He was about seventeen, terribly poor, and the greatest barterer who ever lived. I visited his family often, a stereotypical Asian peasant clan in a ramshackle hovel, with far too many mouths to feed. I took care of Noi, kept him clothed and fed and his *samlaw* repaired, and took groceries to his mother and trinkets to the kids. We shared many wonderful meals in that shack, and I loved Noi like a brother. After the war the American army pulled out of Korat, and I often wonder what happened to Noi. Many *samlaw* drivers were hoodlums, but we gave Noi a key to our house, and he was always straight. Every morning he woke me and any GI who might have crashed overnight, and pedaled us to the bus.

• • • •

Many nights I just wandered the dark streets alone. I loved to sip tea and listen to the old men with their ancient Chinese string band, or visit a tailor from India and talk about Hinduism and psychedelic Nehru shirts and the River Ganges. The neighbors took us in stride and, indeed, into their hearts. They came and laughed, and taught us their language and customs. Any night I might be host to three or four Americans and as many Thais. One girl, a widow, had three breasts and quietly nursed her baby without embarrassment. The guys brought presents for the baby, and she baked snacks for us.

Jerry had been married just a few days before he shipped to Thailand, and his heart ached. He lived with me awhile, smoked too much, and we became dear friends. Watching his agony made me glad I hadn't left a wife at home. One night we rode a Thai bus to stir a breeze and escape the heat, and the conductor was actually timing the laps on a stopwatch. After a few corners on two wheels, we decided to walk home. About the time I felt I could talk to Jerry about the ghosts I had brought from The Nam, a death in the family called him home, and I was alone again.

I was far away from Lin and aching for female company. As often as possible, I visited a girl at a Thai massage parlor. No other Americans visited this humble paradise. It was inexpensive, and my favorite girl had been trained in Japan. She was more chiropractor than masseuse, but it was a soothing, relaxing place. She giggled at my Thai pronunciation, but her fingers resolved tensions in ways no sedative could. We became close friends, and the Thai patrons seemed to enjoy my visits to their secret oasis.

I had formed a special friendship with Stu, a college graduate from Idaho. We arranged a three-day pass to visit Bangkok. Stu did not allow himself to be intimidated by a military haircut. At his urging, we ate at the finest restaurants and shopped at the finest stores. We drank at a tiny jazz club called The Balcony, surrounded by embassy employees and students instead of drunken GIs on R and R.

We visited the most beautiful and sacred temples and shrines, the tourist attractions. This was fantasy, a total environment as unreal as Disneyland or Colonial Williamsburg, but with a special atmosphere which made us feel the presence of God as surely as if we were at the Vatican or Winchester Cathedral.

We returned to Korat early Sunday afternoon, ate dinner, and retired to Stu's room at the Semanut Hotel. We were eager to smoke a joint and tell Eht, Stu's lady, about our adventures. Eht was a beautiful, educated lady, and I think Stu was tempted to fall in love with her. She was nearing thirty, with a personality far different from the bar girls'. Eht had been a teacher but had come into money and retired. Her family was in Vientiane, Laos, and she often visited them. She had a character and sophistication. She spoke impeccable English, dressed with great taste, and discussed literature, music, and art with the ease born of familiarity.

Stu and I settled into comfortable chairs, smoked some grass, and dug into bowls of ice cream. We told Eht about Bangkok with enthusiasm. Rich and Wayne dropped by, we shared another smoke, and ordered more ice cream. I was floating, enjoying the gentle company and the sounds of the Beatles from the corners of my mind. Eht held out the newspaper, pointing to an article. "John, weren't you in Pleiku?"

I took the paper. "Yes, why?" It was apparent from the picture on the front page. Pleiku had been hit. No mention of units or specific locations, but nine Americans were reported killed. That probably meant twenty-nine were actually dead, and my mind raced over a list of my friends. I saw them, one by one, face by face, and I saw my old hootch, and the fields, and I heard Artillery Hill roar, and there was a crash. My ice cream hit the floor. Eht knelt to wipe it up, and I felt my head tripping away to the horror and the fear.

I came back to reality with a start. I was with friends in Korat. The rockets had all been in my head, and the shaking and sweating had concerned my friends. "Are you all right?" "Christ, you really tripped out on that!" "You look like you've seen a ghost!"

I tried to make light of it. "I think I just saw a lot of ghosts!" I added a slight giggle to make them think I was over it.

Eht's eyes were soft, concerned, and very kind. "You didn't even hear us. We were scared for you. Do you not think you should talk about your experience and try to get over it?"

These were dear friends, trusted friends, but I did not want to allow myself to think about The Nam. "I just want to put it all out of my mind." Stu, ever the easygoing, soft-spoken voice of reason, handed me another joint and a Coke.

"If you don't want to get into it, that's fine. But you must know that some day you'll have to sort it all out, get it settled in your head, and go on…" Stu was so reasonable, so able to accept anything. He waited a moment, then continued. "How do you live with it? How does it feel? Are we winning? I mean, the only dead person I've seen in my life was my Uncle Ted, and he was all laid out in a funeral home, with the flowers and all that. I was just a little fellow, and I can't imagine seeing guys blown apart, or just lying in the sun with the life bleeding out of them. How do you keep from letting that mess you up inside?"

I dragged hard at the joint and passed it on to Wayne. How could I describe it? If I let a little bit out, would it crack the dam and cause an uncontrollable flood? I was stoned, and still these were my friends, and I secretly wanted to talk about The Nam and get it out in the open.

"Stu, I *am* messed up inside. I feel like a leper. I guess that's why I'm here. I waited an eternity for my days to go by so I could go home; then, when it got close I got scared to death of home. I wouldn't know what to say to my parents, or friends, or anyone. Suppose I met one of the guys from my class? What would I say to him? I just try not to think about it. Every once in a while a thought hits me, and I gather it up real quick, wrap it up, and tuck it away like a small-town postmaster putting letters into pigeonholes. I get everything all in order, all sorted and put into the proper little holes, and then I read that Pleiku was hit and nine guys died, and it's like a big truckload of Christmas mail arrived. It takes a while to get it all sorted."

Pause. Am I doing okay? They were watching me, anticipating, but not threatening.

"Stu, I've seen dump trucks with torn, battered bodies hanging over the edges. American kids. I've seen them hang on barbed wire in the rain all day, and I've seen the body bags stacked in the mud, waiting for a plane. I've seen half a dozen American kids strung together on a rope, towed behind a personnel carrier, just bouncing and bumping like lifeless rag dolls. The fire was so thick, that was the only way to get the bodies in. I've seen dead North Vietnamese, with pictures of their wives and kids in their pockets. I sat and smoked with some North Vietnamese the night Bobby Kennedy died, and you know what? They're people, scared and tired, and just like us. They don't want to die. They just want to go home. When they're dead, bodies don't have a country. They're just dead, nothing else."

I paused again. Wayne asked if we were winning.

"That's the worst part. I really don't know how they're going to award the trophy. The lifers are getting to try out all their new weapons. They've got their chance of a lifetime for promotions, and Washington says we're winning. I don't know. The only thing I can tell you with any certainty is, the poor people of Vietnam, the peasants, are losing. They're having to see their kids burned by napalm or starving or shot. Their homes are destroyed, and the rice they eat, and it doesn't seem to matter. Saigon could care less; there are starving kids begging at the gates of the presidential palace. Washington doesn't care; they order more bombing missions. The Army doesn't care. They tell us the only good gook is a dead gook, and that we've done something to be proud of when a peasant village is burned to the ground. A war of attrition, that's what they call it. The sad thing is, it could all be settled so simply. If they loaded those B-52s with food and seed and farm implements and clothing and medicine, and painted an American flag on each piece, and a little message like, 'From your friends in America,' the war would be over within hours. Those people are starving and suffering. All they want is a full belly and a better life for their children. That's all anybody wants. If we would just give it to them, no one would have to die. But there's no money in friendship. There's no glory in farming, or healing, or cooperating. The lifers need to kill, and to order helpless people to die, in order to feel powerful. Our industry needs those Pentagon contracts. Business is good! Everybody thought this thing would be over long ago. Death for dollars. That's been the American way, and it doesn't work as foreign policy, but the lifers get their promotions and the big companies sell their napalm, and the government orders it to go on."

An icy cold swallow of Coca-Cola cleared my head. I never should have started this. It was depressing. I got to my feet. Stu stood, grinned, and shook my hand. "Thanks. I guess that was hard for you. You all right?"

I assured him I was. The room was silent as I eased out the door into a hotel hallway, an endless tunnel of doorways. I was high, but the visions I had seen had straightened me out, and I felt good walking home. I was feeling very fortunate to be here in Korat when the voice of Southeast Asia boomed out and shattered my calm. From the deep in the darkness, a "fuck-you" lizard roared his obscene chant and exploded the stillness of the tropical night. I burst into laughter. "You're too late!" I answered at the top of my voice. "The army already got me!" And I wandered home, chuckling at my inside joke.

• • • •

Back at the bungalow I put on a record, poured another Coke, and did another pipe of grass. I couldn't sleep. Rock had married brass, and Blood, Sweat and Tears and a band called the Electric Flag were at the center of the ceremony. I was listening to an Electric Flag album I had picked up at the PX and had grown to love. There was silence, then Lyndon Johnson's familiar drawl boomed, "I speak tonight for the dignity of man, and the destiny of mankind…" interrupted by a burst of laughter and the scream of tortured guitars. "For the dignity of man." LBJ was sitting on his ranch, in the very undignified position of having been forced out of the White House by public protests in the streets. There is no dignity, no glory, in mud up to your ass with bullets overhead. There is fear and loathing, and a sadness so powerful it becomes a part of you. When I visited Gettysburg, I hadn't realized what it meant, the suffering, the waste that had defiled those beautiful rolling green pastures. Why hadn't my teachers, charged with preparing me for the life outside the classroom, told me about this? They must have known that there were bigger crises than third-and-seventeen on your own four-yard line.

The day was fast approaching when I would get back there, eye to eye with the other kids from my graduating class, and they would want to hear about "my trip," as if I had been vacationing in the Bahamas or something. A few would call me Baby Killer, or just ignore me, but nobody would ask, "What was it like?" and really want to know. I wouldn't be able to tell them, and they would go on through life thinking the faculty of Dear Old Avon Central had told it to them like it is.

Where did the conspiracy start? Was it, in fact, a conspiracy? Maybe it was just misguided tradition. One hundred and ninety-three years ago the Founding Fathers had gathered in Philadelphia and, in an inspired fervor, had set down a plan for government unlike anything the human race had ever seen. And the fervor was contagious, moving men to make great sacrifices at places like Bunker Hill, Gettysburg, Belleau Wood, and Iwo Jima. Just as a bowling ball strikes the headpin and unleashes a furious chain reaction fanning out to affect all the waiting pins, this idea called democracy had dispersed itself among today's powers. But, unlike the thinking, driven men of old, we were the bowling pins. Wooden, undistinguished bodies placed into the path of destruction by a machine marked "AMF Pinspotter." Yeah, American military fantasy. In their seats of power, removed from the headpin by nearly two hundred years of reaction, they felt an obligation to prove their commitment in blood and sacrifice. The chain reaction had created chaos far beyond the limits envisioned by the Founding Fathers; numerical odds suggest that a few men of questionable motives had become involved. Greed. Power. Pride. AMF, capable of putting pins into positions of grave danger. I was incurably melancholy.

There were many nuts, bolts, levers, and screws to this machine. Of course, the president was a mainshaft. "For the dignity of man"? Only LBJ knew his motives; he would not be judged until he was gone. New York's public schools teach a curriculum prescribed by a board of regents. That curriculum had failed us, indicting the state. Of course! Just a lower level of the same life-crushing machine, a wider expansion of the force of impact. The teachers, manipulators of minds, had urged us out of our seats each morning to pledge allegiance to the flag. These were not the guilty or corrupt, but unwitting levers designed by the state colleges and universities to guide us into line. And at the farthest reaches, the machine relied upon our families to teach citizenship, obedience. "Values," they called it, and we were expected to fall blindly into place in the path of the great rolling ball while the distant bowler attempted to prove his skill. Surely, Vietnam would go down in history as only a seven-ten split, whereas World War II had been a strike. The shame of it was that the pins were living, breathing, sensitive human beings, helpless to control their destinies, victims of an experiment gone awry and convoluted by too many reactions scattered indiscriminately by well-intentioned or unprincipled politicians who had occupied the seats of power throughout the two centuries of evolution. Acutely aware of America's military heritage, they had constructed a machine that crushed the life out of the very people it was built to protect, and the machine had run away at full throttle. If the Constitution and Bill of Rights were its fuel, the blood of the weak was its lubrication, and it had developed a terrible thirst.

In an engine, the operator notices unprecedented oil consumption and overhauls pistons and rings, but this machine was not mechanical, there was no tachometer to control revolutions and safeguard the future, and it would not stop for rebuilding. There were two hundred years of momentum swirling in its crankcase, and the agony my generation was encountering in Vietnam was no more than an ignition shock from a disconnected spark plug wire. The engine would experience a slight miss, and roll on. We were buoyed by the rhetoric of our great scraps of paper. "We hold these truths to be self-evident." What guarantee do we have that our leaders see those words, acknowledge them? "Life, liberty, and the pursuit of happiness"? The machine had crushed all three into a dump truck loaded with the remains of teenage kids headed for graves registration; into the blackened, bubbled flesh of a Vietnamese kid whose grass hut had stood in the path of a napalm bomb. "Sweet land of liberty," unless you happen to be male and eighteen years of age, with a One-A stamped onto a scrap of paper.

It must be wonderful to believe so deeply that you are willing to give up your life for someone else's two-hundred-year-old idea. But the tragedy begins when that choice is taken from you, and the choices are made by a machine gone mad. That isn't liberty! The machine has crafted us well; thousands have been drafted and have died in too many wars, and still the machine pushes us into line and few protest. Back in The World, right at the gates of the Pentagon, great crowds of Americans were calling out for their constitutional guarantees. And other great crowds of unthinking tenpins are fighting and killing in the name of order, never seeing that they have been placed in order by the AMF.

God, how America loves its machines! Over and over our teachers had preached the Industrial Revolution, the automobile and the airplane, the steamboat and the cotton gin. But now that love affair had brought us the atomic bomb, the ultimate machine. Now all of mankind was lined up, waiting for the great ball to roll. Rumors persisted that there were A-bombs at Udorn, waiting to ride a B-52 to Hanoi. Or waiting for things to get really bad in The Nam, another Khe Sanh or Tet. Crazy! There are half a million Americans in The Nam, lying in the mud, scared shitless, dreaming about 396 Chevelles and round-eyed pussy. Would anyone even dream of unleashing the ultimate killing machine over them, just to save face? Could I really believe they wouldn't?

How can I describe this fear, this terrible knowledge, to the folks back home? There are no rules. When things get uncomfortable, folks back home change channels. A-bombs and H-bombs and multi-megaton bombs aren't real; *Laugh-In* and Ed Sullivan are real. Vietnam isn't real, not an honest-to-goodness war like World War II. Just a conflict, a little brush fire. I should be glad I've never seen a real war. I would start one if I heard that!

What the hell would I say to those guys? They're gonna ask me to join the VFW or American Legion, go to conventions and drink beer and swap war stories, and I wouldn't be able to think about anything but a group of Green Berets standing around with beers, a fire truck and a horrible scream, and an explosion of flesh and high-pressure water, and I'm not about to march down Main Street on the Fourth of July and be proud of *that*!

Values. I remembered the people back home rushing about, frantic and overstressed. What the hell had been so important? The mortgage? The car payment? No crabgrass? Dry underarms? War is okay, sex is dirty. Why weren't single guys allowed to R and R in Hawaii? The powers knew we would want to get laid, and couldn't bring themselves to admit that we had whores in America. Everybody knows the people in those backward countries are barbarians, with prostitutes and all. We'll just smile and look the other way, send lots of penicillin. It will be all right, so long as they don't bring that filth to America the Beautiful. Bullshit! I had been to Times Square. They can't let all the poor, mostly black, horny bastards fuck their fine young American girls. The generals don't jerk off in the officer's latrines, but the sperm from military officers isn't nasty and distasteful and harmful to American women like farm boy sperm or black sperm.

A war on poverty. Who's doing the dying? Guys who can't afford the student deferments. Blacks. Niggers. A uniquely American word. Peasants, unable to drink out of Alabama water fountains or eat in Arkansas diners. If they try, we unleash the dogs on them, or cattle prods. Values? Yeah, them that's got it, value it. And them that wants it can die. Die in The Nam, die in a motel in Memphis, or at a hotel in Los Angeles, or in a limo in Dallas. I pledge allegiance...

Hendrix started into "Are You Experienced?" Man, am I experienced. The kid who graduated in '65 is an old man in '69. I've seen shit most guys never see in their craziest nightmares.

Isn't that what they were asking about earlier tonight? Poor fools. How can anyone describe it to them? They're so close, just a few hundred miles away, seeing the Phantoms head off to Hanoi every day. They still think there's something noble in it all, something macho and glamorous. How can I describe the personnel carrier at Dak To, hauling in stringers of dead kids by the ankle, dragging the lifeless bodies, losing pieces? These guys still think it's like Sergeant Rock comic books or *Combat* on TV. They see all the equipment, the B-52s and Phantoms, and they think we're invincible. But a guy in the mud with a rifle ain't a bit more invincible in The Nam than he was at Little Big Horn. And there's damn little pride in seeing a kid bubbled by napalm. Experienced? Oh God, I wish I wasn't. Oh, how I miss the kid who graduated so long ago.

My stereo allowed me the luxury of piling three or four albums one atop another and drifting off with the musicians leading my mind away from The Nam. Noi woke me every morning and pedaled my numb form to the bus stop. On base, I showered, shaved, ate breakfast, and marched my guys off to work. One morning I borrowed a jeep and visited the office of a large civilian contractor. I picked up an application for employment at a deep-water port being built on the coast, near Sattahip. The pay would be enormous, the benefits even better. Perhaps I should never go home.

Stu spoke far more Thai than I and had admitted to being tempted by similar offers. "Remember, it won't be Korat," he warned. "Sattahip is a dangerous city. Everybody knows there are atomic bombs coming in, and the Communists want desperately to steal one. Americans aren't allowed to go downtown in groups of fewer than five, and one of them has to be armed. After Vietnam, are you ready for that?" My enthusiasm flagged.

Another night, he added another challenging thought. "You survived The Nam, and you're worried about a shady street in the suburbs? You used to live there, and you admit you hated to leave! All right, you've changed. The street hasn't, your house hasn't, and your family hasn't. John, we're not talking about a transfer to another army post. You'll be a civilian. Grow your hair, enjoy weekends off, drive-ins, and drag races...civilian life! You've been away too long, you don't think your memories are real, but they are. You'd better go back and give it a chance before you give up on it. You loved it once, and I bet you'll love it again."

I thought about it off and on, but I never got around to filling out that application and sending it off. I began to build fantasies of home in my head. Stu was right. I didn't really remember what life had been like before the army. At least I could talk with Stu without feeling like a fool.

"Stu, what are you going to do for a job? Sooner or later we'll have to get a job. Have you thought about that?"

He hesitated, sucked at a joint, then grinned a comical smile and said, "I'm going to sell Thai pot!"

"Aw, c'mon, get serious. What are you going to do?"

"I'm going to go back, look things over, and see what looks good. I don't want to get my mind all turned on to something, then go home to find out I can't get into it and get all discouraged."

"I know I want to get away from welding and dented fenders. I wake up in the morning, and my eyes are all red and bloodshot, and my lungs ache, and I don't want to live the rest of my life like that."

Stu was grinning, holding up the joint. "You wake up, light one of these, and *make* your eyes bloodshot and your lungs ache!"

"Well, that too. But I used to look at the guys that have been doing this stuff all their lives, and they're blind at forty, having cataract operations and arthritis operations and coughing up blood. Man, that's nothing to look forward to. I'm gonna grow my hair longer, but I think I'll buy a suit and see if I can't bullshit my way into something respectable. No more work uniforms. Man, I have had uniforms up to here!"

Stu crushed out the joint and stood up abruptly. "That is precisely the reason why you shouldn't take any job in Sattahip. You feel different, the army would tell you they made you a man, but you've been away long enough. You got your head together, probably more by smoking Thai grass than by being a soldier, but now you're ready to go home. You're scared shitless, but you want to go home, and if you just freak on getting your head ready, you're going to find out it's the biggest trip you will ever take. You're going back to start from scratch, you can do anything you want. You can show them! You can, and you will. Then some day twenty years from now we'll get together and be rich and fat, and we'll go down to some bar and puff cigars and wonder what the hell we used to talk about. We'll walk over to a cigarette machine and buy a pack of joints and laugh about the days when pot was illegal and we stayed stoned in Thailand! Hey, I gotta go. Catch ya in the A.M."

Then he was gone, and I was alone. Donovan was singing "Hurdy Gurdy Man," and I settled back and tried to picture what it would be like, back in The World. I decided I couldn't make it today, but I would get my head screwed on before I caught that big Freedom Bird. Imagine! I would soon walk up to a refrigerator full of goodies, ice cream and chocolate syrup and maraschino cherries and whipped cream. Drag races, road races at Watkins Glen. Water skiing. Twenty movie theaters, each with a different feature. A rock concert, with a psychedelic light show. Cornfields and dairy cows. The special scent of wheat when a field is harvested, the dust congestion in your nose, but that beautiful, special scent. The smell of cow manure, so different from water buffalo shit. Mowing the lawn. Ann Landers in the paper, on your porch every morning. Flopped on the couch on a Sunday afternoon, watching football on television, munching popcorn. Dad's home-fried potatoes. Niagara Falls. The earsplitting roar of a fuel dragster breaking two hundred miles an hour. Girls in plaid wool skirts and ruffled silk blouses, with faint perfume behind their ears, a special treat for someone they would let get close enough to notice it. Snow. Christmas trees and jack o' lanterns. I used to walk down the street every day and never, *never* see an army uniform! No olive-drab loose-fitting fatigues. Hell, when Fidel wore fatigues to address the United Nations in New York, the papers called him a barbarian! No olive-drab trucks. No saluting. No rank. No ignorant sergeants. No days to count. Once, long, long ago, I would get up in the morning, and it would be simply and concisely the twelfth of May, and I didn't have to mark off a day on a short-timer's calendar. What would it be like, to not be waiting? What would it be like to get up, open the refrigerator, go to a job I had chosen, knowing I could quit or call in sick or bust my ass and feel as if I had accomplished something? It was too enormous to consider. To have the basic freedom to say, "I don't feel like it today." Wow!

• • • •

I applied for another leave to Penang. While it was fun to pal around with a group of guys, high on pot, laughing and delirious, I was crossing more and more days off my calendar. The return trip to The World was a reality fast approaching, and I needed to see Lin, talk out some of the problems I was sure her profession would present when the paperwork got into the final stages. I needed a transfusion of real affection; the orgasms in massage parlors had become mechanical relief, like scratching an itch. I was finding myself visiting Thai families more and more often, admiring the closeness only a stable loving relationship brings. I dreamed of children, of home-cooked meals, and of long talks with the one person in all creation I had picked to spend my life with.

I had gathered a considerable sum of money, intending to give Lin a special week of first-class treatment. I had to make her believe in me, that I could and would give her everything. I had a plan. If she would emigrate to Thailand and get a job as a secretary, I thought the bureaucracy might get confused or discouraged trying to track her down through the bureaucracies of two other countries. I had no doubt I could bribe some official in Thailand to make the papers acceptable, and at least the fact that she had left prostitution and was working at a "legitimate" job would be in her favor. I wanted to show Lin the country I had learned to love, I wanted to live with her as Jack had with Mai-Lee, perhaps get married in a Buddhist ceremony that would not be recognized by the American authorities, but would be my commitment. I thought we could, we *would* find a way. Yes, I had had doubts. Faced with marriage, all young men experience doubts. I was about to re-enter a world I no longer knew and that would not know me. I looked forward to it and felt afraid of it at the same time. I was convinced it would be a difficult adjustment, one I could approach with far more optimism if I had a course charted and could watch pieces gradually falling into place.

I had lived through three hundred and seventy days in The Nam and another hundred here, clicking them off like mileage posts on the edge of a great interstate highway. I was living the same goal-oriented existence again, coloring out the squares on my calendar until I had served my sentence and could be a free man. I had tried to remember what it would be like to get up in the morning as a civilian and not X out a square, not be a day closer to the end of an ordeal. It was, in my present circumstances, beyond comprehension.

If I could create a goal, if Lin and I, together, could assign a reason for getting out of bed, things would be a lot easier. First, we would get her to America. Then we would set up housekeeping. There would be kids, with all the accompanying paraphernalia; shoes, lunchboxes, a bicycle, a training bra. I couldn't picture any other scenario. It was this or nothing. Oh, I wanted to be clean, wear a shirt and tie; but if the boss expected me to sell my soul to the corporation for a bigger office or a title, I could always go back to the body shop and bang dents out of fenders and go home at quitting time and survive. As long as there weren't any rockets raining down in the backyard, I would be satisfied.

I wrote these things to Lin, hoping to start her thinking, and she said we would talk about it. It was a small step, but I was pleased. When the day came, I collected all the necessary papers, signed out, and caught a bus to Bangkok. I taxied to the airport, checked my luggage, and strolled out onto the white hot concrete toward the waiting plane. At the bottom of the stairs a Thai official checked my visa. It was incomplete!

How could that be? The army had procured it for me, just like last time, and there had been no problem on the train. I was escorted back inside the terminal to an office. A policeman called someone, there was a long wait. I could hear the jet engines whining. What about my luggage? The policeman waved me away. There was an exchange of words in a tone that indicated he was sincerely trying to help. It was no use. He replaced the telephone on its cradle and tossed my passport across the desk. I'm sorry. What about my luggage? The scream of the jets was fading. Another phone call. Pick it up Wednesday after three in the afternoon. What do I do 'til then, without even a toothbrush? He shrugged.

I stepped out of the office into the chaotic terminal. This was some kind of cruel joke. I knew the American Embassy was on Sukhumvit. They should be able to straighten this thing out. No, they explained, it was a visa problem, the visa would have to be granted by the Malaysian government, and that could take three weeks.

I walked back into the bright heat, sat on a low brick wall, lit a cigarette, and tried to decide what to do. I couldn't very well go back to Korat and save the leave days, because Wednesday I had to pick up my luggage at the airport. It was late Monday afternoon. Lin would be expecting me at any moment. I had to call her, tell her what had happened. Fucking army! It wasn't so bad putting up with the incompetence on their time, but this was my time.

There was a hotel next to the embassy, a large and very beautiful hotel Stu had pointed out. Bob Hope stayed there when he came to Bangkok. I could get a room, call Lin. Maybe I could see a little of Bangkok, pick up my luggage, and check in off leave Wednesday night. I still had time to try again. Not even a toothbrush, let alone a change of clothes. Damn!

Lin had been understanding, but there was no time to talk. I had begged her to get a passport, come to Korat. We could talk. I had a few days of leave time left, we could go to Phi Mai or Bangkok. I would send the money for her fare, for the passport. Please come. No, Mama-san would not understand. I did not understand. Did Mama-san want to marry her and take her to America? I would be going home soon, thirteen thousand miles away, and we had so many things to talk about. Casually, much too casually, she suggested I come to Penang. If only I could, but here I was in Bangkok without even a change of clothes, as if in retribution for trying. It wasn't that easy. Well, if I couldn't even arrange a leave to Penang…she had to go now. Love you, good-bye. Twenty-five bucks!

Where was it headed? Her last letter had been so upbeat, so full of excitement and hope and optimism. If she had been there, right there, right then, I would have been too bewildered, too confused, for even her sensuous body to cut through the haze and excite me. I was going back to The World, thirteen thousand miles away, and everyone at home expected me to act "engaged," which would have meant no dating, no girls, but thirteen thousand miles was so far. Why had she let me feel so distant while I was still within reach? Didn't she know how much I needed a friendly word? I was so alone, with such an obstacle ahead. She could have fired my imagination, convinced me I could make it. I needed that, and she had said no. If I went home without the dream, what would they say? What would I say? I spent an extra year in Thailand because I needed...needed what? I felt a need I couldn't put my finger on, a need to justify it all. Why? Why hadn't I just gone to Niagara Falls, crossed the Peace Bridge for a "better view of the American Falls," and gone to Toronto? Scared of being alone in a strange city? Look at me now. I had been so tired, so physically wrung out, so emotionally ravaged at Fort Dix I had wanted to just fall into the snow and lay there. Let them kick me, punch me, haul me off to jail, I didn't care. But I had cared, I pushed myself, and what did it get me? In the final estimation, I had lain in the mud and water and water buffalo shit and didn't give a rat's ass if I lived or died, and I had trouble sleeping sometimes because when I closed my eyes I saw hundreds of little people in black pajamas charging at me, and I drugged myself every day so the day would go by without me noticing.

What a way to live! I had been a round peg, and the army had positioned me over the square hole and hammered me down, 'til the smooth edges were now splintered and ragged. In a few days they would send me back to the round hole, and I wouldn't fit, and I would try to cover the ragged edges with a suit and tie, polished shoes, and clean fingernails. I would go to a job interview, tell some asshole I was a round peg, he would ask where I had been the last few years, and I would say, "In the square hole," and he would know I wouldn't fit his round hole anymore, and what then? If I had had the dream, the plan, I could have said, "I'm a round peg," and pulled it off. I had to hang onto the dream. I had to be able to answer when someone asked, "Why?" and the only thing that had mattered in so long was Lin, I had to have her to dream about, talk about; or just stand there and trip on all the other shit, and I would be arrested for indecent exposure. People in The World were so hung up about seeing a tit or pubic hair or somebody's bare ass, what would they say when they looked into my eyes and saw a hollow ball filled with blood and gore and tortured, ravaged nerve endings all squirming and twisting and begging for some small escape? I could hear them. "We're so glad you're home!" Why? What the fuck did I ever do for you? What do you want me to do for you? "You look good!" You mean, compared to the guys that come home in a box. You look better than they, except the eyes. "What happened to your eyes?" Well, I was watching this whore one day, and she took a douche with a fire hose, and just kinda exploded into a pink mist, and the old eyes ain't been the same since…must've caught some sort of spray. "I'm sorry, sir, the position's been filled by a person who doesn't utter obscenities in every sentence." Fuck ya! "What a beautiful day!" Easy for you to say, sitting in your rocking chair admiring your roses! What you fail to realize is, in a few hours that very same sun is gonna be looking down on a bunch of guys in a hole, and they'll see the dead Charleys hanging on the barbed wire, and they'll smell shit and piss and death and gunpowder; and they'll cross off another day on a calendar, and a lot of them are gonna die. They'll scream and twitch and cry and beg, and grab their intestines with both hands and try to cram them back into the hole where their belly-button used to collect lint, and they'll choke to death on the blood in their throat, or look down and discover their legs aren't there any more. Nice day? No, nice days are for children and fools. "How does it feel to kill somebody?" I don't know. How does it feel to be crueler than death? "I remember when you were only this tall." That was before I died. Now I'm only *this* tall, carrying around this body like a penitent. "Why did you make it and my son die?" Well, I met this Chinese girl, and just gritted my teeth and ducked. What would you like me to say? He was dumb enough to step in front of a bullet? It wasn't that way, but I can't quite find the words to describe it right now.

Would it be fair to saddle Lin with all that responsibility? One look at her, a few words with her, and they would say, "I understand. She's beautiful." We would go home, lock the door, and I would say, "That was a close one!" and she would say, "Love me!" and drop frilly lace things one by one and hold me and make all the ugly things go away.

Suddenly, it was eight o'clock, raining, dark, and I was very alone. Lost in my thoughts, I hadn't noticed it getting dark, and I was sitting in the black void, and I had to get my mind off this. Wish I had a joint and some music. Wish Stu was here to talk to. Wish Lin was here, or Mom and Dad, or somebody. They're all off living their lives, thinking I'm living mine, not particularly worried about me, just knowing I'm off in the distance somewhere. I can't just sit here in the dark.

• • • •

The rain was soft, refreshing. The taxi drivers flocked around like predators. Do it in Thai, blow their minds, keep the price down. I want to go to a place, near the Temple of the Emerald Buddha. I know the temple is closed, but I want to go to a warehouse, a big, big bordello, in a warehouse. I saw it a few weeks ago, a friend showed me. It is a warehouse, maybe four stories tall, a whole city block, with many women, many unusual pleasures. You know the place? How much? Oh, no can do! I give you *yee-sip* baht. Okay, *yee-sip-see*, twenty-four. We go. How do I know this place? My friend showed me. Very expensive, very good? I never go before.

We came to a stop in front of a huge, concrete warehouse. Yes, this is the place. I paid the cabbie, he pointed out the door, and I knocked. A heavyset Thai in white shirt and tie opened the door, urged me in out of the drizzle. I was wet, unkempt. Did I have identification? Yes, my military ID. I presented it, he gave me a quick glance, handed it back, and led me to another door where he rang a buzzer. In a few moments, the door opened and a strikingly beautiful girl smiled and held out her hand. There was a long hallway, carpeted now, another door, the sound of music. Through the door, an abrupt right turn, and we were in a restaurant. It was a bright, airy, cheerful atmosphere; greens and whites, huge plants, ceiling fans softly moving the air, an acoustic guitar off to the left somewhere. The furniture was wicker, with pale green pillows. The table-cloths were emerald green, the napkins white with green bor-ders; the plates and utensils and crystal goblets refracted and reflected the beams of myriad hidden spotlights high above, mostly white, a few green, some blue to add a sensation of cool-ness and zest. I was in slacks and button-down shirt, playing Stu's game, and my hair felt wet and matted against my fore-head. The girl led me to a table for two tucked into a corner, held my chair, lit my cigarette, and bowed. She wore a pale green dress of Thai silk, the wraparound skirt to the floor, the bodice stiff and not revealing. Her hair was done in a flamboy-ant swirl, and long earrings reached toward her shoulders.

"I am Savitri. Do you wish dinner or a drink?" I ordered a light meal and a Scotch, anxious to finish eating and find the brothel. Most Americans had only whispered about this place, and here I was. I watched the other clientele, mostly older Asian businessmen in dark suits, with occasional Caucasians here and there. It was quiet, restrained, cultured. Savitri returned with my dinner and drink, then disappeared to leave me to eat alone. When I finished, she brought the dessert menu, suggested an after-dinner liqueur, and asked me to sign the check. I paid cash, rose to leave, and she accompanied me to the area near where I had entered. An ornate Victorian lamp lit a small table in the corner. On the table rested a large leather-bound book. Instead of the door, Savitri led me to this small table and held the chair. She settled into the other and leaned toward me, her eyes lowered.

"Do you wish to visit a young lady this evening?" It was a dignified, respectful inquiry. How did a gentleman respond with equal good taste? I decided to be direct and not wordy.

"Yes."

She opened the great leather volume. "We are very proud to offer great pleasure. Please read about our facilities while I summon a guide for you. She will accompany you upstairs. It has been my great pleasure to serve you." I offered a tip and she bowed and disappeared. I concentrated on the book.

It was ornate, printed on parchment paper, lettered in elaborate and flowing black script. On the outside edges of the page, tiny watercolor couples bathed together, rested together, or were locked into various positions of the act of love. The English was somewhat broken, but adequate. The first page listed rooms, each with a special motif or atmosphere. There must have been forty choices, wild, exotic-sounding chambers to suit the most adventurous or perverse aficionado. The second page offered combination baths; the Roman emperor, the Finnish sauna, the lotus blossom. Many of these choices included a number of women; you could order the quantity, the field of expertise, the nationality, even the language to be spoken. I turned the page to find detailed lists of costuming: the Cleopatra with sheer harem pantaloons and golden brassiere, the schoolgirl with frilly knickers, the Harlow in shimmering satin, dozens of other choices. Then there were costumes for the male: cowboys, policemen, Roman togas, each with a description of the delights to be imagined while clad in this outfit.

The rest of the book reminded me of my high school yearbook. Page after page of glamorous photographs of beautiful women, a smorgasbord arranged by nationality, with a caption detailing each lady's age, talents, special kinks, and a brief sentence describing her in glowing terms. I almost expected to turn the page and find the girl voted "most likely to succeed." At the rear, a few pages displayed the various rooms or girls in use, the customers' faces hidden, the girls seemingly bursting with unrestrained joy. I noted that the pages were loose-leaf, indicating turnover, but with such a choice I did not feel I would miss much if one or two of the girls were no longer available. I was thumbing through the book for the third time when my guide arrived. She, too, was beautiful, and almost regal in her bearing.

"Have you chosen?"

I laughed nervously. "There is so much to chose from, I am not sure I can decide."

"Would you like to tour our facilities, to see for yourself all that we offer?"

How could I refuse? In the wildest flights of fancy, the most sensuous drug-induced journey through the depths of my sexual subconscious, I had never envisioned anything like this! I wanted to explore it all, choose only when all the choices had been laid out before me. I followed the slim escort to an elevator. "We have three floors," she explained. "I'm sure you will find something that interests you. Privacy and discretion are assured. You need only concern yourself with an evening of total sexual pleasure."

"You speak English very well."

She smiled. "I am a graduate of Florida State University. I hope to begin graduate work next year."

The elevator door opened onto a panorama of golds and reds, oranges and maroons. This was a lobby, a sitting room, with soft music and subdued lighting. My guide led me across the thick carpet, down a short hallway. This floor, she explained, was furnished for the more conventional tastes. Each door had a small light panel, and she stopped at one with no glowing bulb, opened the door, and presented a room featuring a huge bed and the most tasteful decorations. She pointed out the radio controls, bathroom, light dimmer, and fresh flowers. Further down the hall another room featured a round bed and sunken tub, and another had mirrors on the ceiling and walls. There was a room with a massage table, another with pillows instead of furniture, an office with a broad-top desk, a school-room, and a child's room with a giant crib and teddy bears. By the number of glowing lights, it was obvious many of the rooms were occupied.

Her name was Lana. She led me down another hallway, opulent and yet dark and discreet, to a curving stairway with a white marble balustrade. She lifted the hem of her skirt as she ascended the steps. "The next floor offers more unusual delights, the fantasies many men entertain but never expect to experience. Perhaps you will be shocked."

At the top of the stairway long halls led off to the right and left. The doorways were spaced farther apart, but featured the usual light panels. Again, we stopped at rooms with no glowing light.

The first was an adult-sized replica of a child's nursery, with frilly gingham adornments and another huge crib. There were stuffed oversized animals and a large changing table with a stock of adult-size diapers, rubber pants, and baby powders. Along the left wall sat a jolly if enormous rocking horse with a most unusual "saddle horn." The next room was a replica of a beauty shop, with an adjoining women's wear department straight out of a fashionable store, with racks of exotic gowns and dresses. An adjoining cubicle simulated the lingerie counter, a transvestite's dream come true.

At the next door, a sign declared, "Hospital Zone...Quiet, Please" in numerous languages. Inside there was a patient's room, complete with adjustable bed, nightstand, bedpan, even fresh flowers and a wheelchair. Lana led me down a short hall to an operating room, with bright lights and shimmering tiles that seemed about as sexual as a morgue. "We have a staff of professional nurses who are fully certified and able to cure nearly any complaint," she said.

In another room she opened the drapes to exhibit a large window looking in on an ornate bedroom. "We allow exhibitionists to entertain voyeurs," she stated matter-of-factly, "but of course the window is one-way glass. This room features a modern sound system, so one might catch every sound from the room next door." I was getting edgy and could feel a blush painting my cheeks. Next was a shoestore, offering a wide array of styles; then a room decorated like the interior of a sheik's desert tent. I noticed the exquisite water pipe and wished I had a joint.

There was a medieval king's palace with thrones upon a raised dais and suits of armor. There was a peaceful garden, featuring a strange wicker chair suspended over a couch. According to Lana, a girl could be lowered onto the male, the chair was bottomless, and, when lowered to the proper position, could be spun. "A most unusual sensation," she said. It was a beautiful garden, with a gurgling brook, white latticework with creeping roses, and the sounds of birds twittering in the trees.

On down the hall we visited a pirate ship, a saloon from a western movie, a Roman villa prepared for an orgy, and a church. There were two dungeons, cold stone rooms with chains and racks of whips, and strange ladders of heavy wood. Without emotion, Lana showed me the jail cell where the male slave awaited his fate; in the other dungeon four naked women were visible through another one-way glass, their wrists chained above their heads. "We are quite liberal in the punishments we allow the customer to inflict," my guide whispered, "and the dungeons are very well-equipped."

"Are the girls held against their will?" I asked, incredulous. You hear about things like this, but it was incredible to have it presented with no outward emotion. Regardless of the answer, I doubted I would really believe it.

"They are all volunteers. This is the highest-paid position we offer, and there are many volunteers. In a place like this, you soon learn that there are all types of people."

After the dungeons, it was refreshing to climb another stairway to the third floor. These were the exotic baths, and many were apt to be in use, she said. We would hope to find one or two that I could see. There were very few doors on each hallway, and when we found one without the telltale lights and entered I could see why. This was no brothel; this was a set for a Hollywood spectacular! I was in ancient Egypt; far off to the right I could see pyramids. Huge stone pillars supported a temple to my left, and wide stone steps led down to the pool. Straight ahead a tent of translucent pastels sheltered pillows and cushions of various colors and sizes. "This is Cleopatra's garden," Lana whispered. "Imagine the pleasure of bathing with Cleopatra, attended by a dozen beautiful handmaidens. We have a selection of the most exotic oils that will be rubbed deep into your body; soothing, caressing, preparing you for the pleasures only the most beautiful woman in history can provide." She looked at me from under her long, dark lashes. "Once, I was Cleopatra." I didn't know what to say, but this was beyond my budget.

The other rooms were in use. We took an elevator down to the crimson lobby. Lana led me to a tufted leather couch in the rear, handed me the book again, and left me to myself while she fetched a complimentary Scotch and water. I looked around nervously; the room was deserted except for me. What the hell was I doing here? This place was positively outrageous, maybe even perverted! I could feel my cheeks stretch into a grin. I liked it! I couldn't afford it, but I liked it. The average tourist in Bangkok never saw anything like this. I thought back to Stu and our shopping trip on the Rappasong; the way he had bullshitted the merchants. You'll never see a place like this again, I told myself, play the role. You've got a few bucks;

you're not going to Malaysia. What else were you planning to do tonight? Sit in a dark room and feel sorry for yourself? Someday when you're old and gray you'll wish you had. I reached for the book, flipped the pages. Outrageous! I stayed.

• • • •

The next day I toured more temples and the famous floating market. In the evening I went back to The Balcony. As the taxi roared through the rainy streets I caught a glimpse of an incredible automobile in a dealership window. The taxi driver waited while I pressed my nose to the plate glass and fantasized. I was familiar with exotic cars from Ferrari, Lamborghini, or Maserati, but this was something different. Its rounded contours seemed menacing as a torpedo, yet the upswept tail was tasteful and pleasing to the eye. Back in the taxi, I asked the driver to interpret the unintelligible squiggle above the showroom window. Toyota. Made in Nippon. Japan. The Japanese only made children's toys and transistor radios. The idea of Japanese high-performance car was absurd. I laughed as we went on to The Balcony.

• • • •

Wednesday morning I wandered the Rappasong, playing Stu's game, window-shopping, acting rich. I began to get the system down, the merchants were taking me seriously, and it was fun. After lunch I taxied to the airport and retrieved my bags. I had to pass the army counter where I had checked into Thailand, and I stopped in my shoes, riveted by another fantasy become reality. A long line of delirious GIs stretched across the tarmac to a waiting American Airlines jetliner. I heard myself whisper, "The Freedom Bird!" Thoughts of my luggage disappeared. I raced up to the observation deck, cranked a fresh frame into my camera, and waited for the magnificent bird to lift off and turn toward the east. It was beautiful, graceful, awesome. I watched until the tiny black speck disappeared into the eastern clouds. On my way down the stairs I noticed a poster with a pen-and-ink drawing of a jetliner and huge, flamboyant black letters that shouted, "Meet the People Pleaser." I went directly to the airline's counter and talked the attendant out of a poster. This would be my new short-timer's calendar!

That evening I called home. Collect! It was afternoon; Dad was working, my brother was at school. Mom sounded glad to hear from me. I was fine, in Bangkok, and I had just watched a bunch of guys get on a Freedom Bird and fly east. My day was fast approaching. But there was bad news. Brenda Lustine had been killed in a car crash, and her fiancé had volunteered for a transfer to The Nam from Thailand. Bud had been a nice guy, and I was saddened. Could I find him, talk to him, before he got himself killed? I would try. Gotta get off this thing. Tell Dad I'm sorry I missed him. See you in a few months.

What a shame! Brenda had been beautiful, so full of life. I had never dated her, but we were friends. Dead! Now Bud was trying to do something stupid. If he wanted to join her, I could understand that. I would advise him to just commit suicide, escape the agony of The Nam. With death so real to him, so personal, he might go crazy in The Nam. There would be a lot of reminders. Better to just get it over with. Living in Vietnam was no answer to anyone's problems.

Depression was invading me again. I could feel it. So many friends, dead. Gone, never to laugh or speak or cry; just gone. Eighteen months ago, I thought my dad was maudlin when he read obituaries. Now I wondered who would be next, which teenager or twenty-year-old would not be around the neighborhood. How could I have been so callous when Skeeter Patrick had bought the farm? Why had it seemed, well, almost glamorous to die drag racing a Chevy? Dead was dead. Bud was my friend. We had laughed, water-skied, driven through blinding snowstorms for pizza, whispered in study hall. Together. Graduated, together. Yearbook pictures. That's all that was left. A black-and-white likeness of a kid in a tie; and all you could remember was the kid in a T-shirt; and now he would be a kid in the mud and the blood, in jungle fatigues, and he wouldn't be a kid anymore. I would probably never see him again. If I had only known it would be like this, the day we graduated I would have thrown my arms around every one of them and held them close and told them how much band practice and the senior play and those notes in study hall had meant to me. Now it was too late.

I had to get out of this mood. I went to the hotel restaurant for dinner. The hostess was gorgeous. One? Yes, please. The waitress was even more beautiful. I spoke Thai. I had eaten Thai food almost exclusively for months, but it had been the food of peasants. Would she please help me to experience the finest Thai cuisine, the very ultimate in pleasure the chef could prepare for my American tongue? I sipped a Thai beer, waiting to be served, when the hostess interrupted my thoughts. The restaurant was very crowded. A Japanese gentleman wished to eat, but there was no table at which to seat him. Would I consider allowing him...? Of course! Of course! I would welcome the company and the exposure to a new culture.

He was, I guessed, in his late thirties, a salesman for a camera company. He wore a dark blue business suit and spoke textbook English. We talked long into the evening; long after my ultra-dinner was gone. We talked over too many beers. I remember the conversation, but not the dinner. He spoke of technology, transistors, and sophisticated electronics. Yes, I had seen a Japanese sports car the other night, and it was impressive. "We lost the last world war on the battlefield," he said. "We believe the next world war will be fought in the marketplace. After Hiroshima, war is too terrible. We expect the war to be fought in the marketplace; and we are prepared to win. We will conquer the world with technology." I was skeptical, though I didn't tell my friend that. I had seen strong nationalistic pride in these undeveloped countries. Of course, they could never approach the technology of the United States, but it was the struggle to try that gave the people a reason to go on. Pride and dreams of greatness were one thing; world leadership, especially in technology, was something else again. Imagine Japan, devastated by World War II, trying to outdo the United States in technology! It was ridiculous, laughable. I was very respectful, but completely skeptical.

It was June 1969. I had a Yashica camera and a Sony stereo. I did not know that there were Toyota dealerships in California. My guitar was made by Yamaha. In Vietnam, America spent $141 billion, much of it on technology, the technology of death and destruction. We could not defeat people who made watches tick with beer-can mechanisms. We lost forty-nine hundred helicopters, many to cross-bows. History has not made her final judgment on the wisdom of our investments. It was laughable in 1969.

• • • •

I returned to Korat, my fortune squandered. Granny's caught fire, and a few of us went to watch the excitement. To our joy and amazement, a huge crowd had gathered...downwind! Having read about the love-ins in The World, this Saturday afternoon celebration seemed like a Thai version of a modern-day happening. Literally hundreds of people got a free high; but a basket was passed, contributions were quickly forthcoming, and Granny was soon back in business.

The problem was, I decided the next day, that it was all so meaningless. Another day had dawned, another milestone toward the future, but the future was far off and difficult to predict. Until September I was destined to sink in a quagmire of meaningless existence. After The Nam I had needed a time-out from life. The atmosphere of Thailand had been perfect, but it was a superficial satisfaction. I still wore the army insignia on my chest, still made formation at 6:00 every morning. Coloring a square on my calendar was a token acknowledgment of life as it had used to be. Once I had accomplished that daily ritual, my day bore little relevance to the rest of my life. I wasn't building a future, I was serving time, and time had become an insurmountable foe. No longer in the mood for a fight, even against the innocuous calendar, I distorted reality behind a cloud of pot smoke.

One afternoon a group of us were chatting on the barracks steps when I mentioned that I was glad I didn't have to work the next day. Bixby moaned. "You got tomorrow off? How'd you manage that?"

"It's Sunday!" I answered matter-of-factly. "You don't have to work Sundays, do you?"

"Sarge, you better lay off that Thai wacky-baccy. It's Wednesday, tomorrow's Thursday. If tomorrow was Sunday you wouldn't have worked today. You do remember working an hour ago, don't you?"

I didn't remember working today, and I was more surprised to hear the date. It was sixteen days later than I remembered! Somehow, I had stumbled through sixteen days totally unaware, in charge of forty-odd GIs and half a dozen Thais. They were relying on me, their families were relying on me, and I didn't know what I had done for over two weeks. Surely the army had noticed? I asked Bixby if I had done anything particularly outrageous. No, he said, I had acted normal. If I could exist in a fog for sixteen days and seem normal, I was pretty messed up when I was normal. Taking a frank look at myself, I was normally stoned, and the simple fact was, it was illegal. I could go to jail for possession of a bag of grass. I should be going home soon. I was short, almost a ninety-day loss. I didn't smoke any pot that night.

In fact, I didn't smoke any grass for a number of nights, and my suspicions were reinforced when my Thai neighbors asked what was wrong. I explained that I was preparing myself to return to America, and they scoffed. "Don't go home to the States," they advised. "You are more Thai than American now. You will never be happy in the States." I sat on my porch, listening to the same records, eating the same foods, and I wondered if they might be right. Without the drug, my sleep was tormented by human waves and napalm-scarred children.

I sought help. There was an American mission in Korat, and I thought it might offer someone to talk with. My "battlefield religion" had disintegrated to an Oriental form of ecumenism. I saw God in the wonders of Nature, but felt no desire to attend formal services, especially Christian. How could I embrace an American Christian church that openly supported war against Vietnamese Christians? Surely, the one Supreme Being would never condone such actions. With all this in mind, and a growing uneasiness about returning home, I spoke to a "missionary." He was quiet, listened well, then suggested we move to another room. The door opened onto a large room where ten or twelve GIs were talking or reading. He led me to the center of the room, raised his hands, and boomed. His voice trembled with pseudo-emotion, and a dozen pairs of eyes riveted on my chest. "Looooord Jeeeeesus," he moaned at top volume, "our brother has come to us in need." He ordered me to my knees and asked the silent GIs to lay their hands on me. I did not to go to my knees. I did not beg Jesus to take my sins away. I interrupted. I just wanted someone to talk to. I hadn't done anything. He drowned out my embarrassed pleas. "Oh, Jeeesus, we pray for our brother…" I burst out the door and never went back.

One of the neighborhood girls arranged a meeting with a Buddhist monk who spoke English. He was a tiny old man with shaved head and glasses, and the inevitable orange robe. He was calming. We talked in a shaded courtyard beside an ancient temple. I was moved, but he suggested I not allow the past to haunt me and said to concentrate on the present. Accept life as an inevitable burden to be endured as preparation for the next life. It was a pleasant conversation, but I could not, or would not, accept all that I had seen. Did we not have obligations during this life? I felt no guilt, just fear. Fear of being busted, fear of that truck without markings, fear that my nightmares meant I was losing my mind, fear that I would no longer fit into American society or the human race.

I had to overhaul my life. I left my beloved bungalow and the neighborhood I had enjoyed so much. I lived on post a few days, but the military atmosphere wasn't preparing me for home. I rented a room in the Semanut Hotel, just down the hall from Stu. I had a double bed, American-style toilet and shower, air conditioning, wall-to-wall carpet, a closet with wooden hangers, and a huge dresser with a mirror that covered one wall. There was a phone, and round-the-clock room service.

I saw this as a major commitment. I was going home and had to prepare myself. This room, according to my distant memories, was almost American. The walls were pastel, and the bathroom had tiles and chrome. No more bare wooden walls; no more showers by dipping water out of a barrel and throwing it over my head. I gave my pipe to Noi. In America I could not smoke pot. It was illegal, and I had served enough days. I wore my wraparound Chinese pantaloons only as pajamas, and stopped wearing Nehru shirts and love beads. I put away my John Lennon round glasses and wore the military plastic frames. At the very outside, I limited myself to one joint a day. It helped me imagine the life I would soon be rejoining.

More than a little of my concern was for Lin. Once I got her to the States, it would be a disaster if I were busted for pot smoking. In order to build my future, I had to get my head clear. Jobs were scarce, and I would never find one dressed like a hippie. When I returned home, I could be anyone I wanted to be. I wanted to be successful.

In ninety days, I would be a civilian. I was scared to death and looking forward to it at the same time. If I smoked in the evenings, it was usually a single joint after dinner. Then I would sit in front of my mirror, study my face, practice the words I would use on a job interview. "Yes, sir, I spent a year in Vietnam, and then a year in Thailand supporting the war effort. No one was shooting in Thailand. Yes, sir, I saw some action, but I prefer not to talk about it. Yes, sir, we can win the war. The people of Vietnam are not fighting for ideologies or political ideas; they are fighting for food, for survival. If we load all those bombers with rice, and bread, and seed, and planting tools, and paint 'From your friends in the United States' on each one, they will turn to us. The Viet Cong cannot match that. We have to stop trying to match the VC in terror and horror and killing and maiming. If we offer the people peace, and hope, and a future, they will embrace us. It is difficult to embrace ideas, either democracy or communism, when the rhetoric is drowned out by the sound of your children crying from napalm burns and starvation." That seemed to say it, and in a way that no one could dispute. No blood-and-guts war stories, just look 'em in the eye and don't back down. If they don't like it, fuck 'em.

●　●　●　●

No, I couldn't get that close to my own wounds, wounds that weren't healed. "I have satisfied my military obligation." With the draft swallowing up so many young men, that would be a positive statement. Don't ask for trouble. Don't volunteer anything. The fighting had grown increasingly ugly, both in The Nam and in the streets back in The World. Blood was being shed, the government was entrenched, fortified, spitting in the face of public opinion. There were, there would always be, the "my government right or wrong" types. There were wiretaps and indictments, and blood had flowed. I was afraid to face a war in The World. It was obvious the government was committed to this thing. Nixon had said what the people wanted to hear, but was doing nothing. Drop a bomb on Hanoi in the morning, negotiate in the afternoon, express frustration in the evening. How long had we been bombing Hanoi? What had it gotten us? We had already dropped more tons of bombs on Vietnam than we had dropped on Hitler; more than twelve tons for every square mile in both North and South Vietnam. We couldn't even convince Hanoi to agree on the shape of the negotiating table! We had dropped over one hundred pounds of explosive for every man, woman, and child in the two Vietnams. Nixon talked of withdrawing troops, but we could see the bombers overhead every day. A troop withdrawal just meant easier pickings for Charley, and an infuriated South Vietnamese government ordering their already incompetent forces to do even less. I expected another Tet to bring calls for more troops. One out of every four American soldiers was AWOL or deserted, unable to accept the horror, harassment, and genocidal atmosphere. Since my first day in the army, I had been surrounded by the insignia "FTA." In spray paint, ink carvings, embroidery; no matter where you looked, those three letters were there. Everywhere. FTA! Fuck the army! Over one-third of the cost of the Vietnam war was supposedly attributable to sabotage by disgruntled GIs. Now new reports from The Nam indicated that the despair had manifested itself in a more sinister form. "Fragging" had become an epidemic. I wondered if Captain Benedict had lived out his tour of duty.

This was the news from Vietnam. Our slave-labor fighting force was revolting, deserting, getting stoned. Surely the military realized they had gone too far. No, the draft continued, the bombing continued, the newest state-of-the-art technology was arriving. Did they really think pulling out 4 or 5 percent of the troops would quiet the protestors? By now all the maimed, disfigured, shattered hulks of men I had seen in The Nam should be returning home; the survivors of Tet and Khe Sanh and Hill 875, without arms or legs, walking down Main Street, U.S.A., with those eyes. You couldn't hide them. You couldn't ignore them. By now, they should be everywhere; hobbling, wheeling themselves, drinking in bars, taking their kids to school, telling wives, family, neighbors, everyone what was going on. How, in the face of that, could the war go on? How could any parent walk down the street, come face to face with a guy who had been to war, and allow his son to be drafted? The very fact that it continued convinced me they must be bursting into houses and taking away draft-age boys at gunpoint.

There was only one way to win, and the United States always wins. Only one way. There had been only one way in the war with Japan, and it worked. Twenty-five thousand troops being withdrawn? What ranks? They get all the colonels and generals out of there, then drop the Big One and send a lot of letters to the parents. Wait for Hanoi to surrender. Drop another one if the wait was too long. It's sitting in Udorn, just waiting. There aren't many alternatives left. Victory! Intimidate the world. That's what the policy had been since Hiroshima, why not reinforce it? Concern for half a million American kids? I had seen their concern. Swagger sticks and polished boots. Win a medal ten thousand feet in the air, looking down on the jungle where some expendable kid is trying to push his brains back into the hole in the side of his head. "I had dinner with Captain Benedict while he was in Saigon, and I consider him a fine officer…"

Night after night, hour after hour, I sat in front of that mirror, looking deep into myself, hoping to find enough resolve to get me through it. One night I thought I saw it, the next night I knew it wasn't there.

• • • •

There was the mandatory re-enlistment talk, the starched and spit-shined lieutenant. I vowed not to spend one minute in the army I didn't have to. He hadn't been to The Nam. He was sorry I felt that way. I was sorry too.

A whirlwind struck downtown in the form of an international motor rally. Strange little cars with multiple driving lights, crumpled fenders, a crust of mud and dust. Inside, stark rollover bars, stopwatches, aviation lights, and complex mileage instruments. Two-man crews; wild, dirty, sweat-stained men with a twinkle of adventure in their bloodshot eyes. Something here vaguely reminded me of a convoy in Vietnam, unseen hazards, split-second decisions. All around town arc welders flickered late into the night, tired crew members pounded, straightened, replaced, and fabricated; then suddenly the strange and flamboyant little cars formed up and headed south. Crazy, but what adventure isn't a little crazy?

One night four of us crammed into a Toyota taxi and headed downtown. It was twilight. We laughed and joked, trusting our driver to deliver us safely. Suddenly he screamed, there was a violent collision, and we skidded to a stop. The driver was obviously excited, gunned the car into a wide U-turn, and let his headlights play over an incredible scene. We had driven over a python, stretched across the asphalt to savor the heat. Wounded, it coiled and writhed in agony. This was no ordinary snake! It must have been ten feet long and a foot thick, and its tortured struggle was awesome.

Spec 4 Wilson went on sick call to have a wart removed from his finger. The army doctor cut an artery by mistake, bandaged his finger, and sent him back to work. Concerned about the amount of bleeding, he loosed the bandage. Blood sprayed four feet. Wilson passed out. Rushed to the hospital, he came around to the sound of laughter.

Still, my main struggle was with the fear that grew with every square I crossed off the calendar. I needed someone to talk with, someone with answers. There were hours of reflection and confusion. Sixty days. I signed up for an interdenominational retreat at Pattaya, on the Gulf of Siam. Pattaya was a popular Thai resort, with white sand and blue water. We slept on the sand, and toasted hot dogs over campfires. We sang folksongs and talked about sexual morality and drug abuse. We tried scuba diving. You could see a dime in thirty feet of water, and the coral formations and colorful tropical fish combined into the most beautiful sight I had ever seen. God's creation; but when I looked for a private word with the organizers there was no time. On the way back to Korat, my plane landed at Udorn and taxied by rows of B-52s. I saw the bombs being wheeled across the steaming asphalt and wondered if the airmen realized what those bombs would do to the earth.

I took a *tee-loc*, or live-in sex goddess. The sex was great, but one night I had to work late, and she attempted suicide. I visited her in a Thai hospital, with flies swarming, army cots, bloody bandages, and nauseating stink. She loved me, she said, and thought I had left her. I sent Eht to deliver her things. I didn't even like her. The sex had been good, but I was trying to straighten out my head and didn't need a suicide in my bedroom.

On a weekend excursion to Bangkok, and the inevitable late-night pilgrimage to The Balcony, a couple of college students explained the words of a catchy new tune. The Age of Aquarius was dawning. According to astrological predictions, peace and harmony would soon reign over all the earth. It was a simple fact, a physical manifestation of the relative positions of the planets. I was encouraged.

I applied for one last leave to Malaysia, but it was refused. This close to my separation I was not allowed to leave the country. I decided to use my remaining days in Thailand. In an impassioned letter to Lin, I begged her to meet me in Bangkok. She rejected me without listing her reasons. My emotions rose and fell like empty roller coaster cars. I couldn't give up on my dreams of a future with Lin; without her there could be no future.

A pfc asked to talk with me in private. His parents had visited his wife and were concerned that she might be abusing the baby he had never seen. He broke into tears and begged me to help. I piled him into a jeep and raced around the post, to battalion headquarters, the chaplain, the Red Cross. There had to be proof. Regulations. Sorry. There was nothing they could do. We both cried before it was over.

Hours in front of the mirror. If anyone saw me, they'd think I was vain. Going over the lines time and again, picturing the backyard, the living room, my room. I imagined what it would be like to sit on the front porch, surrounded by the wooden railing, watching life trickle past the neighbors as if in slow motion. Perhaps I should go to school; but the thought of sitting still at a desk, listening to a professor talk about the truest meanings of life, seemed absurd. There would be drums, the money was set aside, the catalogs were dog-eared, but it was a necessity. I fantasized about a bath in a tub. Drive-in movies. Root-beer floats. The smell of racing fuel. The moist, dirty scent of a cellar. I hadn't been in a cellar in a long time. Would it freak me out, bring back the trench along the wire where the dirt was moist? The scent of burning leaves in autumn. Peanuts at a baseball game. The sound of locusts overhead on a summer night. Carpet on the floor, thick and cushiony with thick foam padding underneath. Scraping ice off the windshield. Snow! I had almost forgotten snow: the glossy, tranquil surface in the early morning, placid form flickering in the headlights. I imagined Lin with rosy cheeks and wide eyes, her bulky mittens clutching the rails of a Flexible Flyer. How 'bout the midway at a county fair, the freak shows? Cotton candy. Candy apples. Pizza. Imagine, a two-foot pizza with mushrooms and pepperoni and heaps of onions, and a pitcher of beer, and

warm friends on a cold night, discs of dough rising in the background, jukebox thunder. I recalled the men's room at
Eduardo's. When I got home, I'd have to refer to it as a piss
tube; it fit the term. Wouldn't it be strange to see ready-made
clothes and not have to wait for a tailor to make a shirt? To
wear shoes to work, instead of boots? To have no nametag on
your chest, no stripes on your sleeve? To be a mister? Wouldn't
it be strange to open a cupboard, take out a glass, and get water
out of a faucet?

• • • •

One night I stepped off the Thai bus to find the city transformed. I was reminded of sidewalk sales at home. Every shop
had a table out front, loaded with food, drink, and a television
or radio. What was going on? Everyone was on the street, but
it seemed quiet and peaceful. They were deeply absorbed in
the TV. I had given up the news, hoping if I ignored the war it
would go away. That was my strategy. Don't talk about it; don't
think about it; concentrate on home and the future.

As I approached a number of my Thai friends rose,
extended hands with joyous smiles and congratulations.
Congratulations? What had I done? I pushed closer to the TV.
A newsman was bubbling in Thai, in words I did not know. A
middle-aged businessman sprang from his folding chair,
invited me to have a seat. Someone put a drink in my hand. I
leaned toward the silvery tube, strained to find a word I recognized. What is *duang-chun?* A lady pointed above the square to
the soft warm orange ball looming up among the palm fronds.
Apple-O. Apple-O. Americans go *duang-chun.* You will eat
with us? I turned back to the newscast. Good Lord! The moon.
Duang-chun. Moon. The Americans were going to the moon!
Apple-O. Apollo. Apollo Eleven. They were going to land on
the moon, walk upon its surface. The moon was looming over

the square now, unusually large, a soft peach-colored ball in the darkening sky, clearing the tile roofs, serene. A harvest moon, my dad would say. When would they walk? Tonight? Yes, about midnight. Later this evening mankind would know one of the greatest adventures of all time.

A little after 4:00 A.M. Thailand time, Neil Armstrong stepped onto the lunar powder, uttered his famous words, and planted an American flag and the flags of seventy-six free countries. Among them was the flag of Thailand. Buddhist monks burned joss sticks. Parents roused sleeping children to watch flickering black-and-white TVs. Restaurants would not accept money from Americans, and bartenders poured free drinks in the street. The streets were choked with people, standing for hours, celebrating, joyous, awed. Here, deep in the city, Americans rarely shared in the everyday life. Tonight any American was a dear friend, a receptacle into which they poured food and drink, and larger helpings of brotherhood and admiration, gratitude and wonder.

I, too, was overcome with joy. This was an incredible adventure, probably the greatest thrill any man would ever know. How many billions of people had gazed at the moon, and now one would stand in the dust and look at the planet earth in the night sky. I felt an emotion too long forgotten, and too often neglected. Those were Americans up there; the people of the world had to admit it. I had to acknowledge that no other country, no other people could have accomplished this. I felt pride, patriotism. Perhaps, had I been in America, the enormity of the moment might have been obscured? Here, thirteen thousand miles from home, surrounded by peasants, listening to a broadcast in another language, eating fascinating foods, smelling the exotic spices, here this achievement could be appreciated. This triumph simply electrified Korat, Thailand. I supposed that Main Street, U.S.A., was affected; but on Main Street it was "them" making history. NASA. The astronauts. In Thailand,

America made dreams come true, and it was suddenly nice to be an American. I hadn't been proud in a long, long time. In fifty days I would be back there, back in the mainstream. I staggered a bit on my way to the hotel, dizzy and exhausted and very comfortable. I slept soundly, without dreams. It had been a choice seat at a very exclusive event; probably the best vantage point on the entire globe.

• • • •

There were glad signs now. I spent an evening in Stu's room, sharing, chatting, gaining some sort of access to dear friends; sharing the common denominators of pot smoke and Beatles music. The conversation ebbed and flowed, sparred with soft rock from the radio. The room drifted, crystallized, misted again. "Listen!" From the radio, the sounds of John and Yoko, in bed, spending days for peace. If *that* had found its way to Korat, surely John's accent was permeating through America; raising questions, suggesting answers, voicing the emotions our generation all felt but could not express. Not revolution. Revelation. Peace. Brotherhood. Love. Hope. From his honeymoon bed in Europe, he had spoken to the World. Someone would hear. The old times were just that; old times. The dawning was at hand; the Age of Aquarius would bring peace and brotherhood. In a strange land, be it Amsterdam or Thailand, the message was coming through. The earth was a little blue ball in the sky; everything is relative; from the moon you can't see borders or boundaries or demilitarized zones. Mankind couldn't afford hate anymore. Mankind wouldn't tolerate malice anymore.

In a few days I would leave all of this, probably never to see it again. Lin wouldn't come to Bangkok; I couldn't go to Malaysia. I would see the true Thailand. I would immerse myself in Thai culture so deeply it would seep into the very depths of me. I would find the simplicity, the essence of these happy people. If the opulence and commercialism in The World disheartened me, I would have a refuge, a deep inner sanctuary. There was an indefinable something in the eyes of the Thai peasants. I intended to define it, and absorb it. It wasn't in Bangkok. I had seen it in Phi Mai, and in the market. Once, it had been in the eyes of a penniless laborer nursing at the edge of an emerald paddy. Despite her poverty, despite the heat or the exertion demanded by the fragile shoots of rice, despite her lack of material goods, she had gazed upon her beloved child and defied the raw deals of her life. She had what she needed and wanted most, and was satisfied.

The Buddha had wandered among the poor and found enlightenment. He had invested a lifetime; I had a few meager days. I only knew I had to leave Korat behind. The most destitute resident of a city can watch the activity and escape his woes. I would find the truest form of whatever it was I was seeking far from concrete, steel, and bright lights. I wasn't sure I would find it all, but I was sure it was there, and worth the search. I left Korat by bus, hitched a ride on a truck, then another, then walked for hours. I was sweating and tired, but cleansing something inside that had been decaying.

There were flat paddies, endless rectangles in various stages of development. Muddy brown or lush green. Three inches, or twelve inches, or something in between, partitioned by narrow earthen dikes. Clusters of palms rose from the endless plain like oases in the Sahara, shading crude but universal huts of palm thatch and baked mud, flotsam and jetsam and corrugated tin. I was tiring and thirsty, and I turned right at a crossroad to head for an inviting clump of dark green vegetation. There were inhabitants; a family. They were in the paddy, harvesting the tall shoots. An old man, a middle-aged woman, a teenaged girl, and two younger children, both naked. Beautiful. Serene. May I have water? They had probably never seen a *felong*. They gathered around, whispered compliments they didn't think I would understand. Beautiful hair. The older woman wanted to touch it; the man was leery. I leaned in toward her, asked her to be gentle. They grinned, realizing we would communicate. The knot tightened, eager to feel this strange golden hair, curiosity overcoming caution. The naked children were first.

There were two of them, a boy about three and a girl about seven. They seemed to know I would not hurt them, and clambered up onto the road to inspect me. The teenaged girl wore a ragged shirt and the usual wraparound skirt. The boy was ashamed of his nudity; the seven-year-old was clutching her mother's thigh, peeking at me. The mother seemed old to have kids this small; the father brought a filthy bottle of water, and I estimated his age at fifty. Deep furrows creased his cheeks, and his eyes were nearly squinted closed, the effects of too many years in the blazing sun. I lit a cigarette. The girl reached for the pack, inspected it, then shook out an American filter tip and looked at me for permission. I nodded and offered a light from my lighter. She eyed it with great caution and moved closer only when she saw the flame. She asked where I was from, where I was going. I explained that I wanted to visit the people of Thailand, which seemed to puzzle her. America didn't seem to ring a bell, but I mentioned Korat, in the old Thai name, Nakhonratchassima, and she grinned and explained to the elders. They moved closer. Why was I here? To see how life is lived here. Still puzzled. Is this good rice, a good crop? I was into my dictionary already and hadn't broken through defenses yet. The old man nodded, grinned. I gazed out over the paddy, probably three to four acres. Only a small corner had been harvested, a corner of placid water that abutted the wall of eighteen-inch green. The mother had returned to the shoots, reaching low to pull them loose, wrapping them into bundles, lining up bundles in formation. There was a small wooden platform for settling the shoots, making them uniform. Papa-san asked again, what do you want? I kicked off my boots, removed my socks, and rolled up my pant legs. "I want to learn about rice." I headed down into the water, hesitated? "Snakes?" Everyone grinned. No, only rarely. "Good!" They laughed. I walked toward the woman, feeling the soft ooze between my toes, the cool water on my calves. The little tyke hid behind her skirts. I resorted to the dictionary again, before my hands got wet. "Tell me how to do this. I will help."

The vermilion sun rested on the horizon when we stopped. My back felt as if it was broken, permanently bent. The backs of my thighs burned. I was hot, dirty, sweaty, and very comfortable. As I pulled on my worn pointed-toed, Cuban-heeled "Beatle boots," the old man asked where I was going. I did not know; where could I find food and a hotel? He pointed to twinkling lights in the distance but asked if I would eat with them. It was getting dark, I was in the middle of nowhere, and I thought I should find a hotel before it got too dark. You sleep with us? No, you are poor, I would be a burden. No, no, we can talk, eat, then sleep. Tomorrow I will show you more about the rice. You are too kind. I will pay, you buy food. No, we want to talk. Please eat with us. You eat Thai food? Yes, but not hot things. More laughter. Okay. I tell Mama-san. Come.

I was too stiff and tired to walk to those distant lights. Okay. Thank you very much. You are too kind, but it would be a great honor.

Dinner consisted of fried rice, wide green beans, and a small portion of chicken. We ate with chopsticks, and they were amazed that I could handle them. (I often won bets with Thais by picking up an American dime with chopsticks. They used chopsticks more as a shovel and were not used to pinpoint accuracy.) There was chicken broth with a spinach-like vegetable. Mama-san took the children to bed, filthy woven mats near the back wall of the house. I gave each a goodnight hug.

The little girl was still shy. I should have brought candy. Papa-san took out a long tin pipe with a stone bowl and a tin can of smoking material. I had seen the garden behind the house. With a single match, he lit a candle and the pipe. I asked to try it, and he grinned. My head was overloaded long before the pot smoke reached it. I struggled to communicate, complimented the beautiful children, thanked him again and again for his kindness. He held out the pipe again.

Mama-san joined us, with a small tray of sugarcane sections. She refilled the pipe, lit it from the candle, and inhaled deeply. I took out my dictionary and tried to make conversation. We touched on many subjects that evening, struggled to understand worlds we would never know. Papa-san had heard of America; his wife had not. They were familiar with trucks and buses, but not automobiles. My lighter fascinated them. Mama-san asked about my hair. What could I say? From the opening that served as a door we could see the moon's glow moving in and out of the clouds. I tried to explain that two men had walked on the moon. Papa-san laughed. I was not used to smoking pot! I tried to convince them by building a tiny rocket from a match and the foil from the cigarette pack. They followed quietly to the launching pad, the front porch, and jumped back when the tiny projectile ignited and flew into the darkness. Papa-san grinned. Would I show him how to do this? I tried to describe a similar machine, higher than the trees, with men in a special room, traveling to the moon. The old woman seemed to comprehend and tried to explain it to her husband. It just wouldn't fit into reality as he perceived it, and he settled for my tiny flying machines built from book matches. I slept on the hard wooden floor, felt the rain seep through the cracks in the middle of the night, and was awakened by the return of the relentless sun.

Before we returned to the backbreaking paddy we had to show the neighbors the miniature rockets. I was running out of foil, but there was no lack of enthusiasm from my audience. The secret of the rockets was to provide an exit by slipping a pin under the foil to guide the combustion gases out the tail. I had accomplished this with a sliver of wood, and my host guarded the sliver as if it contained some magical power. The neighbors ooohed and aaahed at each flight, despaired at the frequent duds, and scurried to retrieve the good ones and examine them in awe. Mama-san fried some sweet pancakes in a crusted wok, produced some short, stubby, but incredibly sweet bananas, and we went to work. Mama-san had attempted to convince her neighbor women that I had described a giant rocket that had taken two men to the moon, but they weren't buying that. The poor woman was probably the laughingstock of her community as a result of my visit. I hoped someday a newspaper or book would back her up.

I left them in mid-morning. Their good-byes were warm and genuine, and as I trudged through the heat toward the distant village I formed a plan. It turned out to be a tiny village, but I was able to buy a few things I needed. I bought a dozen eggs, a package of dried fish, a jar of squid oil, tomatoes, an onion, and a pint of Thai whiskey. I found a few bottles of Coca-Cola and a watermelon. There were magazines, two bolts of cotton print, and fluorescent orange rubber balls. I couldn't find any news of the moon walk, but I brought a package of joss sticks and a plastic sheet. I got a few candles, a comb, and a mirror. I had a cardboard box full of goodies, far too heavy to carry, so I bribed an old man at the market to drive me back to the paddy where my friends were working. The battered truck couldn't make twenty miles an hour; it wheezed like an asthmatic and rumbled as though the gears were square, but we made it. My adopted family stood in the paddy, staring in disbelief. My driver was amused by it all. I retrieved the box from the back of the battered truck and summoned my friends. "Mama-san," I explained, "tonight we have much food, much party. Tomorrow I go. You are very kind; this is to thank you. You make food, okay?" Her eyes went wide at the sight of the material, the watermelon, and the food. I had a special treat I knew would provide the *piece de resistance*. A bag of ice. She motioned to the rest of the family, calling them up, out of the paddy. She was excited beyond my wildest expectation. She threw her arms around me, then handed ice cubes to the kids. Papa-san spoke to my driver, motioned my way, and smiled broadly. He pointed to my matches, repeated, "Can do? Can do?" and arched his right arm in a flying motion. We built a rocket for my driver, who was duly impressed at the wonders of modern science and technology. The older daughter had one of the balls and ran up to hug my thigh. Her smile was worth a million dollars; I had spent less than twenty. The average Thai peasant family has an annual income of under three hundred dollars.

It was as if I had arrived in a red suit and beard, in a flying sleigh propelled by reindeer. The neighbors gathered around, and Mama-san invited them to eat. The kids flitted from the balls to the watermelon to the ice, and back again. I offered some chewing gum to one of the neighbor girls, a beautiful teenager, and she followed me about with eyes wide. Papa-san lit his pipe and hailed me, and the neighbors gathered and laughed and tried to understand.

In the morning, I walked away from them. The older girl followed me for a while, then turned back. I wondered what her life would be. Surely there were worse things than early wrinkles.

• • • •

It was a long and lonely walk back to "civilization," with plenty of time for thinking. Had I found what I was looking for? I had felt something, but was it the essence of Thailand? No, I decided, the rat race in Bangkok was as Thai as the timeless struggle in the paddies. I had visited the poor, probably among the least capitalized societies in the Free World. In a few days I would return to the land of two-car garages and color TVs. This long walk would lay the groundwork. From the ragged hootch and the simple people, my feet would carry me back to Korat, where I had to give up my beloved room and move back on post. I had to give up Thai food, Thai clothes, and pot. The fantasy was over; reality grew nearer with each step. In order to survive the transition, I had to prepare myself. Very few Americans would experience Thailand as intimately as I had. Now it was time to divorce myself. I had been out of The Nam for eleven months; it was time to put the memories in a box on the shelf and go on with my life. Thailand had to go into another box.

The experiences of the past two years had shaped me, there was no denying that; but I would return home physically whole and with an opportunity to make a new start. If those experiences had strengthened me, they were valuable. The hottest flame tempers the strongest steel. If, on the other hand, I allowed them to be a negative, knowing full well how immense and profound they had been, there was no telling how destructive they might be. I was twenty-one years old. I wasn't about to give up; I was about to start struggling. Struggling for myself, in an atmosphere of free enterprise, unhampered by rank or regulations. I was going to do my own thing. Anyone who could spend two days in the rice paddy, communicating with a worn Thai dictionary, and find the entire experience to be beautiful and uplifting, was ready to face life in the American suburbs. There would be bad days, but I would never have to live in such conditions again; and if I did, I knew I could. I had proven to myself that I could survive and enjoy life anywhere. That was the essence. Call it enlightenment, call it anything you like. I knew it had been a profound experience.

I had rejected American life, tried some alternatives, and now it was time to go home. I had come to this land emotionally battered and bleeding. The Thai people had nursed me back to health, allowed my emotions to decompress. That was it. Like a deep-sea diver who has to rise slowly to the surface or suffer the agonies of "the bends," I had spent the last eleven months rising from the depths. Nobody wants to stay on the bottom. High school was a past experience. Vietnam was a past experience. I had taken a long rest, slowly rising to my full height. Now, with the box on the shelf, it was time to go on. To stay in this environment any longer would be like treading water.

At the end of the long, hot, dusty road was Korat. I showered, packed, paid my bill, and called a taxi. Back on post, I sorted my things into two piles; the things I would ship in a "hold baggage" wooden crate, and the things I would hand-carry on the plane. I had to have a set of civilian clothes. The minute I was out of the army the o.d. green fatigues were going into the nearest trash barrel. The records and stereo would go into the box. I would carry my camera and guitar, but the box of pictures was too bulky. I sat on the bunk and looked back at images of Pleiku and Dak To and Penang. I would hand-carry Lin's pictures. I held the coarse Montagnard shirt in my hands. I could almost smell the rot; I nearly let my mind go back to Pleiku.

I hadn't smoked any Thai weed in days, but my mind journeyed back. It had been almost two years since I had entered the barracks at Fort Dix to await my flight to Vietnam. I saw the polished metal mirrors to discourage suicide, the empty gaping holes where window panes should have been. At the time, thoughts of suicide had seemed ridiculous. I remembered the giant air force Starlifter, the long hours of silent contemplation, the wave of heat as they opened the door at Tan Son Nhut. It had only been a year ago, back at Tan Son

Nhut, lying under wooden benches listening to rockets crashing on the airstrip. I could feel the floor tremble against my chest, the sickening fear bubbling in my throat and twisting in my gut.

This flight would be different. I would be going back; back to my room, my car, a simpler place and time. I struggled to picture the old neighborhood. Surely, I would be running into the old gang, the kids I had graduated with. They would be getting ready to go back to school, it being early September. I counted fingers. I had graduated from high school in '65. Why, they've graduated from college! They're getting jobs or going on to graduate school to stay out of the draft. What in the world (I grinned at my own pun) would I say to them? Newly armed with a diploma, they wouldn't want to hear about my experiences. They would be on their way to success. Smug and confident, they would pity me because I had not been smart enough to beat the draft. Goddamn it, I had seen life stripped to the essence, and they would laugh in my face! It wouldn't be so bad that they laughed at me; I should have taken my scholarship and stayed out of the draft too. I couldn't debate that. But their laughter would be directed at everyone who had gone to The Nam: at the two guys driving a flatbed of ammo up a muddy road toward Dak To, at Archie, and Stu, and Digger, and Bones, and Ohio, and hundreds of others. Fine people, good people, whose only crime had been poverty or a different set of values. Some of them had died, and if anybody laughed at that…well, I would have to be awful damn careful. After The Nam, a college diploma didn't seem very relevant.

No, I decided, it wouldn't go that way. They would slap me on the back and shake my hand, and be genuinely glad I was home in one piece. The horror stories we had been hearing were just army bull, trying to intimidate us into signing up for a couple more years. The guys running past my memory were friends, and nothing could ruin that. Not Vietnam, not college, not the army, nothing. I would have to be careful, of course. It just wasn't socially acceptable to sit in a pizza joint and talk about kids disfigured by napalm or with limbs blown away by explosive. I would have to buy records, catch up on things, get with it. Put the boxes on the shelf and fit back in and go on. They could never know. I could only be successful if I could rejoin their world; the events of the past few years weren't relevant. It was sad, but I couldn't acknowledge any of it and succeed in The World.

I had to push those thoughts out of my mind. I had to concentrate on home, the shady street, green lawns, glass-pack mufflers, and drive-in movies. I was short! My replacement had arrived, a he-man Korean War veteran staff sergeant. I had few responsibilities. I joked with the Thais, reminisced with the older guys, begged the new arrivals to describe The World.

Disaster struck. I had forsaken Thai food, knowing I would not be able to get it in a small town in upstate New York. I was almost religious about it. I had seen the mess personnel tossing hamburger like snowballs, scraping it off the walls into our lunch. I never gave it a thought. I didn't feel good one night and went to bed early. I was awakened in the middle of the night by an attack of vomiting and diarrhea that would last a week. The doctors attributed it to *Stringella sonnei* bacteria, a form of typhoid. A number of people had been infected, obviously by the mess hall. I lost twenty-three pounds in five days, racked by fever and cramps. Surely, they would delay my trip home. It seemed absurd. For months I had ignored the army's warnings about the Thai food. Now, eating the army's food to prepare myself for civilian life, I had contracted typhoid. I was weak, discouraged, and angry. My strength was gone. For three days I hadn't even X'd my calendar. The World was far away.

I resolved to eat at the PX cafeteria and the club. I was feeling better. They couldn't justify keeping me here, they hadn't even allowed me bed rest. If I hadn't been so short I would have been expected to work every day.

One morning, breakfast at the PX was particularly uplifting. I was really short now and had been relieved of all responsibilities except packing and waiting. I placed the dishes and silverware on the table, put the fiberglass tray on a stack, and picked up a discarded newspaper. It was an English-language daily from Bangkok, several days old, but the news was exciting. A half-million people had gathered in a farm pasture in upstate New York for a monumental rock concert called Woodstock. Although there had been an abundance of marijuana and nudity and a shortage of food, water, and sanitary facilities, peace and cooperation had prevailed. The authorities were amazed at the gentleness and compassion, the bizarre dress and behavior. Hendrix was there. Janis Joplin had knocked them out, a bottle of Southern Comfort in one hand and the mike in the other. Country Joe & The Fish. Richie Havens. John Sebastian. Crosby, Stills & Nash. Sly & The Family Stone. The roads had been choked; the state was in shock. No trouble. I imagined the fertile fields of home, imagined half a million free people enjoying life without threatening anyone else's. That was what the atmosphere was like at home. The Age of Aquarius. Peace on earth. Body paint and bellbottom jeans with frayed cuffs. Births. A half-million people shouting "Fuck" in unison, but hurting no one. A sound as big as all outdoors. A movement that the establishment couldn't ignore. Flower Children. Hippies. Peacenicks. The labels didn't matter. Peace on earth, good will to men. I had missed it, but in a few days I could join that moment. I could tell them what I had seen, describe what hate could do. I could relax, dress, and say and do and think what I wanted. Free again. Starting over. Doing my thing and letting everyone else do theirs.

• • • •

I packed and shipped my crate. There was a weekend of calm before the storm. Monday and Tuesday I would process out, traveling from office to office getting signatures. First, I would enjoy. The past month had rolled by slowly, but I had succeeded. No pot, no Thai food, no strange behavior. I felt calm inside, prepared for home. Six days! I spent the weekend in a room at the Semanut Hotel, with Stu and Rich and Wayne, great heaps of food from the market, a dwindling bag of smoking material. Would I try to smuggle some home? No, I would never smoke again after I left here. I was freaked on succeeding in The World. I wasn't about to go to jail for smoking a cigarette. I had served enough time. What was I going to do for a job? First, I would just take a few weeks, buy some drums and beat 'em to death, look things over. Roll in the grass in the backyard, scratch the dog's ears, grow my hair. I had to look it over. I had been away a long time. A lifetime. Two days away from civilian life, Emery had deserted in Bangkok. He was in the south, near Song Khla, working as a laborer on a pot plantation. Crazy. I wanted those separation papers. I wouldn't give the army the satisfaction of deserting. Not one extra minute would I remain with my life dictated by a lifer.

On Sunday, stoned, I visited the neighbors and Noi at my old bungalow. I gave Noi a few bucks, and he took me on a tour of the city in his *samlaw*. It was an eerie feeling, looking at familiar places, remembering adventures, but knowing that I was going away and would probably never return. The last time I had felt it, my family had driven me to the airport. Familiar people hustled and bustled amongst familiar surroundings. Divorced from the mainstream, it was like watching a TV program. In a few days, someone would switch the channel forever. You try to soak up every detail and absorb the ordinary, which will soon be extraordinary.

I bought an elaborate dinner for Noi and myself. He tried to convince me to stay. No, that decision had been made long ago.

Was I scared? A little, but I had been more scared when I had left home to go to Vietnam. I had survived, and I would survive. I delivered a bottle of expensive French champagne to my favorite massage girl, listened to the Chinese string band one more time, then Noi took me to the hotel. The last ride in a *samlaw*. On the sidewalk, Noi threw his arms around me, tears in his eyes. My eyes were wet too, as I watched him pedal away.

The last bus ride to the base. Dizzy speeds, bumping, lurching. I carried a clipboard of documents for two days, collecting signatures, absorbing sights and sounds and smells.

Then it was the last night. I bought a case of beer, and my guys had a last cool one with the sarge. I felt the beer, probably because my emotions were running at a high pitch. The suitcase was packed, my dress khakis laid out. I took a set of jungle fatigues out into the parking lot, soaked them with lighter fluid, and set them ablaze. More beer, handshakes, memories. I had worn those fatigues in The Nam. The beer affected my urinary tract as much as my head. I put the fire out. Piss on The Nam! Piss on the army!

The lights went out for the last time. I smoked the last joint with friends, walked into the darkened barracks. There had to be one more act of defiance. That's the way they did it in The Nam, and I had felt it building for two years. And five days; can't forget those five days at Tan Son Nhut. A year ago tonight. I had smoked the last joint as a gesture of farewell with dear friends, but there was another reason. I needed to freak on this one, do it as it had never been down before. No deep breaths, no interruptions. I filled my lungs with air, controlled it. It started low, built in intensity, built in volume. I wanted them to hear it in Pleiku, to know I had made it. Louder and louder, emotional, powerful. "SssshhhhhhhoooooooOOOOOOOO RRRRTTTT!"

I didn't sleep well. I was shaved and showered when the wakeup man slammed the door. More good-byes. Over breakfast. After formation. Handshakes and embraces. Was that a tear in Stu's eye? Had the sunglasses hidden mine?

I signed out, got a last jeep ride to the air base. A last C-130 with that wretched nylon webbing seat. Process in at the airport. The plane would leave at 8:00 that night. I took a taxi downtown. The Balcony was closed. I should have a last fling, visit the warehouse, but I would probably catch a dose of something. I got a hotel room, parked my suitcase, wandered. There was so much I hadn't seen. Shops. People. I had never gone northwest. I joined a tour to watch classical Thai dancing. I shopped, but bought nothing. I watched the milling crowds of shoppers. I sat on a low concrete bridge watching children swim in a *klong*. I ate *cow-pot-moo* and drank the syrupy tea for dinner. I cried, thinking about dear friends I would never see again. I pulled a wrinkled news clipping about Woodstock from my wallet. It would work out. It had to. I bargained with a taxi driver and finally agreed upon a price for the trip to Don Muang Airport.

Surprisingly, the paperwork didn't take long. I had a couple hours to kill. The giant silver bird sat on the tarmac, regal, waiting to take us home. There was one more thing to do. I changed a twenty-dollar bill into coins and found a secluded phone booth. "Operator? I want to call Penang, Malaysia." I shoveled handfuls of coins into the slot.

Lin was awaiting my call. All of the kindness, all of the intimacy and compassion we had ever known together flowed through electrical wires that night. She sounded soft, warm. She cried; she pledged undying love. She would be waiting. I was so scared and alone. It was so far away. Soon, she promised, she would join me, and we would never be sad or lonely again. She was crying now, softly. Please be careful. Please take care of yourself. Please don't forget me. The coins were dwindling away; the sun was sinking low. "I love you." "I love you, too." "Never a good-bye, but farewell." "Farewell." Click.

Scotch on the rocks. Make it a double. Long, long ago, on a train from Buffalo to Fort Dix, a boy had gulped Scotch. Now, a lifetime later, devastated, ravished, defiled, a hollow shell rose from the stool, dried his eyes, felt the familiar warmth spreading through his belly. The bartender approached. "Thank you. In my heart, Thailand is my homeland. I will never forget." A last splash of the pungent liquid, a tip of the glass, one last tear, and the boy lifts the heavy suitcase, turns, and walks away. This part of his life is over.

• • • •

Unrestrained joy all around me, I fit into the line and move toward the gleaming Freedom Bird. I have to fight back the tears. I am surrounded by jubilation. Up the stairs, eyes awash, everything blurring. A window seat near the back, crude remarks all around as the stewardess comes into view. Is her blouse really open one button too many? Is that really a hint of cleavage, a suggestion of lace? She looks good, smells better. A drink? Sure! Scotch on the rocks. The engines whine. I press my forehead to the plexiglass window, my eyes blinking away the tears in an attempt to catch one last glimpse. As we roll toward the final separation I see the terminal building, and my thoughts race back to another plane, another day, just one year ago. I had been scared to death in that warrant officer's jeep; scared of every shadow, every movement. Then, a few days ago I walked out into nowhere, alone, and delighted in the free-dom of it. Thailand had done me a lot of good. If I can make that adjustment, I can cope with home. I'm ready! The engines begin to turn, we taxi, and a surge of acceleration pushes me deep into the seat. Everyone else roars with approval. I tip the rim of the clear plastic glass in a last toast to the sparkling lights falling away, then swallow a hard belt of the Scotch. Never good-bye. Farewell. I want to close my eyes, but there can be no sleep for a while. We have to be pampered first. More drinks, hot rolled washcloths, peanuts, pillows, magazines, cheerful smiles, that glimpse of swelling breastflesh. I can feel the scotch adding weight to my limbs. The cabin lights are dim, everyone is settling in. It's getting quiet, the emotions are spent. It is going to be a long flight.

"This is Captain Moore. We are cruising at thirty-seven thousand feet. We plan to stop for refueling in Okinawa at approximately 8:00 A.M. 'Til then, gentlemen, may I be the first to welcome you home and thank you for a job well done. We want you to enjoy your stay with us. If there is anything we can do to make your flight a little more enjoyable we urge you to let our flight attendants know. Uhh, the flights attendants have asked me to say *almost* anything!" A roar from the crowd. The girls play shy. "In a few minutes we will be flying over the Republic of South Vietnam. I understand the weather is particularly cloudy tonight, ground action is reported to be light, but you may see some artillery flashes. Again, welcome aboard, and we hope you enjoy your flight."

I lay my head against the window frame. There. And there. Red circles appear and disappear in the darkness below. A burst of fire. Ground action is reported to be light? Somebody's getting the shit kicked out of them down there! I buzz for the stewardess. Are we near Pleiku? No, farther south. Thank you. For fifteen minutes the tiny red flashes excite the crowd. They lean across each other to see. They oooh and aaah like spectators at a fireworks display. I am cold. Another Scotch, we're out over the South China Sea, and I close my eyes. Once and for all, Vietnam is behind me.

We refuel in Okinawa. I buy a pack of postcards, just so I can say I've been there. Eleven hours to Oakland. It will be 6:00 A.M. when we arrive. I sleep, as if exhausted by events of two years and five days. When I awake there are eggs and toast. Dawn will be breaking soon. It's cloudy. The whine of the engines changes pitch, my ears pop. There. The Golden Gate Bridge! Magnificent! Low over the water. Brown bush-covered hills. Land. The wheels touch down. Another roar.

Outside there are three olive-drab buses, with no screen wire on the windows. So this is California, home of the hot rods and busty blondes. I see neither. Another army post. By 7:00 A.M. I'm in the first of many slow-moving lines. No respite, no place to sit down. Line after line after interminable line. At 10:00 P.M. they pay me. At 11:15 I get my plane ticket. At 11:30 they hand me my discharge paper. God, I'm tired.

Outside, taxis are waiting to take us to the San Francisco airport; it will be an hour's drive. Four of us squeeze into a Dodge with heavy-gauge vinyl seats. There is an MP on duty at the gate. We laugh and giggle and holler. "Short." He waves us through. Four voices in unison. "Going...gone!"

I'm not in the army anymore. Well, I've got to wear the uniform all the way home to get the military rate, but I'm actually a civilian. I don't have to get up in the morning. The long, dark ride lets my mind trip back over it all; the KP, Fatso, Pleiku, Dak To, Saigon, Tan Son Nhut, Bangkok, Korat, Penang. Thousands of miles away! How far are we from the Haight-Ashbury? About ten miles and driving away from it. Look at the freeway! Biggest damned road I've ever seen, five lanes each way. Look! A Chevy. A Corvette. A convertible with the top down, and a blonde with hair dancing on the night air. Wow!

I've got about twenty minutes to spare when we arrive at the airport. The terminal curls alongside the drive, an endless expanse of plate glass. Inside, milling crowds. At this hour? Look! A hippie. Blonde Afro hairdo, beard, round glasses and a rainbow-striped shirt. Miniskirts. Jeesus! I check my bag, get my seat assignment, and am shown to the plane. A simple flat tire and we wouldn't have made it. The stewardess leads me back to my seat, on the aisle next to a businessman in a suit. Eyeing my uniform, he whispers to the stewardess and moves to another seat. I fall into the window seat eager for the plane to lift off so I can lean the seat back and catch some sleep. Strange, there is no real excitement; just fatigue, accumulated over two years, or was it three? The stewardess smiles, offers a miniature pillow and a blanket. God, she smells good! I close my eyes, try to picture my family. Will I recognize them? Will they recognize me? We rush into the air, the lights are dim, and I nod off.

• • • •

I have to change planes in Dallas, with an hour's layover. Now, halfway across America, seeing the dawn breaking, I begin to feel the excitement. I've got an important phone call to make, but I want to watch the people. First things first. The dime falls, I dial, and Dad answers. Why is he home? You took the whole week for vacation! I'm fine. The plane will be in about noon. I'm fine! Really, I'm great. Can't wait! I probably should be bringing gifts. There are things in the hold baggage box, but who knows when that'll arrive? I walk up the corridor, marveling at the wall-to-wall indoor-outdoor carpet, toward a gift kiosk. Something from cowboy country would be different. Just a little something. I see a rack of postcards. No! It can't be! Three-by-five, living color images of Dallas assail my senses; photos of the Texas Book Depository with one familiar window yawning open, Jackie in her bloodstained pink suit, an intersection lined with flowers, the Lincoln convertible, the spray of blood and brain matter. My stomach contracts, my knees threaten to buckle. The muscles in my legs have lost their elasticity, quivering, trembling deep inside with a violence that drives me backward. I turn, stride away, my thoughts reeling. Is that the image they mean to project? The city's claim to fame? Murder? My God, what kind of people are these? Have they ever seen a red-pink spray? Have they ever wiped it out of their eyes? Felt it, wet and warm, on their chest? You don't send it to a loved one. There were guys, over *there*, who got off on the blood and the strange sound a bullet makes when it hits flesh and bone; but not *here*? Not here! Those guys were fucked up by the miles, the loneliness and fear and horror of it all. That was *there*, and *here* it's different! It has to be different, 'cause I can't take any more of that. I'll just scream and fall on the floor and fucking give up, and they can put me in a room somewhere. Just let me sit and get old; they can peek in the door and whisper, "He's a little weird," and shake their heads and walk away.

It's not like this at home. It's not, it never was, and it can't be. I am aware that I am walking funny, struggling to move. I get an orange juice and a donut. There are so many people flittering around, wrapped in their own pursuits, I don't even want to take the time to look at the wonders of the snack counter. I've got a hole in my belly, and maybe if I fill it with something...

Another plane, moving closer. Early morning sunshine, a breath of fresh air, then the crowded aisle leading deep into the fuselage, a window seat this time. I try to focus on a magazine, get my mind off the excitement growing to a bursting point. A tall, thin guy in a rust-colored corduroy suit, cowboy hat, metal-frame glasses, and string tie checks the number of the seat next to mine. He looks down, I look up, and he turns abruptly and fights the flow of traffic to the stewardess. I see him gesturing; she shows him another seat, glances nervously at me. I don't understand, but fuck it, I go back to my magazine. The aisle seat remains empty all the way to Detroit. There is conversation all around me. I become acutely aware of the fact that, for the first time in a long, long time, I can understand peripheral conversations. You lose that in a foreign country. Breakfast, without a smile. Mass-produced food. Army quality. The stewardess refills my coffee cup, lowers her eyelashes. "Are you coming from Vietnam?"

"No. Thailand." She looks very relieved, looks at me, smiles. I think I'm in love. Why did I say that? I think I'll add, "But I was in The Nam before that" and watch the reaction. No, I like her eyes too much to chase them back into hiding. Blue shadow, long fake lashes. So clean and fresh. I bet she smells good all over.

"How long have you been away?" Don't press it, honey, I'm off the hook and I want to stay that way; just keep smiling at me and batting those long, black lashes, and don't push for answers.

"Two years." Don't volunteer.

The smile widens. "Well, welcome home."

She's gone. "Thank you..."

Is there a lesson to be learned? She changed, visibly changed, when I mentioned Thailand. Relieved. What if I had told the whole truth? How would she have reacted?

The Detroit airport is outside of the city, in an area of rolling green farmland divided into rectangles by darker trees. I see the lake, and the combination reminds me of home. This time the layover is an hour-and-a-half. I sit on a plastic chair in a cinderblock-and-dull-aluminum modern-architectural-style wing, single-story, pastel and sterile. Too many cigarettes, too much coffee, not enough sleep, far too many emotions. I feel it in my chest, thudding against the walls, growing stronger by the moment. I remember Christmas Eves long past, eager to see if Santa had remembered. The same feeling. I take comfort from it, from the realization that I really *want* to go home. In a couple of hours I'll have made it, and it won't be so hard. All the past two years seem impossible now. Far, far away, left behind, impossible. Stored in a box on the shelf, souvenirs, but not applicable to this. Far, far away.

I buy a paper. Gotta know what's going on in the world. The World? In The World! Right here, right now! The World exists, the dream's come true, it's a beautiful day, and in a little while

I'll be in the kitchen with a cup of the finest coffee anywhere, and tonight we'll barbecue burgers in the backyard. The news in Detroit concerns corporate profits and stock market closings. I don't understand those things. The protestors claim they're evil, but I don't know. Nothing wrong with selling cars. Cars oughta be a lot of fun.

Jane Fonda is criticized for trying to talk to the North Vietnamese. A traitor. A traitor? God bless her! If she can help to end it, communicate, maybe all the guys over there can come home and feel what I'm feeling, see what I'm seeing. Everything so neat and clean and orderly, just like before. If I was still there I'd be grateful to anyone who could get me out. Bombs haven't done anything; what's wrong with a little conversation and understanding?

This plane is smaller, the aisle more congested. Sold out. I get another window seat. Maybe I'll be able to see my family from the window. Maybe even the house. Can't let myself get too excited, I'll have to pee and excuse myself every five minutes. A guy settles into the seat next to me. Joe College. Open-neck shirt, cardigan sweater, jeans, brass belt buckle. I look up from my paper to say, "Hi."

"Listen, I want to get one thing straight. I got nothing to say to you, and you got nothing to say that I want to hear. Understand?" He opens a textbook forcefully.

I lower my head to the newspaper, but my eyes don't comprehend the words. Why? What had I done to him? I was warned about this, but that was so long ago, so far away. I'm here now, just like before. I'm the same person I always was. This never happened before. It's the uniform. Stinking, fucking army! Even fucks up coming home! When I get to the airport, get my suitcase, I'm gonna...

The stewardess brings more coffee. Time sure has accelerated lately. After all those nights, all those long, lonely days, X's on the calendar; suddenly the time is rushing by way too fast.

After waiting for it so long, I've traveled halfway around the planet, and I can't really remember much of the trip. Just a few minutes. Just minutes 'til I see Mom and Dad, and Ken. What will I say? Is it socially acceptable for a combat veteran to cry? Better not cry. I'm changed, harder, stronger. I've dealt with so many goddamn emotions in the last two years, I can deal with this. If I start bawling I might never stop.

• • • •

The whine cuts. We're gliding down. My ears pop. My chest is gonna burst. There's something in my throat, big, stuck. Need to swallow, but I can't seem to force it out of the way. Now I can see the ground rising. Beautiful, green, with multicolored splotches of houses around cul-de-sacs. I see swimming pools, the familiar low profile of a school, the cluster of golden buses. Esso. Texaco. Chevrolet. Star Market. Traffic. Pine trees, maples, shrubs around the houses. Kodak tower. Gulf. A shopping plaza, orderly rows of parked cars, trees, grass and pavement, blue lights, red-and-white cones, the radar, the terminal...bump...bump. The engines howl in reverse, I feel myself shift forward in the seat, then we're crawling across the flat. I see the guy waving paddles, guiding us into place, the whine dies, everyone stirs, rises. Jesus, I'm at the back, I can't wait much longer, stooped under the luggage compartment, then out into the aisle, shuffling forward. Slowly. Very slowly. Closer and closer, I see the sunlight streaming in, the stewardess says, "Bye." I turn left and the sun blinds me, I step out. Grip the railing, strain to see, nothing but the bricks and dark glass, down the steps, across the blacktop, swing open the door, darkness, crowded, bumping, shoving, milling, searching...THERE! I fight my way, Mom's arms are outstretched, Ken's waving to get my attention, Dad's eyes are wet. Mom's crying, the lump is growing in my throat, I push forward, straining, reaching...closer. The crush surprises me. Arms, wet kisses, tears, hugs, people bumping, and we're in the way, and it all starts to come out, and the lump is so big, and my eyes are so wet. Then, it has to break. We can't spend the rest of our lives like this. Handshakes. Another hug. They're crying too much. Gotta keep my shit together. A lot of words, none of them as important as the sights and feelings. Mom won't let go of my arm. We wait for my suitcase, then I kind of peel her off. I've gotta visit the men's room. There's something I got to do, and it's nothing as trivial as taking a leak. In the cool tiled room I lay open the suitcase, push back the overflow. I strip the emblems and badges and ribbons off my uniform, toss them into a suitcase. I strip, slip into jeans and a T-shirt and my boots. I wad up the khaki army uniform, walk to the basket. I bend the arm at the elbow, rigid, holding that wad close in front of my nose, shaking with emotion. I speak to the clothing, inanimate objects that suddenly symbolize two years and nine months of agony. Quivering, looking at a shirt and pants but seeing Fort Dix and Pleiku and Dak To and Korat, I say my final words to the army. "*Fuck* you!" And I throw them in the basket with the soiled paper towels. I stomp the dark green dress hat into a pancake, scuff its spit-shined brim, utter the same message, and push it deep into the toweling. I close the suitcase, rinse my face, look at my eyes. My God, how they've changed! I splash more cold water over them, towel off, lift the suitcase, and walk out into The World. A free man.

The T-Bird is beautiful; its new blue paint catches the sun like an exposed diamond mine. I haven't driven in The World's traffic, so I take the shotgun seat. For an instant, just a brief, blinding instant, there's a shiver. That is not a good word to use here. That word should have been left over there, forgotten along with all those other things that don't fit here. We stop. Gotta get some ice cream. Things are gay now, almost giddy. I'm goofing! Crazy. A trip. I haven't smoked in...let's see, it must be…thirteen thousand miles! Doesn't matter. It's a trip! Aisle upon aisle. The packaging is unbelievable. The displays are a work of art. The light. The clean freshness. Four half-gallons of ice cream; chocolate, butterscotch, and marshmallow topping; whipped cream in an icy can; peanuts, maraschino cherries; apples, grapes, pears, and bananas; a pack of Snicker bars; and a carton of cigarettes. Fifty bucks. Not a damn thing that's good for me, and it's fifty bucks.

Then the right turn, deceleration, left into the driveway, up the porch steps, into the foyer. The eyes are getting wet again, more hugs and kisses. Into the kitchen, the same except the postcards of Saigon, Penang, or Bangkok taped to the refrigerator. The dog wiggles and whines, shivers, and piddles a little; she remembers me! She explodes into my arms, licking and wiggling, and I kiss her too, 'cause I've had a lot filthier things in my mouth and I'm still alive. The backyard. The living room. The Vietnamese doll in her *au dai*, a Christmas present so long ago. Up the stairs to my room, just as I left it. I open the closet, look at some of the clothes I used to wear. Shit. Kid's stuff. I gotta buy some more. Jeans with fringed cuffs. Into the bathroom. Back downstairs. Out on the porch; then around the house. Back inside. The cellar. When I open the door the cat explodes out and, in typical cat fashion, could give a shit. Around and around I go, looking, touching, reinforcing, discovering knicknacks and keepsakes I hadn't thought about. How could I have forgotten so many things? Important things. The things that make this home. Every time I realize I'm acting like a fool and sit down, the nervous energy lifts me out of the chair and my explorations begin again. The family sits, somewhat bewildered, more than a little amused, watching. Trying to make conversation, but my head is too overloaded and my attention span too short.

• • • •

In a couple of days we go to the city, to the music store. I come away with maroon sparkle drums, cymbals, chrome stands, pedal, stool, sticks. I'm driving around town now, back and forth to the drugstore for more records. The Fifth Dimension. Zager and Evans. Three Dog Night. I tell my folks, "You should see The Balcony!" as though it were next door and not thirteen thousand miles away.

Steaks and roasts and pork chops, a green tossed salad with every meal, milk and ice cream and cake and a coconut cream pie. The phone rings, and I jump out of my skin. The doorbell rings, and I roll off the couch in a flurry of pillows. I haven't heard a doorbell in a long time. TV. Football seems less exciting than I remember. The news is obscene. *Playboy* shows pubic hair now, and people think that's perverted, but they sit in the living room and watch some grunt coming home in a green bag, and that's respectable. What the fuck is wrong around here? Do you realize that that is somebody's kid, and they're gonna unzip that bag and find just an arm, or just a leg, and the rest of him is part of the Vietnamese terrain now? You didn't mean to upset me? You didn't upset me! The war upset me! You're fine, it's the casual way you all look at hell and sip your coffee that fucks my head up. Oops! Sorry. That's a pretty acceptable word over there. Yeah, I realize I'm not there anymore and that I can't say that here. (But I can fucking well think it!)

I find I'm asking how the neighbors are. *Where* are they? Did you tell them I was coming home? Why don't they come over? Well, I can understand that they don't know what to say; I don't know what to say either, but "hello" might do for a start. What do you mean, "It's hard"? There are a lot harder things to do than say "hello."

The wooden crate arrives. The treasures seem paltry. These few trinkets, remembrances of the most enormous experience of my life. Trivial. I thought they would help me tell you, help me explain. There's hardly anything here!

It's good to sleep in your own bed. Kind of like returning to the womb or something. The windows are open, a soft breeze is rustling the shade. I'm almost asleep. The siren summons the volunteer fire department, at its first scream I explode out of bed, crashing and banging into walls. Then I'm crouched on the stair landing, I realize where I am and what I'm hearing, and I'm crying, and the lights come on. They look down at me, and say, "It's all right," over and over, I feel very pathetic and very fucked up. I haven't heard a siren since the night...shit, you wouldn't understand. When we got hit, a siren woke us. Except we were already awake, but the siren would go on and on and on....Sorry. I know you've got to work tomorrow. Sorry.

Then I'm beatin' the shit out of the drums, and it isn't music, it's just noise, but it feels so good to just beat something. The stereo speakers are inches away from my ears, full blast, and I'm making thunder, thunder like a 155 howitzer on Artillery Hill, and I suddenly realize I could have been one of those other guys. I could have lost a leg, or both legs, and not be able to perch on the stool any more. My right foot jerks involuntarily on the foot pedal, and thunder shakes the living room, and my fingers have bloody blisters where there used to be calluses, but it seems so good to beat something. The Beatles are into such heavy stuff now, I used to be able to keep up with them, but they've been practicing, and I've been....And I get so goddamned fucking out-of-my-head mad that I throw the sticks and beat the cymbals with my bare knuckles, and it hurts and the tears come. It could be worse. You could be in a wheelchair with a bag of piss strapped to your waist, but why did you have to go at all? Why did it happen to me, and will it ever just stay in its box, on the shelf? Souvenirs.

There's a letter. I recognize it across the room, the color and size of the paper, the Malaysian stamps. I thought it would never get here. Oh, I need her so bad. It isn't as easy as I thought it would be. I tear into the envelope, unfold two small sheets.

Dear John,

You are home now, and I hope you are happy and healthy. You can start to go on with your life now, as I must start to go on with mine. You are far away, and it would not be good for you to work to get money to marry me. Use your money for your own happiness and future.

I am going to change my address. Please do not try to find me. I will be okay. I hope you will be happy. Good luck. I love you.

Lin

I scream. That night my Dad is drying dishes. I ask him what I should do. "Forget her," he says, as matter-of-factly as if she were a lost ballpoint pen. "She's just a whore. You'll get over it."

Another scream. Into the T-Bird, out the driveway, put it into low, the engine roars and the tires scream, and there is only smoke in the rearview mirror. Broadside the stop sign, headlong flight to...to where? No money. No family, no friends, nobody I can talk to. She's thirteen thousand miles away; they never met her; how could they know? When I was a kid, I'd ask Dad for a baseball glove or a bicycle horn, and somehow, I'd get it. Delivering papers, or selling cherries, or mowing lawns; somehow I always got it.

Now, after a war, after a lifetime away, the first time I ask him for something, the most important something in the entire world, now he says no. If I'd known, I woulda stayed in Sattahip. Been a welder on the deep-water port. Married Lin, be in her arms tonight.

But no, I gotta be the All-American boy and come home! To what? A chill wind, grass tickling my cheek. The moon is straining to break through the clouds. I'm back in The World.

Big fucking deal! Isn't it grand? Sitting in the grass shivering and alone; helpless, hopeless, and thirteen thousand miles from my Lin. Crying like a baby and almost out of cigarettes, and I don't even know where the fuck I am. It's quiet, peaceful. How did I get here? How long have I been here? Long enough to relive a war in my head, to visit Malaysia and Thailand and exotic ports of call. Now what? Where do I go from here? How? If I had a jacket, I'd stay here. It's so quiet. The moon pushes through a cloud, and I see the shadows of my legs spread out in front of me. I light a cigarette, and the lighter illuminates the block of granite I am leaning against:

MARGARET EDMUNDS
1903–1967
R.I.P.

• • • •

The Boxer
I am just a poor boy
Though my story's seldom told,
I have squandered my resistance
For a pocketful of mumbles,
Such are promises
All lies and jest,
Still, a man hears what he wants to hear
And disregards the rest.

When I left my home
And my family,
I was no more than a boy
In the company of strangers
In the quiet of the railway station
Running scared,

Laying low,
Seeking out the poorer quarters
Where the ragged people go,
Looking for the places
Only they would know…

Asking only workman's wages
I come looking for a job,
But I get no offers,
Just a come-on from the whores
On Seventh Avenue
I do declare,
There were times when I was so lonesome
I took some comfort there…

Then I'm laying out my winter clothes
And wishing I was gone,
Going home
Where the New York City winters
Aren't bleeding me,
Leading me,
Going home.

In the clearing stands a boxer,
And a fighter by his trade
And he carries the reminders
Of ev'ry glove that laid him down
Or cut him 'til he cried out
In his anger and his shame,
"I am leaving, I am leaving."
But the fighter still remains…

—Paul Simon
Copyright 1968 Paul Simon

The Aftermath

"What did you see, my blue-eyed son?
And what did you see, my darling young one?"
— Bob Dylan, A *Hard Rain's A-Gonna Fall*

Not long after my return, I was invited to a birthday party for one of my high school classmates. The party was in Buffalo, where she was doing graduate work. Another former classmate drove, and I was amazed by his Fiat roadster. For so long I had dreamed of returning to "muscle cars," the awesome 427 Chevies and Hemi-Dodges. I found it difficult to accept the high-backed bucket seats, federally mandated safety features that made it impossible to retrieve anything from the back of the car, or the asthmatic wheezing of the smog-controlled seventy-horsepower engine. But the car was nimble, agile, and fun. It was a cold and rainy autumn day, otherwise we could have put the top down. I was disoriented. The world (The World?) I had come home to had changed so significantly, and yet it had a great deal to offer. Surely, this little buzz bomb was reminiscent of the tiny Japanese cars I had grown to accept in Thailand?

The party was also disquieting. Many of my classmates were there, and I was buoyed by their warm greetings. We reminisced, and for a few moments the carefree, optimistic joy we had shared comforted me. Then their conversations turned to college life, and I watched raindrops weaving psychedelic patterns down a steamy windowpane. Since graduation, we had little in common. Once we had been seedlings on the same stalk. They had fallen upon the fertile soil, and I had been blown among the rocks and briars. They saw a rosebud and anticipated beauty. I recognized its teardrop shape and felt sadness that it would wither away so soon.

I had come to know despair and disgust. I had lived in a world characterized by the stink of death and the horror of disfigured, hopeless children. I had seen poverty, starvation, atrocity, corruption, incompetence, brutality, and suicide. Their world revolved around graded papers and a professor's outrageous neckties. I had lived among the rodents and reptiles while they had been carrying laundry home on weekends. They had never seen a religious penitent; I was unimpressed by athletic letters on cardigan sweaters. The girls pretended to be shy virgins. The guys snickered about sexual adventures at drive-in movies. A letter from exotic Malaysia had widowed me.

I had been cleaning a rifle while they were cramming for exams. They spoke with great conviction of the agony of studying without sleep, the enormous amount of No-Doz and coffee it took to pass a trig final. I remember Dak To, Ohio, Tet. They protested the war. They had diplomas to prove their wisdom, implying subtly that my views were not being sought because they lacked credentials. I had no diploma, no report card granting a 2.5 in horror or a 3.8 in social studies for my research into the peasantry of Thailand's rice paddies. Almost apologetically, their eyes avoiding mine, they said they had taken part in marches against the war, then changed the subject.

I, too, protested the war. I had my reasons. I had known the thunder of a B-52 at work, the difference in sounds of an M-16 and an AK-47. I could sleep through an outgoing artillery bombardment but be awake and screaming a warning to my friends before a first incoming round struck. I had seen body bags and coffins stacked like cordwood, had seen American boys hanging lifeless on barbed wire, spilling over the sides of dump trucks, dragging behind an APC like tin cans behind a wedding party bumper. I had seen a legless man's blood drip off a stretcher to the hospital floor and a napalmed child's haunting eyes. I knew the spirit of the bayonet and the sizzle of a rocket tearing across the night sky. I slumped in a faded armchair sipping wine while the stereo played the score from the musical *Hair*. It sang of the joys of masturbation while I sat alone, remembering a place called The Warehouse. They opposed the war. They didn't ask my opinion. They had diplomas. I guess they thought I was stupid for having gone. If you weren't part of the solution, you were part of the problem. I, too, opposed the war. They were twenty-one, eager to try their wings. I was twenty-one, my life nearly over. We recalled the prom and the pizzas and went on with our lives.

• • • •

I was on unemployment, reading the classifieds. I saw Arlo Guthrie in concert, then Country Joe & The Fish. I caught *Yellow Submarine* at the movies. The disk jockeys wondered if Paul McCartney had died. The Beatles' newest album, *Abbey Road*, was everywhere on the airwaves. Onja had gotten pregnant, and the Loose Ends had broken up. Everyone told me to relax, take a few weeks to rest. I had rested in Thailand. I was eager to get on with my life, to build a future. I was eager to put the past behind me.

In a shiny silk suit hand-stitched by a Malaysian tailor, I arrived for an interview at an employment agency. Without a degree, I was referred to life insurance companies as a management trainee. For days I bounced off the walls of a concrete canyon, filled in the squares of the aptitude tests, and endured rejections because I wasn't "aggressive enough."

My clothes had been custom tailored in the Orient, part of my preparation ritual. They were hopelessly out of style. My hair was unfashionably short, my army-issue glasses weren't "cool." Overweight middle-aged men in brightly colored dress shirts, their hair "styled" to transform receding hairlines into Beatles bangs, asked if I had any "management experience."

I had been a platoon sergeant in Thailand, in charge of forty-three Americans and numerous Thais. It counted for nothing. In fact, it counted against me. I might as well have arrived for the interviews dressed in jungle fatigues and carrying an M-16. No one knew what to say to a Vietnam veteran, and no one wanted to meet one at the water cooler.

I ate lunch at the greasy restaurant across the street from the Chevy dealership where I had worked. I sat with Harry, who had been one of my best friends. I had looked up to him. While I was away, he had dumped his wife and baby to live with a go-go dancer. He was into drugs and motorcycles, and wearing an earring. "Fuck the world," he said, and I had just spent two years dreaming of returning to The World, and we didn't have very much in common anymore.

I found a job selling cars in a quiet, out-of-the-way foreign car dealership. Before the army, I had worked with Detroit iron. The World had changed, and so had I. Perhaps no aspect of my outward personality was more changed than my automotive tastes. I had always read the sports car magazines, but the foreign cars seemed exotic and unapproachable. I could understand Fords and Chevies, and the straightforward acceleration of drag racing. Now I surrounded myself with complex little Triumphs, MGs, Fiats, Jaguars, Lotuses, Volvos, and Saabs. Front wheel drive. Rear engine, rear wheel drive. Air-cooled engines. Exotica. I heard about, and began to try, apexing corners and four-wheel drifts. I sold my beloved T-Bird and bought an outrageous Triumph with a roll bar, a multitude of high-power driving lights, and a rally odometer. Rallying was a passion at this dealership, and the bug bit me. My car was anything but basic, but I was learning. Alone on twisting country roads, I pushed the Triumph and myself to death-defying limits. Perhaps the memories of the road to Dak To entered into it; I don't know. I had great confidence in my driving ability. This was freedom!

The responsibilities of job and car payments brought frustrations. Thousands of Vietnam veterans gathered in Washington to protest the war and throw their medals onto the steps of the Capitol. I knew I should have been there, but I also knew I wasn't ready to say anything in public. The job gave me a convenient excuse. I read the papers and felt a knot in my stomach, and sadness and disappointment in myself. Once again I had conveniently sidestepped the issue. Might my presence have kept someone alive? But I told myself the war hadn't happened, and I was usually able to fool myself.

There was a blind date, a disaster. I wasn't much for beer or crowds anymore. The psychedelic light show reminded me of the past, and I was concentrating on the future. The girl was ill-at-ease, alone with a Vietnam veteran. I was thinking with my glands. I said the wrong thing and offended her, and took her home. I tried a few taverns; I needed a drink now and then, but the taverns were full of college students laughing about their draft deferments. I sat quietly in the shadows, feeling terribly out of place, even frightened, though I didn't know why.

For almost three years the word *home* had brought a mental picture of the big yellow house on the shaded suburban street. Dad's job was twenty-five miles away, and the family decided to move to the city. I had nowhere else to go, I didn't want to be alone, so I went along. It was disquieting, the loss of something dear. The city was intimidating, and I retreated to my small room. It began to snow in October. The fun lasted only a few minutes. I was cold, and resented the time spent scraping a windshield or shoveling the driveway.

• • • •

One night I sat cross-legged on the floor of my room, handling the feeble mementos I had brought home, thinking back to another time when I had been better able to cope. I had so little in common with the people here. My world was thirteen thousand miles away, as fleeting as the smoke from my cigarette. The idea came from nowhere. I attacked the phone book. I had a friend from The Nam, someone who had known me in that context and had never been ashamed of me. The number was local. I hadn't written to Carolynn in a year. At the very least, I owed her a thank you for her wonderful letters. If things didn't work out I could easily hang up. We talked for over four hours that first night. She seemed so glad to hear from me. One of the other guys to whom she had been writing hadn't made it home. She invited me to her house. Eager to have a friend, and ever mindful of parents who were about to see their daughter invite a Vietnam veteran into the living room, I shut the car off and coasted into the driveway. She was far prettier than her pictures, far kinder than even her letters had indicated. We dated. I took her to a bar where an all-woman band from Thailand was playing, a band I had seen in Korat just a few weeks before. She seemed to understand and had the courage to ask questions. I had written about Lin. Was I married? At a rock concert a joint was passed my way, and I took a hit. In a huff, Carolynn demanded I drive her home and warned that she wouldn't see me again if I used drugs.

We found a little coffeehouse where we sat on the floor in the dim light of flickering candles, drinking hot cider with cinnamon sticks. The place was owned by two young folksingers and named after their cat. It was always crowded, but it felt warm and intimate when Carolynn and I were together. The snow melting off hundreds of boots made the floor damp, but we didn't mind. She hooked her arm in mine, and we swayed as the soft voices and acoustic guitars led us down a path neither of us had traveled before. We talked her mother into allowing Carolynn to spend the night with me, not in passionate love-making, but strapped into a rally car, racing at unconscionable speeds across miles of snow and treacherous road conditions. Carolynn was the navigator, reading the complex route instructions as I wrestled against Mother Nature and fatigue. There was a heavy snowfall, about eighteen inches, and I managed to lay the car on its side in a ditch. We scrambled out Carolynn's door into a raging blizzard. I rushed to the trunk to get the shovel and winch, and when I returned she was gone. I found her under the front of the car on her belly, frantically pulling out snow with her arms. At that moment I knew I would never find another girl like this.

I spent long hours alone in my room. I had to resolve Lin before I could accept Carolynn's affections. My passionate letters to Malaysia had gone unanswered for months. I had been dumped, and it hurt. As soon as I had taken my wallet back to America, Lin's passion had cooled. She was an artist, able to make five-day dreams come true, but unable to break out of that time barrier and dream dreams of months or years. Outside of a bedroom Lin's imagination was limited. She had never taken a ferry to the mainland, a scant half-mile away. She talked about New York or California with ease, but her worldliness was a façade she slipped into as easily as her clothes. She always reserved the ability to slip back to the comfortable familiarity of Penang's peasantry. When there was no GI to be entertained she wore cotton nightgowns. Nudity was her business suit, and nostalgia about The World was the balm she used to soothe the wounds of war.

She had learned her craft well. Many tormented visitors had vacationed between her thighs. She had learned from each of them, compiled a repertoire of illusions designed to invite dreams. On a five-day holiday from hell, her man was supposed to dream of a better future, but only within limits she would set. She wasn't ready to leave her island or her family to face the future in an unknown land. She was a relief pitcher, talented for an inning or two but unable to start the game and face the challenge of going all the way. It wasn't that she was afraid, I decided; she had made the simple choice.

I remembered the inner agony when I had left Pleiku, left my friends behind. There had been a strong urge to stick it out to the end, to apply what I had learned that they might have a better chance of surviving. Perhaps Lin knew better than I the value of what she was doing for men in dire need. The nurses comforted the physically wounded. Lin nursed the emotionally wounded.

Yes, she was a prostitute. A whore. I had accepted that fact for eighteen months, dared to dream of a lifelong relationship. I had committed myself, "'til death do us part." Had her simple handwritten note altered my values? Had my return to The World signaled some mysterious moral awakening? Had I shed immorality and lust when I had stripped off my army uniform? Certainly the protestors, with their "baby killer" accusations, had made morality a question of prime importance. To ascribe responsibility for the immorality to the uniform would be to condemn my friends. Every kid in uniform was somebody's next-door neighbor. My life had rested in their hands, and theirs in mine. They were not degenerate or immoral because they had slept with whores. They were lonely, afraid, and confused; caught up in a merciless web, shipped halfway around the world, and subjected to violence and death the next-door neighbors would never imagine. I felt no remorse, and I would make no excuses to the detriment of the guys I had left behind.

I had seen friends in Vietnam react to "Dear John" letters. Lin had been a sensitive, caring person. She had waited until I was back in The World to shatter my fantasies. She knew there would be a kaleidoscope of diversions to ease the hurt, that I would have different perspectives. She would not be hurt. She had freed me to find another woman; fate had been kind and I hadn't waited long. Carolynn offered more kindness and understanding than I was likely to find again. I would be a damn fool to live in the past.

It was fate! I had been thirteen thousand miles away. I could picture the mail shack. Carolynn had chosen three names with her eyes closed. Her finger had come to rest on my name, and she had accepted me in olive-drab, now again in jeans and sweaters. She seemed to know far more than her words could say about the hurt I felt inside. I needed her, and I willingly accepted her kindness without regret. Lin became a pleasant memory in the midst of a nightmare, and Carolynn became my future.

• • • •

The war continued, both in Southeast Asia and at home. Four antiwar protestors were gunned down at Kent State University. Thousands were arrested in Washington, D.C. There was an invasion of Cambodia, and a lot of Americans died when the South Vietnamese ran. It all seemed far, far away. Carolynn and I were planning a wedding, and the world stopped turning. Oh, I knew I should have been with the protestors, trying to save the helpless kids. Tired of the war, I had found something so beautiful, so wonderful, I very selfishly enjoyed it. I had given far too much to the war. Carolynn had rescued me from myself, and I committed myself to her. The economy was not good, and I needed to apply myself if we were to have a future. The war was the past. We concentrated on finding an apartment and furniture. I was so wrapped up in wedding plans I scarcely noticed that we had set the date for September 12, barely a year since I had returned.

Of course, there were reminders. One Saturday morning I woke with a terrible headache. My eyeballs had swelled until they literally grated against the sockets. I was rushed to the hospital, where I underwent a spinal tap. The doctors were rushing in and out, obviously concerned. Carolynn was frantic, but the swelling finally went away. The doctors explained that they really didn't know what it was, but there had been about a dozen cases reported...all in Vietnam veterans!

• • • •

Carolynn and I were married on September 12, 1970. We had hoped to have the folksingers from the coffeehouse sing, but we couldn't work it out. The church organist played our song, Simon & Garfunkel's "For Emily, Whenever I May Find Her." Our apartment had been the servant's quarters in the attic of a stately mansion in the finest section of the city. Our landlord and his family lived downstairs, and their kindness did a great deal toward starting our marriage on the right foot. It was a long climb to our third-floor hideaway, but worth it. Converted gaslights with crystalline globes arched out of the walls, the woodwork was polished wood, and the bathtub was a Victorian clawfoot antique. Learning to live with each other was a great adventure. Like kids in a tree house, we retreated from the dizzying world. We never seemed to have extra money; it was years before we had a couch, but Carolynn covered a foam mattress with corduroy, and we made ourselves very comfortable. At Christmas we built elaborate Victorian decorations. I fashioned a peace sign out of cardboard and lights, and let it shine down upon the richest neighborhood in the city.

• • • •

We found some Thai friends, students and doctors, and rang in the New Year 1971 with a Thai feast and good fellowship. In February, Laos was officially invaded. Fully half of the South Vietnamese invaders were casualties, and President Nixon declared his policy of Vietnamization a success. The *Pentagon Papers* were released, a mind-numbing exposé of our government's long history of lies and distortions concerning Vietnam. I read it nights, while Carolynn was at work. We didn't talk much about The Nam, but I had a peace sign in the window of my car. Lieutenant Calley was found guilty of the My Lai massacre. Carolynn thought he should go to jail, and the public wondered how anything like that could have happened. They couldn't accept what the war had done to their sons, the realities of survival and betrayal. I couldn't give my reasons for seeing Calley as a scapegoat. I might have been prosecuted for the incident with the fire truck, and I had a wife to think about. It was better to just leave the past behind.

There were hard times. Dock strikes and assembly-line strikes dried up our flow of cars, leaving me with a salary of $75.00 a week, or $54.23 after taxes. I became a salesman and deliveryman for a foreign auto parts store, and took a few night courses at the community college. The VA benefits were meager, so I couldn't afford to consider full-time school. In 1972, Carolynn and I won a rally championship and put on a charity event to buy toys for kids confined to local hospitals. The papers said American troops were coming home from Vietnam, but I didn't believe it because I didn't see the amputees and paraplegics on the street. Richard Nixon campaigned for reelection, and the Young Republicans in three-piece suits cried out for "four more years" while less fortunate Americans continued to bleed into the Southeast Asian swamps. I was convinced Nixon was postponing the peace to aid his reelection hopes, and predicted peace would come November 1. The announcement came October 26, and "Tricky Dick" was reelected November 7. He didn't get my vote. I pulled George McGovern's lever, opened the curtain, and loudly announced, "That's for all the guys who have died in Vietnam while the president played politics with peace!" A lot of matronly ladies were shocked, and I was hurried to the door. On December 18, the president ordered the most concentrated bombing in history. Over a hundred thousand bombs fell on Hanoi in just twelve days. Thirty-three American planes were lost, twenty-six of our fliers killed, and another twenty-six captured. Damage to civilian areas of Hanoi was heavy. The war continued.

• • • •

American combat troops left Vietnam in 1973, and (some of?) our POWs were released. I found a job opportunity in a South Carolina Toyota dealership, and in two weeks had moved Carolynn and the furniture a thousand miles from home. My new boss admitted he couldn't pay what he had promised, so Carolynn drove more than sixty miles a day to and from work. Richard Nixon was "tormented" by Watergate. Carolynn miscarried. I decided our best hopes depended on my success in the new job, not for the boss, but in spite of him. We managed to buy a house. A "gas crisis" brought long lines at service stations. The endless supply of fuel that had been keeping our troops moving in Vietnam had mysteriously dried up when the troops came home. Richard Nixon left office in disgrace but was pardoned by his successor, Gerald Ford. The American people never seemed to connect the deceptions of Watergate to the deceptions of Vietnam, although they may simply have been too bone-weary to demand an accounting. The vets and protestors seemed to forget their differences, and amid the silence they raised families and gained car payments and mortgages. I was no different, at least outwardly, but started a beard. The boss ordered me to shave it. I refused. I quit, and we moved again. I gave Carolynn two paperback books for Christmas, and she gave me three pairs of undershorts.

Nineteen seventy-five was a better year. I did well at my new job, earned a promotion, and we built a new house. Carolynn got pregnant. She was working in labor and delivery, and wanted a baby of her own. I had been in no hurry to have children. Although I never attributed my feelings to Vietnam, I'm sure the memories of starving or napalmed children made me hesitant to bring an innocent child into the world. Once we were sure she was pregnant, it was full speed ahead. Carolynn was the authority on these matters, and we were careful to do

everything just right. We attended Lamaze classes and pre-
pared a nursery. Meanwhile, Saigon fell to the Communists on
April 30. Ironically, on the same day, CBS-TV cancelled
Gunsmoke after twenty years. Our son was born December 31.
Our joy was indescribable, and I smuggled a bottle of cham-
pagne into the hospital.

On the morning of January 14, 1976, I received an emergency phone call at work. Carolynn was hysterical; the baby was
dead. I dropped the phone and started running toward home, a
distance of sixteen miles, until one of the ladies from the business office caught me and gave me a ride. I burst in the door to
find Carolynn holding him, singing soft lullabies through great,
choking sobs. In the distance, the ambulance siren came and
went, as they couldn't find our house. I was frantic, refusing to
believe the unbelievable, and I drove madly to the hospital.
Carolynn, of course, knew he was gone, and her face was hor-
rifying. It became official, and a terrible numbness set in.

I had seen horrors before, but never anything like the sight
of Carolynn cradling that baby. I had felt loss before, but never
a loss like this. Here it was again. Within seconds, everything
important to me had been snatched away. Carolynn, the most
precious thing I had ever known, was a desolated shell of her
former self. All our plans had been an illusion. Our parents
were heartbroken. The nursery, once a joyous room, had
become a chamber of horrors. They call it crib death, or
Sudden Infant Death Syndrome (SIDS). It takes thousands of
American babies a year. No one expects it to happen to them.

The autopsy showed certain anomalies. The baby had three
spleens. That, in itself, was not life-threatening, but I went
berserk. Long, long ago in a place far away, I had smoked some
marijuana. I quit before I came home, had puffed a joint only
twice in the past seven years. There was research suggesting
marijuana might cause genetic defects, but research has indicated almost everything causes diseases. You ignore most of it.

Now it was thrust into my face in the most terrible manner. Had I brought this heartbreak and suffering down upon the woman I loved? The pediatrician assured us it had been SIDS, that there was nothing we might have done to avoid it. The questions and the guilt remained.

• • • •

I had forgotten lessons learned; forgotten that life is, in essence, only day-to-day survival. I had allowed my good fortune to become my reality. A loving wife, a son, a comfortable house, two cars in the driveway…you can't take any of it for granted. I knew. Why hadn't I prepared Carolynn? For the first time in years, my thoughts returned to Southeast Asia. At times during the next few months Carolynn thought I was insensitive. I was sad, confused, and bitter. We had to go on. But had Vietnam scarred my emotions until I could scarcely shed a tear at my son's funeral? Our marriage was a commitment to life, which, I knew, included an unspoken pledge to love our children fully and without reservation. The war was far behind me. Or was it? Had it rendered me incapable of loving, at least of loving in the same sense of the word Carolynn expected? If, though using the same word, we were saying two different things, was that a misrepresentation of the very foundations upon which our marriage had been built? Of course I loved her, and I had loved my son. But was it love in the conventional sense, or love with conditions? I hadn't cried at the funeral. Death, I told Carolynn, was an inevitable part of life. We just had to go on. Was I a monster? Was I truly insensitive, or simply realistic? Sadness overwhelmed me; I contemplated suicide, but I couldn't cause Carolynn any more pain, so we struggled on. I resented our Lamaze classmates, playing with their healthy children. Carolynn saw a baby at the supermarket, burst into tears and fled the store, abandoning a cart full of groceries. She found work as an industrial nurse. I concentrated on rallying and my job, and earned honors in both.

On St. Patrick's Day of 1977, Carolynn presented me with a beautiful, healthy, red-haired daughter. For all these years, the Simon & Garfunkel song had been special to our relationship. We named the baby Emily. At long last, we had found her. There was little relief, however. We flew to her crib at every burp or gurgle, sat watching her sleep by the hour, and prayed that she would survive each night's sleep.

The job began to go poorly. I tried to start my own business, but the financing fell through. We moved again, to the suburbs of Washington, D.C., and scratched to pay both rent and mortgage until the old house was sold.

A second daughter, Thersa, was born in June 1980. Another redhead, she was the clown to counter Emily's seriousness. There is no boy to carry on the family name, but girls are especially close to their daddies. We have chosen to do without a lot of material things so that Carolynn could be a full-time mommy. I've been fortunate. I have a successful career, and a beautiful and loving family.

● ● ● ●

I think the war started to creep back into my life in the spring of 1980. *The Deer Hunter* had won a bouquet of Academy Awards. I thought Vietnam was far behind me, but the prisoner-of-war scenes started me shaking uncontrollably, and then I was crying and I had to leave the theater and smoke a cigarette. The American military had botched the Iranian hostage rescue attempt and was pleading for funds. A new militarism was dawning in America, and the presidential election brought us Ronald Reagan as its chief spokesman. The rhetoric tightened my stomach. Had we learned nothing? I had been unable to shed a tear when my son died, but one

December morning I pulled my car over to the edge of the road and cried great gasping sobs. John Lennon had been gunned down. For the first time in years, we fashioned a peace sign from cardboard and Christmas lights and hung it in an upstairs window.

In late 1981, *Newsweek* did an article about a company of Vietnam veterans, what they remembered and what they felt today. The article lifted the lid of my secret box. I begged my parents to read it, the first time I had acknowledged my war memories in years. Nightmares woke me more often now.

Everything exploded one January night in 1982. There was snow on the lawn, but the fireplace was crackling a cheerful tune. The kids were tucked in and I was twisting the TV dial, looking for mindless escapism. I found the famous CBS documentary about phony enemy troop counts during the Vietnam war. My box fell off its shelf, and the contents scattered all across the living room floor. "It's coming out! My God, it's finally coming out!" Here was General Westmoreland, the commander of the American forces in Vietnam, a genuine four-star lifer of lifers. Questionable troop strength reports had been relayed back to Washington for "political reasons," and the larger-than-expected enemy force shocked the world (and The World!) with the Tet Offensive of 1968. I fell apart that night, and dawn was breaking before Carolynn was able to settle me down. I wrote for a transcript of the program and carried it for days, reading and rereading it. This was the war I had seen. All of the deception, agony, treachery, and waste of Vietnam were wrapped up in those few sheets of paper. The lifers had felt so much contempt for us they had even lied to the president of the United States to earn their goddamn oak leaf clusters! We had been expendable. Now everyone would know and understand!

But despite the enormous implications, the methods used to uncover the story attracted as much attention as the story itself.

Westmoreland sued CBS for besmirching his professional reputation. When his officer staff began to testify that he had indeed created a ceiling of enemy troop counts that could be relayed back to Washington, he quickly abandoned the suit. Sadly, CBS agreed to shelve the story. The implications of this story were enormous, and the losers in this case were all the kids who will ever find themselves serving in the U.S. military. The precedent is clear: an officer can blatantly lie about the strength of enemy forces facing our troops, even for "political reasons," and get away with it! How many died needlessly? How many more will die needlessly in the future? I will never forget the terror of the Tet offensive. The truth has been obscured. I wrote numerous letters to my senators and congressmen pleading for an official investigation into this travesty, but I never received so much as a reply. I liken it to another letter to another congressman, so long ago. "I've had dinner with..."

After the TV documentary, I got myself back together. Vietnam was eating away at me now. The warlike rhetoric flowed out of Reagan's Washington in ominous torrents, and my stomach twisted into knots. My children were in danger. All of humanity was in danger. Why were we quietly accepting this terror, these distortions? I wanted to speak out, but I couldn't even talk to Carolynn about the things I had seen in The Nam. I felt trapped and powerless.

I enjoy books and bookstores, but it was Carolynn who discovered our first book about Vietnam. I had never imagined that someone might write about that awful place. How could they let it out? I was stunned! I rushed to a bookstore and filled a shopping bag with books about the war. There were strange, almost biblical titles: *A Rumor of War, The End of the Line, Fire in the Lake, Hell in a Very Small Place, Winners and Losers, Nam.* I devoured each one and attacked another. I have collected hundreds of books about the war, trying to understand what happened. Each time I start another book about Vietnam

I am on edge. Is it anticipation, or fear, or the pain of memories? I only know that I'm searching for something, I need to find it, and I don't even know what it is.

Hindsight can be confusing. Vietnam had fallen to the Communists. So had Cambodia. Saigon was now called Ho Chi Minh City. Cambodia had become Kampuchea. Had the architects of America's policy been right? Would the Communist horde sweep into my beloved Thailand, then Malaysia? Cambodia died an ugly death; perhaps uglier than even the Nazi holocaust. Nicaragua. El Salvador. Afghanistan. I watched my children learning to walk and talk, heard the news reports about "windows of vulnerability," "freedom fighters," and "covert" forays into foreign politics. This would be the world my children would inherit, if it lasted long enough! I attempted to make sense of Contras and Sandinistas, mined harbors and death squads. I wanted to leave my children a better world. I needed to settle whatever was gnawing at my guts. I started swallowing ulcer medicine before each meal. Once before I had been unknowing, and I carried the scars. Vietnam carried the scars! The newspaper articles seemed ominously familiar. I had to take sides! I had to resolve Vietnam, but I didn't know where to begin.

It had been fourteen years. I didn't want to be cross-examined or interrupted until I had reached a conclusion I could defend. Until I was satisfied and at peace with my memories. There was no cataclysmic decision to blurt it out. One Saturday afternoon, I jotted down a list of the most important incidents I had seen. That evening I began to type. I would describe my experiences. Perhaps Carolynn would read and understand. Perhaps I would save the papers until the girls were older, and they might learn from their Daddy's memories. Carolynn encouraged me, then left me alone. After about two weeks of typing, I added to my list. I had expected this project to consume about twenty sheets of paper. Incidents long buried were surfacing at an alarming rate. I got up in the middle of the night to jot a note, or pulled over to the edge of the road to record another memory that had just exploded out of my subconscious. I typed late at night, every night. The old records that had been background music to many of my adventures helped bring those adventures back to life. It was a difficult, painful journey. I relived all of the horror and the fear in the living room. Sometimes Carolynn had to come downstairs to help me through the ordeal. I was obsessed; there was no stopping. The pages accumulated.

Carolynn was concerned. Where would this explosion lead? She sought out the author of that first book about Vietnam, a nurse who had worked with civilian casualties. I worked up enough courage to meet the lady and she was as honest as her book. She knew; I could see it in her eyes. She said her nightmares didn't take her back to The Nam, but brought Vietnam into the present.

Sometimes, in the night I dream I'm looking out toward our backyard. The kids are in the sandbox, Carolynn is puttering with her flowers, and the neighboring yards are teaming with Viet Cong sappers in black pajamas. I scream, but my girls cannot hear me. I am frozen, and the approaching Vietnamese are all grinning that maniacal grin I once saw on the road to Dak To, twenty-three days before I was due to leave The Nam. I am prickly with terror! Insane! Frantic. I can feel each hair jumping out of my skin. Sweat lies cold upon my ribcage, burns my eyes. Then I wake with a start and prowl the house. I see the children sleeping peacefully, looking like angels, and I sit and read magazines until I am able to go back to bed.

I dream I am leaning over the bed to kiss a forehead goodnight, and there is a stir, and a beautiful, trusting face has been transformed into the bubbled, flaking, disfigured black horror of the kid I once saw at the hospital in Pleiku.

I dream we are crouched behind the sandbags, watching the horde of Charleys approaching. There is no escape. There are only four bullets left. I remember the fire truck in the midst of a clearing, and know what I have to do to keep my girls from being violated. But the girls look at me with eyes full of love and trust, and I can't do it, and I am deeply sorry I brought them into the world. There is a frantic explosion of action, and I wake to find the blankets wrapped tight around me, the sheets soaked with sweat, and my fists twisted frantically into the pillow. The dream never reaches its unspeakable conclusion, and I lie awake and quake at the awesome responsibilities of parenthood.

I'm not the only one with nightmares. Talking with other Vietnam vets has taught me that. I wonder if I'm crazy, but I know the psycho wards could never hold all of us. The experts say we are normal, just more aware than other people, and better for it. This is, after all, our "duty" to our country!

I was typing every night now, the story bubbling out of me like pus from an infection. I couldn't stop the flow. And as my writing progressed, so did my nerve. I began to talk with other vets, to check details, compare feelings. I became aware of the Agent Orange controversy. I have no idea if I was ever exposed to this state-of-the-art military miracle. Outside our barbed-wire perimeter there was a free-fire zone of six-inch grass for about fifty yards, then a wall of ten-foot elephant grass. The free-fire zone was booby-trapped with mines and flares. No one mowed that grass, but it never grew! Why? One night I took an ominous inventory of the Vietnam veterans I knew personally. At that time there were nine, plus myself. (One has since committed suicide.) Two had never fathered children since the war. Of the remaining eight, one was a woman. She has suffered numerous miscarriages, and many very severe health problems. Another vet's first child was stillborn. Four of us had known the agony of SIDS. Seventy-five percent of all the

Vietnam veterans I knew had buried their children! A macabre coincidence? Perhaps, but I began to ask questions of acquaintances, my students, total strangers. The percentage who have lost children has never fallen below 65. Did we lose our sons in The Nam? Are our beautiful daughters carrying a time bomb in their bodies? Might our grandchildren become Vietnam casualties? Had we been aware of the Agent Orange connection to infant death, we would not have risked having other children. Our daughters are beautiful and healthy. We wonder what their future holds.

I didn't ask to go to Vietnam. I tried to avoid it, but the authorities said it was my "duty" and they had a relentless force of agents ready to invade any neighborhood to force compliance. No such show of force exists today to answer the questions about Agent Orange. The VA often suggests psychiatric help. The air force's "Ranch Hand" study reported three times the normal mortality rate in children under twenty-eight days of age, children of Vietnam vets exposed to Agent Orange. But, in announcing the findings, the air force was quick to add "we see no reason not to use it again." All we ask for are some honest answers, but our government fears the costs...both in medical compensations, and in the morale of potential recruits! During Operation Desert Storm, an unprecedented number of military personnel had their sperm frozen before shipping out to the combat zone, "just in case." The government's efforts to suppress "Gulf War Syndrome" have mirrored their disregard for Agent Orange victims. "Be all you can be" indeed!

With the dawn of the twenty-first century, the army has abandoned its "Be all you can be" recruiting slogan, luring today's recruits with the image of "an army of one!" Teamwork be damned! How appropriate. Still, cigarette commercials have long been banned from TV because smoking has been found to be hazardous to your health. Since Vietnam, nothing offends me so much as hypocrisy! I understand that those recruiting messages are just propaganda, as insidious as any brainwashing by our supposed enemies! To air recruiting commercials on Saturday mornings, interspersed with the cartoons for preschoolers, is unconscionable to my eyes.

• • • •

I was deep into my story when I found the key. I was searching for a word, and *expendable* came into my head. My dictionary defines *expendable* as "in military usage, designating equipment (and hence, men) expected to be used up (or sacrificed) in service." I cannot be expected to experience the war and its after-effects, to relive it in hundreds of hours of self-analysis, punching out hundreds of typewritten pages with only one finger, without reaching conclusions. The Vietnam War is too deeply significant for me to have learned nothing. I am not comfortable with my conclusions, but I am satisfied that they are realistic.

I'm afraid that our leaders, civilian or military, are so obsessed with power that they have come to view us all as expendable! What mother cradles a child to her breast and considers him "cannon fodder," or wants to think of him as "expected to be sacrificed?" By law, we are allowed, even required, to nurture and teach our children until they reach the tender age of eighteen. After that, the state can seize them for military service, and waste them in the most ill-conceived of adventures. The authorities speak of a child's "duty," of his "obligation to his country." These same officials have long ignored the majority public opinions, repeatedly demonstrated in referenda, polls, and surveys that the American people favor a halt to the arms race, that they favor gun control, and that they favor a woman's right to choose. Democracy in the age of corporations and television does not conform to the model created by our founding fathers.

In the wake of the Tet offensive, an American military officer described the action around the village of Ben Tre with the words, "We had to destroy it in order to save it." Did America's military leaders lie to Congress and the president about enemy troop strengths and expose half a million Americans, mostly teenagers, to unnecessary suffering and death? On December 27, 1983, President Reagan publicly accepted "full blame and responsibility" for the deaths of 241 marines in Beirut, despite a Pentagon report outlining critical errors by marine lifers on the scene that had contributed to the slaughter, perhaps caused it. Ironically, just across town that day, General Westmoreland told a press conference, "If I were guilty as charged by the CBS broadcast, I could be court-martialed." Clearly, there is no precedent to cause the general any concern, no matter how guilty he may be!

Under the guise of "security," the press was not allowed to accompany our marines to the invasion of Grenada. Approximately five thousand Americans took part. More died as a result of accidents and "friendly fire" than by hostile action. There was no disciplinary action, and in fact, at least 8,666 medals were awarded, many to lifers safely ensconced in their Pentagon offices!

The tragedy of Agent Orange continues. The only assurances we have seen from our government or the military are statements that they would not hesitate to use it again, birth defects, premature deaths, and suffering notwithstanding. Indeed, late in 2001, in the wake of a flurry of anthrax terrorism, it was discovered that the deadly spores had not originated overseas, but from weapons-grade specimens propagated by the army despite clear national laws outlawing such practice. As this is written, no public or congressional outcry has resulted. I wonder if a subtle coup has occurred, rendering all things military in America exempt from legal interference, and unrecognized by "we the people."

The sacrifices made by American veterans in all wars have been terrifying and heroic, but once their usefulness has been "used up," the VA hospitals to which they are committed are often a disgrace. Ron Kovic had volunteered for his second tour in Vietnam when a Viet Cong bullet smashed his spine and left him paralyzed. In his book and the ensuing movie, *Born on the Fourth of July*, Kovic describes life in a VA hospital. The patients tossed bread crumbs onto the floor at night so that marauding rats would not gnaw at their lifeless toes. (Ron Kovic, *Born on the Fourth of July*. New York: McGraw-Hill, 1976). Conditions in VA hospitals are little improved, and numerous budget cuts have not helped. Meanwhile, America's arsenal, and corresponding budget deficits, have mushroomed.

Disquieting numbers of American children see nuclear war as inevitable within their lifetime. Many see no reason to apply themselves. Our children are conditioned to accept that our government finds them "expendable."

During the Reagan years, government officials assured us that we could survive a nuclear war, if we would just dig a hole in the backyard, place a door over the hole and cover it with dirt. I refuse to spend any more time in a muddy hole at my government's pleasure! If they have a nuclear war, the survivors will just have to bury me or live with the stink. I'll be damned if I will quietly and conveniently dig my own grave to make it convenient for them!

I am not anti-American. The wholesale murder of civilians is horrible regardless of whether it is done by American, Communist, or terrorist forces. The bloodbaths in Vietnam, Cambodia, Afghanistan, Nicaragua, Northern Ireland, Israel-Palestine, and throughout the world are all equally repugnant to me. I was horrified the morning of September 11, 2001. I hope every individual in any way responsible for that tragedy, or who helped the terrorists responsible, will be systematically hunted down and eliminated, without lengthy and expensive trials or concerns for their "rights." Still, I understand that significant portions of the world's peasants hate America, because they have been victimized and manipulated by our country. Our politicians pay tribute to America's values and inherent morality, but those qualities are never allowed to interfere with corporate profiteering or military adventuring. All too often, as in the case of Ho Chi Minh and Vietnam, America's hypocrisy and clandestine policies have forced the world's peasants to embrace Communism and other ill-begotten ideologies as a means of self-preservation. Our leaders have shown utter contempt for the poor of our own country, as well as the poor in Lebanon, Afghanistan, Palestine, Grenada, El Salvador, Nicaragua, South Africa, Somalia...the list is endless. America tries to hold all the world hostage with our military might. Is it too much of a stretch to fear the day they decide to destroy all the planet "in order to save it"? Long ago the army pointed to my IQ scores and suggested I volunteer for Officer Candidate School. I never attended OCS, but I think I gained a certain awareness from my military experience.

• • • •

November of 1982 brought into my life a tidal wave of emotions and long-suppressed memories, all centered around a shaded corner of the mall in Washington, D.C., where a Vietnam Memorial was being constructed. A television camera scanned the vast wall of names as it neared completion, my eyes recognized a ghost from the past, and I burst into tears. I didn't know he hadn't made it. The children were upset at the sight of their daddy crying. We hustled them into the car and drove into Washington. The memorial was surrounded by a snow fence and security guards, waiting quietly to be dedicated the following weekend. Television hadn't prepared me for the power of those huge, black walls; it takes a lot of space to print 57,939 names. We stood on a small knoll beneath the naked branches of hickories in winter dress. Perhaps a hundred strangers were scattered around us, many sobbing, none ashamed. My eyes were watering uncontrollably when the children spotted a squirrel and rescued me with their delighted chatter.

• • • •

Saturday, November 13, began as a scarlet glow on the eastern horizon. A neighbor was sitting with the children while Carolynn and I drove toward a special event. Bundled in our heaviest winter clothes, we parked the car and rode the subway into Washington. We adjusted hats and scarves and climbed the steps to the mall, near the Smithsonian Institution. The exuberance of dawn had faded to a cloudy gray, and a chill wind swirled off the Potomac and resisted our march across the mall. The fence had been rolled back this morning, and we shrugged our way into the crowd, deep into the terrible V, past a wrinkled woman in a folding chair. Her eyes watered as she sat quietly, gazing at the awesome walls without seeing. She held a faded photograph in a gilded frame and a sign that read, "My Son Died in Vain."

Many years before, Carolynn closed her eyes and picked three names from a long list of lonely soldiers in a far-off land. Not all her letters had been answered. She searched out a special name among the thousands and laid a rose against the cold, hard granite. There was another name, another rose, and I thought back to fourth-period study hall, the Audio-Visual Club, and high school graduation. We found a panel, the names of the dead from November 1967. Somewhere on that panel were the names of two men who had tried to drive a truckload of ammo to Dak To; names I would never know, men I would never forget. Somewhere, among these hundreds, a name would remind a family of the living thing that had become a broken shadow hanging on the barbed wire and a twisted shadow behind an APC in the night. I prayed that Carolynn wouldn't say anything. I had something growing in my throat that would make answering impossible.

One rose remained. A very special person had shared a nightmare kaleidoscope of emotions with me; friendship and compassion, then sadness, understanding, pain, and fear. There had been a magic moment when she had shared grief. She had loved in Vietnam, and lost. We found the name, fit a rose into the pages of a novel, and leaned them against the base of that cursed wall amongst the thousands of flowers and flags. I had never known him, but his name embodied all the body bags and silver boxes I had seen on runways long ago, broken limbs I had witnessed spilling over the sides of a muddied dump truck. They were memories now, just names upon an awesome tombstone, and it was fitting that they have an epitaph for their suffering.

The Capitol Dome and the Washington Monument reflected off the polished granite walls; soft gray-black forms offering a poignant urgency to the title of the tiny red novel, *Forever Sad the Hearts.*

The parade started at ten. We stood on the curb, hunched against the wind. Not long ago, I swore I would never come to the memorial, let alone a parade. Now I needed to be there, to see it and be a part of it, but from a distance. State by state, the waves of veterans came. Phalanxes of wheelchairs, ragged clusters out for a stroll, paunchy, nearing middle age, often irreverent. Clad in three-piece suits, jungle fatigues, green berets, and Indian war bonnets. Jeans and T-shirts. On crutches and canes. There was a disproportionate amount of long hair, as if overcompensating. Orange banners defying America to admit to Agent Orange, and black banners remembering POWs and MIAs. Too often, someone broke ranks to rush to the curb to share a hug and a tear with a ghost come to life. I strained my eyes when the Ohio contingent passed. Perhaps it's best I didn't recognize the barrel chest and wavy blonde hair I had known for less than a day. I called Archie's name, and no one answered.

I was expecting the end of the parade when I saw an approaching solution to years of regret. They looked like all the others, except some carried outrageous signs.

I am a Vietnam veteran.
I like the memorial.
And if it makes it difficult
To send people into battle again…
I'll like it even more!

I could hear them now, chanting as they must have chanted in 1969 when I stayed home. "HELL NO, OUR KIDS WON'T GO!" I hesitated, as I had hesitated in 1969. No, I couldn't wait another thirteen years! I pulled Carolynn off the curb and into the midst of them. I added my voice to theirs, fighting back years of emotion and frustration that threatened to crack my throat. I was amazed as people stepped from the curb to shake our hands or slap our backs.

Someone thrust a cassette recorder to my face and asked what I was feeling. I was too emotional. "We can't allow this to be the end of it. The war isn't over. We can't allow Vietnam to be swept under the rug as past history, because many of the men responsible for Vietnam are right over there," I pointed to the Pentagon, "hard at work, trying to involve us in Nicaragua, or El Salvador, or Libya, or Angola, or anywhere they can try out their terrible toys! It's not past history. It's a terrible, terrible threat, and we have children of our own now. We don't want to raise them to die in some swamp for no good reason." The recorder disappeared, and Carolynn worried that it might have been some form of government surveillance. I didn't care; I had an American right to my opinion, and to voice it. It was a free and glorious feeling, and we followed along to the memorial amid overwhelming joy and sadness. Rain had left the lawn a shambles. Behind us, an ironic voice declared, "Nice of them to provide all this mud to make us feel at home." A worn guitar hung neck-down from a backpack. A wrinkled old man welcomed us home, his World War I uniform immaculate and proud.

I didn't need speeches to remember The Nam. Carolynn and I lunched on crepes and wine at the Smithsonian Associates' restaurant, enjoying a rare meal without bibs or potty breaks. By the time we returned to the memorial it was dedicated. The crowd was enormous, and I tugged Carolynn into the midst of it. These were my peers, my generation. I didn't know them, but I wanted to soak up their company. Just being here, I was making a statement I had been unable to make for many years.

Finally the sun faded, the November chill returned, and we headed home. We walked hand-in-hand under Lincoln's stony gaze, through the trees where the antiwar protestors had been beaten and teargassed. To our right, the bronze image of Thomas Jefferson watched us retreat; to our left, the White House glowed in the glare of electric lights. Carolynn asked if I was okay.

Behind us, there were no proud sabers or prancing horses. There was only a black wall with 57,939 terrible reminders of the American blood shed in The Nam. Every morning, members of Congress would see it, feel it. It stood out, black and somber, and it couldn't be ignored. I was fine.

In early January of 1983, a group of "scholars and analysts," many from the Defense Department and the Army War College, met at the Smithsonian Institution in Washington, D.C. Officially known as The Smithsonian Institution's Wilson International Center for Scholars, they hoped to define

368 | John Ketwig

"the lessons of Vietnam." The conference lasted two days. The *Baltimore Sun* reported, "There was disagreement and criticism, but little in the way of raw emotion." Half a mile away, a veteran stood before a black wall and shivered...

...and a hard rain fell.

I had only twenty-three days to go when a convoy
was ambushed. After the action quieted, we gazed
at the dead Vietcong like tourists at a museum.

Our "hootch." Home sweet home...to a lot of rats that were as big as small dogs. Rabies was a constant threat. The best defense was to kill a rat and burn it so that the smoke permeated the tent.

Dak To. Vietnamese kids watching a convoy getting ready to depart.

Scenes from convoys to Kontum and Dak To.

Trucks on the convoy.

Armored personnel carrier (APC) after it hit a mine.

Montagnards near Pleiku.

The author with a Montagnard child.

Aboard the Thai train to Penang, Malaysia.

The author on R&R in Penang, Malaysia,
being blessed by a Buddhist monk.

The temple of Phi Mai.

Another Thai temple.

The dedication of the Vietnam Veterans Memorial.

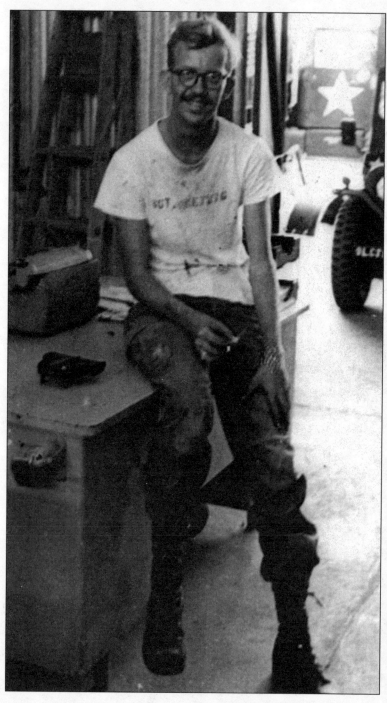

"Sergeant" Ketwig in Thailand.

About the Author

John Ketwig was sent to Vietnam in September of 1967, and completed his tour a year later. Because he felt there was a civil war occurring at home, he chose to serve out his military obligation in Thailand, where he could not be called upon to stand against fellow Americans who were protesting the war. In 1982, John began to examine the Vietnam tragedy and his role in it. He started to write about his experiences in a letter to his wife and children, in hopes someday they might understand and know the truth of what he had experienced. He had never written anything before. His account was originally published in 1985. Widely quoted, the book has attracted critical praise, and is a staple of many college and university courses on the war.

Mr. Ketwig has spoken at many of America's high schools, colleges, and universities. He is an outspoken adversary of American militarism, and passionately urges young people to become knowledgeable about political trends that may involve them in future combat situations. He is currently working on a novel.

John grew up in the Finger Lakes region of western New York. From the first, he was interested in automobiles. He has enjoyed a varied and colorful automotive career, including management positions with Toyota and Rolls-Royce/Bentley. He now works as a District Parts and Service Manager with Hyundai Motors America, and lives in northwest New Jersey with his wife Carolynn. Their two daughters are college students.

Acknowledgments

For Emily and Thersa, our beautiful daughters. I hope someday you will appreciate that your Dad wrote this for you, in hopes that you might inherit a better world.

And for Carolynn, my wife. Our love is the most wonderful experience of my life. I like to think of this book as a love story, *our* love story, every bit as much as it is a war story!

Thanks to Horace Bracey, Mike Lockaby, Dr. John A. Parrish, Kate Walker, and Bill Elder.

Very special thanks to John Beam, Robert and Gloria Horner, Winona Jackson, and Ed and Patricia Walsh. Also, very especially, our most grateful thanks to Jacky Sach.

And, for their understanding and encouragement, thanks to Joe and Jane Fusco, in memory of their son Paul Richard Fusco, Class of '65, Avon Central School, who never got the chance…